Volume 10

Sun Tracks
An American Indian Literary Series

SPIRIT MOUNTAIN

Sun Tracks and the University of Arizona Press / Tucson, Arizona

SPIRIT MOUNTAIN

An Anthology of Yuman Story and Song

LEANNE HINTON and LUCILLE J. WATAHOMIGIE, *Editors*

About the Editors

LEANNE HINTON has worked with the Havasupai for many years, first as an undergraduate student, then as a researcher and a consultant for the tribe. Her studies have included anthropology and ethnomusicology. She received her Ph.D. in linguistics in 1977 from the University of California at San Diego and joined the faculty at the University of California at Berkeley. She has also studied Hualapai and La Huerta Diegueño.

LUCILLE J. WATAHOMIGIE was raised at Milkweed with her parents, her grandparents, and other relatives. Her childhood was quite traditional, with the family living based in large part on agriculture, hunting, and the gathering of wild foods. After earning her Master's degree in education from the University of Arizona in 1973, she became the Associate Director of the Teacher Education Program for Indian students at that institution. In 1976 she returned to the Hualapai reservation to serve as the director of the new Hualapai Bilingual Education Program. Under her direction, this program has become one of the most successful in the country, receiving a grant as a Demonstration Program for 1983–85. She has been responsible for the collection, transcription, and translation of most of the Hualapai selections in this book.

SUN TRACKS and THE UNIVERSITY OF ARIZONA PRESS

This book was set in 11 on 13 Linotron Palatino.
Manufactured in U.S.A.

SUN TRACKS
is an American Indian literary series sponsored by the American Indian Studies Program and the Department of English, University of Arizona, Tucson, Arizona. All correspondence concerning text should be sent to: *Sun Tracks*, Department of English, Modern Languages Building #67, University of Arizona, Tucson, Arizona 85721. All orders should be sent to: University of Arizona Press, 1615 E. Speedway, Tucson, AZ 85719. Volumes 1–5 of *Sun Tracks* are out of print. They are available on microfiche from Clearwater Publishing Company, Inc., 1995 Broadway, New York, NY 10023.

Library of Congress Cataloging in Publication Data

Main entry under title:

Spirit mountain.

(Sun tracks; 10)
Bibliography: p.
1. Yuman literature. 2. Yuman Indians—Legends.
3. Indians of North America—Southwest, New—Legends.
4. Yuman languages—Texts. I. Hinton, Leanne.
II. Watahomigie, Lucille J. III. Series.
PM2701.Z77 1984 897'.5 84-112

ISBN 0-8165-0843-7
ISBN 0-8165-0817-8 (pbk.)

In memory of
John Rouillard

Contents

Preface

Innumerable people have helped to bring this volume together. It began with the wisdom of many old people in many different communities, each independently realizing that the old knowledge was threatened, that traditional ways of passing on this knowledge were eroding, and that something different had to be done in order to give it to the coming generations. This understanding led them each to consent to pass on some of their knowledge to unlikely sorts of folks: Indians and Anglos, staff members of bilingual education programs, students of anthropology or linguistics—a motley crew who commended themselves to the elders primarily by their curiosity about tradition.

It is this odd assortment of people that form the second stage in the making of this book—they recorded the stories and songs and descriptions of old ways, wrote them down, worked long hours with many patient people to translate them, and then saved them for opportunities like this one.

But beyond these elders and their scribes, who are listed as the contributors in this volume, there are others to whom special acknowledgment must be given.

One person who was extremely important to the Yuman communities until his death in 1983 is John Rouillard. Since 1978, Yuman communities have been sending native speakers to the Yuman Language summer institutes, to be trained in practical linguistics for community use. John Rouillard was instrumental in the original funding for these institutes and in their organization and implementation. To a large extent, this volume is a result of the training and the writing that has occurred at these summer institutes. In fact, the first planning sessions for this book occurred in John Rouillard's offices, with himself organizing and directing the sessions in his inimitably talented way.

The editors wish also to thank Professor Margaret Langdon, who has done more than any other single person to bring about active scholarship among Yuman tribes and at the same time to develop linguistics in the service of the Indian community. She developed the first practical writing system for a Yuman language, and trained many students who, besides doing active research, were able to be of use to Yuman communities in their own search for revival of traditional knowledge. Besides training scholars, she has also given much aid and encouragement to Indian people developing community language programs and writing systems. Almost every section editor in this book has been trained or aided in some way by her.

Thanks also go to Professor Akira Yamamoto, a gifted linguist and teacher, who has taught in most of the Yuman summer institutes and has therefore been instrumental in the training of many of the section editors and contributors to this volume. He would devote sixteen- and eighteen-hour days to his duties, often working far into the night with students who wished it. He has also exhibited the same dedication to consulting for the Hualapai community, training the Hualapai in linguistics, and helping in the preparation of language materials. To those who know him, his inspiration is strongly visible in this book.

Since many of the organizers of this book have received much of their training through Title VII funding, thanks are also due to the U.S. Government, along with our fervent hopes for continued funding of Indian bilingual programs, which have had enormous importance to Indian communities in recent years.

Thanks are also due to the University of California at Berkeley and to Peach Springs Elementary School, the home bases of the editors. These institutions provided the working space and supplies for the editing of this volume. Also, the Survey of California and Other Indian Languages kindly covered some of the costs in the preparation of this manuscript.

Finally we wish to thank Larry Evers, editor of the Sun Tracks Series, and Ofelia Zepeda, who together envisioned a Yuman anthology and asked us to put it together.

Leanne Hinton
Lucille J. Watahomogie

SPIRIT MOUNTAIN

Victor Masayesva

Introduction

In the deserts and along the waterways of the lower Colorado River, in the oak and pine forests, the canyons, plateaus, and mountains, the land sings through its people. When the song seems to be fading from living memories, it is time to write it down. In confining the song to markings on paper, there is a risk of freezing and paralyzing it, robbing it of vitality. In this collection of stories and songs from the Yuman Indian peoples, we have tried to preserve the song in ways that will turn the hearts of modern readers, as it turned the hearts of men and women before they began to forget. The song must continue as full of life as earth's own celebration.

Spirit Mountain represents the beginning. It rises from the desert floor at the Colorado River near what is now Davis Dam, capped by white granite bluffs, dwarfing other landmarks. At its base, inhabitants long since gone have left behind a rich legacy of petroglyphs as an account of human origins. Versions of the name Wi Kahme', "The Highest Mountain Range," are known to exist in Hualapai, Havasupai, Mojave, Diegueño, Maricopa, and Paipai. It is known as a sacred place to all the tribes. Yuman oral tradition names Spirit Mountain as the source of human emergence from the earth. Narratives describe the original unity of the Yuman peoples, as well as the events which led to their dispersion over the land from Spirit Mountain.

The Yuman Tribes are so-named because they speak closely related languages. The Yuman communities represented in this volume are the Hualapai, Havasupai, Yavapai, Paipai, Diegueño, Mojave, Maricopa, and Quechan (Yuma). When people speak related languages, it means that they shared some history somewhere back in time. Thousands of years ago, the ancestors of modern Yuman peoples probably spoke a single language, and perhaps lived somewhat closer together. "Yuman," of course, is not a term that has ever been applied to this group of communities by themselves; but the people do recognize their kinship in some of their origin tales.

The first four languages mentioned above are closely enough related to be subgrouped together as the "Pai" languages. Havasupai and Hualapai are so alike as to have only minor dialectal differences; Yavapai (which has several dialects) can also be understood quite easily by the Havasupai and the Hualapai; and Paipai is slightly but not fully intelligible to people speaking the other Pai languages. A second subgrouping within the Yuman family is sometimes called the "River Tribes," consisting of the Mojave, Maricopa, and Quechan. Their languages are very similar to each other, and relatively different from the other Yuman languages. Diegueño enters into a subgroup with Cocopa (the latter not represented in this volume), sometimes called "Delta Yuman." Kiliwa (also not represented here) is a branch unto itself, showing major differences from

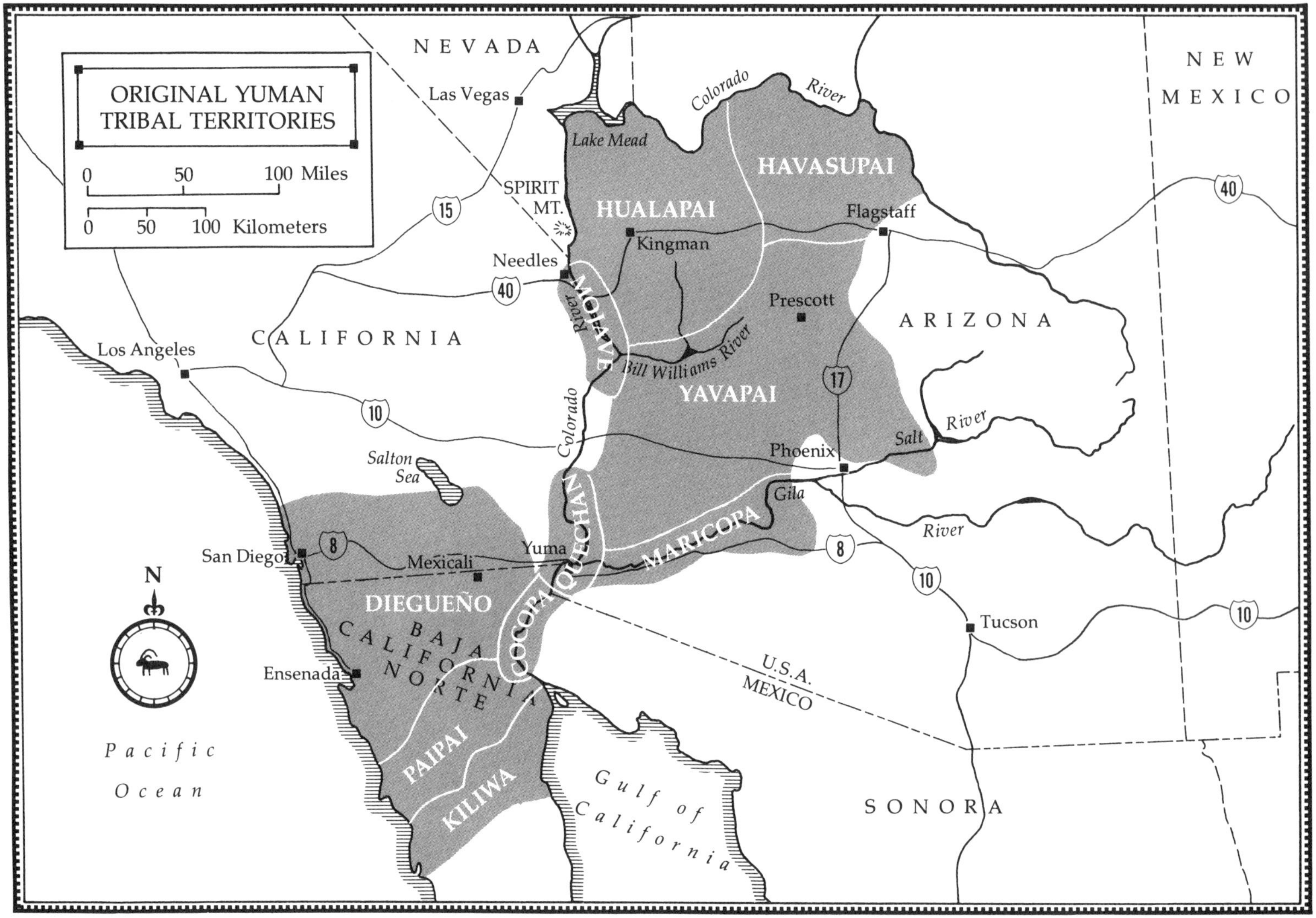
ORIGINAL YUMAN TRIBAL TERRITORIES
0 50 100 Miles
0 50 100 Kilometers
NEVADA
Las Vegas
Lake Mead
Colorado River
HAVASUPAI
HUALAPAI
SPIRIT MT.
Kingman
Flagstaff
Needles
Prescott
MOJAVE
Bill Williams River
YAVAPAI
ARIZONA
NEW MEXICO
CALIFORNIA
Los Angeles
Salton Sea
Phoenix
Salt River
Gila River
QUECHAN
MARICOPA
Yuma
San Diego
Mexicali
DIEGUEÑO
COCOPA
BAJA CALIFORNIA NORTE
Ensenada
PAIPAI
KILIWA
Tucson
U.S.A.
MEXICO
SONORA
Pacific Ocean
Gulf of California
N

the other Yuman languages, but still clearly belonging to the same family. These groupings are represented below as a "family tree."

When people who once lived together separate and lose contact with each other, their languages—imperceptibly slowly—begin to differ from each other. Given enough time, and little enough contact, the dialects can diverge so strongly that their speakers can no longer understand each other, and then they would have to be defined as separate languages. In this manner, the Yuman languages have diverged over the millenia.

The Yuman peoples have developed different ways of life from each other in response to the varying opportunities of their lands. Agriculture was and is practiced by all Yuman communities that had sufficient water, most extensively by the tribes living along the Colorado and Gila rivers, where large permanent settlements arose. The Havasupai also have a large year-round water supply, and have an intricate canal system for irrigation. Smaller gardens were tended near springs and small watercourses by other Yuman peoples. In southern California, even where irrigation was not possible, wild and semi-domesticated grasses, seeds, bushes, and trees were planted by the Diegueños. Along the coast, seafood was collected regularly in the old days; and such coastal products as abalone and other seashells were traded along inland routes. Abalone shell has been found in archaeological sites as far away as Ohio, indicating the complexity of the trading networks in traditional America. Where the oak grows, the acorn was a staple. In the higher mountainous and plateau regions the piñon replaces the acorn as the staple. All Yuman peoples also practiced much hunting and gathering of wild foods. While all these traditional modes of living are still practiced by many individuals among the Yuman peoples, they have tended to become less easy to follow in modern times, as land and wild resources have been taken away. Newer ways of living, such as raising horses and cattle, and earning wages in order to buy food from stores, have come to be dominant.

Along with these different ways of life, the Yuman peoples developed different patterns of knowledge, different religious traditions, different stories and songs. Many of the same themes run through all the oral traditions of the Yuman territory, and indeed a considerably larger area than that.

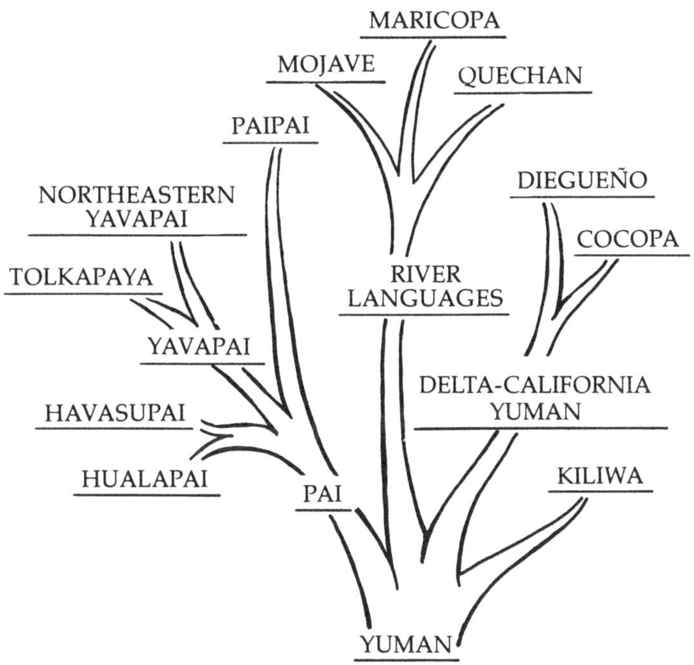

But every community also has many themes and many songs and tales entirely their own. This variety produces such a rich set of traditions that a book of this sort can hope only to touch the surface. We can, however, provide representative and authentic examples of this continuum of imaginative verbal expression.

The Traditional Role of Oral Literature

Traditionally, oral literature was not merely a means of entertainment—not merely something to do because television had not yet been invented. Instead it was the means by which the generations transmitted cultural mores. All human activities are part of a universal scheme, and the wise person always knows the relationship of himself and his behavior to this universal pattern of nature. The traditional tales and songs helped people learn about the world and their place in it, how to behave toward other people, and how to lead a life harmonious with nature. It also taught people how to respect other species and how to respect the places on the land, by telling their own place in the pattern of the universe. Many of the tales have morals, but few of them actually say "such-and-such a behavior is wrong." Instead, they are designed to cause people to contemplate their own behavior, to understand something about the consequences of such behavior, and to give them insights that allow them to change their behavior when necessary. "Coyote Law," as some Yumans call it, is the law of the land—sometimes capricious and unreasonable like Coyote himself—but nevertheless, the way things are. The tales tell about Coyote Law.

Traditionally, most Yumans did not expect a large and attentive audience for singing and story telling. Most of the traditional songs and stories in this book were told to members of the family during a winter's night. Adults would often sit and listen well, but children would probably go off to play, or fall asleep. Yet they would hear bits and snatches over and over, and listen with greater and greater attention as they grew older—and in the end, would know enough to lead a wise life, and perhaps to begin telling the stories to their own children. Through these songs and tales, everything in their daily lives would be imbued with powerful significance. Every plant, every hill, every spring was the actual site of some historic or spiritual event in a tale, and the harvesting of a plant or arrival at some location would recall the rich set of events depicted in the tales. The associational framework attached to events in our daily lives now must be so pale by comparison!

Transcription and Translation

Since Yuman languages were not traditionally written, once the decision has been made to write, the first task is to find a writing system. There are many different writing systems presented in this volume. Some are slightly modified versions of technical writing systems used for linguistic scholarship. Others are practical writing systems devised by native speakers, often Indian educators with the goal of designing a writing system that ensures readability by children in elementary grades. Some communities, such as the Hualapai and Havasuapai, have agreed upon official writing systems, now in wide use. Some other communities are still in the process of designing writing systems for their own use. Because of the complexity of the status of writing systems in Yuman communities, we have not tried to regularize the orthographies. We have generally left it up to each contributor to decide how he or she wishes to write the language.

Oral literature in many of its forms has sometimes been captured by scholars and written down as faithfully as possible to the spoken word. These scholarly transcriptions and translations of oral masterpieces are invaluable for linguistic and ethnographic research, and they form an important resource for people interested in these works for their artistic merit. And yet the artistic merit itself is not well portrayed in scholarly transcriptions. Lost are the intonation patterns, the gestures, the performance context, and the enormous background of cultural knowledge surrounding these performances. The format of presentations rarely allows easy reading. And their translations are, quite appropriately, based not on artistic goals, but rather on the goal of being as literal a translation as possible. The translation itself, then—that part of a presentation of Native American oral literature most frequently read—has little of the beauty and power of the original language.

Many poets and some linguists have made attempts to overcome this barrier by the development of free translations of Native American performances that attempt to create the same emotional impact on its English-speaking audience that the original might have on the Indian audience. Many of the results are artistic masterpieces. And yet they are sometimes so far removed from the original that no one can tell if they bear any resemblance at all to it.

There is also an audience left out by both these styles of translations: many of the American Indians themselves. Among the tribes whose works are represented in this book are many native speakers, with varying degrees of experience in reading their language, as well as people who do not know the traditional language but have some knowledge of the stories and songs. The arcane transcriptions and transliterations of linguistic scholarship are close to unreadable by native speakers of the languages so written. The artistic translations that are without the checks and balances of the presence of the original language leave a gap for people steeped in traditional culture. There is, then, a large audience who wants to read an English version of Indian oral literature which is moving and beautiful and true to the original—and at the same time wants to have before them the same piece in the native language, for the sound and the rhythm and for all those subtleties of meaning that no translation can hope to achieve with total success.

In this book, therefore, we have tried to combine approaches in the richest way possible. The literature is presented bilingually in the Indian languages and in English. In the case of Paipai, the presentation is trilingual—the third language being Spanish. We have attempted to present the book in an attractive and readable format; we have labored over translations to make them as true as possible to the literal text of the native languages, but also to give them something of the same flow and tone of the original performance. In some cases, contributors have added extra devices to preserve aspects of rhythm and intonation. Of course, there is a power in these tales that can never be transmitted through writing or translation. But the Sun Tracks Series has dedicated itself to continued improvement in the presentation of Native American literature and has provided us with the opportunity to attempt to put these Yuman stories and songs into a form that can communicate more of their feeling to readers.

The Yuman communities have always enjoyed the oral literature of their neighbors. Traditionally, there were always people in every community who had learned and could perform the songs and stories of other groups. Thus, by compiling the literature of various communities together, we are doing nothing that is new to Indian communities. And we hope people will enjoy these selections as they enjoyed them in the past—to delight in the retelling of stories they know, and to delight in the novelty of those they have never heard. ◇

LUCILLE J. WATAHOMIGIE, MALINDA POWSKEY, JORIGINE BENDER,
JOSIE UQUALLA, and AKIRA YAMAMOTO, *Editors*

The Hualapai

The Hualapai Tribe once occupied approximately one-fourth of the state of Arizona in the northwest portion. The Hualapai reservation of 999,000 square acres, which is one-tenth of the original territory, was set aside by executive order in January 1883. There are estimated to be 1,200 Hualapai members. The name Hualapai is translated as "People of the Ponderosa." Huala means "Ponderosa Pine" and pai means "people." The name originally designated just one of the bands of the people. There were fourteen bands, each consisting of a number of family units.

The Hualapai Tribe adapted ingeniously to their environment. Baskets and pottery were essential utensils in their mode of existence. Wild plants were gathered for food and medicine and for making necessary utilitarian items. The game, including deer, elk, and mountain sheep, were hunted for meat, and the skins were tanned and processed for clothing and for other uses. There were many Indian gardens wherever there was sufficient water available for irrigation.

The oral tradition of the Hualapai transmits the language, history, values, and mores of the culture. Oral tradition teaches the way things are to be: sharing, helping one another, living in harmony with nature, and the basic philosophy of the culture. Oral tradition is the conveyer of memories, passed on from generation to generation, memories of the land once occupied by the Hualapai, contacts with other tribes, their history; it tells the people who they are today on the basis of who they were yesterday.

The oral tradition committed to writing and translated into English cannot do justice to the powerful narration of the Hualapai language. The format of the English translations given here tries to capture the flow of the narration by writing the complete thoughts or phrases line by line.

Kate Crozier's life story is further transcribed by incorporating his pauses as part of the written format. Each line (beginning with a capital letter) represents a segment of speech. If the word before a pause ends in a rising intonation (indicating an unfinished statement), the following line is indented. If the word before a pause ends in a falling intonation, the following line is not indented. A blank line is an indication that an entire section of the story is over. By presenting this narration in the format of poetry, we hope that the beauty and richness of the Hualapai oration is better captured on paper. ◇

The Contributors

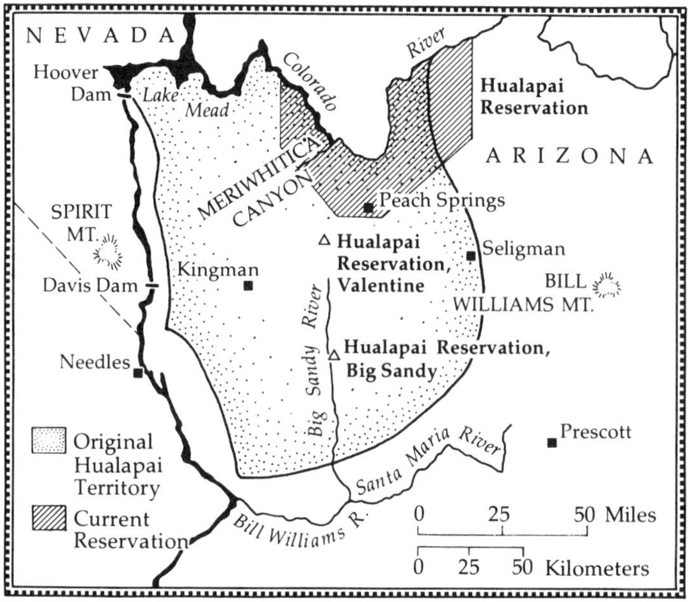

Jorigine Paya Bender is half Hualapai and half Havasupai. She grew up in Supai but is now a resident of Peach Springs. She is working for a bachelor's degree in education and is working full time with the Hualapai Bilingual Education Program as their best transcriber and translator. She has been instrumental in the development of many books and materials that have come out of that program.

Kate Crozier, a Hualapai man born in the 1860s, lived a full, rich life. The forced march to La Paz, which occurred when he was nineteen years old, and the events that precipitated it were vivid memories. He lived for well over a hundred years and saw many drastic changes in Hualapai life. He survived to tell the stories, traditional and personal. Kate Crozier was from the Milkweed Band through the line of Chief Hitchi Hitchi.

Robert Jackson, or "Bobby," as he was known to friends, lived his lifetime on the Hualapai Indian Reservation. Born in Chloride, he spent his childhood years learning the oral traditions and living the Hualapai way of life. Among the special qualities that made him a respected member of the tribe was his knowledge of the language and traditional culture. He was a largely self-educated man, learning through jobs and contacts with others, driven by strong self-motivation. He used his learning not only for himself but for his family and for the whole tribe. His ability to get along with others and his understanding and compassion for those he loved all combined to make him a man greatly beloved by his community. Robert Jackson died in February 1980 and is well remembered, especially for the services he gave to the children of the school, to the community, and to the church in which he was a leader.

Elenora Mapatis was born in Hackberry in 1903, where she lived until she was of school age. Her family moved often to go where there was work to do. Throughout her childhood, she listened to the stories of Hualapai people, and she has a vivid memory of them. She has retained the language intact through the years, a tremendous aid to future linguistic studies. Elenora Mapatis has been invited to many workshops and conferences to display her vast knowledge in any area, whether cultural or linguistic. With only a moment's notice she can sum up a topic and give a superb performance. She has the gift of a singer and knows many of the Hualapai Salt Songs. She learned how to make baskets from her mother and also makes cradle boards for families and does some beadwork. Her vast knowledge of plants made possible the publication of *Ethnobotany of the Hualapai*.

La Van Martineau lived with Shivwits Paiute relatives in Utah during much of his childhood; there he learned the language, culture, and traditional ways of the people. During these years he was exposed to the Indian rock paintings that were to consume his interest and time as an adult. In the armed services he worked as a decoder, a skill that he later used, together with his knowledge of sign language and Indian ways, to begin to decode the language of the rock paintings. His ability to share and transmit information has made him a popular consultant to several Indian tribes, who have come to respect the validity of his work. His work with the petroglyphs on and near the Hualapai reservation has added insight into that people's history and legends.

Malinda Majenty Powskey was raised on the Big Sandy. From her grandfather, Kate Crozier, she learned many traditional ways and developed a strong commitment to the preservation of the knowledge of the older generations. She has worked with the Hualapai Bilingual Education Program since its inception in 1975–76. Her work has made her an expert in linguistics, and she has authored and co-authored several scholarly articles on the Hualapai language, as well as many books and materials developed through the Program. A graduate of Northern Arizona University, she teaches at Peach Springs School and has taught courses on the Hualapai language through Mohave Community College.

Paul Talieje was born around the middle 1880s and was the oldest living Hualapai at the time of this book's publication. He has retained the legends and stories of the Hualapai as they were told to him by his grandfather as part of the tribe's oral tradition. Most of his life has been spent around the Hualapai reservation.

Josephine Uqualla is part Havasupai and part Hualapai. She lived in Supai as a baby but grew up in Grand Canyon Village. Now a resident of Peach Springs, she has taught preschool and is working for her degree in elementary education. She has worked for the Hualapai Bilingual Education Program since 1979 as a curriculum specialist and as an instructor in the classrooms. She has been a key staff member for the development of curriculum guides and materials, as well as many of the books on traditional stories and knowledge.

Akira Yamamoto is a linguist and anthropologist at the University of Kansas. He has spent many years working with the Yuman languages. In 1973 he began research on the Hualapai language. Since 1976 he has worked closely with the Hualapai Bilingual Program helping to prepare classroom materials and curricula, and assisting the staff in grammatical analysis and other aspects of language study. He has coauthored many papers with other members of the Hualapai Bilingual staff, and they have given many presentations together. He has also been a regular key staff member at summer training institutes. Born in Shimane, Japan, Yamamoto studied at Indiana University, where he received his M.A. in linguistics in 1970 and his Ph.D. in anthropology in 1974. As a bilingual, bicultural person himself, he has brought an extra sensitivity and understanding to his work with the Hualapai that is uncommon among social scientists.

The Hualapai Alphabet

Vowels

In Hualapai there are six short vowels and six long vowels. The short vowels are represented by one letter; the long vowels are represented by adding a colon (:) to the short vowels. Vowels may also occur in diphthongs, which are short or long vowels followed by the letter *w* or *y*.

Short vowels

a *wava*, 'ten'. Like the vowel in English h*o*t.

ae *baeqk*, 'to hit'. Like the vowel in s*a*t.

e *bes*, 'money'. Like the vowel in English b*e*t or b*ai*t, or Spanish p*e*so.

i *siđa*, 'one'. Like the vowel in b*ea*t, but shorter.

o *op*, 'no'. Like the vowel in b*oa*t, but shorter.

u *gula*, 'rabbit'. Like the vowel in b*oo*t, but shorter.

Long vowels

a: *va:m*, 'now'. Like the vowel in f*a*ther.

ae: *gae:k*, 'to shoot'. Like the vowel in b*a*d.

e: *be:mk*, 'to be no more'. Like the vowel in b*e*d.

i: *misi:*, 'girl'. Like the vowel in sh*ee*p.

o: *vo:k*, 'walk'. Like the vowel in b*o*ne.

u: *hu:*, 'head'. Like the vowel in p*oo*l.

Consonants

b *ba'*, 'man'. Somewhat between English *p* and *b*. A weak p, as in s*p*in.

ch *chu:d*, 'winter'. As in *ch*op.

d *thadab*, 'five'. A flap; a tap of the tongue against the gum; like the *tt* in bu*tt*er when said rapidly in English.

đ *điyach*, 'corn'. A dental *d*; the tongue tip is just behind the teeth or touching the teeth.

f *yafok*, 'to be first'. Like the *f* in *f*ist.

g *gwa*, 'horn of animal'. A sound between *k* and *g*; a weak *k*, as in s*k*ip.

h *'ha*, 'water'. A weak *ch* sound, somewhat between *ch* and *j*.

k *ko'*, 'piñon'. Like the *k* in *k*ite, or the *c* in *c*ool.

l *lu:thk*, 'to burst'. Like *l*, as in *l*ook.

m *mank*, 'to fall'. Like *m*, as in *m*oon.

n *ni:s*, 'spider'. Like *n*, as in *n*oise.

ny *nya:*, 'sun'. As in ca*ny*on.

ng *misma:hingyu*, 'you will sleep'. As in si*ng*.

p *yapa:k*, 'night'. Like the *p* in *p*at.

q *qwaq*, 'deer'. Like *k*, but the back of the tongue is farther back in the throat.

s *sal*, 'hand'. Like *s*, as in *s*ell.

t *tuyk*, 'to take off'. Like *t*, as in *t*op.

th *thambo:*, 'bee'. Like th, as in *th*in.

ŧ *aŧa*, 'reed'. Like *t*, but with the tongue tip touching the teeth.

v *va:m*, 'now'. Sometimes this is said like English *v*, but other times more like Spanish, with the air coming out between the two lips.

w *waksi*, 'cow'. Like *w*, as in *w*et.

y *yal*, 'under'. Like *y*, as in *y*ell.

' *i'i*, 'wood'. Glottal stop. Sound is momentarily stopped by closing the vocal cords, such as the break between the two "uh"'s in the English expression "uh-uh" (meaning 'no').

Wikahme'

Paul Talieje, Narrator

Ya 'ha:vch 'ha:vche gwivok gwivok
gwivok gwivok 'ha:vch mađ bay lumk

'ba:v' val vowa:vk
'ba:vch yabayk
val vowavk yuđika
ba:y ba lumk

bay ba jigwa:nk
gwivok ya yuk yuwke smak
[haygu' hayguvch spo'j kimo
hayguvch i'ka
vwav hubak thadapk ji'al kyukjik yu:jik]

nyiham be vak baya
ba jigwa:n kwij ki:je

bay ba jigwa:nka wime
nyiha nyiha nyiha' gwe: gwe gwe gav yujivch yu gav
    yujivch yuk
ge wak yuđik

Water, water; it rained and rained,
It rained and rained, flooding the whole earth.

There were people who roamed this land;
People were making their living;
On this land they had their homes
When water covered them all.

It killed all the people,
Raining day and night.
The white, white men, as if they know it,
White men now say:
For forty-five days it rained, so it happened.

During the flood period,
All those people were destroyed, so it was said.

When the flood killed them all,
That one, that, that one; there was someone, some
    body, something; some one was there;.
There was someone living there.

nyiha ba ha: ba bavđa:y i'jik
nyihach hak wa'kyu i'k
nyiha Davis Dam 'wi' hak wa:h Wikahme i'ja i:k
[Spirit Mountain mi Newberry Mountain si:joki hayguv']

nyiha nyiha nyihak jiwom hak wa'ha
gwe gayu:v' hwak'k ga yuh đ'o
đu siđthik yuđik

ya 'ha:vch bay nyi lum'm
đu đu wajimak'vim yuđ
hak yunya
đu nyihak wak yunyik hak wak yunyik yunyik

đuway'k nyuv'om
nyiha nyiha nyiha nyaji'alo đi:yup' ha:mk
nyaji'alo đi:yup' ha:m'
hak wak

ha:mk hak wak wa đik
"gwe gayu:vch be nyihe yuwk
miyah yuwk he nya: qidud'k'k yu?" yik ha:mk ha:mk

yuk yuđika:
v'va:'k v'va:'ik yum
nyiha nyiha
nyiha nyiha Guwi:hch yuwkyu i'k

Guwi:hch yuwk hak va:k 'u:k 'u:ka
"yume nyivak mu waka mi yuk yu: i'jik gi'i'jij i'k Giyo:v Guwijache jikna:k i'k

nyi e:m 'mi yam' 'u:h nyu yujivch he wa'kyu' ik
im nyiva 'yuk
'yuwk va:k nyi 'u: yukyu

nyi 'u:k 'yuva:
gwe'e: 'mu gwa'

That one, the man was getting old, so it was told.
This man lived there, so it was told,
There toward Davis Dam, on the mountain called Wikahme', so they say,
Spirit Mountain or Newberry Mountain, white men would call it now.

There, on that mountain, he was placed, and there he lived;
To live with him, he had no one,
He was all alone, so he was.

When water covered everything,
Very very lonesome he really was, but
There he remained,
There at that very place he lived and there he was; he lived there; he remained there.

Later as time passed,
Toward the east that one was gazing,
He was facing the east
And there he sat.

As he was looking while sitting there,
"What on earth is it that is coming,
Descending, small and dark?" so he wondered and looked and looked.

There it was, there it was, then,
It finally arrived, and here it was;
That, it was that;
That, it was that; it was Dove that came, so it was told.

It was Dove that came; there he came and he saw him, he saw the old man.
"So, in this very place you make your home, here you live, just as the Creator and Maker has told me and instructed me;

'mu gwa mi yok mu wik
han yova han qwidqwida
han ya mađ đu:v' va mi đathhwalk'k va mu wik
nyuwim 'ha:vch ham ham ham thađ đik ham buvk
thađ đik yuk yu:hikyu i'jim i'm i'k
i'k nyiva nyi ganavom vam wih i'jik nyi ganavok va
va:k yum" mija

mijik i'k i'đe bahch yuđe vigak yuđe gwaw'k giyu ga
i'nya đ'opki
'opm

yuđe va gwe wive gwe i:ha gwe gainavnyik i:ha
ha wiđ đinyuk đinyuk nyuv wi:ha

'mu gwa yok ha mađ nyi wawok gavgiyujim gav
wimk
hak hal jiya:mk
wa:l dav jiya:mk
mađ' hal đithgwalk'm hak đithhwalk' kwiki:

wik wim hahch ha yumk hal hal thađ'mk
ya yumk
ham buvm'k yamk yamk
yamk yuk yuk

yuk nyi đuwa:y'm qech'm yav yu: imk yamk
vithnya:p imk yamk
yu: ika: Guwi' va:kyu i: yu yik

He commanded me, 'You go and see him; there is a
person living there,' He said;
So He told me; that's why I have come here;
I have come here and now I am looking at you.

Now that I have seen you,
Ah, that thing, a mountain sheep's horn,
A mountain sheep's horn, you obtain it, you do that,
A nice, sharp and pointed one,
With that good one dig a hole in the middle of the
ground, you do this,
If you do that, water will drain into, into the hole; it
will dash in and drain through the hole, and so
it will be; thusly He has instructed me.
This He told me to tell you; so I have come to tell
you this."

So he stated, but the old man did not speak; no, not
a word.

The old man followed that, and he did as he was
told to do.
He took the mountain sheep's horn; the ground
where he was, that's where he started,
There, into the ground, he drove it,
Far deep into the ground he drove it.
Into the ground he dug; digging that place was what
he did.

As he did this, the water went out, into that hole it
drained;
There it went,
Through the hole it seeped; went out and went out;
Out it went, and that was what happened.

As time passed, slowly the water kept draining, it
went away and away.
So it was. Ah, Dove came back, I tell you.

nyiha yuwo ha:mi đim
nyihe yuw'im nyi ha:mk
hak wak ha:mk ha:mk
nyiha guwi:hch vamikyu i'k
vamika yuw'm nyi 'u:k i'ka:
ya bahch i'nyik "gayuk yuhiyu vava wikwi vava wih
mij' miny
nyuva wikwi nyu wik vak wa'kyu

mi a:mik mi yamik viya:dmik mi yavk
ya mi yavik đikivjud'v mi 'u:h
vige vige mađ nyu' yav yu:'ik
ge mađch u:vk duvk yoh yuk yijivch
mi yaming yum" i'k

nyi'i'k Guwi: jiyamk
"e:h" nyi i'k
yam' yamk
miyav' điga:vk ya yuk

miyav' điga:vk yum ye midmidmik guwev
midmidmik
ve gavgiyuj mađ gayujich ham nyov'oka
nyiha mađ'ch nyiha mađ'ch hak u:vk
mađ'ch hak u:vk
ha wilch ha'jibak
vayuk vasuwk

vasuwk yum nyi 'u:k
ha Guwi:je: yamk he gilwik'
jigaeđik yok jiłav'k
ha jiłav'k hany wik

nyiha nyiha nyi yuwom yuw'ik
yuwk he va:'ik hany wawoh'k va:'ik
ha bakđay wawo hak va: nyi'i:ka "yum nyiha jiłavk
va:k yum
yal havch thađ đik thađ đik ye v'ok yuwk
ya wil givasuw ya gaeđik ya nyi 'u:wok

That one was looking toward the east again, then,
There he saw Dove coming again.
He sat there looking and gazing at it.
There Dove appeared again.
Seeing him arrive again, the old man said,
The old man said, "What might it be? I have
followed the instruction that you gave me.
I actually did so. After I did so, I remained here.

Go along again; go and fly high above again;
Go up high in the sky again; circle the earth and see.
Somewhere, at some place, the earth must have
formed again;
Somewhere the ground has shown up and it has
dried; that should have happened.
Go forth," he said.

So saying he sent Dove away.
"Yes," he said.
He went and left.
Up went into the sky; he went searching around
here.

He flew straight this way, straight to the south.
There, over there somewhere, he arrived;
There the earth was visible,
The ground was visible,
There the grass was growing;
The grass was there and was green.

When he saw the grass was green,
Dove went to it, and that's what he did.
He cut it off and clenched it in his mouth;
He clenched it in his mouth; this way he did it.

That very same route he followed again,
He followed it and returned again to where the old
man lived; he came back again;

va gimi:k wim" ih
nyi'i:k wiđe bavđa:y i'k nyi yuji kyuđ

nyihach yuđe yiwayach đu a'diyek vayum kyuđ hak wah
"hanokyu" i'k 'kyuđ hak wah hak wak
yum yuđ yum nyi 'u:ka yav yuk yuđ

đuwaya hak nyov 'om yuđe "e'e" i'k Guwi'hch yiđ ham 'om yuđ yamik
ham 'om ha yum ha yumim
gak sinyuvk med gak ham gak vok vaya đ'o
ham 'om yuđ gwehch ha yuk yuđ hahch ham 'om yuđ

đuway ham 'om hahch yuđ thađ đik
ham 'om đu mađch bay duva
mađch bay duv' ha yuyiđ
mađche đu 'hayk vithe kyu i'j mij

đu hayk vithek gak duv dava đ'o gwad đik
nyu yu kyujk
yuk i'k hak wa'k hak wa'k

hak wa'kyuny đika
nyi đuway'm nyi đuwayme
nyiha nyiha guwavch bavđa:y'im nyi yujik đujiv bađayk vayum nyi yujika

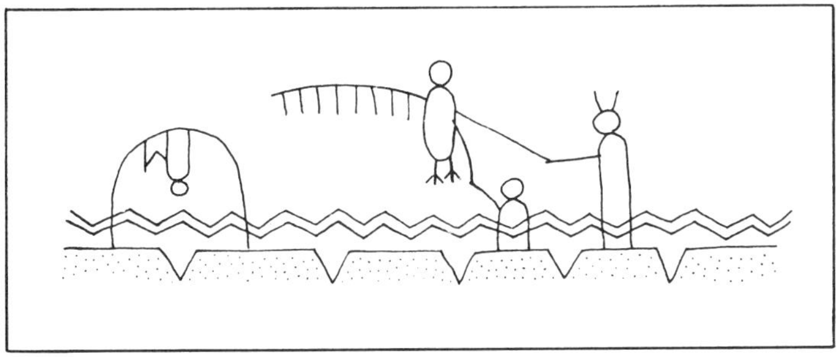

Reaching the old man's home, he said, "Thus I have clenched this in my mouth and I have returned;
There the water has gone down and drained to this point;
I have cut this green grass to show you;
I have brought it back to you," he said.
So it was, and he was aging.

As he was, he was very happy in his heart; so he was, as he sat there.
"It is good," he said as he sat there.
It happened this way, as he saw it happen; it happened thusly.

Later as time passed, Dove said, "yes," and made a final departure.
He is gone, never coming there, never returning there again,
No, from then on, no, he did not return.

No more return he made; so it happened; water no longer stayed;
Gradually water was there no more; it drained.
No more water; the very land became dry all over,
The earth everywhere was drying, so it seemed. . . .

The earth was still damp, it was said,
It was damp and not completely dry,
So it was. So it seemed and he stayed there, he remained there.

As he stayed there,
Time passed, it elapsed.
That one who lived there grew older, and so it continued; he grew very old, and that's what happened.

So it went on; there at that very place it went on; then,

yujke nyihak be đuway i'k nyov 'om
hach nyihach hak bi:'imk nyihak bemk
hak yo kyu:jki:je

bemk hak yom yom
nyiha nyi 'uka
hak yuyk Gwegiwijich Gweksiyabewch Giyovch Giwijich nyihach hach nyi đuwayk nyov 'om
đuwayk nyov 'om sinyuk
sinyuk ba kay yovik
ba kay ha be
ha be mađ giny' mađ ni:'m hwak'm ba yovk

nyiha nyiha hwaka puko
ba hwaka pukok hak bayk
hak ba jigwam hak bayk
hak bayk

nyiha nyiha qechik ba bavđay guwijivch ha nyiha nyiha mulch Mađvil mul kyujk
Mađvil Mađvil nyi mul'm

nyiha nyi ginach yuđe nyiha Judaba:h muljuny
Judaba:h mulnya ya yuk
ha muljach ya yuk hak baya
ya yuk hak bayk hak baya
đu đu ya yuk yabayach hak bayk yuk yuk
yuji đika

đuwayk nya gud'k đuwayk yu: nyime kyumo yume
Bakđay Guwijch i' ka yapam yapam nyi smajik gwe đismajim 'yujik nyuv yuk nyuv yuy
Bavđay Gwijich gwe đismajik
đismajika gwe ganavk i'k
gwe e:jim wasivka yujik i'jivj yu

yum hany hany nyi manik
yek đim nyi manik ha nyi gina ganavok "va yapame

That, that old man passed away, that one was gone;
This was what happened.

He was gone and this was what happened, and now . . .
Upon seeing this,
The Doer of Things, Giver of Life, Maker of Things, Keeper of the Universe, this very one, He, later as time passed,
Later as time passed, again,
Once again, He created a different being,
A different being, indeed,
Indeed, a younger Earth-Brother and an older Earth-brother, two beings He created.

These two beings, they were the first ones;
The two beings that He created anew, they lived there;
There He placed them; there they lived;
There they stayed.

That one, slightly older, the Steward of the Old, that one, his name, Mađvil, he was named,
Mađvil, Mađvil was his name.

That one's younger brother was then named Judaba:h;
Judaba:h was his name and this was so.
Thusly they were named and the two lived there.
In this way the two lived there, the two stayed there;
In this way these two lived there, so it went on and on, on and on it went.

Later a long long time afterward, so it seems,
The Steward of the Old said: night after night when sleeping, he had a dream; this happened again and again;

gwe đismaj'k gweny ganavjom
gwe va wih i'jik
gwe va wija i'jik i'ka mijki: i'jim

vak 'wak yum ih
waka ya ta:va 'ta:v 'ya:k ya wik
đem yok 'ke:mk ya wik vak nya jakjik

vak nya jakjik ham hath'k ya wik yahank ya nya wijik

đo:wi:m gyulok g'yafo'h gyulok
g'yafo'h qechm gyulk ya wimk ya wimk
ya wimjik đu đađek va va wimk ya 'juwida mijikiny" i'k

nyu wika ha wik wiđe gwe i'j gwe gwe ba ganavok gwe i: wiđe wija
nyu wik
nyu wik yuđ hak baya
nyu wik

ha nyiha ta yo:k ya wik 'kek ya wik hak jak'k
hath'k
jijgaeđ'k jijgaeđ'k
ya wik gilwik wik
wik wika wik

"gak đu jilwimth ge v'ge v'ge
v'ye v'ge nyihak mi jigwahak i'đe
'op đu nya'ji'alo mi điya:k hak mi điluiluik ham mi jijmijim jijmijik
jijmijik ya mu wim ya mu wik

bay mi jiwidayng wi mi jiwidayng wim i'k yavik i'k nyi'i'k nyi e:jim nyi ganavjom đismajik
vak 'wa'kyu ya wija yivch yum" i'k nyi ginya evo'

The Steward of the Old dreamed a dream,
A dream, in it he was told,
He would be given a gift to think about, to contemplate, to make sense out of, in his heart.

So, when, when he rose
In the morning, when he rose, he told it to his younger brother:
"Last night I dreamed a dream,
I was told that I do this,
That we do this, it has been said, it has been told."

Living here, as we are;
Staying here; these, the canes, gather them; you do this,
Get many, haul them; you do this; pile them here.

When we pile them here, scrape them;
We are to do this; make them clean; we are to do this.

Some of them, we leave long; the first ones, we leave long.
The first ones, a bit more, are to be long; we are to do this.
We are to do this, a lot and lot; this we are to do, then we can stop; so it has been said," he said.

What had been told to them, that was what they did; what had been said, that which had been instructed, that they performed.
So they did.
So they did, and they remained there.

Those, the canes they gathered; they did this; they hauled them; they did this; they piled them there;
They scraped them;
They cut them, they split them;

yava wik nyu wik ya:k be:mk ya wik wik
ha kek jak ya wij'k
gwe ih gwe i'ny jinyu:jik
gwe ba ganavom i:ny
"gwe va mu wijayng wim" i'k
đinyu:jik hak vonuwk
hak jijmijik jijmijik
jijmijik hak bay wi:d i'jik

bay nyi jiwidim
nyi i:y'k "v'yak v'yak gayuhim i:
i:' nyich i'giyak vache thavgabaya yiha
yeka ba:ya gak nyaji'al'm yuh đ'opk
yek giba:yam nyu wij yabayaykyu i'jik

yuktho mi eva
ya' yuktho nya đismak v'gak gayuk diw diw'ik nya 'om gavayujik yuja i'ja i'ya đ'opok
đu thuwayk va va imk 'yuja i'k va i'k bany i'k banya nyi e:vjoki:
nyi ganavjom nyuva yuja yivch yum i'm i:ja"

i' kyuđ hak yuđe đis'mway i'ma

They did this; they measured the canes; they did this;
This they did on and on.

"No, not just haphazardly, anywhere, any place, any spot here or there, right there, don't put them just anywhere, I mean;
Toward the east you place them, there you line them up, there lay them down,
Lay them down,
Lay them down; you do this again and again.

You do the whole thing, so it was said; this has been said and given to me, it was told to me, so I dreamed.
Right here we will stay and we will do this," he said, telling his younger brother.

They worked and worked, fetching and gathering canes; they did this on and on;
Carrying them back and piling them there;
What had been told to them, the instruction, they followed it;
The instruction they had been given:
"You are to perform this," it was said,
Obeying it, they went on;
There they laid them more and more;
They laid them down, then at long last the whole job was completed, it is said.

When the whole job was completed,
He said again: "What now is to happen here, he says;
The canes that are lying here, these, before dawn, at that time,
Before dawn, not at sunrise it will be,
Just before dawn, those ones there will come alive," he said;

gwe nyu widjik g'the nyu wijika đa:d'vk
yuth'ka yuk yuk yuthika:
yume nyiha yapach vilwi:v g'baye' gayum be

nyiham be gwe nyihak gwe he nyi jigwajach hak be
v'a: i'đa:mk
ma:nk mi:jvika
jijgwa:dka
gavyujik vogwajim e:vjik
evk hak đadv'k
evk hak đadv'k đadv'k i'k

yuk yuthika:
yuk yuthik nya:v'ch mađ'm nyaji'ala đ'o đim
mađ'ch va han nyi i'k'm
"mah bavch nova:ka yu kimo i'k
va yamk ba 'u:jayu" ih Mađvilach i'k "ba 'u:k 'yujay
yum" i'k

hak nyihak smaje yuk
nyi man'k be:mk hak be:m kyuki:

ha baka đevch hma:ny'vch bay viyulvik
hak wayok yuj kyumo yujom ha ba 'u:k
ba 'u:ka i'ka: i'k i'k Bakđaych hake Mađvilach i'k
nyihak đuwayim be hak bany 'u:k yuk yuđ'ke
nyiha gwawk ba gwawok ba ganavok hak vogwak
"vav nyi yuk nyi yume nyu mi yujika
nyume nyume nyach bany wiyik
nyach bany ja:ka 'yuk 'yuk
vak 'waka yuha yivch yu i'k jikna:k nyi e:jkwi
Gwegjiknahch Gwegiyo:vach va i'k nyi e:m vak
'wakyum'" ih i'm

"i'ke yuka bavch mi nova:ng yuva
ma hank nyuk wa'm yok

"So it will be, but hear me!
So it will be, but . . . when we sleep, no, no way are
we to wiggle or shake; no, nothing; we are not
to do so, He has said.

Very very quiet we are to keep, this should be so;
this and all He told me, this and all He gave me;
This is what we have been told to do; this is what we
will follow, this is what He has said."

When they talked thus, they retired for the night.

When they finished their work, when they did those
things they had to do, they lay down.
Then after awhile, before too long,
Perhaps the time was approaching the midnight, so
it may have been.

Then, it was then, those that they had put there
began to make noises;
Awakening and crying, laughing and giggling;
These things, noises they were making, they heard
them.
They listened to them while lying there.
They listened to them, while lying there without
getting up; so it was said.

Thus it took place;
Thus it happened; then, before the sun rose from
the horizon,
When the land was just becoming pretty,
"All right, the people have arrived, it seems," he
said,
"We will go and see them," said Mađvila.
"We are going to see them," he said.

There, right there they had slept.
Up on their feet the two went to that place, they
went there, so it is said.

ma hank miyujik miyujik mađ mi điyujik
mađ mi nuwah'k

mađ gayuj mi 'uj'ka: miyuja' mivch yuh
v'gake gwe hiyanma wamsivk
gwe hiyan'm gak mi yuja mi yivch yuh đ'opkyu
a' v'gake mađ-wam' mi:k nya 'opk mađ-wam'jibek
a: ma hwayv'k mi go:ka gwe gayuj gamija mivch
yuh đ'opk

đu gwe han'
đu gwe wasivja han
nyiva pida va pid mi đugwiv'k

va pida wamsi:vk mi yuk vak wamiyoh" i'k ba
gwawok
ya ganavk hak wa'k ba evok hak vogwak

"nyu yujime
yuđik ga yuka yuđik nyu yuk yujik v'gake gwemav
nyi mu wi:yik
gwemav nyu yuch
gayujich nyi jiwadv'
gayujich gayuk yuw'm nyim u:k

gayum uđ'k bavđay nyik gwe gayuk đu yak
gwedavk nya'om gayum nyim u:k

nyuk ma ba:vch nyuk wamyo:k nyim yujik
nyiha gwe mi wiwo' mi yivch yuh

wa mi yo:vk wahch jiwad vim nyim 'u:k wah mi
yovk
nyum gwedav'm nyim 'uka
nyiha wah 'wila h'kay hang jak
wila h'kay mi yomk ma ke:mk jang mi jigwa:k

There were people after people, mixed with
children;
There they were; they were there, it appeared; the
two saw that they were there;
Seeing those people, he said; the Old, ah, Mađvil
said;
It was there, later when he saw all those people
there, as he saw them,
He spoke, he spoke to them, he told them, he
advised them:
"Thus it has happened; this has come about; and
thus you are; you have come about;
So, it is so; now I will rule over you;
I will be your leader, I am to be and I will.
I have lived here; I have been given orders;
The Creator, the Maker, He has said this and He has
given me the orders, so I have lived here," he
said.

"You people, you have appeared;
Be good; live a proper life;
Be good, you be that way, you be good; since you
are related to each other,
Be friends with each other.

When you see a land, any land, you shall do this;
this is to be.
At any time you are not to think of bad things,
Do not be bad, do not have bad feelings, this is not
to be.
At any time do not hate or resent anyone,
Do not quarrel or complain or any such thing.

Only good things,
Think of only good things,
Only these things, these only, you must follow.

Think only of these things, be like that and live

yom yuk yuk muwek hank yuthik yabek yuthik
gavgiyujim nyov 'omk be:mahivch yuk nyuk
yokyu" i'k

"v'gak wami:k nya 'om ga mi yuja' mi yivch yuh
đ'op i'k
i'k gwe gayu be:mk gwe ma:h yi be:mk
o'đuh yi be:mk
o'muweyk yuk nyuk wah yich be:m nyim 'u:k
ma ba:jivch yak wamyok nyim yujik

gwe gayuvch gak gavyuk yuk yuk va muwiwo va
muwiwo i'm mu wiha'
nyu mi vg'ok mi 'u:k mi yam' mi 'u:k mi visok
yamyuk mi yuđik
gwevch juwadok
gwevch vayum nyim u:k
mi wiwo' mi wija 'mivjuk
ya v'ya v'ya wija 'ivch" i'k

"gwe han' gwe yuja han'
gwe wasivja han'"
ya ba gwawok ya ba ganavk hak vogwak i'k
ha v'wi:d i:y'k

v'wi:d nyim gwe đem i: yiđ
gwe đem ganavk gwe đem gwawk va i: yiđe

here," he said, so he advised the people.
He told this to them; there he stayed; he gave them
this advice; there he lived.

"Then, somehow it will happen and it will be so.
Sometime when you have food, you think;
The kind of food
Someone will be in need of,
When you see that someone is somehow in need.

One way or other, one ages; for some reason one
gets ill, or something will happen;
You may see this happen.

You people that live here, you will be this way,
You are to help that one, your thinking is to be so.

Make your homes; when the house needs restoring,
Build a house;
When you see illness,
To that house, haul more wood and pile it there,
More wood you haul and carry and pile on high.

When it is done so, he will be warm and good, he
will be alive; but sometime or other it will reach
a point when he shall perish, it is so," he said.

"Do not hate, or do not be or feel anything bad," he
said;
He said: "When he is in need, in need of food,
In need of firewood for building a fire,
Being warm that is what he is out of, that you will
see,
You people that live here, so it is to be.

Someone is asking for help, for help; you do that for
him, help him then, do that;
Notice this, see it, pay attention to it, watch it, and
be this way; then,

i'k "yuyiđe
nyach gava yuk vayuk yabek
yak hak wak vak wak 'yuka

yuka 'gud'ka yuk yuka đuwaya hiyivch yu đ'opa
'yu yivche juwadv'
yamche juwadv'
gwe wasiv' juwadivka
yum yume v'gake 'yuk yabe:k 'đuwaya hivch ih đ'opa

yuđik nya be:m yuđik nya bi:k nya yuk nya yam'm
nya yum ya nya giny'ch vak wa'k
ya gwe nya i:va gwe wanyasi:v i'k vak vogwam mi e:vjingyu miyu:va
nyivach vach bay yok
vach bay i'k vach bay yuk yum yuk

nyuv yum nyivache: ba:m wi:yik
nya yu:v luwik nya i:v luwik nya gwe wanyasi:v luwik i'm
mi e:vja hi:vch yu yum ik

yuđik yak nya bi:k
nya be:m nya yam'me yuhivch vak wa'kyu" i'k

yav i'k yav vilwiwok e:vo ba ganavom evjik ki:k
yuk yu i'k i' đika đuway ik'k nyov'om
hak yuk yuyđika yuythik đuway'k nyov'ome

nyihake: suwa suwa [guda ha ne:m'k wij muwij'k nyu wik yovjik wij muwijom 'u: miyuj']
nyu yuk ha ke:m muwij'ka

'thi:j muwijkwi
gwe gawij muwijkwi i'k i'jkiđe
duvk duva ha:ch duva
suwach duvo kyum nyi'i'k

When there is a need,
When you see there is a need,
You help, that you do, you shall do this," he said.

"Good things, good beings, good beliefs,"
This he told them, he advised them; he resided there;
Thus he completed this.

Many an instruction he told them; many an advice he spoke to them; that he said;
He said: "It will be that
I will, one way or other, keep living,
Here, I will live; right here I will live and I will be doing so;
I will be doing this so long, for a long time; when time is up, however, it will not be so.

My sight will weaken,
My walk will weaken,
My ability of thinking will weaken.
So in no way will I live forever, that I can't say.

When I am gone, however, when I die, however, when I go,
When I go, this younger brother of mine who lives here,
The things I have told you, my beliefs I have told you, here I have placed you, and you have heard them all, you have done so;
This very one, he will take them all,
He will say them all; he will follow them all and it will be so.

So it will be; my brother here will lead you,
Just like I have been, like I have spoken, like my beliefs, he will say:
You shall obey me and it shall be so, he will say.

đina:lk ha:vch jibak hak yok gayu' yum yuk yamk
ha bakđayach yamk ha yumk
ha: yamk ha: ke:mak

"ha: yamk yomay wim" i'k
yamk ha yum' yu:mk ya yumk ha yumk
ha:vch jiba:k he:lkyum
nyiha thi:k yumo yuk hak ba:yk yumo yujika:

gilyuj gwevche: yamhom nya' yamhom
'ha:hk g'ba:yk ha:h g'bayk ha:hk va:ma nyik
hak hanya'ch hanya'ch nya: davak yamok
hak wa'k hak wa'k

hak wam 'u:h đ'opkyu'
u:h đ'ope gavyuk yu:
nya:' nya 'om qech'm yu:hch juwadve
gayum nyiha nyiha jakji:k

haka jakji:ka hav hav' msalv'i'wok
ha v'lap'i'wo kwij ki:je
hak v'lap i'k nyi yujik kwi i'k

nyuvkyuny 'ha:h yamk
hak hak nyi buk nyi wi:d'k nyi wi:d'k h'ke:k yamk
vomk wa:h nyi va:mk
nyihak gita:vich nyihak be i' đa:mk
gwevda:v'k hak yok
yuk đako:h'l yuk

đako: h'l i'k'm đako:h'l i'k'm
yany i'me yuk yuđika nyihake: gavyuk yuh
đay sma:h đ'op đik đu nyihak be:mk yo kyujki
hak bi:'imk yum
yujike yujivje yume: i'me

nyihak 'u:k wayok
bagađe:vch hak 'u:k wayok i'jike

So, here, when I die,
When I am gone, when I go, he will take over and
he will live here," so he said.

He said this; he prepared them for his instructions;
he told them as they listened, it is said.
This was so, as it was said, and time passed on.
He was there, he lived there; though he lived there,
much later;

There, a water jug, a water-container. (Long ago
water was hauled, so, it used to be so, they
used to make that and that I used to see.)
It was so, and he hauled water; and he would do so.

They drank this, and they would do so;
They used to do these things, he said; so it is said;
But, it dried and dried; the water dried up,
The water jug dried up, so it is said.

Nearby water came out; it was abundant; somehow
it was so, and he went.
He, the old man went toward the water,
To the water he went; he hauled water back.

"I will go and get water," he said.
He went; there he went this way,
He went to the water, he went.
Water came out, flowing out and out,
That they drank, that was so; they lived there, it was
probably so.

There was something, something, where he walked,
where he was walking,
Near the water, near the water, to the water as he
was almost there,
There the frog, the frog, on the very road that he
was going,
There it sat, it sat there.

hak wamwad'vik wamwad'vik nyihak nyihak
    suwad'k vonuwk
hak e' mi:k yunyihayvik

g'gwawach gwawk ba wajimaka i'jivche i'k gwawk
    va i'k yamk
gisuwadivch hak vogwak yav ik
hak vonuwk ik
hak vonuwk yuđik yuđik

nyiva nyiva nyi ginyach nyi ginyach Judaba:vch i'k
i:ka "e'e wamjimakjika
e' ma ba:jivche: yak wamyokng yuva yuđe:
i'i: mi giyad'k yam muwijka mi đ'na:lk yany mu
    wijika
i:' mu wik hak hak mi jak ya mu wik
hak mi jigwak mu wijik
i:' mu wime wijime va ja: nyuk jimimjika đah'tavjay
    wim
v'i:'ik i'k ba evo'

ba e:vom nyu wik hak vonuwa
nyu wik i' giyad'k hak vonuwk hak vonuwk
va wik va hmi: i'wok

He did not see it sitting there,
He did not see it for some reason,
Or, or, his sight must have weakened a little,
Whatever, that, he stepped on that.

It was there he stepped on it, the stomach, its
    stomach he crushed,
He flattened it, so he did; it is said.
There, it was flattened, he did, that was what
    happened, he told.

So it was, to the water he went,
There, there, he put water in, finishing this, when
    he finished it, he hauled it, he started to go
    back, and to home he returned.
There, the pain began, there the pain overcame him.
He became ill, he became so.
It was, it was his stomach.

From the inside of his stomach, the pain started.
When this happened, right there, somehow.
Before he could sleep many nights, he passed away,
    it is said.
There he died of a sudden death, so it was.
So it was, it was the way, truly so, so it happened.

There they witnessed this,
The crowd saw it and stayed there, they say.
There, sorrow stricken, in sorrow, right there at the
    very site, they sang, they were doing these
    things,
There they cried, they were in tears.

The orator spoke; we have to bear it, we are to do so,
    he said; this was the way he spoke.
A singer, there, he sounded, this is what he did.
There, that was what the people were doing,
That was what was happening; then, then,

hak wik wij' đik
nyiha nyiha ja:hke
nyihak v'jimi:'imjik hak v'jimi:'ik

gwe gayu wi:yim gwe gayu nyi wi:yim
ham bay điyek hal hal mađ nyi mađ'l đu:jom
hal jigwa:m jikwijki
ja:hk wik va wijik wimo wij đik wijime:

yum nyihak nyihake: i'k i:ka
ha Judaba:hch i'k i:ka "gwe osji:ya 'yuka 'yuviny ge
ga wik be gava wik be 'đu:jaym imo yume
'yuk simye:kyum"
i'k hak vogwa: 'ik
ba evok hak vogwak i'me

"mi evk mi yu thim" đuway nyim i'k i:ka "Kathad
suje" ih "Kathad suje: mi yamk wa O'giwi:yache
v'ya guwe:vk guwe:vk O'giwi:yach wa'kyu
wa'k nyim yamka ba yav hubach nyu mijiny mi
yam'k mi viyam'k mi yam'k mi yuk yuk mi
va:m'k o'sji:ya m' gavak mi gamim
ya nya ya' ya đu:jay i'm" i'k

i'm i'm nyi evk Kathad'ch Kathad sujach ika "e'
nyivath wi:hi nyithja: nyivath yuhiyu" i'k
"nya' nyivath yuhiyu bavithyama hothbachijivch
yum" i'k

nyi 'i'k yam kyujki
"mi ya:m hoka v'gake: ye mak'l vi'yadmik
v'gak nyu mi yuh mi đ'opa
đu mi midmid'k đu siđthik nyuk đu nyuk mi ha:m'
mi yama
đu mi yam đu miny yujđik mi va:ma" mija i'k evom

yamk ha yumk yamk ha yumk yamk
hak đu baya bayk gwe sqid'vima đ'ok yamk

He, that one, the younger brother, his younger
brother Judaba:h said,
He said, "Yes, be strong and bear this,
Ah, you people who are living in this place, even
though you are doing so,
Gather and haul wood, do this, nearby, here you do
this;
Get wood; there, there,
Put them there, you do that.
Do that with the wood; we will lay wood one on top
of each other; we will burn him,"
This he said, he spoke to them.

He told them so and they did their job,
They did that; wood they gathered, gathered and
gathered.
They did this and made the pile high.
There they did so, so they did; then,
There, there, on the top,
There, they laid him, they laid him there.

Whatever he owned, whatever belonged to him,
All his belongings, in the ground they made a fire,
They placed them in, so it is said.
On top, they did this; they probably did this; they
must have done so.

Then, right there, at that place he said,
He, Judaba:h said, "Firestarter, that we need, that
kind, how in the world we do that, how will we
burn him, I wonder.
This, I do not know," he said, he spoke to them.
He told them, he spoke so,
"You have heard me speak, now what do you
think?"

Later, he said, "Cousin Coyote,"
He said, "Cousin Coyote, you go to that Firekeeper,

ha yum thik gayuk yuhiyu mađ vilwi:vo'
nya 'om ge điyavk va:ma gi'baye'
gayuk yuđik
he he gwe wih i'j eva đ'ok

ya mak viyadv'k ha:kok
yuwme ha nyiha đu:j mi yuk yumo
gwal hol hol'm nyi ha:k'k
hak vok' ik yujiki:
vok i'k

nyiha nyiha đu:ja yi nyiha ga wik đu:jkwi mi yik mi yijam đe o'ga:k wik o'ga:k gwe gayu wimo ya wik
gwe gayu qwinyth hak nyi jiwoj kwimo ya wik ya wijim h'lu:v i'm yujokyuny' nyu wi kwijki

nyu wa wa gina:ch nyime thimbud'k givasuwa
il giyov' nimnyuv yov muwiji'
nyiha vasuw juwkyuny
qilyev i'jim il yov đu nimnyuwok qilyayviwo muwijokwiny
nyiha' nyiha gina:jik

ya wik ya wik đu v'hluv i'wok
ha ha nyiha' gwal hol hol'm nyi ha:k'k
ha yuk he yuwk he yuwk
ha yu'k ha yu'k

ya ba: nyu nyi đu:jime
ya ma:đviche đe bilk bem yiđe
nyu va wik wiyim 'uhiyu
nyuva wik ba đuk hmuke mi gayum yumo ba đuk wim yach jigwal yiway nyiche nyuch gak nimnyuv bilk

this very one, to the south, to the south,
Firekeeper, he lives there.
All right, so you go; you have said that you are equal to four men,
Go, run, go;
When you are there, when you arrive there,
Ask for firestarter and bring it back,
Then we can cremate him," he said.

He said, when he heard him say this, Coyote, Cousin Coyote said,
"Yeth, thith I will doth, Uncleth, I will doth thith," he said.
"I will doth thith; I runth the speeth of four men puth thogether," he said.

He said this and started on his way.
"When you go off, never, never glance back,
Never, do not, do this.
Go just straight ahead, just that, and do that.
You look straight ahead and go.
Just keep going at a steady pace and you get there," he spoke to him.

He went; that he did. He went on and on.
He took off with a great speed, and off he went.
He did so, then, he reached somehow, a halfway place,
Or when he almost arrived at his destination,
Somehow, then, he did not heed Judaba:h's words.

"Behind me, I will have a quick glance, I will look,"
He did so. That, that, the fire must have been started,
A billowing smoke he saw in that way;
There he turned back, that was what happened, he turned back, he said.

bilk gak muhul nya đ'opa 'opk
đu ya wik i' kay jigwak ya wi:jik ya wijim
nyuch nyu nyuk bay đu muhul miyujokyu

nyuch bay nyuv yuk nyuv yuk nyiha ma:đach yach
bay bilk bem yiđ
vach pid bijvik hak o'h'l o'la:wk ya yuk hak yom
hach v'hlu:vik gwadvi yiđ
ge yuwk nyihak va:'ik
ha nyiha nyiha gwe hal giwa:ja
nyiha nyiha ha viyaw i' kwijk

ha jiƚavk yok wiđ đu nyadopov ye điyavk yum
nyiha điđgwijivk
ha ha gwanjaykwi i'jik i'j mij ki:

thak yav yuk ga vilwik yujkyu yujik
nyiha nyu nyu yayach nya: đi'o:n kyu i'ch
nyi nyiha nyuv wi:yim [nyiha yayach nya: đi'o:n im

The fire flamed; that was how the fire started, you may wonder; you people may wonder, but don't. Kindling, kindling, it was something similar.
Something soft they must have put there.
The fire started; that's how they started fire; this is what they did.

That very one, that one they appointed, the blue-green one.
Fly, the one that produced worms rapidly,
It was the blue-green one,
Large ones, it made, large fat worms, he produced them,
They appointed him, that very one.

In this way, in this way, he started the fire,
That one, he, that very one saw the blazing fire;
He turned back, went around, and turned back.
He kept on coming.

They cremated this man, the flesh burnt to ashes;
But, in this condition he probably saw it,
It happened, people were cremated after three or so many days,
They cremated people; when they did this, the liver, heart, those things, those did not burn right then;

They do not burn, no, they do not burn to ashes;
When that happens, they just have to add wood, they must do that again and again,
Then, and only then, they burn to ashes.

That was exactly what happened, so it happened to the body, the body had burnt, but,
The heart, lungs, and liver, they remained in the hot coals,

yujim nyiha nyuv yujivch yu:wk
nyiha nyu wim 'hađ'ch nyuv yuk
smad'kinych yuđ bay nyu yum] nyu yuk nyiha

nyiha nyu yuk hak bilkyu ij mijki:
nyivav luwik vak yokyu
gwegayu i'ka i'k hak vogwak yav i:j mi'jk
nyuv iha "mađ'che yuwo'che
yuwoch mi viyayka nyuv i'm

nyiha Judaba' nyihache
nyihach wiđe ba ja:k
ba wi:yik wi:yik wiđ hak waha
wak yuđ nyuv iha

nyuv i'k ganavoh "nyivav nyi yuk vav yuk nyi bik
'ni:ch vayuk nyi bik nyi be:m' nyi yam'm
gwe wi'wo gwe i'wo gwe jij'ginaj'ka
gwawk gwe wasivk uk i'k ba mi gwawoka
ga i'k yuk yuva 'yuh mij kijime
yuka mi evjik' yujik
nyuva yuha yivch
nyuv yuha yivch vak 'wak yum" ih

i'k ba ganavo'
ba ganavom evk "gayuk yuđe ya mađ'vch hana đ'op'me
yuwovch hana đ'op'om
Miviyaych misevk vayuk yum
yum i' v'gake smak gavayuk yuk yum hana đ'ome
'yuk gavayuk vak gayuk wayo:ha yivch yuka: 'opk
ya đu v'ya ya ya đu namak'ka

ya ha: val g'a:m'v gake:mk
gake:mk 'nyaji'alo givya:h
he he wayo:hiyum" i'k
i'k i'j đika yuk yamk yuđik yav yuk

They were still burning, but
From somewhere, Cousin Coyote appeared,
The organs that remained in the coals,
That one, he grabbed them.

He clenched them in his mouth, and he ran toward the west,
That one, they all chased him,
That, that is why they are going to kill him, they always say.

There, when this happened, about one-half of the people stayed,
That one, his nose is black and upturned, they say.
That, he clenched the burning heart in his mouth.
(That, that is why his nose is black and upturned, it is so.
That is the way it is, it is so.
Because he did that, dogs are like that,
Even their ears are all like that.)

It was that way, it was that way, it burned; this is how it happened, it is said.
This is how it is today,
Whatever it was, he said, he was talking, that is what they say.
He said this, "The body, his path, his life, something bad happened to them."

Judaba:h, he,
He led the people living there,
He led them, ruled them and lived there,
He lived there; he said this.

That was what was told: "When a person dies this way,
When the people are gone and no longer here,
What he did, what he said, what he commanded,
His thoughts, his beliefs that he told you people,

nyuv yuk ha:h hmu:k bay ya yuk ha:h'm gake:mk
hach nyaji'alo givyave nyiva ha:v wa'k jik wi he
wayo:kyu i'j ki:je
he wayo:k hak wayok

nyuv i'k gwe iha gwe gwawa gwe wasiva a: ba
gwawok
ba ganavok ya wik ba jithwe:k yamk gak v'oma đ'ok
yekđ'm i'k va i'ka
nya: v'wa:m i'k
nya: nal'mik vav i:jik
yamk ya i'k kyu i'ka:

yujiđ nyihake đuwa:y i'k nyov 'om
đuwa:y i'k nya: gud'jik nyov 'om

yuk yuke yuk yuka: nyiha Judabahch i'k i:ka
nyihak ba: gađev' hak wayok yum yuk yuva: ba
gwawok
ba i'k ba ganavok "ma ba:vche ma ba:jivche vak
wamyok
'đek vak wamyok mi yu:va gava i'k wasi:vk i'k yuh
đa'op'
mi yama mađ'vch ye yo:k mađ'vch ye yo:mk
ha'vch yuka i'k

gweđay giyov gwethov gwe gayuv vilwivk yuk
mađ'v'm bay vilwik vak yok
yok yu:va mi yamik gavgiyuch' wi' mađyawa gayujik
yawa mi 'u:k han mi 'u:k mi yuk nyihak
wamyo:hing yum" i'k ba jiyama

"nyuv yujay'yum" i'k
i'k ba e:vom ba ganavk
yav i'm evk nyuv yuja [nyuv yujik gwe gayuvche
hayguv'ch yu:w'm ga i'ja đ'opki:

This is what is going to happen to me, he told us;
This is what you heard,
This is the way it will be for me."

This he told the people.
They heard what he said, "What is happening is that
this land is not good,
My walk on earth is not good,
The disaster is overpowering, it is so,
It is so, I am saying, I cannot sleep good; I don't
know why it is not good;
I do not know how; there is no way we can live here;
No. Just leave this place here.

The water that is flowing down here, we cross that,
Cross that to the other side to the east,
There we will live," he said.
He said this and they went, and it was how it was.

It is how it was; they moved across the water; they
all did so, they crossed the water.
They settled at a mountain in the east, they settled
there, it is told.
They settled there, they lived there.

He spoke to them, his sayings, his thoughts, he
orated to the people,
He told the people; in this way he had managed,
continuously, never stopping;
In the morning he spoke, he spoke;
Late in the afternoon, he spoke;
In the evening, he spoke;
At sunset, he spoke; it is told.

They did this way there; later on it ceased.
Later on, as time passed, it ceased.

That was how it was, that was how it happened; that
one, Judaba:h said,

hayguvch val yunyik gwe gayu mulva 'kay'v haygu-
    đaha:n mi nya 'om gwe gayu:vch yumo val
    wayo:hm nyu nyuch val yu:w'm ga i'ja đ'oki:]
    đu ba:j dava pid kyujki
ba:j dava
ya bay mađ'v bay vonu:k mađ'v'm bay vilwi:'im
    kyujki:je

i'jim yuk yamk galwik yamk yamk yamk yam đik
bay mađ'm ba:y vilwi:'imk vilwi:'imk
nyach jivch yal wayokyu
yal wayok
ya mađ'vk wayok 'yuv
nyach jivch nyach jivch nyihal nyihal ginyi:vjik
    yumo yuk
nyihak ginyi:vjim nyajiv gak ba: gany i'h đ'op
yaj đowi:m đ'kyujik
nyajiv ba: gav nyi ih đ'opa

o'pk o'pk
ga ih yi đu wasi:vk

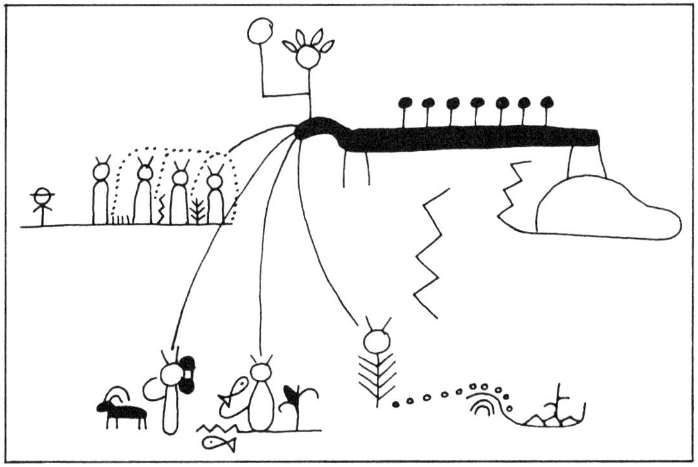

There, where the crowd lived, where they were, he
    spoke to them,
He said to them, he told them, "You people who live
    here,
There are many of you here, you are; what I am
    thinking is not random,
You go, there is land over here, over there,
There is also water," he said.

"There are things plentiful there, there is game,
    everything all over,
It is all over the land.
This is so, go and find the land somewhere; search
    for a good land,
Find a good land and live there, this is to be," he
    said, telling them to go.

"This is what we will do," he said.
This is what he told them, that is what he spoke.
When they heard him say this, they did this. (They
    did so; some others like white people, they were
    not mentioned.
White men were included in here,
Some other kinds of names,
Mexicans or something else that might have been,
In here they lived, the very kind, in here they came,
They were never mentioned, never.)
Real people, Indians,
Throughout the land they roamed;
All over the land they spread, it is told.

Throughout the land they went, some left first and
    others followed;
They inhabited all of the land;
We stayed here on this land;
Here we lived,
On this land we lived,

ih yi:
yuh yi:
wasivk hak wa'k
gak nimnyuv wasivk "va mi yuh va mi yunya va mi yujnya" i'k
gak ba ih đ'ok
đu ba 'u:k
đu đu ha đu ba yigwithe'
mi ba gawik wihwi
ba gawim yumo yujika
ya yuja đ'op miyujkyu
ba ga i'ja đoki: yij miyujkyu i'jom
ga i'ja đ'opki:

hak đuway i'k nyov 'om
ha nyuv i'k nyuv i'ka i'kimo
nyiva Wamu:ha Mu:ka nyihachva
nyihachiv gwe ba e:h puk kwijki
gwe ba e:k
gwe ganelo wika savađo'v nyiva be e:jik
va ba e:jik i'k

"ma:ch yam yok mi yamk
mi nyihađja mi yok mi yamk
ya v'ya gwethov nyi ma h'na:qjik nyu mi yok v'ya ya mi gwank mi tho:k
nyu mu wik ya nyimiy'v nyu mu wik nyivam mi jibevk
vam jibev mi jiyovk gwe giyu ga mu wik mi yovk
nyiva va mahnyoyk
nyivam mi jibev nya hi:vjum" i'k
yav i'k yav i'k ba e:m yamjik
ba e:m yamjik yum
ve điya:vk yam'l điya:vk yuwk

yam'l điya:vk hav yuk yuwk
hav yuk hav yuk hav yuk hav yuk yuwk yuwka

We did, we did; we refused to leave,
We refused to leave the place; he did not say anything to us,
Some of the other people began to leave,
He did not say anything to us,

No, no,
What he wanted to say, he contemplated,
His speech,
His belief, he sat thinking,
He did not think just a short time, "You do this, you be this way, you all be this way," he thought.
He never said that to them.
He just watched them.
Just, he just spared them,
Or he might have talked to them.
You do not act this way;
He never did speak to them, it is said.
It is not mentioned.

Later, as time passed,
It was then he spoke, he said.
The Navajos, Hopis, they,
It was to them, he gave rules first.
He gave laws to them,
Sheep, it was goats, he gave to them,
He gave to them, it is said.

"You take this and go,
Get your animals and go;
When you desire meat
Take them and kill them and feast on them;
Do this, the fur you use for covering,
With this, make blankets, something you make,
This, wear as shoes,
Cover with this, you are to do this," he said.
He said this, he gave it to them and they went.

yuk yuk yu i'ja
yuk yu i'jik i'jivch

vav i'k i'k i'k nyiva va gwe kaya i:va
va Wamkava nyiva be va: be
ba i'k "Wamkave mach ya ha: vam giyakve
nyiha guwev gavgiyujik mađ 'uk
mach mađ mi 'u:k mi hanik mi 'u:k
hak nyihak gwem hwalk
hak mu' wak hak mu' wak
'yuj mi ma:k hak mi yuh mivch yuny kyum" i'k

nyiha gwe yach ba gwe yach ba e:m
nyihach hmu:k'k he yamnyik
yam'l nyiha guwevk
hak thukije
nyuwa Bullhead City guway'le nyihal wayom
  kyujki:je

nyihal wayomk yuk
nyiha wiđ
"mach gwethova
gwe gayu:'u 'yuj mu winya mi yi:vch yu đ'op
mi yunyah mivch yu đ'op
ya ha:v'l ichi:vch gwevch ichi:v val gowa:jiv
nyul giyu:ny
nyiva mitho:nyah mivch
vak yokyu yuk yum" i'k "nyuwi iyo: nyu 'ha: nyu
  gwe nyu thaeq nyu gilyuch nyu
nyinyu nyinyum he mi yovk
ga mu wim wik baqich he:'
mahnyo mu wik mu wim mahnyo giyalv mi yov'm
  wik mu wim nyu mahnyoyk
nyu mi yuh mivch yu" i'k
yav i'k nyiva ba e:k

Judabahch i'k i'm
Wamkavach yuđ hmu:k'k Wamkavach yuđ đihinyvik

He gave this to them and they left, so,
To this way, down here in this direction, they came.

They came in this direction, they came on,
They came on this way, on and on.
This way, this way, they came.
It was so, it is told.
It was so, it is told.

This is what he said, this, to a different one he said
  that also,
This, the Mojave, they,
He said to them, "You Mojaves, the water that lies
  here,
Somewhere to the south there, find a land,
Search for a good land, find a good land,
There, plant crops, live there, you live there,
Those plants you will eat and live there, this is to be
  so," he said.

He gave them seeds, gave them seeds;
They moved; they went over there,
Down to the south,
There they turned,
At Bullhead City, down there they settled; it is told.
They settled there, they did this.

To them, he said,
"Your meat,
The kinds of things you will not have,
That is your being, it is not to be.
In the water here, there are fish, they are in here,
These are in there,
These you are to feast on;
This is what is to be," he said, "That, the water-
  willow,
Those, the leaves of those that are there,
With those make dresses,

val nyihal wal hal yamk
hal wayom kyu i'j mijki:
[Ft. Mohave'l ba jijya:jmik] "ma:ch vam yuk mi yunya
gwevch yivilwivk i'i:vch ha:vch gwevch gwemtho:h yivch
gwe gayu ga mu wik mi tho:nya mivch
gwe giyu yilwivk đu ham vowa:vk
ham vonu:kyu" i' ki:k

ya mađ'm mađ'm bay vilwik
yak wayokyu
wik gwe mu:lv gwe gayu mu:lvch yu Hwa:j yu gwe gayu: mu:lv
ba si:đjikimo i' va
yum yav yujkyu i'ja
ya vilwi: gavyuj kyuij yiđe
nyajiva med' dav 'mi:vik i'k i'k "mach Hwalbay Hwalbaye
mach ya yuch mi gimu:l'vche
v'gak ge gud'm mađ
nyi mađja kay mađ nyi wija kay'
yuk mi yamk ge ga mi yunyah mivch yu đ'ok

ya: ha vam giyak'm
mađ vak giyo:va
vam giyujiv
nyiva nyivak mowa:vik
vak monuwik
vak mi yujnyah mivch vak yokyu
gwevch
i:vch
ha:vch
habaqch jiba:k vayujik yuva
ha nyuch nyuva i'i nyuch gwe gayu gwemtho:' miyivch yivilwi:vk
nyum vonu:k

Somehow do so for the women to wear;
Shoes, you make; make sandals, you make, you do so to wear;
This is what you will do," he said.
He said this and gave this to them.

Judaba:h said, he said,
The Mojaves moved, the Mojaves moved,
Down there, they went down there,
They settled down there, that is what they say.
(He sent them to Fort Mohave.) "You are to be this way.
Things are prepared, the fish, water, food you are to eat,
The things you are to do; things you are going to eat,
Those things are prepared; they are around there;
They are there," he said.

Throughout they spread all over the land,
They were living there,
Names, whatever names they were, Apaches, whatever their name might have been,
He named them; he said,
This is how they were, it is told;
They were like this, somehow, but,
Us, later, next, he said, he said: "You Hualapai, you, Hualapai,
This is what your name is going to be,
Nowhere, no far away lands,
Different lands, some strange lands belonging to others,
You are not to go or be anywhere;

Here, the water that lies here
The land here, the land along this river,
Here, you roam here,
Be around here,

ya havch 'chi:v va ma nyi ma hina:qk
nyivach nyiva mi yuwka mi yuk'k mi yok mi
    jgwa:nk mi tho:k
va mi yujah mivch vak yokyu" i'k

ya mak'dav va nyiva nyajiv bany e:ny kwiki:
Judabahch wik wik bany e:k wi i'k

nyu yuk nyum wayo:kyu
nyuv yuk ba đek đu yumk nyum wayo:kyu
bay ya mađ'vch bay đudo luwikyu i'ji:
i'jik yujik yuj đik đu đu vak yoha
vak yom nyuv yuj miyujik
nyuv yujik nyihal wayomka
'chi: tho:ka va wijnyim muwijk
vayuk yamk vam vowa:v'k vam vowa:v'k

yuthik đuway'me yuk đuway'm hak nyov 'om
đuway i'k nyov 'om
nyihak be hak be a:mjik
hak be a:mk
ya yuk vam naga:mk ya yuk yuj'k

ye ye v'ye đowi:k nyiwa Hwal-yigwilak
nyihak dowi:k hak đi:gav kyujik
hak đi:gavk đowi:k vam noga:mk
vam vayuk yuth'k nyivam vam vowa:vk
yam vowa:vk yam ya yuk yuj thik
Hwalyigwilak đowi:k he nibaj i'k
vayuk va lwi:j hak wayokyu i'jik
[gwe gayuvch hayguvch
janmich
nya 'om gwe gayuch val yujnyom i'jo ga i'ja đ'opk]
đu ba:j dava pid'k

đu mađ'm bay vilwik
mađ'm bay đu:dkyu i'j mijki: kyu i'j ki:jtho

You are to be here, it is destined,
Things,
The fish, the water,
Springs flow, it is so;
That water, that wood, whatever you are to eat is
    prepared,
They are around here.

This water, this fish, when you desire this,
Here, come here and get them, kill them and eat
    them,
This is what you are to do, it is so," he said.

This he gave to us at the very last, it is told.
Judaba:h did this, gave this to us, it is told.

This is how the people lived here,
This is how, many people, lived throughout here,
All the land seemed overcrowded, it is said.
It is said, they were, this is how it was.
This is how they were,
That is how they settled around there,
They ate fish, this is what they did,
This is how they lived around the land.

Then, later, as time passed, much later,
There they were; they traveled,
There they traveled.
They did this, through here they departed, they
    departed.

Over here, some of them, at Hwal-yigwila,
There, some of them gathered, it is told.
They gathered there, some of them departed
    through here,
It was here then, through this land they roamed,
They roamed through here, this is the way it was
    until

đu nyu giyu:ch vak yokyu i'j ki:je kyu: i'jik
i'jith'ka yum nyiha nyuv i'jim qech'm evk vam qech'm evk yujtho
Wamkavach hach gayujik yuka nyihak hak gayuk wasivk yuk
yamk nyadopov ba ba guv'nu:v he guv'nu:
he gavgiyujik yuk yamk he siyek
mađ he siyek yamnyik
Barstow gavgiyuj'k nyu yuch 'ha vam g'a:m'v lwich hak yok yuthik
hak yok yuthik đuway'k nyov 'om
hach 'hach duv'm nyi 'u:k Wamkavach he vok'k

he vok'k yake nyiva val mađ ba e:h puk'k
val wayoh pukov
nyival va:k
wayo kyuj ki:je

nyach nyajivch nyi giđiyev'ch Suđul'g'bay'm vayuk hal vonuwk
hal vonu:k yuđik
ha yujim nyi 'u:k
mak'l hinyk mak'l vok

vam voya:k vam vonu:k
yamk vam 'vowa:vij 'vowa:vyu i'j mij ki:
ya yujik yuk yujđik nyim 'om yuđ
hach yuđe nyiha
ha nyiha novo:k nyuk wayo:kyu
đowi:k nyum wayo:k
yamk wa Mađgahwalal ha yumj'
Wamkavach ya yuk nyuk wayokyu

nyihal ba 'kay hal vonu:k
"'hach duvkyu" i'jik
hal giv'nu:w'v gwe gayu mul'vch yuha

At Hwal-yigwila, some of the people lived, it is said.
This is how, like this, they lived there, it is said.
(Other beings, Anglos,
Japanese,
Or other peoples, in here they might not have been, it was never mentioned.)
Just real people, Indians, only,

Through all the land,
All the land was overcrowded, it is said, it was told; then,
That is the only beings that were, it is said, it was so, it is told.
It was said, that is what was told, the little that I have heard; then,
The Mojaves, they, somehow, thought of something,
Some of them went to the west; People, there are people
Over there, somewhere. They went,
They went toward that land,
Somewhere at Barstow, where they went, there was a river that flowed through there, like here,
It was there, but much later,
The water in the river dried up, they saw this, the Mojaves returned.

They returned from there, and came here, here to the land he gave first,
Here, where they settled first,
There they arrived,
They settled there, they did, it is told.

We, our people, People of the South, with them they lived,
This way we were living about,
We lived around there.
When we saw them do this,

ha nyiha mulv gwe mulv ba sij yiđ simyech mijki:
nyiha Wamkavach ha simyenye mi spo'ch nyi yiđe
gak ga i'jim eva đa'op
đu nyuv yujivch yuk yuj

nyihach bay be:m i'mo i'jiny
nyihach 'ha yaduvk bay be:mk
mijayk bay buyk bemk
ya siđ gayuj yabe:kyu ih ha

Barstow gavgiyujik nyi mađ'k hak wayaw'vjuny thik
bay be:mkyu i'jki:
đu mađ dava pidk
[haygu:v dava pid'k yujivch yu i'j mij ki:je]
yuk gana:v'm nyuv i'k i'kiny

yalwi: ya yukyu i'jivch
hak wayok yujik wayokyu i'jivch
vak wayok wi:'l nyu đowi:k vak wayok yuthik
ya v'ya v'yal nyu wal Mađwiđa'l đowi:k vam wayo:k

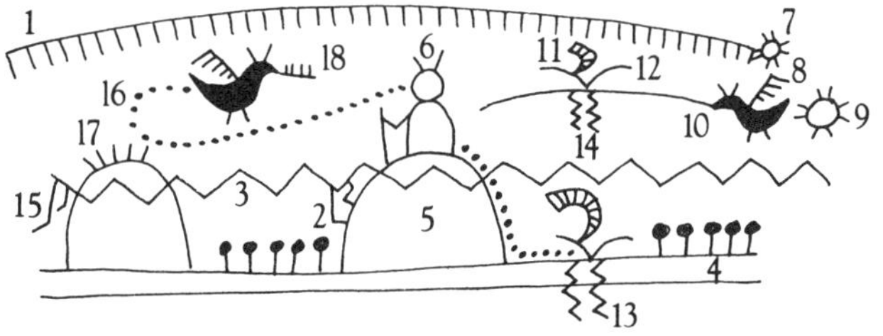

(1) Raining 45 days. (2) Legs climbing (water rising). (3) Water. (4) People wiped out. (5) Wikahme'. (6) Old man on mountain. (7) Sun (days). (8) Bird obeying Creator. (9) Bird coming from East. (10) Bird telling man to dig with ram's horn to drain water. (11) Ram's horn. (12) Open up (dig). (13) Old man going down and digging hole; water drains out. (14) Water going. (15) Legs (water) descending. (16) Old man telling bird to go; bird finds. (17) Grass on mountain. (18) Grass in mouth.

The Hualapai moved back, we came back to this area.

In this direction, they roamed about,
Through here they roamed, so it is said;
In this way they were, until
It was that way, it was;
They all returned, and they lived there;
There some of them settled down,
This way toward the Hualapai Mountains, they came,
The Mojaves, this way here, they settled.

There were different peoples around there,
"The water dried up," they say.
Around there, people were there, some kind of name they were,
Their name, whatever they were called by, they did not know,
They, the Mojaves, they have forgotten, or they might remember it; I have never heard them say,
Just that kind they were,
Those ones, they were all gone, they say,

They died of thirst,
They died of hunger,
Maybe one of them may have survived.

Somewhere, around Barstow, their land there, the people lived there,
They were all gone, it is said,
Just only that land,
(Now only Anglo remained there, it is said.)
It is told, he said this.

This is how it was;
There they lived, it was meant for them to live there,
They lived here and some lived in the mountains, they lived here; then,

yam wayo:k ye yav yujik yuj kyu i'jivch
yujik yujive ha Hwal-yigwilach hal đek hak wayo đik
đowi:ka nyuv yuk nyiha nyiha

nyiha mu:lvch hak nyihaje g'gwawvch ha nyiha
nyuwa Judabah lwi:yivch
ha nyuv lwi:yivch hak wayok
gwa:wk ba mu:lv'ch hubam hak yovij'k
ba yovjim nyihak wayok

yuktho đowi:k hak đowi:k hak wayok
đowi:k hak ginyi:vk wayok
đowi:k yam yuwk yal nyival wayoy kyujki
ba ka:y'm đi:gevk Mađwiđ'vle
Mađwiđ'l wayok va yu kyu i'j ki:je ◇

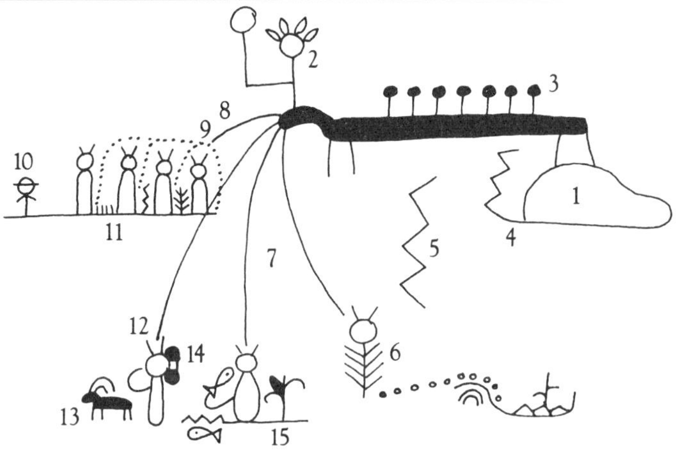

(1) Wikahme'. (2) Younger brother as Chief. (3) Younger brother carrying people (taking them) away from Wikahme' and across the water. (4) Where the water rose (flood). (5) Water they crossed. (6) Pine People (Hualapais). (7) Instructing. (8) Instructing people. (9) Telling people to scatter and dwell all over the land. (10) No white men living here. (11) Grass, water, trees—for food and drink on land. (12) Lower positioning equals later instructions. (13) Instructions to Navajos to have sheep and eat them. (14) Navajo hairdo. (15) Instructions to Mojaves to live by water, eat first and plant corn.

Here, here, down here, in Mađwiđa, some of them settled,
Here they lived, over here, they were, so it is told;
They were there, up Hwal-yigwila, many people lived; then,
Some of them, that way, there, there,

The leaders there, they, the spokesmen, just like Judaba:h,
The same as he, they lived there,
Talking, they appointed four leaders,
They appointed them and they lived there.

Some of them, however, there, some of them lived there,
Some of them refused to leave there and remained there;
Some of them came through here, down in here they lived, so they say;
With different peoples together, in Mađwiđa,
Down in Mađwiđa, they lived, this is how they did, so it is said. ◇

Mađwiđa

Elenora Mapatis, Narrator

nyul va:mjik kyujki
yal Mađwiđal
Mađwiđal va:mjika
bagađevch nyul wayok
gwe:hch yuha
Gija:nch yuha
Wamkavach yuha
Jimwavach yuha
Jimwavach yunythik
yake gweny ge
wik Bullhead City i'jim
ha đivgo:jokwi
nyu gagiyuj nyum ha sake:jivch
sake:ja yijithik
hach gak yamja đ'ok
đu vokjim ih ma:đki:
yuja i'k wasi:vk yujthik
nyi vokjik đu ba đagwivjika

They say they arrived there
Down there in Mađwiđa
They arrived in Mađwiđa
Many people settled there
They were
Quechan
Mojave
Chemehuevi
The Paiutes were going too but
Around here somewhere
[There at Bullhead City is a dam]
Somewhere there was a bridge
They were going to cross there
But they did not go
They returned, they say,
They planned to cross, but
They returned and followed the people
Down to Mađwiđa

val yuwjik val yuwjik
bay yuwjik yuwjik yuwjik
hal Mađwiđal wany yomk
yuđe ba:y dav hal Mađwiđa bay wayo:ha
Wamkavach Wikahme wayoha
hal wayoka
"nyach Wamkava yu" i'j ki:ki
i'jim yuđe nyuch đowi:k yale Mađwiđa
nyul wayom kyujki:
wayok nyul wayoka
bagađehch ba:y dava hal no'va:mk
nyul wayo kyujki
Mađwiđa ba:y dav nyul wayok
nyithal wayok gwe hwa:lk
hal wayok gwe'e điyach wiha
hamđe wiha
midi:k nyuv yuj wijika
gwe ham gabe:h ya:k
ko' ny wih
'manađ nyu
viyal nyu
nyu yu:j yo:k maji muwi:ja
nyiv ya ma:jika
nyu wi:jik nyum gwe jijyovjika
gwe'e gabdo:
suwa' va wi:jika
han' hal wayok a'diyayk'
gwe dayk
wisđo wi'ka
đasvika
no:fika
đudvika
nyu yujik nya 'op' jigaevika
jigwi:thvika
va' yu:jiđik
'thal wayo đika

All the people arrived
Down in Mađwiđa they settled
All the people lived in Mađwiđa
The Mojaves remained at Wikahme'
They lived there
"I shall remain a Mojave," they said
They said this, but some of them went down in
Mađwiđa
Down there they lived
They lived down there
All the people arrived down there
It is said they made their homes there
They all lived in Mađwiđa
Down there, they lived and planted crops
They lived down there and planted corn
Squash they planted
Beans and other crops they planted
Native plants they gathered
The piñons
The banana yucca
The mescal agave
These they harvested and ate
These they ate
They also made useful items from these plants
The bowl-shaped baskets
The water jug they would make
They happily lived together
They played games
The stick game
The shinney game
The hidden ball game
The hoop and pole game
They played these games or they raced
They wrestled
They survived in this way
They survived and then

Maďwiđal wayok
wayo đik
[yak hma:ny qachich 'nyudm'u:jik
gwem đi:yek day day mij mij'ngmi
đu đi:yek mi'mi' i'j mijki
nyuv yujk yujki:]
chud 'wava hwak'e mi 'wava hmuk'e
[20-30 years i'je mi ganyyujik hal wayoka]
i'j đika đu hmany giđiyeh i'jik
điyek mi:k day day i'k mik
baeqja đ'o yiđe
[nyu yum vak nyuv i'ji gwadva maďki:]
gweny nyuv yu đim
Maďwiđal nyuv yuk yu:jki
hal yuwk hak yuđ juhway kyujki:
yujim yuđe hmanyach nyi mi:m i'đ
bagđa:yach yuđe bay yuđ hwa:yka i'jki:
yuđim hmanyach nyi mi:m i'đe
yav i'k i: iha
"hmanya nyi giđi:yewach wanyi wa daywa daywa
nyiya we nyiwa nyi i:m we
gake nyi bagađe:hach
gaje nyi ja:wvik wayalayk
'wanyi yujika jiha
hale nyi đigavik
vanyi nyi yuđi: ga nyihake nyi hijihwayik
gake nyi vida:d i'k wanyi yuwme
yava nya yujika
ba ganyiđayach hame hwayika
wi:v'm nyi đađanehvika iv'm i'j baeqvi đam'ka
yavi nyi wanyi hwiji:ch vanyi:h yum
yuwa nyi i:m i'ki:
i'wa 'yoka nyi miwo: thake nyi jihwa nyi qechi thake nyivi dadik yumo
yava nya i'ka u:liwanye
nyiyake yokame" ik i:k

They lived in Maďwiđa
They lived there and then
[Here some children at school
cry over nothing
Just cry over every little thing
That is what happened down there, they say]
It was about 20 or 30 years later
[They lived there 20 or 30 years]
It was so, that the crybaby
Would cry over every little thing
Even though he wasn't hit
[Maybe some children might act like that here]
Something like that happened and so
They say that it came to pass that in Maďwiđa
On account of that, there was a battle
When the crybaby cried
All the people fought, they say
When the crybaby cried
This is the song they sang
"Crybaby cry cry
When he cried
All the people
All fought in anger
So they did
In a mass
This way they battled
They couldn't get up
This way we are
The old people joined in the battle
They hurled stones and they hit with sticks
This they did then
This happened, they say
He got the stick and put it there where the battle originated
This I will say
This is the place," it is said

hmany suwad'k
ba:ha siđ'k suwadk
hmany giđiye:h điyav'm
bagađa:yach wiv'm điđanehvik
i'vm ji'baeqvi đa:mk
jihway yik jihwa qech yo:vkwi ik i:jki:
hmany gi'điyehk điyavik
hak nyi ja:wvim đo:wik buy'ya
đo:wim ba jigwanja
gavyuj đinhmi:dvija
i'jim yuđe nyi đ'opk nyi o'pk
Waqiyasma ga'mulvch nyihe gwe jikna:vj yuh đ'opm
"đu 'nyach yuwo lwi'm vam 'om gwedavk nya bim ya 'wahavol mijimi:ja
gak ge muwamk miđu:h miđ'opa
wahavo ih nyul mijimi:jim val đu 'yaka" ik vany ik
gweha Wasi:yoma Waqiyasma Jiqyal-Giđi:dva Joq-Gijsi:va mij i: nyi thajivch i'đe
"maha gak ahanja đa'op nya yujika
vam 'ome gak baya asiđ'k gwawjiya đa'opay
vam 'om đu 'ya:jimka vilwaqmik
g'odvak hak nya jibamjiktho
đu mi ya:jmik đu tha mi yumk đu mi ya:jmik
mi novo:ka
mađ'm ba:y mi juyavangyu" i'jik
ba gwawjo ki:jki
ba gwawjok ba ganavjok
"vam 'ome gak sinyuvka mađ 'ya evika
mađa spoyka
'điyevk wayoya yivch yu đ'opk
vam 'ome đowi:ka jihwa qech vak
jihway qech vak jivda:djik nya yuj'ka
ba:v đowi:k buyme:
vam 'om đu vam vijiyawa yivch siđ thikyu" i'k

He sang about the crybaby
One man sang
Blaming the crybaby
The people were hurling stones at each other
Hitting each other with sticks
They created a small battle, they say
On account of the crybaby
There some people died
Some people were killed
Some people were injured
They say some were and some weren't
Waqiyasma, the Chief, did not order this battle, so
"Since it appears to be my doing, when I get sick and die, bury me in this cave dwelling.
Don't take me anywhere to cremate me.
Just lay me in this cliff dwelling," he said
Wasi:yoma, Waqiyasma, Jiqyal-Giđi:dva, Jog-Gijsi:va, all said
"This battle is not good
From now on our language will not be one
From now on we all will leave and scatter one by one
When we come out at the rim
Just continue on your way
On foot
You will settle throughout the land," they said
They commanded them, they say
They commanded them, they told them
"From now on, never again will you understand each other
You will be exiled from this land
You cannot live together anymore
Because some of the people, a small battle here,
Since we were involved in a small battle,
Some of the people died

"vam 'ome gak 'gwawjivch đu đisivu:kvik 'kayme"
"nya gak mađ ya' eviya đa'opyu" i'k ham vilwaqk'k
vam yuwja nyuv yuji gwadva giyafo'jach yuwk nyuv yukjik
yak đowi:ka yak gweh si:ja Hagivgwach i'jki:
nyuk smakjika Qivjudak smakjika
yak gweny ge He:l nyuk
nyuk smak'k vav yu:jik
đu 'diye:jika
hanjik yujik nyujik
"đu yem mađ 'u:k wayo:hiyu" i'k vam yuwjik nyuk smak
galwi: gayuj sið hwak smak
hmuk smak hubach smak vayujivch
gijyujik vam yuwk vam yuwk
nyum nyuv yukjik vav yukjika
v'yake gweny ge yale I'qađ i'jik
nyival nyival va:jik
đu thugwayk novo:k nyuv yuj'k
đowi:k val va:k
nyival wayok vav yujik
gidnyu:vach we đu yuwk vad
v'ye nyuv yujik vam yamk val wayo:ka
hiny'k yamk ye Gwadal nyihal wayomka
đu hi:nyik vam yamk hav yumk Havsuwal wayomk vav yuj kyujki:
Havsuwal wayomk yuthik ham yamik
ha yum đik yujik
vam yamk we'e Mađnyu:h wayomk
đowi:k hav yumk yamk
wale Indian Garden i'jokiny nyihal wayoma
hal wayom thik giyujik vam yamk
hav yumk we'e Tuba City yuk hav yumk đu đu hinyik yamk

From now on there is no other way but to separate," they said
"From now on there will be many languages."
"I do not understand you," they said and started branching out
This way they came, the first ones did so,
Some of the people at Ha Givgwach
There they slept and made their camp at Qivjuda
Here at this place He:l
There they slept and made their camp, this they did
They all were happy
Since they all were going to be all right
"We are going to find a place and make our home," they said as they were coming along making their camps
It might have been one or two nights
Sometimes they spent three or four nights
They continued on like this
This way they all came
There at Iqađ they say
Down there they arrived
They all walked fast
Some arrived down there first
They made their camp down there
Some of the people were still coming
Over here they went and made their home
Some moved to Gwada and made their home
They moved around, to Supai and other places
Some settled in Supai and decided to move on
On and on
From there some settled at Drift Fence
Some continued from there
Down into Indian Gardens and lived there
Some journeyed on
To Tuba City, moving on and on

ham 'om gak mađ ya evjiya đ'o kyujki:
đu ham 'om yuđ gwawjach kaya
hav yumk vam yam đu vam yamk hav yumk we'e gweny ge Tuba City' kyuha
ha yumk we Mu:kach wayoma
Hwamu:hch we hav yumk yamk Gallup nyuwe'e gavgiyuje he hav yumk
đu bagađe:vch vam yamk
viyak be yak nyov'oka Frazier Wells i'ny kyu
mi: wale Hađigevo i'jki: hak gavgiyujak nyuv'ok
yach Nyavbehch vam si:yub' kyujiki:
yam gwevme Hakthigwavam nyum nyuv yumk yamk
vam vav yumk yamk ye'e ye đu đi:yav nyik
yuk nyihach Nyavbey kyu i'ja
Nyabevch nyul wayo:ka
đuwaym nyihach đowi:k gihanyik yam we dav Whiteriver i'jk
nyihe 'hwa:jach wayomkyu i'k vav i:jik
ham 'om gak mađyany evya nyi đ'opm
ye giđya:vach ha yumk Lagunach yuha
gwehch yuha
Puebloch yuka
nyuv yujivch vam yamk nyu we'e
gavyuch Blackfoot
nyihach đu yamk đu hav yumk
"mah nyach vam 'om Hwalabaya yu" ih
"nyach Havasuwa yu" ih
"nyach Nyavbeya yu" ih
"nyach Mu:ka yu" ih
"nyach Hwamu:vch yuh" i'k
đu nyuv i'jik vam yamk
nyivach ba:gađevch mađ'm vilwikyu i'k
Waqiyasmach đowi:m vam ba' ja:k vam ba' oyk vilwaqk'k yuwk yuwk hayuk
Kathadnyiha:m ham nalja

From then on they did not understand each other, so it is said
From then on their languages were different
From there they went on past Tuba City,
There the Hopis settled
The Navajos settled around Gallup
Many people went on from here
Here at Frazier Wells they stopped
Or at Lagoon, when they arrived there
The Yavapai departed here, they say
Past Rose Well, they went on
Here they continued in that direction
So they are called the People of the East
The Yavapai settled there
Later some of these people moved to Whiteriver
There the Apache had settled
Nevermore did they understand each other
The people that went in this other direction were the Laguna
They might have been
The Pueblos
These people continued
Some were Blackfoot
They continued on and on
"Mah, I will remain Hualapai"
"I will be Havasupai"
"I will be Yavapai"
"I will be Hopi" they said
"I will be Navajo," they said
This is what they said as they went
These people settled throughout the land, they say
Waqiyasma led some of the people and came
To Coyote Springs they came down
They descended and came to Gwaljilway

ham nyi naljik hayuk yuwk yuwk yuwk yuwk
Gwaljilway i:hm
nyihak hak wayoke mi gany yuk
nyihach Gwaljilway mulaykyu ik
wih qech'k yawik hak nyi ja:k
nyiha gwad'm yawik đahwađ'k namaka
namak vam yuwk
gwevch 'gwavch hak wam nyiha ha u:jom habaq'vch nyihal yoh
yum nyi u:k "yach yavyuch mulaykyu"
nyik qwaq he yok hak i'i:h si'onk namaka
nyuk ham yuwk ba ja:k vam yuwk vam yuwk vam yuwk
'Yachgame ihk nyiv'ojik
'yach mijk gwech be miyujkyu
nyu yuch ha yeny ja:j'k
ya wim' nyiha 'Yachgame mula ik
vam nyi yamka gak gudma đo' đim
kwa mađ a:vim
ya wik a:vk
ya wik hak đi:yupkok wijim
đu mađ'ch gweny mađiny hnuk yavyuk gwe ja:j nyu lwik
mađ'ch yayuk ham medmed'm
ya mađch đu đek yuw'm ha:vch hak yom miyuj
"Nyiha vam'om nyu yuch mulaykyu" nyi i'k vam yamk
"Hachuway Gi'sya mulaykyu" ik
hachuway nidik ya wik jijnidik
gigilyuj yo:k hak ja:h ja:k
nyi hak nyi namak
Ham yuwik yache "Gahwa:đ mulaykyu" ik
wi:hch hwađ'k hak yom
ha gwe gwad'm ya wik jaj'k đahwa:đ'k
ha ha yoh'yi: ya wik thiluyok
nyiva nyiva nyiva 'ba:vch si:jk

There they might have camped
"This place will be named Red Hill," he said
A small pile of rocks he poured there
He turned that red with Indian red paint
They left and came on
They saw antlers where there is a spring
When he saw it, "This place will be so-named"
He took a deer tail and hung it on the antlers
He led the people on and on
When they arrived at 'Yachgame
Seeds from which something always grows
That kind he scattered about
This way this place will be kown as Abundance of Seeds, he said
They continued not far from this place
With a pick
He struck the land
In this way he left it
Like a hole in the ground
The ground was like it was plowed up
There was always water settled there
"This is what this place will always be known as," he said
"Hachuway Gi'sya will be the name," he said
The sand sifted through his hands
Some of it he took and poured on top
Thereupon he left
He continued on and said, "This place will be known as Gahwa:đ"
The mountain was the shade of red
There he poured Indian red paint on
In order to get this, he dug holes in the mountain
And so the people know it by this name
"The people who live there have to call it this," he said
He left there and continued on.

"ba: a:mivch si:ja yivchyu" ih
nyihak nyi namak'k vam yamk vam yamk"
Mađgaŧi:d mulaykyu" ik
mađch ya yuk hank hwiny hwiny'm sijik ya wik hak namak'm
"Mađgaŧi:d mulakwi" ik
vam yamik
ham yamka ye Hak'nyimsav mij
nyiha 'ha qech'vch mađch ya yuk qech'k jikav'm
nyiha 'havch hal yom
ha hwalk ya wik nyi namak'k ya "Hak'nyimsav mulaykyu" ik namaka
nyi namak'k vam yamk' vayumik haba:qch ya yuk ham yak'm nyi u:k nyihak
nyihak "Yach Ŧa:game mulakwi" nyi ikyuđ
ŧa: yach wihi gayujiny gayuj yo:k ham ja:j namak'm
hach be:k hach "Ta:game mulaykyu" ik
vam yamk va yumk va yumk
"Jimwav sivyowo ijay" ya mađch qech'm jimed medk hak nyi namak
habaq hwalk ham 'ha:ch nyijijbajik
"yach Jimwav Sivyowo mulaykyu" ik
hmany hmany lay ha yok
nyiha yevk withik nyiha nyigwanik
ha wik đisivyo:k nyihak nyiha "Jimwav Sivyowo mulaykyu" ik hak namaka
hak nyi namak vam yamik
gak gudma đop đim nyihak yach jibay gayu: vasuw'ch yam yam v'ok nyimsavk
hwak ham yavyujim "Hanyaq" mijik jad ik i:
mi gany ik i:mo yuđ
vis'on nyik "jaq" ik ki: mi nyihach "nyaq" nyi ik
ga ik i:mo "nyaq" ik ik i:mijokiny nyuch yabek vak a:mjik vad'k
[nyiva si:jivchyum mij nyu gana:jim u: miyujyuny]
hach nyuv yuch mula

"Round Valley is the name," he said.
The land was good and shaped like a bowl, and he named it and left
"It will be known as Round Valley," he said
He went on
On to Hak'nyimsav
There was a small canyon
There was water in there
He dug a hole and said, "White Water is its name"
He left there and continued on until he came to another spring
There he said, "Yach Ŧa:game is the name," he said, and then
He scattered cane seeds about and left
"The seed will grow and be known as Cane Springs," he said
He went on and on
"Jimwav Sivyowo will be the name of this place," he said
He dug out a spring
"This will be Jimwav Sivyowo," he said
A lame child he got
Who was traveling with them; he was killed
And dragged there: "Place where the Chemehuevi is Dragged is the name," he said and left
He left there and continued on
Not far from there were blue birds who had white marks
There were two and they called out "Hanyaq"
Or something like that
He speared them. They said either "Jaq" or "Nyaq"
Whatever the bird means, he says "nyaq" and is still about
[This place which is called that has been pointed out to me and I have seen it]
That place is named that

vam yamk vam yamk ha nyi yumk
mađ mađ đu qach giyo:ny sik đu namak'k
hmuk'm nyi ik yach
"'Hak'bi mulak wim" ik
"ba gwedavivch ge yuwch 'ha: đaduik mađ'm đu jijbajk'k Hakbi mula ba gwedavivch ya 'hav'l deva nyik deva" ik "vach yuyiđ manihkyu" ik
ik vam yamk hayumk yumk mađ mađ' yal yavyumk yal yavyumk
gak u:v wam jikme:m đik
yav yum miyujk nyuv yuh đ'ok
yal yayuk gak u:va đ'om nyiha nyiha Ha Gadup ijik
nyihak nyi sma:k
hak wany yok gwawk
"Mađ gavgiyujiny mi'vok
mađiny mahanok gavgiyujim miđi:yav gwal nyim mi yiktho mi yuh"
im nyiha ha Jimwavach
nyihach ham siyuba
Qwaq Ha Thiwo g'mulam siyub'k
hach hak đowi:k hak wayom miyujokyuny
Isba'a:m nyi g'muloch hak wah
hak wam nyi yujik
nyi nyum yamik ye đi:yavk vam yamk
"Wiyalgivov ijki:m" ik
"ya:l nyi vo:m nyihach hwaw hwaw i' mi:jim nyiha Wiyalgivov" ijik
ham yamk hayumk ye đi:yavk mađi:lgivasuwa hmi:davch hak wak
"Nyiha Mađ đu:l Suwgiskwi:" ija ik
nyihach vam yamik vam yamik mađch ye gijkavm đu giđ'odv'm
mađch gayuk nyimthav' hak me:w lwim nyitha Muhuljamo Game ija
hak hak wayok
"Hwamu:v' nyu ha Geronimo ba wi:vj yuha

He went on and on
Small landmarks he named and left
After naming three other places, he said
"Hakbi will be the name of this place," he said
"Hot Springs is the name, and sick men will be cured there
Sick men will be healed in these hot springs," he said
He said that and went on in this direction
It was not visible but he headed toward it
This way it is visible but it was not
In this way it was not visible, there is a place named Ha Gadup
There they made camp
There they sat as he lectured.
"As you walk the lands
If you like the land, in any direction you want to go, do so,"
He said this, and the Chemehuevis
They turned there
Toward Deer's Drinking Water they turned
There some of them settled
A man called Isba'a:m lived there
Since he lived there
They continued on and went in this other direction
"A place called Wiyalgivov," he said
"If you walk under, it will echo, Wiyalgivov will," and so they call it
They went on and continued toward a steep blue mountain
"This place will be known as Blue Mountain in the Middle of the Land," he said
They went on and on, to a place of canyons and rims
The land is grayish and piled in a heap. "It is named Big Heap of Ashes," they said
Some of the people settled there

gavgiyujik va mađ' gavgiyujik mi đi:yav gwal nyim
miyik wamsi:ve
đi:yema nyu ha
banya:' nyu ha
gwe gayu: nyim g'mulach đu nyivak miv'ok mi
jiyawk
đu mađ gayu:ny mi hanok mi yamjayngyu" ik
nyihak ba tuim
nyihach ha mađ'm v'lwi:mkyu ija
ev ve' nyivach nyiva lwik nyivam'oh ◇

"Navajos, Geronimo's people
And other tribes
Go into any direction of the land that you wish
Maricopa
Pima
Whatever you name yourself, here you will separate
Whatever land that you like, go and settle there," he
said
There he sent them on their way
The people went and settled throughout the land
Do you understand this? This is the way it was. It is
finished. ◇

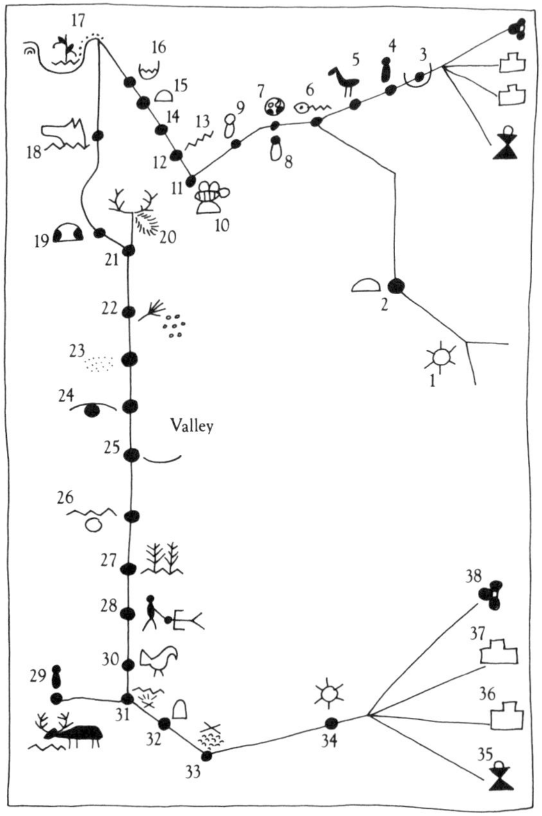

(1) Yavapai. (2)Thavgiyalyala. (3) Indian garden. (4) Mađnyuh. (5) Havasu. (6) Ha'đigevo (water hole). (7) Gwada (red paint). (8) People stayed. (9) People stayed. (10) Withambo (bee hill). (11) Iqađ. (12) Stops on a journey. (13) He:l (running water). (14) Qivjudak. (15) Wi'mhlu (pipe hill). (16) Hagawa (water pool). (17) Mađwiđa. (18) Coyote spring. (19) Qwaljiway (red paint on a hill). (20) Deer tail on a pole. (21) Qwaqwe. (22) Yachgame (hand throwing out seeds). (23) Hachwaygisiyava (sandy). (24) Gahwađa (red earth). (25) Madgaŧi:đ (round valley). (26) Haknyimsav (white water). (27) Ta'gaminy va. (28) Jimwav sivyowo (dragged Paiute). (29) Qwaq ha thi:wo. (30) Nyaq (bird sound). (31) Hakbi (hot spring). (32) Mad:il suwgiskwi (steep blue mountain). (33) Muhuljamo (ashes piled there). (34) Yavapai. (35) Apache. (36) Pueblo. (37) Hopi. (38) Navajo.

'Sa Ba: 'Sa Baqi

Robert Jackson, Narrator

Guda
Kathad gana:v đik-ng ba:j-ng Kathad gana:v đik
'Sa 'Sa Ba:hch-ng 'Sa Baqi:hm hwak'k nyihak
Ye'e' gweve: Qa'nyiwa:ja (White Hills ijki)
Ve' mađ giđiya:vm gavgyujiv wayo:nyk wayo:nyk
Ba:jich ham wayo:k
Gwevch yuha
Gulach yuha Kathadach yuha qoqotach yuha nyimiđach yuha
Ham ba:y đik
Ham ba:y đik yujik-ng
(Yu đik nya wanyasi:vnyich
va nyach qech đam va nyi gana:vom
va nya jiđach nya nyi gana:vnyom evm
nya wanyasi:vch ba:jich yuj đik yujk yu:ki i'
nyimiđach yuđ nya ma:đjyuv lwih ma:đga' yik đu wasi:vnyiyu)

Nyi yuk hak wayo:nyk yuny đam
Baqi: Baqi:ch yu'đe 'Sa Ba:vch gwe nyek nyi ya:m'm nyiva

Long ago,
As Coyote stories tell,
Eagle Man and Eagle Woman
Lived together at White Hills.
People lived around there.
They were the Gula, Kathad, Qoqot, Nyimiđa,
All of them were people.
(When I was young I heard my mother tell this story.
In my thinking, the Mountain Lion was human like us,
That is what I think.)

That's how they lived there.
Eagle Woman, when Eagle Man went hunting, like some women
Would stay home and then think,
"Yes, that person has fine things,
Fine things for sewing, washing and grinding.
I am going over there to sew and wash."
She must have thought that

Nyiva 'Sa Baqi:vach ga yuk yuđ
Baqi:nyich nyuk wa' thik
"e'e' nyiwach gwe ha:n wi:yokwiny
gwevanami han wi:yokwiny
gweđathgwi:li han wi:yokwiny
nyiha gwewi:jach hanam nyihal ya:m'
nyihe' gwe vanam gwe đathgwi:laywi"
Yik wasi:vk yuk yumo yum
Nyihal ya:mk Baqi:
Baqi: nyu yunyk "Nyihach pi' han wi:yim
hankyuny" ih
đu điđkayvk ya:mk
'Sa Ba:vch gwe nyek nyi ya:m'm
Nyi vok nyi va:k
Gwe gwank nyi gami:k
Wi tham
Gak gwe đa'olk nyiha 'Sa Ba:v đi:yuma đ'opm nyi
yum nyi 'u:k
đu ye:vm gwe galwik nyi ma:k
Nyuk đu ya:km nyi 'u:k
Va yuk Baqi:hch vok va:k nyum nyi yujk
Hak bay thik
đu nyi ya:m'm
Nyi yuk
"Ye hankyuny nyihe' ya:may'yu
Gwe mi wi:ny gak hana đa'opkyu
Gak hana đa'opkyu" i'

And she went down there.
Since she was a woman, she would say,
"They have a better grinding stone."
She would act childish
And leave when Eagle Man went hunting.
Eagle Man would come back with his kill,
But Eagle Woman would not cook for him.
When he saw that,
He would just cook for himself.
Eagle Woman would just lie around
And this happened all the time.
This is how they lived.
When Eagle Man left,
Eagle Woman said,
"It is good over there,
I will go over there,
Your things are not very good," she would say.
"Your grinding stone is not very good, it is old."

The Coyote head with lines coming from the mouth means "Coyote Talking" or "Coyote Tale." The two circles joined by a line mean "long ago." Eagle was human; the name "Eagle" is shown by a line coming from the man to the eagle. Eagle's wife is to his left; they are shown to be married by the lines joining them. A hill is a symbol for any dwelling place; pictures of Fox, Rabbit, and Coyote show that they were also dwelling there.

"Gwe đa:yi mi wi:ny gak hana đa'opkyu
nyikwaykyu"
ih mi nyuk ya:mk
Yam'm nyi 'u:k
Med ham 'Sa Ba:hach đu nyimi:lo lwik va:m miyuj
đik
đu ye:vm gwe đa'olk ma:k va wi:jik wi đik

đuwaym ham nyiv om'm hak wasi:vk ih
"Mah! nyiha gwe wi:hich
nyi wa'woch hank yukiny
Mah! ha gwe wi:jach han' ham yo:k yukiny mah" ik
wanysi:vk
"Ga yuk vak wah đe ya:may'yu" ih mi yuk
wanysi:vk

Nyiha yuk'k Qaqwadam (Red Lake i'joki) nyi nyum
gake:k
Ha yuk yuwk
Nyiha Haduva joq buk'm nyiham nya qechich
yakam ham yuwk
Yu thik nyihak gayuk wasi:vk hak đugwekvik
Kathad-nyi-ha'm ham nyi ya:mk nal me mi ga
yum'm

She said this and left.
He would see her leave.
Later Eagle Man started returning home on purpose
And he would have to cook for himself.
He would do this and then . . .

. . . as time went by, he finally thought,
"All right, their things, their house is better
All right, their things are better over there.
Why should I stay here?
I am leaving."
This is how he felt or thought.

He crossed Red Lake
To Clay Springs.
At the edge of the juniper,
There was a small trail that he followed.
He came this way.
Then for some reason
He changed his mind and turned back.
He journeyed to Coyote Springs
And went down.

Eagle Woman returned home
And found him gone.
When she heard that he had gone,
She had a change of heart
And followed him across Red Lake.

Eagle's wife is shown embracing another man; the black circle by her shows that the act was performed secretly. The small symbol for Eagle attached to her identifies her as Eagle's wife. The two lines coming from Eagle's head show that he is searching (i.e., hunting). The line that spirals at each end means "going and returning"; since the line emanates from a hill, it means "going and returning home." The dots show Eagle's path as he goes hunting (signified by the bow and arrow).

Nyiha 'Sa Baqi:ch nyi va:m đik yuđ nyi same:k
Nyiva yuk ya:mk
Ya:mkyu i'je mi i'jm nyi evk
Nyihak wayvakay'ik đugwi:vk
Nyi Qaqwadam gake:k' yu:ki
Qaqwadam gake:k

Nyuk ya 'Sa Ba:v gul jigwa:nk
Galwik silk bavk nyi ma:k
đuwa:y nyim 'Sa Baqi:hch nyi va:m'm
Yapa nyim nya do'pm nyi va:mk "Nya mi e:nya
Mijayyu
Nya nyahmi:
Mi e:nya mijay'yu" i' thim
"Joh! Nyiha gwe wi:jach hankyu miny
Gweđa:yi wi:hch hankyu miny
Ha gwe ma:jach hankyu miny
Ha wa'woch hankyu miny
Ga yum nyihe' mi yuh mi đa'ope? Nya ga muwihk mi đugwi:vka?
Nyach gwe kay mađ mun jikna:k ya:mayk
Hwa:la jikna:k wasi:v vak wa'kiyu
Mivom ma
Nyiha gwewi:jach hankyu miny
Mi ya:mk mivom' nyiha ba mi nyiwe:vk m'wah" ih
ih thim nyiva 'Sa Ba:vch gul nyi ma:h jiya:ka đu hak jam'm
Nyiha jimo:dk

Eagle Man would kill rabbits,
Roast them and eat them.
Sometime later Eagle Woman arrived
At nighttime or in the evening.
"Give me some, I am hungry, my husband.
Give me some, I am hungry," she said.
"Jo! You said their things were better.
Their grinding stone was better, you said.
Their food was better,
Their home was better, you said
Why aren't you over there?
Why are you chasing me around?
I am going to a different place, a cold place.
I am sitting here thinking of the Hualapai Mountains.
Go home!
You said their things were better.
Go home and live with them," he said.
When Eagle Man finished eating,
He would throw away the rabbit bones.
Eagle Woman would get the bones and gnaw on them.
That's what they say she would do.

The dotted line shows Eagle's wife returning from her secret doings (the dark circle) and finding nobody at home (the dash signifies "nothing there, no one there"). Her arms upraised mean she is requesting something (the return of Eagle), and the two lines emanating from her head suggest she is searching for him. Eagle has left home, as shown by the pack on his back. The dotted line takes him past the Red Lake and the counterclockwise spiral shows him descending toward the symbol for water.

Nyiva 'Sa Baqi:hch nyiha jimo:d nyi muwi:jkwi i'ja
Nyiha gul nyimi:ya nyi yo:k
Nyiha skwidk skwidk skwidk
Skwidk nyiha ye:vim jibevi (gu'hul) nyi yo:vm nyi
 viyevk wi đik

Nyiha 'Sa Ba:che nyiham nyi gake:k
Nyiva yuk ya:mk nyiha Hwa:l jikna:k nyihal va:m
 ma
Nyiham hanbachk yu mo yum
Mađach va:m hanbach miyujk nya điminyvim nyu
 yum nyi 'u:k
Nyu yum mi yum nyi va:mk yu đik nyiha wi:bad
 davm
Tha Hwa:l
Hwa:la hmi: Hwa:l gahmi: dava nyiha su:nk
Nyihal jikba:vk
Nyihal va:mk
Hal wa yo:va
Nyihal wak

Eagle Man got the rabbit skin
And wove it
And made a blanket for himself
This he packed with him.

Eagle Man crossed the Red Lake valley
Toward Hualapai Mountains.
This is how he arrived there
At his destination.
At this time it was snowing
And the ground was covered with snow.
Since it was well past the time for it to snow,
He searched for the highest peak in the mountain.
He searched for the tallest ponderosa pine.
He picked the tallest ponderosa pine
And climbed to the top and made his home there.

Eagle Woman followed him to the Hualapai
 Mountains.
She lay down at the bottom of the tree.
And she called to him using affectionate terms.
She begged him to not be mad at her.
But Eagle Man had made up his mind.
He only had one thought (feeling) in his heart
And would not change this.

The footprints at the right show Eagle ascending a mountain (clockwise spiral means ascension) with his wife behind him as shown by the other foot's inferior position. Eagle is now at the top of the highest tree after having ascended the mountain. Still in his fur robe, he is warm in a cold place, as shown by the group of lines above his head. The wavy lines are the symbol of cold. Neither he nor his wife has legs in this picture, a sign for "dwelling somewhere." The lines emanating from the heads of Eagle and his wife show they are facing opposite directions, meaning they are separated. Eagle's wife bears the sign for "covered with snow" above her head; her clenched fist is sign language for "cold."

Nyiha 'Sa Baqi:vch đu đugwi:vk đu đugwi:vk đu
    đugwi:vk đu vam nyuk
Bukal đu yak nyuk
Yuyiđ ya i'k điđyu:j ya i'j yiđ
Ham om yiway gasi:đk yo:ve mi wik
Nyum nyi yujk gak yiway gowe:ka đa'opk
đu gwe nyi ih davam đinyu:vk

Ham om gud wasi:vk yo:vk nyi yujk
"Gwevch ga yuk be yuk yukyu? Gak ahana đa'opm
    yuny mi?
Gak wany'mi:ya đa'op yuny mi?
Nyiha gwe wi:jach hank yuk
Mi qathk mi mi: yiđ
Ham om nyi namakaywi"
Ham om wasi:v yo:vk nyihe ya:mk nyiha Hwa:la
    bad'l nyihal wayo:vk
Nyihal wa'nyk
Nyiha 'Sa Baqi:vch nyiha bulk đu wa'nyk "Mi
    yo:knya mun'm bi:yu" i'k va i'j yiđ

Hanbachkame
hanbachk Hwa:lal hanbachkm
"Mi yo:knya" i'k ya i'j yiđ
đu opk
đu hal yak
đu evk
đu muwe:k hal yak đu evk
đu evk
Hanbach bay silwi:m
Miya:l bay silwi:m
Yapacha hwake mi ga yu kyuhiyu
Yuyiđ ham om hanbachach ham jiwe:vm'm

Ham ji'alk ha:k thim
Hanbachach đu ba:y đu nyimsavk ham đilđilm

Since he had his mind made up,
He followed his decision.
"What has happened?
You said I was no good.
Do you think I have forgiven you?
You said his things were better.
Even though you come begging for me,
I have divorced you."
He had made up his mind,
And made his home in the highest ponderosa pine
On the highest peak of the Hualapai Mountains.
Eagle Woman lived at the bottom of his home.
"Come get me, I am cold,"
She begged but he would not.
"Come get me, I am cold,"
She would say.
It snowed and snowed
In the Hualapai Mountains.
"Come get me,"
She begged.
But he did not.
He just lay up in his house
And heard her crying.
He was warm
And lay comfortable in his home.
It snowed for about two nights
Or maybe more.
The earth was all covered with snow.

He peered down and looked for her.
The land was blanketed by the snow.
When he saw this, he thought,
"I wonder how she is?"
He saw her at the bottom
And he climbed down to see.
She was lying there in a heap.
He saw that

Nyi 'u:k "Ga yu kyuh ma?" yik wasi:vye mi gany' yuk
Nyiham nalk'k
Nyihal 'u:wm
Hal đu yakom nyihal đu gi'oskim nyi 'u:k
điv'vom
Hanbacha jigwe:k
Bay nyi qwa:dok wi:m
điv'vom
Bay thaba:k yuk yum
Nyi 'u:k
Nyuk i'qach i'ya:k nyihak jak'k nyihak o'ny đuk
đumwe:k điđgwayk'k
đumwe:k hak vonu:k hak vonu:k hak vonu:k
đuwa:ym hak muwe:k hak liw liw i'm
Nyiha yuk điv'vom nyi 'u:k
Nyiha nyiva đako:v jakji:m
Wih
đako: jaknyiji:m

Nyiva gwegakayvich vam jiba:k
Nyiva luwi:vich yuha
Liyayđivch yuha
Mithulđach yuha
đilgwam'ch yuha
Gađu:lach yuha gwegayu:v mithulđich gwegamu:lviny nyu va:m nyu yu:j mađm miny 'u:k
Nyiva luwi:da (nyiva rattlesnake i'jm) nyiva nyivach yuđ vayu:jm
đowi:m nyiham jiba:m ba jibaeqk

She was with child.
He uncovered all
The snow from her body.
She was frozen
And she was with child.
This he saw.
He gathered wood and piled it up
And built a fire.
He warmed her
And massaged her, warming her up.
He kept doing this
Until she got warm.
Her body began to twitch/move.
Since he saw that she was with child,
He helped her deliver
By stepping on her stomach.
He stepped on her stomach.

This is when all these poisonous animals came about
The rattlesnake, bullsnake, Gila monster,

The lines emanating from Eagle's wife's frozen body signify the giving of birth, and all the other pictures are the dangerous things to which she gave birth. Eagle is portrayed above her, fighting the animals with a stick; Eagle's small size indicates that he is no match for them.

Nyihak vonu:k wi thik
Ye:vm ba jigwa:nk
Nyu wik hak vonu:k
đuwi:m ba gijba:jm
Nyi ye:vim
Ha luwi:dava ham jijba:jm vilwim
Nyum gwegayuny nya: nyim đa:dvk nyu miny 'u:k
Nyiha 'Sa Baqi:vch tha:wch yujm
Nyi gana:vjm hmany đim nyi gana:vm ev miyujm
Nyiha 'Sa Ba:v gana:vm ha wasi:vnyik
Nyihak ba:y đik
Ba:yk nya yujiv lwiny đik
Nyiha đu wasi:vk 'Sa Baqi:vch nyiha gamu:lvch
Nyihe wayo: đik yujk yuki
Hak ba:y đik yujk yuki
Nya jiđ' gana:vka gana:vjm nyiva
Hađgwilach
Nago:ch
Nyimiđach
Ba Kathadach
Qoqotach
Muhwa:ch
Hami:dach
Nyihak ba:ykyu i'jk
Nyu gana:vjom
Nyu nya wanyasi:vnyich yunyim
đu nyiha nya ma:đjva lwika yi miyujyuny
Nyiva gana:vji đam nyiva evyuny
Nyiva mi evjang yumo miyujm
đu ye:vm nya jiji:vch nyu i'ny mijm ev miyujk yuk yuny đik
Nyu yuk vak a:mja dav miyuj yiđ
Mise:v mijki
Mah nyivam otha
Ha nyiva yuh◇

Horned toad, Chuckawalla lizards,
And all kinds of poisonous animals.
Then some came out,
He hit them,

Trying to kill them.
He did this with the rest.
He killed some by himself
And some came out.
A rattlesnake came out.
If you see a snake lying around a road,
You'll know it's Eagle Woman's child.
This is what they told me,
About Eagle Man's story and his thoughts.
Eagle Man and Eagle Woman lived there like we live,
Eagle Man and men like him lived there.
My mother told this story.
This is what they told
And I heard it.
This is what you want to hear.
My mother would tell me these legends.
When I roam around and think:
What if the rattlesnake
Was killed by Eagle Man?
Would it be better?
This is all.
And this is how it is
(That the poisonous reptiles came into the world).◇

The Life of Kate Crozier

Kate Crozier, Narrator

Recording and first transcription by Werner Winter

Translated and transcribed by Malinda M. Powskey, Jorigine Bender, Lucille J. Watahomigie

Guda 'hmanyđik
Gak haygu 'u:h đa'op'yu
Ba nya đayach
Haygu gwa:w 'eva đ'opa
Nya nabo:hch gak haygu gwa:w 'eva đa'oh
Nya nyagwa:wach gak haygu gwa:w 'eva đa'oh
Nya godach nya monyach gak haygu gwa:w 'eva gak haygu 'u:ja đa'opa

Ham gav'giyujm ya'bek
Yumoyu
Mađ Widiđa
Gud jikna:k
Bagiyo:vach yo:vk ba'e:h
Nyihak'wayo:h
Wi:h'le wi: gsqa:kva
Gwe ga yu ma:k gwe ga yu ga wik
Hank yuh đ'o yiđ
Viyal nyu siđik nyuch ba giya be:wch
Nyuk siđthim yabe:jik

Long ago when I was a child
I had not seen a white man.
My old man
Had not heard the white man's language.
My father's father had not heard the white man's language.
My mother's father had not heard the white man's language.
My mother's mother, my father's mother, had not heard the white man's language, had not seen the white man.

About that time I came into being,
Or so it was.
Meriwitika.
Long ago it was planned,
The Creator made it and gave it to the people
There they lived,
In the mountains, the canyons.
They ate various types of food

Nya:nya duyim
'Wilnyuch nyi bak'm
Yach nyu ma:k
Nyu jigna:k
Ba 'e:jivchyu
'yabe:jik
Gak tho: nyu gulach, hlo nyu, hmalg, qwaq,ma'ul, 'mu nyu
Nyuk siđthik nyiyabe:jik

Guda
Bagiyo:vach
Ba nyi yabe:wjom
Mađwidiđa gana:mk "ma:m nyi mađivchyu"
I:yk
Hak siya:vjik

Yuyk nya nabohch nyi yuyk bim gak 'uh đa'op
Nya nagwawo gak 'uh đa'op bih
Nya monya gak 'uh đa'op bih
Nya goda gak 'uh đa'op bih
Nya đala 'u:thik gak u:k spoh đa'op
đu n'qe:cha dav đim
Hach bi:ya
Gak 'spoh đa'opa ma:đa
Nya jiđa siđthik yabe:h
Nya 'ni:ya pidik yabe:ji
Ha pida 'spoh

Juv nya đa:yk
'Avo:k
'Gwa:wk
Ba 'gij wi:jik
Nya 'yum
Hayguhch m'ŧavk yuwh
Nyiha Mormon'vch yuh
Nya ji'alovk ya:ma

It was not easy, but
As mescal was the only thing there
To keep them alive
They lived on that alone.
In the summertime
When the plants were in season
They would eat the seeds.
This was planned
And given to the people.
They survived.
They had no game to eat—jackrabbit, cottontail, packrat, deer, antelope, or mountain sheep.
On that (the seeds) alone they survived.

Long ago
The Creator
When he brought the people to life
He pointed toward Meriwitika. "That is your land,"
He said.
They went toward that direction. But

My father's father died, I did not see him.
And my mother's father I did not see, he was dead.
And my father's mother I did not see, she was dead.
And my mother's mother I did not see, she was dead.
Whether I saw my father, I do not remember.
When I was just very small,
He also died.
I suppose I do not remember him.
Only my mother was alive,
Only my older siblings survived.
This is all I remember.

When I grew older,
I walked,
I talked,

Qwa:q Weh'k
Gwad vam giyakva
Ham yuw'm
Hayguhch miyala ba'e:k
Dutch Oven ik miyalik ba'e:m
O'm jijgaeđik ba e:m
Nyi'e:jim 'manyak ijthim
'a'opok
"Sahak
"Gak hana đa'op'm"
Im 'ijik gak maha đa'opwi
'Spokyu

Yuđ hayguh gak ba'u:h đa'op yu
đu nyiwal dav 'a:mjik
đu 'nya:h'm ya:mk
Nya ji'alovk điya:vk ya:mk
Nyiha pida spoh

Yuk nya đalch nyi bim
Nya jiga:va pidik bijivk
Vach hmukđik ya'ba:ya
Nya jiđa ni:ya bayo:vich
Nya jiga:v davch

Thak 'ya:mk va nya 'yum
Nya jiđch he ba nyi wa:m
he wa nya yom

Qechk juv nya đayk
Nya vo:k
Nya yum
Nya jiga:v đu:l giyujich
Gasta nyi nabow'
Va guwi:jik
Hayguch gav nyum nova:k yuhiyu
Nya:h spoh đa'op

I would tag along with the men,
So I did, and then

The white man came from the north.
These were the Mormons.
They went toward the east,
To Hackberry,
Toward the open valley that is there.
They came along here.

The white man gave our people bread.
In a Dutch Oven they would bake it and would give it to them.
Or he would divide it up and give it to them.
They would give me some to eat but I would refuse.
"It smells.
It isn't any good."
I kept saying that, I would not eat it.
I remember that.

But I did not become acquainted with the white man.
I just roamed farther away.
I just went along the trail
Toward the east I went,
That is all I remember.

When my father died,
Only my cousins remained.
All three of them survived,
My mother's older sibling's children,
My true cousins.

When I went there
My mother took us there
And we lived there
Still small, but growing up,
When I walked,

Hla: chu:da
Spoh đa'op yu
Ham nya jigavach haygu đadaha:doh
Muwada sugada goth gwe:yu
Ba nyi'em
Ham 'đa:ya
Qanuwa:jah'k
Hak yum

Nya jiga:va nyu we:vjim
Va nya jiga:va Gasta nyi nabo:w'
"Navahu" ch
Vach ba nyi ja:k
đadaha:dk

Ham 'Wi g'hwalach nava:m
'Wi:h 'nuwaja Mineral Park, Chloride, Cerbat, Hualapai Mountains, ham ha:yum
Hayguhch
Va:h pukja

Hak qech'm nyađayk qechm nya vo:k haygu nyuwah nya ya:m'm
Wi g'hwalvich
Wi g'hwala' prospectorch
Nyu va:m
Nyu qech'm haygu nya'um
Miyal nyi ny'e:k
Goth gwe ga yu nyi ny'e:jim
Nyu'ma:m
Qwad 'id 'idk
Gak nyigwa:yva đa'opa
Kamhwidv
Gwega yu nyigwa:yk
Mahnyo:vk

When I was like so,
My cousin—the middle one—
Augustus Walema's grandfather,
Him we joined.

When the white man arrived, I do not know.
The day I do not know,
The month, the year
I do not know.
At that time, my cousin worked for the white man.
Flour, sugar, coffee, other things
He gave to us,
And so I grew.
At Mineral Park
Right there, it was.

My cousin that I lived with
This cousin, Gasta's father's father
"Navaho," he was called
He was our leader,
He worked for them.

About that time the prospectors came.
Mineral Park, Chloride, Cerbat, Hualapai Mountains, along there it was,
The white man
First arrived.

Then when I had grown a little, when I could walk a little, I went to the white man's place.
The prospector
The prospector
When I got there
When I was small, I saw the white man.
He gave me bread,
Coffee and other things he gave me.
I ate them.

    Yuh'đa'opk
    đu qwada 'id 'id a
    (va:m yiđ)
Haygu:ch 'oda hwalk
    Yung nyi ya:mayk
    Midi:k đa'olk
    Namak'k
Hayguy gwa:w gak'eva đa'op
Kwa silok qecha
    can
    can ga yu:
    a'ha:h
'Hach guda đ'ok nyi yujik
    "Ha:h" nyi ik ya nyi gana:k
"we miya:mk
    'Ha:h gowe:k
    Midi:k đa'ol'ny m'jah"
    Nyi 'ik
"Nya: vilwi:vim 'va:jay yu"
"Nya:vilwi: davim 'va:hi yu."
"Ya midi:ka đa'olv'"
I'i: i'i:vch hak yom
    I: qach hak yom
Nyi ha nyi yok nyiny' u:wok
    "We miya:mk
    Ya vilwi: miyok migami:k
    Ya'a
    Midi:k
    Ya 'om đum
    Yach
    Midi:kch mam
    Nya: vilwi:vim 'va:jih yu" i'jim
Nyiha nyu nyuva wim 'muwijik
Miyal jigaeđik mola:sim jiyalk
    Nyi e:muwijik

I was naked
I was not clothed.
Pants,
    To have something to wear,
    Shoes,
    I did not have them,
    I was just bare
    (even now).
The white man, the gold digger,
    Before he left
    He would cook beans
    And leave them
The white man's language I did not understand.
A little metal bucket
    Can
    A can of some kind
    The water
The water was not too far off.
    "Water," he said, pointing to it.
"Go over there,
    Bring water back,
    Pour it in the boiling beans."
    He said this, and
"At noon we will return."
"Right at noon I will return."
These beans that are cooking,
There was some wood there,
    There were some small sticks there,
He picked that up and showed it to me.
    "Go over there,
    Get ones like these and bring them back.
    This,
    The beans,
    Keep this fire burning,
    This,

Ma:k nya đo:k
Gwe i:v 'đinyuk đu wik
    Gak gwa:w' eva đok
    Đu was'ik gwe nyu đinyum
Ham hach hayguhch hak bayk
Ham gwe'spoh

Vayuk vayuđik
    Haygu gwa:w qech'm
    Nya ni:ych ya'eva
Nya ni:ych
    Nya ni:y dav nya hwaki
Vach
    Miki mij Mickey Beecher 'ija
Vach va va nya nya ni:ya nya nya hwaki davch đayk
Nyivach haygu ya'eva
Vach goyujik gwe nyi gana:vo mijim
    'Ev'yu
'Yujika đayk hal 'yuwa

A'oda hwal 'spoh đa'op yu
Nyu'a
A'oda juwe:k đisyahwink
Nyu gak nyu gak gwethabida gige:y đadaha:da
        'đa'op
Nya 'đayk đu 'i'i đigaeđa
Halavu:dovk i'i: đabeh juv nya đayk
Nyu pida 'wi muwija
'Yibad'k ham đayk
    Hak 'điya:vk haygu
    Nya đayk

Gak gwe—hmanych gak gwe'spoh
    đa'op mi yujkyu
Nyu yuk
Hayguhch
    'A'oda hwal nya đek

    The beans will be cooked.
    We will be here at noon."
This I used to do time and again.
The bread he cut, spread it with molasses,
    He would give it to me,
And I ate until I was full.
I would just do as he did.
    His language I did not know,
    Just by his gestures he would instruct.
There the white man came to live.
Thus I learned.

It went on like this.
    A little of the white man's language
    My older brother understood.
My older brother,
    My true older brother,
This one,
    His name was Mickey, Mickey Beecher.
This one, this one, my older brother, my real
        partner, he, he was older,
This one, he understood the white man's language.
And from there he would tell me
    And I would know.
This is how it was, I was brought up in this way.

I did not know how to dig for gold.
That
To mine for gold, to turn the soil,
I did not know—
There was no hard, strenuous labor that I did
As I grew older, I just chopped wood.
I would pack the wood on the donkey as I grew older.
That was all I used to do.
I learned the tasks as I grew.
    From there with the white man
    I grew up.

Qanuwaj'k Mineral Park im i:'jik
Hak nyađek

Gwe mava
    Fort Moha:v'l yomjim
Gadeđa đu 'guwik ya:mk
    Gak mahnyov'k
    Nyigwayvik ga yuh đa'opk
    'Gway be:mk

đu'guwik gadeđ'l 'wa mi yuch
    Nyu wa:m jim muwijik
    hwak nyi sinyu:v'm
Nyi hach nyigwaya kamhwida
    Mahnyoh
    Bud'
    Gwe gayu ba:y
    Nyi hach nyi yo:wjo

Nyi ham 'nyigwa:yv'k
    đu'ba:
    đu'ba hmanya hana 'lwih

Gadeđa 'guwik
Olo:ny
    Nya vilwi:v'm tuym
Nyavdo:p nyi'im nyi sma:jim tuyjim

Wila 'wa:mk nyu we jiyumk
    wa:mk
    wila ba'e:m
Ga yukyuh gak gud ih đ'ok
    One hour i:
    Ganyi yum gowe:k Wim 'uwij nyik
Tha pidik
    Gwe yu đadaha:d đu wima đ'oh

Ham đayk hak điyavk
    Hayguny 'spoh

Things . . .
As a small child does not know things,
That's how I was.
The white man,
    The gold miners were many.
At Mineral Park as I said,
There were many there.

Food
    They got from Fort Mohave.
I would just go along with the wagon.
    I wore no shoes,
    No shirt or anything on,
    I had no clothes.

I would go along sitting in the wagon.
    They would take me along.
    When they did this twice,
They bought me clothes, pants,
    Shoes,
    Hat,
    All sort of things,
    They bought for me.

That's when I became clothed.
    Just a man,
    Just like a handsome young man I was.
I went with the wagon,
The horses
    At noon I would unharness
At sundown when they were going to sleep, they unharnessed the horses.
I would take hay, herding them over there,
    I would take
    The hay and feed them.

However it was, it did not take long.
    One hour or so.

Ham nya đayk
Qech'm nya đayk
Hayguny nya spok

V'olo: va'ula waksigwijich gak đek đa'opa

George Bonelli 'ijich
waksi nyihađa puk

'Młavk
Gwe ve
Ha:va nya nyi mađjach
Ha:ve g'a:mva gwevk ge
Boulder Dam 'ijiv
Hayguch ga yuh đa'op đim
Hajich 'młavk yuwk

Waski:h
Hakjak jik 'jij bajik

Gahlo wi:yik
Ha' ha' bagohoke:k
Hach puk yiđ
Nyi đuway'm bany đigavjim
Ha'gumwe:h'k wa nya yom
Gak gud'k gud'k gak yuh đ'op đik
Bert Groundach
Nya ji'alok
Wi yuwk
Ha ba:hmil'm điye:vk
Kingman a
Nyu:gam Ga Yoda Gayoda i'đe
Gwe:h 'a:
Union Pass mij ki:
Nyi hak waksi:h jak'a

Bany đi gavjim
Waksi:h gaga:vk

I would bring it back, I would do this,
Only that.
I did not have to work too hard.

From there on as I grew
I understood the white man

As I grew older,
A little older,
I understood the white man.

There were not many cowboys.

George Bonelli they call him,
He was the first to own cattle

To the north.
This place here,
The water, our land,
This water, the Colorado River, over at this place,
Boulder Dam they call it,
When there was no white man there,
This man came from the north.

The cattle
They unloaded, brought them out.

They had boats (steam).
They would bring them across the water.
They were the first. But
Later when they rounded us up
When we were placed at Beale Springs
It was not long after that,
Bert Grounds,
From the east
He brought them (cattle)
He, along with his brother's-in-law.
Kingman
Farther up from there, Ga Yoda,

Ham nyi va:m gaga:vk
Tho:jim 'wija

Spo'nya

Hak điya:vk
Waksi:ny'
Hachiv ba đadaha:doh

Haygu:ny đu ahmanyk
Ba nyuwe:vk gak 'namaka đa'opa
Nya jiđach siđthik yabe:h
Nya niyach pidik yabe:j
Ha ba nyuwe:vah đa'opk
Hayguny nyujwe:v đik
Nyum ba'đayk

Ya:mk ya:m đik
Chuda wa:vk halthuyk ji'ale ga nyi yum

Ha La Basal bany wa:m ja
Gwe gava wijim wih
gak ha spoh đa'opa yiđ'đe
'spo yiđ đe
Ha La Basal bany wa:mja

Hal bany wa:mja đo đik
General Crook Sulđa:w
Hwalbay
Bay sul đa:wok
Hwa:ja
Nyabeh
Hach haygu jigwa:nk
Gwe nyihađ hwayo:vk
Waksi: nyu 'olo: nyu gweny
Hayguny đu jigwa:nk wijivch

Nyi vach
General Crookch ba:j

Somewhere
They call Union Pass,
There they brought the cattle.

When they would round them up
They would buy cattle.
When they arrived, we bought
And ate meat.

I remember that.

From then on
The cattle,
Those people I worked for.

The white man—since the time I was young
I have lived with them—I did not leave them.
Only my mother was still living.
My older siblings were still living.
I did not live with them.
I lived with the white man.
Thus I grew into a man.

I went on like this
Until I was about nineteen years old or how many years or so.

The time they took us to La Paz
Whatever it was that we did
I do not know, but
I know this:
The time they took us to La Paz.

Before they took us down there
General Crook, the soldiers,
Hualapai,
He commissioned them all soldiers.
Apaches,
Yavapai,

Hwalba:y sulđa:w
Ham'sulđa:w nya

Chud vwava hmukspek ya:mk
Nyi ham juv nya đayk
Chudwav nya hwak'k
Gava yuk nya ji'alk nya yuk
Ga yuk yuh qech nya đaminy'k
Ham'sulđa:w nya

đu ya vo:k vam ya:mk
Qwaqwehk 'ya:mk
Vo:k
Prescott ak nya va:mk
Vo:k 'ya:mk
McDowell ak 'va:mi

Nyi hak nyov'ok
olo nyi e:jim 'v'ulk
Gwe ga yu:gava wik
đa'opa yiđe
Hak wayok six months' nya'ijik

Hwa:jivch
Haygum mađa neh'k
Gweg'ji:jivk
gwevk olo:k gwe:vk jiya:k
vak haygu jigwa:nja
Hwa:jach

Hach six months guwich
Ham ba sahajay'k
Nyi hak wa'yok
Sulđa:wk hak wa'yok
McDowell-le

Ma'h nyi 'im
Hla:ch ham nyi vilwim
Ham 'olo nyi 'e:jim va'ul nya

They killed the white man,
They stole his livestock,
The cattle, horses, things,
They just killed the white man, it was their doings
These
General Crook, the Indians,
Hualapai soldiers
That's when I became a soldier.

I was past eighteen years old.
When I was almost grown up
I was twenty
And some years
Or how many years past
That's when I joined with the soldiers.

Just on foot I went from here
I went to Hackberry
Walking.
When I got to Prescott,
I went on walking,
And arrived at Fort McDowell.

When I reached this destination
They gave me a horse to ride.
We did not do much,
But after we had
Stayed there six months, then
The Apaches
They fought with the white man over land, or
Things they stole, or over
the horses, whatever was the cause,
there they (Apaches) killed the white man
The Apaches.

Within those six months
They were going to hang some people.

McDowella 'i:hk wa'yo thik
    Vam 'ya:mk Banya:nyuwah
    Vam a:mk nya dopov 'điya:vk
    Madagob we:v
Wamboda guvgaeđik hak'wa yoh
Wa'yok ya:mk
A:h
Wambod' nyonya station
    si:jich ha
A:h,
Nyi hak bany jinaljik
Goyujik
    San Ca:la mid mida
Mađim vil wi:vik
Hwa:j saha:ja yih hak bajigwa:jik

'Ijik thak 'ya:mja
    Nya vilwi:vim
    'Ya:mjik
    Nyavdo:p im 'va:mja
    Hwa:j jigwa:ja
    Sahajah yiwohk
    'Va:mja

Ha mađak
    Ha Camp Grounds sijich yuh

Yuđik haygunyuwa' nyi đuv đe:k
    Fort Grounds iđe Fort Grant si:ja
    Fort Grant-Grant Fort ik mi
        Grants gayuch si:jkimo
Nyihak hwa:ja jigwa:jik
'Va:m ja

Nyiye:k nya nyivilwi:vim
    ba saha:ja 'u:h
    Hwa:ja hmuk'm'sahaja

We stayed there. We stayed there.
    We were in the Military and stayed there
At Fort McDowell.

When he said "It's time,"
When it was the right month,
They would then give me a horse to ride.

We stayed at Fort McDowell. But
    We went from here to Phoenix,
    We went by there toward the west
    South of Maricopa land.
We intercepted the train there and we stayed there.
We stayed there and went on from there
Ah
The railroad "station"
    They call it.
Ah
When they let them off (the train)
Right from there
    Straight from San Carlos
Halfway between there and Fort
The Apaches that were going to be hanged were
        kept there.

They were going to do this. So we went there.
    At noon
    We left.
    At sundown we arrived.
    Where they kept the Apaches
    Where the gallows were
    We arrived there.

The Land there
    It was called Camp Grounds.

Then later on as the town grew
    Fort Grounds—no—Fort Grant it was named

Hwa:ja
    Baydava San Ca:la wag'yoh bahe:dk
    Nyu wijik gahmuka bahe:dja
    Ha bagana:k
        nyuch wi i'jim
    Ba ba sahajim u:'yu

Giyafoh'
    Ba:h mula Dandy Chief mijki:
    Dandy Chief 'ihch ha điyafok
        hak jivskwi:kja

Mak'l g'beva
    Nyiha Dead Shot
    Nyiha ba hmivch qech'm hmik
Ham nya hwak'm

Gav'oma
    Ba:ny qech đu'nya vilwi:
    Ha Skip si:ji
Ham hav yuk hmuka
Ba sahajim 'u:k
'Ahmany nya yu:jik
    đu 'mi:k hak 'skwi:h
    Ba sahajim
Gwe sgwidiv
Hmuk'm
'Iv'ye nyi sa'jak
    Yam i'qalyev nyi sahkek
    Nyi hak hwal g'hiyalk
Gwe sgwidvach
    Siđa
    Hwaka
    Hmuk
    Yuk ham đu đu đishajiv

    Fort Grant or Grant Fort
        Grant something or other they call it.
There they kept the Apaches.
We arrived there.

The next day at noon
    I saw the hanging.
    The three Apaches they hanged.

Apaches
    All of them at San Carlos were captured
    And they jailed these three,
    They blamed these (three),
        They said "they did it."
    I saw the hanging of them.

The first one
    A man named Dandy Chief they called him,
    Dandy Chief they put him first,
        they stood him up first.

The next one behind him
    That one was Dead Shot
    That one was kind of tall,
That makes two of three.

The one at the end
    Was just a small man like myself,
    He was called Skip.
That makes the three of them,
I saw them being hanged.
Since I was still young
    I just stood there crying
    At the hanging of the men.
Ropes
Three of them
The poles they posted

Juv yuvluwik yam đahakjah yi:h
    Sal mak ya hwakđim gijilgiyom
    Ya sal g'v badvk gijilgiyo' nyi'ijim

đu hal g'ge:vk
Gavwik ba sahajaykwih wima yik 'u:h
    Gak spoh đa'opa

Nya: nyivilwi:vim
    Wasa'ami nyi vilwi:vi
    Yak g'ge:vol sa'amk
    đige: viye viye đige:k

Nyuk hayguch đek yal yujthik
    bay nyi namakjik
"Mah" nyi i'jik
Nya nyiv'lwi:vim
Yak gweđige:v gadeđa đige:v lwiwjothk
Nyivav tuyv i'wok đu vam sodik
Yam
    Yam milgijik gwe gwesgwidva đita:k jim nyi yujik

Ba sahajik
đu hal điswelvik
'u:h
Ham'oh

đu ba 'hmany đik ha-ni-tha:la đadahada
    General Crook
        đadahadik spok

'Vok nya va:k
Hayguny đu ba nyuwe:vik
Gak gwegayu gawik spoh đa'op

Ba'nyuwe:vik
    olo gak va'ulk

    Along here they put beam across
    And put up the split boards.
The ropes
    One
    Two
    Three, there were,
Just hanging there.

Making ready where they will drop from,
    Their hands were tied behind them.
    The hands were tied at the wrist.

They just stood there.
I looked on wondering how they were going to hang the men.
    I did not know.

At noon
    When they made ready the door-like latch/trap
    Here where the men stood they snapped them in,
    they pushed it over this way.
And there were many men underneath this but
    They all left (it).
"Ready," they said
When it was noon
There was a latch, like the brakes on a wagon and this
This they released and the men just dropped off suddenly.
Here
    since they had ropes around their necks tied securely around their necks
They hanged them.
They just hanged from there.
    I saw it.
That's all.

Waksi
    gak gawik 'spoh đa'o: đik
Ba nyuwe:vik
    haygu waksi g'nyihađa
Ed Imus ijim
Mađ si:jich ye mid mida
    Willows
    Ij
    Hak'wak
Olo v'ulk
    Waksi jiyu:mk
    Waksi may h'li'yomk
        Ba nyuwe:v miyuja

Hak 'olo v'u:lk
    Waksi u:k
    Ham spoh
    Waksi he:d'muwija
    Waksi tha:wa điđnyu:da
Olo wanaw nyi e:m v'ulk
Hak điya:vk waksi
    Cowboy wij'nyiham 'yibada

Nya vok'k
Cha:l Bensach
    Hach mađ'k wah
    He:l'k
    Hach Indian Agent-a puka
    Nyihache Cha:l Bensach
Charlie Spencer ij mijki
    dadaha:da
Waksi
    Waksi 'điđnyudik đe: dav'm
Sam Crozier
    hak điya:k Sam Crozier đadha:dik

Spoh

From the time I was young I worked for the
        government.
    General Crook,
        I worked for.

When I came back
I just stayed with the white man.
I did not learn a trade.

I lived with them.
    I did not ride horses.
    Cattle,
    I did not know how to handle them. Then
I lived with them
    The white man who owned cattle,
A man named Ed Imus.
A place straight from over here,
    Willows
    They call it.
    He stayed there.
I would ride a horse,
    Herd cattle,
    Go after the milk cows,
        I would live with them.

There I learned to ride a horse,
    Look after cattle,
    That's when I learned.
    I would rope the cattle,
    I would brand the calves.
He gave me a tame horse to ride
From then on the cattle
    What the cowboys do—I became skilled at.

When I came back
Charlie Spencer
    He lived on this land
    At Milkweed.

Fred Nodman-a ha
    Waksi nyihađ jiv
    olo gwe yu bay ba yahanok
    Ham 'spoh

Juv nya đayka
    Juv nya ba:yk
    Juv thirty years old i: 'mi
        gava yuk yuh yu
'Withik gwe gayu hiyan'm gayuh đa'opk
Nyiham ha'dav thi:jiv 'spoh

Ha'dava 'thi:h yu yiđ
  v'gak ba'gwank gwe ga yu
        haygu gwank gwe ga yu ga wik i'jivch
    Gak nyu 'spoh đa'op
đu ya nya g'bedik
Va:m Ba:jich ja:wvik wiđ
    đu nyi ha vilwih
    Ha spo'nya đa'opk

đu va hadav'ny gwe bakspowch yuh đ'op
    đu wa'yu: i'vim

đu nyu jo:v'im yujik
    nyu pida spo miyujik

He:dik gak nyi namakja đo'm
Gwe ga yu u:k gavawim nyi he:djivch yuh đa'op
    đu yag'bedik 'jo:vim nyi he:dik nyi hedja pida
        spok
    yujik vam

Bav đa:y imk
Gwe wij nya yibadik
Sam Crozier hach nyu wi:yik
    Hach waksi đay nyihađk
    Bert Groun'ach waksi đay nyihađk
    Hach ba đadaha:dok

    He was the first Indian Agent,
    That one Charlie Spencer.
They call him Charlie Spencer.
    I worked for him
Cattle,
    I branded very many of them.

Sam Crozier
    And from there I worked for Sam Crozier.
I learned.

Fred Nodman—him
    His cattle
    Horse, other things I took care of,
    That's when I learned.

I was almost grown,
    Become a man
    About thirty years old
        or so it was
But I did not get into anything bad
I knew then about the hard liquor.

I drank hard liquor but
    I did not kill people or anything like
        to kill a white man, or anything like that they
        do.
    I did not know those things.
I would just get drunk.
Today people fight
    I was just like that
    Since I did not know.

The liquor makes one not know what he is doing.
    It makes one become angry.

I would just get into fights,
    I remember only that.

Charley Spencer i:j
    Hach waksi đay nyihađ'k

Ha ba đadaha:doh
Nya yibadik
    Sandy 'ya:mk đadaha:dik

Ye gwe ve
    Willows 'mi:jik ih
    Fort Rock i:
    Waksi đay nyihađja bađadaha:dok 'spoh
    Gwe yibadik

Yu yiđ haygu gwa:wk qech'm 'evk
    Haygu ba gwik all my life i:yiđ
    Gak haygu ya'evk
    đu yuma đa'opk
Yuk juv nya đayk
    over forty i'me mi gav nya yuk
    Waksigwich ga pid nyu
đu haygu nya lwih
    đu waksi nyihađny' bany đadaha:dok
    Vuj pida davk
    đadaha:dik
    'Makah đa'op

Juv nya đayka fifty i'me mi gav nya yuk
Chud vava lwik
Nyitham
    Nyuk đu a:mja yiđ đe
    Indian Agent-a
    ba đadaha:da gwadi ya
Indian Agent-a ga pukach
    Charley Spencer ch yuk 'ih

Meda Indian Agent
    yo:j yach
    A:

They were forever putting me in jail.
Whatever I set out to see or do, I was not arrested
        for anything like that.
    I would just get drunk and get into fights, that's
        all I know.
    And from there—

Since I was getting to be an older man
And learned the things they do,
Sam Crozier, he took care of me.
    He owned many cattle.
    Bert Grounds, he owned many cattle.
    These men I worked for.
Charley Spencer (one called),
    He owned many cattle.

These men I worked for.
When I became skilled
    I went to Sandy to work.

Over this way here
    At Willows I said (before)
    At a place called Fort Rock
    There they had many cattle these (men) I work
        for. I remember.
    I learned a trade.

But then I knew little of the
    White man's language, although I had been with
        them all my life.
    I did not understand the language
    Very well.
When I was older
    over forty or so, or however many years old I was
    Cowboy—working only with the cattle
Just like the white man
    I worked the owner's cattle
    Only at that

Doctor ga yuch mij kimo doctor
Doctor i:hch
  Cha:l Bensa nyi gwanjim
    hayguhch ye:m gwanja
  Partnership ij'ivch
  hach waksi nyihađik
  Waksi gav'ik besa đem wi:dik im'yuk
  Cha:l Bensa gwanja

Yu:ch Hwalbay baqi luwe:yim
  hma:ny hwak'm wi:ya
  Vuch gak yabaya đa'op kyu
  Hmany nyu wi:hch misivch yuh
  nyiha Mamie Spencer i:
  nyiha nya dopov jiyam a Cha:l'Bensach

Sammy Spencer i:hch
  Vak wađik
  nyi va mađik bi:kyu
Ham Cha:l Bensa gwanjim
Ham nyiv'om
Sam Crozier đadaha:doh
  Namakah đa'opa
Yu:đ

Indian Agent ba đadaha:da gwadik
Gwe ga yuch mi ya:mk mi ganavok
  gwe gayu ga nyi i'jim
  mi yamk mi ganava
  mi ya:m ba mi e:voh
Nyiva ba:h ba mi e:voh
Ba ba mi ganavoh i'jik
Nyu
Ba ganavok va yuk

đu ya:ja jikduk jikyujik
đuway'm ba: v'đay nyam'k
Sixty nya i'me mi gav nya yuk

  I worked very hand,
  I did not stop.

When I was older at fifty or so
About that many years
Then
  I just wandered around.
  The Indian Agent, I still
  Worked for him.
The first Indian Agent
  was Charley Spencer, I said.

Later, the Indian Agent
  they were going to get
  Ah
Doctor—something they called him,
Doctor he was called
When they killed Charley Spencer,
    the white men themselves killed him,
  One of the partnership,
  He owned the cattle,
  Over the cattle and money spent
  They killed Charley Spencer.

He was married to a Hualapai woman.
  She had two children,
  They are not living.
  She had a boy and a girl,
  the one named Mamie Spencer,
  that one was sent west by Charley Spencer.

The one named Sammy Spencer
  He lived here,
  He died on this land.
That's when they killed Charley Spencer,
When that was done.
I worked for Sam Crozier,

mi chud vwava hwakspe'
mi gav nya yuk
Indian Agent đadaha:da đa:mk
Police-ivch 'yuh

Range Rider'vch 'yuh
Haksaha 'vsoh
Range Rider nyi e:jim
Haksaha 'vsoh

Mađ ba:ya u:j va Reservation-ivch yum nya yu:jik
mađ baya 'u:h
Baya 'vsoh

Ha'nyu wam ga'a:ma ba nyu mađ nyu bay
Gana:vch baya 'vsoh

Hak điya:mk
mađa u:k u:đik
Wi'hwa:l jivch
Gak ba hwalch yuh đ'ok

Hayguhch

Giyafođik ha La Bas'l
ba'nyu wa:mjik wi yik
Hal ba nyiny wa:mjim
Hayguch bany
Nyihal bu:vk wiđe
'wi:h ujik

wi hwaljich
wi hwal namakjivch hak yom
Nyi ha hayguch nyi gana:wch
Nyi hach "high grade-ik hak yok yum" im
nyiha yigwithich hak yoh
Ham Ranger Rider nyi nyi e:jim Nyiha ha baya 'igwith

I did not leave that
But then

I still worked for the Indian Agent
Whatever it was, "Go and tell them."
Whatever it was they said,
"Go and tell."
"Go and tell to the people."
This, you go and tell it to the people.
Go tell this to the people.
This
I would go tell, like this.

Just what they told me to do I just would do that.
Later on when I was older
Sixty years old or however,
or sixty years old
or however many it was,
I started working for the Indian Agent.
I was a policeman.

I was a range rider,
I was to guard Pine Springs.
I was made range rider
and I guarded Pine Springs.

All this land. Since it was made reservation. I guarded.
All the land I would oversee.
I would guard it all.

The water the Colorado River, all the land of the people,
All that was pointed out I would guard.

From that point on
Since I was tending the land
The Prospecting
It was not done by the Hualapai

Med i'dava
    hla si:đja chu:d'v gak spoh đa'opyu

    Vava yuha yi:ny
    gak hayguhch gwe gana:va yi:ny
    gak nyum vilwih đa'om mij

Hayguh Arizonak wak'yovch
Wi:hch a'o:d'm
Wi:nya u:hch' a'o:d'm
besk Hwa:lbay mađ wijich
    reservation wijivch
    a'o:d'm 'm besk
Ca:pach yuk
    gwe mu:lva đek đu yuma
'Wi:hche

Ha ga'a:ma ja:vk ga'odivk
Nyiny tha hwalja u:m
        yigwithm hak yok

Nya: gud'm
    hayguch ha 'wi:h
    ga wik hwal u:j nyi kyu đo'yiđ
Arizona'v Banya:nyuwah
    Prescott ge wakyo:hch
    bay nyi hak ja:w vik
        gijnyi:wva
Juvgaevik yohyik
Ijich
    gak evk bay đuvluwih đa'opa yiđ

Mountain time ch
    Western time 'i:hch
nyiham gujnyi:wvik
    jugaevik gayujich
    twelve o'clock guwijim

The white man

At first when they took us to La Paz
    The one I said they took us on
    When they had taken us there
The white man when they did that to us,
        they poured into this area and saw the
        minerals.

    The prospectors,
    The abandoned mines they left were there.
This the white man pointed to me.
That is high grade that is there,
        this I held on to is there.
They gave me the job as Range Rider and all of this I
        would hold onto.
Much later
    The names of the months, years, I do not know.

    Things that would be like this.
    What the white man will say
    Is not always so.

When the white man came to live here in Arizona,
The mountains have gold.
The mountains I saw had gold.
The Hualapai land is worth money
    The reservation that is ours
    There is money in gold.
There is the copper,
    and many other materials are there,
The mountains have this.

At the rim of the Colorado River
There the prospecting I saw.
    We hold on to that, it's there.

Long time ago
    The white man, the hills,

nyiham vawidik
'wi:h va:mk
Wi:h yo:jay kwijim

Nyiha nyach Indian "cherish v'k" đadaha:dk nya
yujik
ha Range Rider'vch yuk nya yujk
vak kwa đalam gwe bay'wi:yik
hak 'wak nya yujik

Hwalbay bagana:voh
ham Indian Agent-'a:

Indian Agent-'a:h Mr. Shell Shell si:j
Nyiha đadaha:do
Nyiha ya:l đadaha:da
Ha ya:l vo:nya'

Mr. Shell Mr. Shell i'gana:vok i'gwithaywi
a'o:d hwalch a'yigwithk juv gud'k đujiv ya:mk
chud vwav thadapm yigwitha yivch yum
gava wik i'gwith aywi
'ih
đu ye:vm ma ba:ny
ma' reservation muwijivch yum nyi yujik
ba:h mi gana:vk
ma đek nya wijivchyu mija
mi'h
Mountain time-ich
Western time-ich
nyiva wi:ja đa'ok
Ma reservation mu wijivchyu
yum đa:m nyuv yum me

General Crookch gud reservation sik
ba:ja banyi e:m
ya:mk ya:mk chud nya đe:m

How it is prospected, they saw the place and—
In Arizona, Phoenix,
Prescott, wherever they lived,
They all fought, all wanting the land.
They fought over it
They raced to get it.
This is told
And I did not hear this in the complete form,
but—

Mountain time
And Western time,
They were fighting over the land
The ones who were going to run the race.
At twelve o'clock
That's when they were going to run
And reach the mountain
They intended to claim the mountain.

That. Since I was working as the Indian Sheriff,
Since I was the Range Rider
I had on a badge and possessed credentials, and
I was placed there.

I told this to the Hualapai people,
Then the Indian Agent.

The Indian Agent was called Mr. Shell.
I worked for him.
I worked under him.
I followed his orders.

I told this to Mr. Shell, I am holding on to this.
The gold mining I have held on to this has gone
on for a long time past.
It has gone on for fifty years, it is impertinent to
hold on to the land.
How will I hold onto this (land),

Reservationa kwavm sivgok
    title i'wok
    ba nyi e:jm nyi vak yo:me
    gak 'namaka đa'opaywik'e im 'i:jik
    hal v'skwi:k

Mountain time-ich va:h puk i'ja
Lagu:n mij i'
    vah "two mile" im'm
    hak wi:h'k
    Nyihak jugaevik yo:vjim

'wi nya wi:hch two mile im me miyum
Ye 'wihch 'hmi'm nyi ve yoh
    yu yiđe

Tha hayguhch ha yo:h nyimi:lk wijim
    ha yigwithik

Sunyadamach chiefch yuk
    chief yuh đo'pk captainch yuk
Nyi ha mađ'ny gi nyi mađoch yuh
        'a:h
He:dama-ch yuh
Prescott Jim-ch yuh
Old Mahone-ch yuh
Jr. Mahone-ch yuh
    'a:h
Bakin' Powda-ch yuh
Hajiv ba ja:k
    wi:h mi yigwithja'
Wi:h yaygwithjay
    'a:h
Hmuk'm wi:hwaljach u:vik
    Ca:pow wijom 'u:vk hak yom

Nyachivch Lagu:n two mile gwijik g'yoh'k
    Nyi hak wijaym

    I ask.
It is among yourselves, since this is your reservation.
    Tell the people
    All of you get together and voice your claim to
        this land.
    Say this.
Mountain time and
Western time
    They have no claim to this.
It is your reservation.

Long ago General Crook set aside the reservation
    And gave it to the people.
    This has gone on and on for many years.

They fenced the reservation area.
    Titled it,
    And gave it to us. And here it is.
    I will not let this go, I said.
    I stood down there.

Mountain time arrived first
At a place called Lagoon.
    Here for two miles,
    There at the hill,
    There they set points for the race.

My hill was two miles or so.
Here the mountains were high, it was over here, but
        then

That one, that's what the white man intended to get
        a hold of
    That's what I held on to.

Susanyatame was chief,
    Not really chief but captain.
He was the holder of the land.
There was He:dama

Nyach hal yuhiyu
Jim Mahone Jr. mach 'claim' nya wi:h wi:h mijuwoh
gak haygu:hch ha va:mk gak u:ja đ'ok wa:dvkyu
'Twelve o'clock' nyi da:vm
wi:h mijuwoh
đinyudk hak mi juwoh

Nyach ja:wvidaval
guwijal yuh'i yu
Bakin' Powder 'onyi:hi wi
ik nyach hal yu'h

Su'nyadame mach mulvm nyi'yujk
Hedmach-yu
Prescott Jimch-yu
Mahone-ch yu
Bagađev ch
Mi ya:mk nyu we National Canyon'iji:m
Nyu:k he yok
Nya ji'alo yok
Mađqwada hmuk'spe me mi vwave mi k'yumo
he yok
Hak mach mi ya:mk mi yigwith jinya
Nyach 'yal đu:vl 'yu hik
Haygu wij davl yu 'hikyu mij

Tham nyi ham 'mulvk 'ah' Range Rider nya yujik
Hal gwe va 'star'
gwe baya'wi: yik
đinyuda wi:yik nya yujik
hal'yuh

Yuyiđ
ba siđthim vonyi:h
Bakin Powder siđ thim'vonyi:h
Mountain time ich
eleven thirty iđim yumi:

And Prescott Jim,
Old Mahone,
Jr. Mahone,
Baking Powder.
These men I led.
"Hold on to the mountains."
We are going to hold on to the mountains.
There were three mines there that were noted.
It was copper mining it was plain to see.

We were at Lagoon at the two-mile mark.
This is where they will start.
I will be down there.
Jim Mahone, Jr. you take my claim, put a rock there
A white man has not been there or has seen it yet.
Right at twelve o'clock
place the rock there
put a mark there.

I will be in the actual fighting,
right where it will be happening
I will take with me Baking Powder
I said. So I was there.

Susanyatame, since you are the leader/captain,
There was Hedama
Prescott Jim,
Mahone,
With all the people,
Go over there, over there called National Canyon,
A little farther away
Toward the east
It might be 8 miles or it might be 10 or so.
You go there, you hold on to that.
Me, I will be in the middle of this,
Right where the white man will be (fighting), I
said that.

hach hal wa yoh puka
Ba ja:hch wal wa'yoh puka
Ha ba gija:hch 'eleven thirty' 'i mi: yum
thach va:h

Twelve o'clock guwijich
Ferwe:yja
Frazier Well mađ qwad galwik yuhiyu
Nyi hak 'police' Dude Calfach police-k
Hach hak bađigavk
'pu' v'luth nyi i'wom
Hach vawidk ya:m thik

Twelve'k gav nyi yum
đaminyk va:mjinyk yuđik hak ja:w vayk
a'opo:ha
Nyach'wi:h joli:k yak nya jiwok
Wi:hkaya jol'iđik yak nya juwoyk
đu:l 'vskwi:h
H'yal wa yoka pukivch gak 'u:h đa'op đik
'Wi:h hwalk giji:mk galwik yuhiyu
20 step im-me mi
30 im me mi yuk

Nyive'wi:hch hwalk mahliwjok
Guweyok nyiyujk
Hayguhch hal skwi:h

Nya dopov giyuwach va:k wi:h juwoh kwithim
O'pok
Wal givskwi:hch o'pok
i:yiđ
Yak gava:ch wihik wi:k'i
jigana:jivch yu 'ijim
'im
O'pok
Gak mi juwohk i'đ
a'opok i:h

That's when I was Range Rider, since I was that.
I had the badge
And other things
Since I had these papers I was in there.

But
I only took one man along with me.
Only Baking Powder I will take with me.

Mountain time
when it was only eleven thirty
They were the first ones down there.
The people were there already.
The leader, when it was eleven-thirty or so,
he arrived.

The twelve o'clock set time.
Frazier's Well,
I don't know how many miles it is.
At that place Dude Calfee was the police
He had gathered them there.
He fired the shot to signal
They all took off running.

About twelve o'clock
Or past that time, the others got there, and were going to fight.
I told them not to.
I had staked out the area with a rock.
Another rock I staked out,
And I stood between the points.
The ones that got there first, I did not see but
The prospecting area was about
20 steps or
30 steps away or so.

Over here the prospectors had dug deep like a bowl shape,

Gak aha:ma da'o đik
gak u:h đa'op đim
Gak 'pu yigokwima yih đa'opk
h'pu:h yok
ya wik nyi u:wom
tham pida "he:'" 'mi:ja

Gak jawva đ'opa
Nya mađ nyi gigwithoch
yal yak v'skwik'yu
I'm the one responsible ik
mađ va ya reservation
nya wijva
Hwalbay wijivch yu
Ma gak

Frank Beecher-ch

Gud dava
Bill Ridenour ch
ha La Bas'l
ba nyiny wa:mjim
nyiham nyuwa 'wi:h
nyival đu juwaqvik yuđik
Nyuwa ba:hch bijiv'm bamise:k

Jimwavach
hach haygu:h gwanjim
Ha La Bas'l ba nyi wa:mjich
Jimwavch Hakumwe:h wayo'đik
ba ye:vk he wayo'đik

Banyiny wamjim vok 'đim
Sulđawch ba jigwa:nim
'ba:jivch wik ik
i'thim

Since it was made deep,
The white man there stood down there.

The ones from the west arrived, and were going to
place the rock, but
They were told not to.
The one standing down there said no,
Though he was told not to
The one who arrived said he was going to.
I am appointed to do that.
He said
But he was told not to
Don't put it down, I'm telling you,
I am telling you not to.

Before I looked out
Before I saw it,
I did not think he would have a gun.
I took the gun
He showed it to me.
Only then I said "he:'."

They did not fight.
I am the one who holds this land.
I am standing here.
I'm the one responsible, I said.
This land, this reservation belongs to us.
It belongs to the Hualapai people.
You don't . . .

Frank Beecher,

A long time ago
Bill Ridenour,
At the time they took us to La Paz,
That's when the mountain,
They just poured into this area, but
Those men who were left, he was afraid of them.

'opjok
gak nyach wija đ'opk

Hayguhch
Sulđawch wije i'jim
Ha Bill Ridenour ch haygu gayu:m điye:vk yuj đim
Ha ba:jich ba ga wija đ'op yiđ
Jimwavch wi:hime

Juwaqvik ya:m đik
He Bill Ridenour ch
ha ca:ba Mine
nyu wal dava Ha Ga'a:mk ga'odval
hal yaw u:k u:ny
ha gud hak yaw
hwalk namakja
Bill Ridenourch nyi bim
Bill Ridenour Jr-ch hak bany
Hak ba ja:k viyamk ha đik
Ha ha yok
Ha 'mađ
Ya'wi nya wi: u:j ha bay wi:yik i'jiny
a'opok
Gak nyu wijich yuh đ'opk yu
đu nyu wal dav yokyu
'20 mile' im me mi
19 mile im me mi kyumo
nyu wal dav yok'
Gak nyi va gak u:j nya đ'opk im'i:j
Nyach va yigwithk
Nya:m nyach i'yigwithk
Ba:j wijich
Hwalbay wijich
Haygu ga yu:vch nyi thima:vah nyi yik
jivyamay nyi yik tho
Ya jivyam'm

Chemehuevi,
They killed the white man.
When they took us to La Paz
The Chemehuevi were at Beale Springs,
they were there with the Hualapai.

After they took us down, on the
Way back, the soldiers killed (those white men)
and said the Hualapai did it.
They said this, but
They said "no,"
"We did not do it."

The white man
The soldiers did it, they said.
Bill Ridenour and some other white man were
together.
The Hualapai did not do anything to them, but
It's the doings of the Chemehuevi.

When they (white man) poured into this area
Bill Ridenour—
There at Copper Mine,
It is way down there at the tip of the
Colorado River,
Those (metals) that he saw there
Those that have long been there,
They mined and left it
when Bill Ridenour died.
Bill Ridenour, Jr. He was,
He was the leader of his group then.
He took that (mine)
The land
He claimed this land that I saw
But I told him "not so."
It does not belong to them.
That is just way down there,

Ba:ja gwe ba e:h yivch yuh
yuyiđ
Nyach'yigwitha
Gak e:'e ih đa'op
Im 'i:j vak yoh

Gud ba ahmany đik
waksi guwicha wih i'ja
'Good hand' 'good roper'
olo yaha:na
waksi jiyumk yaha:na
Baya yibada
work complete mi mijing
Nyu gwe ga yu đu baya
Gweny spok bay đivilwik
ij nyu vilwik
Haygu 'nyuwe:vk

Sam Crozierch nyi spoh
Bert Groundsch nyi spoh
Billy Groundsch sidthik bijvik
nyuk wak
mi jigwing eva'ja
nyuch nyuk wakyu
Crozier Ranch'k wakyu
ha mi u:h miyik
Yu yiđ đe
v'ge haygu gwank
ba: ge gwank
'đahođik
gak eva đa'opivchyu

đu ba hiyanma nyi sik
đadaha:dik gwehan nya wi:yik
olo hana nya nyihađ'm

It is twenty miles or so,
Nineteen maybe.
It is located way down there.
They have not seen this, I told them.
I hold to this land,
Now, this day I hold this land.
It belongs to the Indians
It belongs to the Hualapai
If any white man wishes to lease
And work the place then
If they want to run (mining)
They will have to give the Indians something.
Even so.

I am holding this land,
I will not grant you permission,
I say this, it is noted.
Long ago when I was a young man,
A cowboy,
A good hand, a good roper,
I trained horses,
Herd cattle,
All of this I have become skilled at,
"work complete" you call it,
Just anything and all things.
I know all the necessary things to know,
that's how it seems to be
Living among the white man.

Sam Crozier he knows me,
Bert Grounds knows me.
Only Billy Grounds is still alive
and he's there.
Ask him and find out,
He is living there.
He is living at Crozier Ranch

đivgaeli gwe ga yu wi:k
đu han nya wi:yik
Nyach nyu haygu jigwa:nk
hwayovik ika
Ba:j điyevich wa nyimij mij ki
Vak 'wak yu
Vam bav đa:y imk vak 'wak yu
Gwe yu' ya hiyanmik yih đa'opk vak 'wak yu
yuktho

Vach va yum
bav đa:y'ak vak yak yu

yuk'tho
Gud 'thad gana:v đik ba nyi yovjik wijivch
Bak đa:ych ganav'm ev thim
Ha miyahch ba: nyi yo:vk wi: yiđ đe

Miyahch ba:ny yo:va nya h'pukoch
yuh đa'opk
Bakđa:ych ganav thik
'opo

Nyajivch yuja đa'ova

Gwe g'tho:vich
gwe g'wa:livch
qwa:qach
gwe g'mu:lvach
Mađ g'jija:vch gwe g'qacha
iluwi:h
'mthula
gwe ga yu g'mu:liv
Mađ đam'oda
ha ba yo:va puk kwij ki:
Miyahch

If you want to see him.
But even so,
At any time I have not killed a white man
Or killed any Indian
And hid this from anyone.
I have not experienced this.

But they just call me a bad person
I work and have good things,
A good horse I own.

A saddle and other things,
Just good things.
They say I killed the
White man and stole his things.
My own people dislike me.
And here I am.
Now I am an old man living here.
I have not been involved in any bad things, here I am.
But,

This is how it is.
I have become an old man and lie here.

But then
Long ago when the Creator made the people,
I hear this from the old people,
The Creator above made us.

The ones they first made,
we are not those ones.
The old people tell us this.
It is not so.

We are not those people.

The game—animals,
The winged animals,

Ba nyi yo:v'm
    Nya 'mađ jiv luwik
    Mahanik gwe mi ma:k
    'Mađ nyi mađ'k vak wamiyoh ik
Ba yo:v thik
    Nya ya nyi yabe:k
đu yimak yimak yimak yimak
    Gak 'maka đ'op

'Nya:hch gith'ye: yo:vk
Mach ba mivsoh
    'Mijithwe:h
    Namaka mih
đu nyuwevk han a mih
đu gwe mav ma:k
Gwe ga yu yuh yi nyu pidik yuja mih
Im
Gith'ye:hch ba jithwe:k
    ba jithwe:h

Gi yima:hch
    misi:ch baqu:ich
    misi:ch hmadach wih pukja

Meda nyi đuway'm
    g' đuy g'lwevjach
    Hma:ny g'wi:yach
    Baquich
    Ba:jach
        Bay yimak nyu jik

Gith'yeh wa mi:k
    yuh'k mađ jamk
    ha'jibah'k
    jelq'ch
        thuj
        yuh'm đađboq kwijk

    The deer,
    These various named animals,
They covered the land. The small animals,
    The snake,
    Chuckwalla
    These various named animals,
The land was filled up with them
These he made first they say,
The Creator.
When he made them
    They were like us.
    Be of good nature, eat
    Live on this land, he planned this
And made them accordingly
    When they came to life.
They just danced and danced and danced and
        danced
    And did not stop.

The sun he made a medicine man.
You watch over them,
    Lecture to them,
    Tell them to stop it,
Tell them to live right,
Eat the foods.
Whatever goals they have, tell them to stay with that.
The medicine man admonished them,
    He admonished them and admonished them.

The dancers,
    The girls, the women,
    The girls and boys were dancing first.

Later on
    The married couples,
    The ones with children,
    The women,

'Nya:hch gak miyayk ya vilwih đ'op đik
Mađ'k đu jiqlamđik yu'i i:
Bak 'đa:yach nyiva ganavja
Hach gak u:ny'k ih đo' yiđ
Giyabe:hch gav gi yuch ha gana:v'm i'mo i'je
Hach we dav yuwk

Vach va yum v'om

Hwalbaych yabe:đik
V'gak juhwayk we yamk
Haygu jigwa:nja đ'opm
    Nyach 'spoy 'yu
    Haygu đu yam 'nuwk
        đu jilwimtha
    gak gwanja đ'opm

Hayguch nya ji'alov yuwk
    Nya dopov yuwh yam nyonyay yim
V'olo hwayoh
đu gwe ga yu nyu pida wih
Wi:yim
Ba jigwa:n'm me
v'gak đuy wi ja đ'ok
Hayguch đu ba jigwa:n
    đu ya:mk nyuwe:vik
Ba:h điyuj wik
    đu gwank gwanjim nyu 'u:k

Olo hwayoh
    gadeđa đu:j—
        gadeđ so'yoch
    Gwe wij
    olo bay hwayok
    wij muwijik

Haygu bajigwa:n jiny
    gak eva đa'op

    The men,
        they all danced and they,

They hated the Medicine Man
    They threw dirt at his face.
    They spit on him.
    Excrement,
        urine,
        they dumped on his face.

The sun at that time was not up in sky like it is now.
It was just here flat on the earth.
The old people tell this.
I am not saying I have seen this.
It has been told from the ones who were living then
That comes from way back.

This is how it is.

When the Hualapai were living here
They did not make war, go out and
Kill the white man.
    I know this too.
    The white man in this area,
        for no specific purpose
    was he killed by the Hualapai.

The white man came from the east.
    They came from the west along this trail.
They stole his horses
And just other things.
For this doing
They killed the Indians.
They did not ignore the deed.
The white man just killed off
    The Indians living here and
Their relatives too.
    They went on killing, this I saw.

Ha pid'k hal yuwkyu i'jach

Med mađ nyi nuwa:hm
    General Crook sulđaw ba nyi yovkwi
Nyi ham pid
    Nyabeh jigwa:nja pida 'spoy yu
Tha pida u:k
Baquiya han dav yo:k

Nyabehch đu:y wija đ'om
General Crook'ch ba ya han yiđ đe
        han yiđ đe
            hank yu yiđ
Nyabehch
Hwajach
Pajimha:wach yuh
Pajiyumach yuh
Paji'ło:nđach yuh
đu gwe mu:lv 'Paji ga đe:hch
Sulđawa General Crook wihch
    Nyihal wal dav wa'yoh 'a:h
Mađkhwal
    Sulđaw wihch Ft. Whipple (ak) wayoh
Hach hla siđ'm
    Bes ba e:m muwijik
Wimuwijim

Gadeđa dawk
    Pa:k'k sulđaw wakyoh
        ba e:m'm
Hayguvch Ft. Whipple (ak) yamk
        ha jiyamjim
    wa:mk ba e:m muwij đik

Nyitha
    Hwajach
    Fort Whipple'm Pa:ka mađ vilwi:vok

The horse they stole,
    The wagon they burn, a wagon train—
    Other things they had,
    They stole these things. They claim, but

The killings of the white men
    I have heard nothing of it.

This is all they did in the beginning.

Later on when they
    Made peace with General Crook, commissioned
        us soldiers, only then
The killings of the
    Yavapai, I know only that.
Only that I saw.
Beautiful women they took.

The Yavapai did not do this for no cause but
General Crook treated them good,
        treated them well.
        It was good, but
Yavapai
Apache
Chiricahua Apache
Mohave Apache
Tonto Apache
Just all the many named Apaches;
General Crook's soldier
    Down there, way down there
At Hualapai Mountain (Camp Hualapai)
    His soldiers were stationed at Ft. Whipple.
They, at month's time,
    He would send them money.
This was their schedule.

On a stage coach
    The soldiers at (near) Parker

Hayguh g'vgaeđik
  Wamkav'm hwak'm
  Hwakđim ba jigwa:nja
Besa đay wija bay yo:ja
Gadeđa bay yok đahođja
olo bay yok
Gwe yu bay yok
đahođja

Nyi hak jiya:k
  Bany đigavja
Gwe ga yu mulvch yu
  tribe ga yuvch yu ik
Bay mađ'v vilwija

Nyachiv Ha'kumwe:h'k bany đigavjinyk
Wiđim
Hwajach u:k
'mbes'ch mađ khwal'l u:va
aLa Bas'k bes vwava hwak đake:vjim sa'adach spok
Bes'v ge mi yong wi i'thim
đadaha:d'k 'yok hayguhch đadaha:dok wim
Hayguhch opok
Gak nyu yujivk bes đadaha:d'k mi yoh mi đo'pa
Yal 'mbes simejik sulđaw wijivch yu
Mi ganavhing mim im
E'nyiva Nyavbe:vik 'yokwi

Nyabevch
  Fort Mohava ba:vch gwe dav'm
  Ha jevik jevik jevik
Nyi man'm
  Ya bes nyiva nyi e:m wi im

E' nyuv mih
Hanokyu

  he would send to them.
The white man from Ft. Whipple, they sent him.
  He would take the money to them regularly.

This one,
  the Apaches
  The land between Ft. Whipple and Parker,

They intercepted the white man
  Along with a Mohave man.
  Both of them, they killed them.
The payroll they carried, that was all taken.
The whole wagon, taken and hidden.
The horses and everything else,
They hid these.

From this event on
  They captured us.
The name of the group or
  Tribe that did this, they questioned.
They searched the whole territory.

They took us to Beale Springs
They held us captive and then
The Apaches were the ones—
The money showed up at Hualapai Mountain
At La Paz a twenty dollar bill was changed
  The store keeper knew this bill.
He asked "Where did you get this money?"
"I worked for a white man and got this money."
But the white man said no.
"You did not get this money from working," he said.
The money is lost from here it belongs to the military.
"You better tell the truth," he said.
"Yes." I got this from a Yavapai.

A Yavapai man—
  "A man from Ft. Mohave

Hach wijokwi
I' be sulđaw bes ba e:m jim wijach
Nyi hak điyak
Nyabehch yuy đugwilvim
    Hak g'jihwaych

Baj sulđaw yov me
Gwehch General Crook
        Sulđaw yovm
Bay Nyavbeh jigwank đek jađ'm jigwank
    nyi juwid'k
Ba đigavk
San Ca:la bajam jim
Hak wayoh

Va yum 'spokyu

Mah Vam 'o kyu ◇

    Was ill and I doctored and doctored him. And
When he got well, he
    Gave me this money," he said.

"Yes" that's the way to tell it.
"That is good."
They were the ones who did it.
That's how they would send
The military payroll, and on account of this,
The Yavapai deeds,
    Was the worst offense. They made war.

He made soldiers of the Indians.
That person, General Crook,
        He made them soldiers.
All of the Yavapai, they killed a great many of them,
    They killed and when they had finished
They captured (the others).
They took them and placed them at San Carlos.
They stayed there.

I know this to be so.

Mah, that is all. ◇

Bibliography

Dobyns, Henry F., and Euler, Robert C. 1976. *The Walapai people.* Phoenix: Indian Tribal Series.

Kroeber, Alfred L., Ed. 1935. *Walapai ethnography.* American Anthropological Association Memoirs Number 42.

Langdon, Margaret, Ed. 1976. *Yuman texts.* International Journal of American Linguistics: Native American Text Series, Number 3.

Manners, Robert A. 1974. *Hualapai Indians II: An ethnographical report on the Hualapai (Walapai) Indians of Arizona.* New York: Garland Publishing Co.

Powskey, Malinda; Watahomigie, Lucille J.; and Yamamoto, Akira Y. 1979. Structure of nominal modifiers in Walapai. In *Occasional Papers in Linguistics 5,* ed. James E. Redden. Carbondale, Ill.: Department of Linguistics, Southern Illinois University. Pp. 35–42.

Powskey, Malinda; Watahomigie, Lucille J.; and Yamamoto, Akira Y. 1980. Language use: explorations in language and meaning. In *Occasional Papers in Linguistics 7,* ed. James E. Redden. Carbondale, Ill.: Department of Linguistics, Southern Illinois University. Pp. 60–67.

Redden, James E. 1966. Walapai I: Phonology. *International Journal of American Linguistics* 32: 1–16.

———. 1966. Walapai II: Morphology. *International Journal of American Linguistics* 32: 141–63.

Watahomigie, Lucille J., and Yamamoto, Akira Y. 1983. Literacy education: language awareness through creative writing. Paper presented at the First Native American Studies Conference at the Oklahoma State University, Stillwater, Oklahoma. March 12–15.

Watahomigie, Lucille J., and Yamamoto, Akira Y. 1983. Hualapai Bilingual/Bicultural Education Program, a case of action linguistics. Paper presented at the International Congress of Anthropological and Ethnological Sciences at Vancouver, Canada. August 25.

Watahomigie, Lucille J. and Yamamoto, Akira Y., Eds. 1983. *Gigyayk Vo:jka!—Yuman poetry with linguistic analysis.* California: Malki Museum Press.

Watahomigie, Lucille J.; Bender, Jorigine; and Yamamoto, Akira Y. with Elenora Mapatis, Josie Manakaja and Malinda Powskey. 1982. *Hualapai reference grammar.* California: American Indian Studies Center, University of California at Los Angeles.

Watahomigie, Lucille J., Bender, Jorigine; and Yamamoto, Akira Y. 1981. Possession expressions and semantic classification of nouns. In *Occasional Papers in Linguistics 9,* ed. James E. Redden. Carbondale, Ill.: Department of Linguistics, Southern Illinois University. Pp. 100–11.

Winter, Werner. 1966. Yuman languages II: Wolf's Son—A Walapai text. *International Journal of American Linguistics* 32: 17–40.

Yamamoto, Akira Y.; Watahomigie, Lucille J.; Powskey, Malinda; and Bender, Jorigine. 1982. Narrative devices in Hualapai: i:jki and ki:jki. Paper presented at the 21st SSILA Annual Meeting at Washington, D.C. December 6.

Notes, Acknowledgments, and Credits

"Wikahme'." Hualapai version from Kathad Ganav, 1981, Peach Springs School District No. 8, Peach Springs, AZ.

"Mađwiđa." Hualapai version from Kathad Ganav, 1981, Peach Springs School District No. 8, Peach Springs, AZ.

"Life of Kate Crozier." The recording was made in the summer of 1956, with funds provided by the University of Kansas. Later work on the analysis of the text was funded by the Deutsche Forschungs-gemeinschaft. Copies of the tape were given to the school at Peach Springs, to the Museum of Northern Arizona at Flagstaff, and to the Yuma Archives at the University of California at San Diego. A copy of the text accompanied by a linguistic analysis and a translation has been deposited by Werner Winter at the Archives for consultation by interested persons.

Photo credits: pp. 9 and 54—Bob Ilumin; pp. 10, 53, and 63—Victor Masayesva; p. 42—Gary Scott; p. 64—Barry Goldwater (courtesy of the Heard Museum).

Drawings for "'Sa Ba: 'Sa Baqi" by Leanne Hinton.

LEANNE HINTON, *Editor*

The Havasupai

From time immemorial, the Havasupai have been the stewards of a verdant tributary of the Grand Canyon. Their name, *Ha vasuwa 'baaje*, translates as "People of the Blue/Green Water." So isolated is their home, and so difficult of access, that not even horses could enter the canyon until the nineteenth century when they built a horse trail. Their canyon can still be reached only by foot, horse, or helicopter; and they have the only post office in the United States which is serviced by mule train. Entering their canyon home used to be so difficult that Garces, the first explorer to reach them, wrote in his diary that his soldiers—fierce, hardened men all, accustomed to facing hardships and possible death with frequency—wept and trembled with fear as they negotiated the trail into the canyon on hands and knees (Coues, 1900). The Havasupai themselves, on the other hand, were accustomed to entering and leaving with frequency. They stayed in the canyon only in the summertime, to plant and irrigate their crops. In the winter, all but the sick and the old left the canyon to camp on the high plateau, to hunt game and gather piñons. It was only in the late nineteenth century, when ranchers began to fence off the water holes and the government decided to take over the plateau land, that the Havasupai were forced to live year-round in the canyon. There was not enough firewood in the canyon for the full population of 500 or more to keep warm all winter; nor could they survive without seasonal hunting and gathering on the plateau. Thus began a period of hardship for the Havasupai, a period of epidemics and economic deprivation. But they never stopped fighting to regain their lost plateau land, and in 1975 they finally won back the right to sole use of over 180,000 acres of land along the Coconino Plateau.

Their relative isolation has allowed their entry into modern living to be somewhat slower and more gentle than it was for other Indians in the Southwest. They were left alone in the mid-nineteenth century while other Arizona tribes were forcibly taken to concentration camps. Almost all Havasupai are fully proficient in their traditional language; most do not speak English until they are of school age.

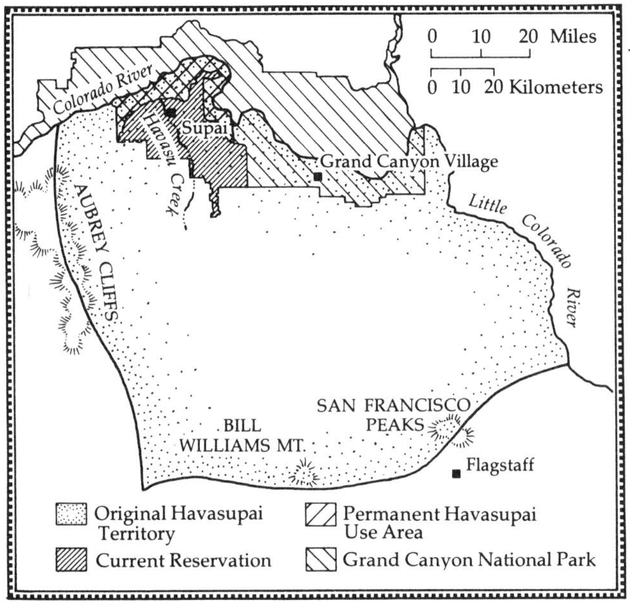

They still refuse to build jeep trails or tramways into the canyon despite many proposals from outsiders to do so. In fact, a major source of income at present is through tourists coming into the canyon as back-packers or on horses. The Havasupai are expert horsemen and packers, and most families have members that make their living at packing.

The Havasupai speak almost the same language as the Hualapai, with only small dialect differences. They have always had close kinship ties with them as well. Beyond this, their most important friends and trading partners, at least in recent centuries, are the Hopis. The Hopis live several hundred miles away, but most Havasupai have made journeys to visit them at least a few times during their lives, and Hopis are known to have come to live among the Havasupai for years at a time during droughts. A Havasupai community was present in Hopi territory near Tuba City in the eighteenth century. The Hopis even have a Havasupai katsina ("Cohonino," a hispanicized pronunciation of the Hopi word for the Havasupai, is the name of their katsina).

Songs and stories clearly express the Havasupai's love of their homeland. The first song printed here describes the canyon in detail; the last song, a farewell to the land, was composed long ago by an ancestor of the singer. The Havasupai know—in a way that many other peoples rarely seem to know—that it is the land which makes us what we are. ◇

The Contributors

Dan Hanna learned many songs and stories from his father, Henry Hanna, and even more from his uncle, Mark Hanna, a shaman. Until his untimely death in 1968, Dan Hanna was respected as one of the best and most knowledgeable singers among the Havasupai, specializing in traditional tales, sweathouse songs, and medicine songs. When anthropologists came to the community, he was willing to work long hours with them. A great many of his songs are preserved on tape as a result of his generosity with his time and knowledge. Most of the songs presented here were sung by him. Dan Hanna left the canyon for ten years under a government project to relocate people in cities. He lived and worked in Los Angeles during that time, but then he came back—as all Havasupai do—to the better life in his canyon home, where he stayed until he died. He is survived by his wife and by many children and grandchildren.

Henry Hanna was the descendant of singers and the father of singers. His brother, Mark, was a well-known medicine man. Henry himself was approached by spirits several times, but he told them to go away. He did not want to bring upon himself all the troubles that being a medicine man entails. Instead, he contented himself with working hard and well all his life, and raising four sons who in their turn became important and respected members of their community. His jobs—like the jobs of other Havasupai of that period—reflected the changing times. He worked for the railroad as it was first coming into Arizona. He worked for ranchers, doing roundup, punching cattle. He worked with horses, learning the trade of packing. At the same time, he had a great fund of traditional knowledge, which he shared freely with his children. On a winter night he would tell stories and sing songs, in the traditional way—never forcing his children to listen, just singing softly for himself and for anyone who wanted to hear. In this gentle manner he transmitted his knowledge. And as with all children, some never gained enough interest to listen well, while others began to hear more and more as they grew up and were thus able to gain a great deal of the knowledge Henry had to share.

Earl Paya, born in 1919, is the oldest son of Lemuel Paya, who was one of the most prolific singers and storytellers of his generation. Earl Paya's mother was Esther Manakadja, daughter of Chief Manakadja and the Paiute woman Baa Ñuwa. Earl Paya, like his father, retains much of the important tribal knowledge. He knows many traditional tales and songs, and is perhaps the most knowledgeable person about the geography of Havasupai territory, having traveled over almost all of it by horseback or on foot.

Earl Paya served overseas in World War II and has been tribal chairman several times, as well as tribal tourist manager, mailman, and packer. He brough the first tractor to the canyon: he took it down the switchbacks, dismantling it several times in order to take it past obstacles.

The eight-mile trip took three days. His wife Lillian Siyuja died in 1975. He has children and many grandchildren living with him and around him, with whom he makes an effort to share his great knowledge as his own father shared with him.

Sinyella was a chief under the old system of tribal government. Born in the early nineteenth century, Sinyella grew up leading a fully traditional life. It was not until well into his adult years that the white man began to encroach seriously on his territory. For several years beginning in 1918, Sinyella—who by then spoke excellent English—collaborated with Leslie Spier in his writing of the now-classic *Havasupai Ethnography.* He has many descendants among the Havasupai today, who bear his name as their family name. Mount Sinyella and several other landmarks are named after him.

Leslie Spier, who was trained by Franz Boas, was one of a group of talented ethnographers who did research among American Indians in the early twentieth century. At that time, there were many people living who had grown up before the white invasion of the West, and it is due in large part to Spier and his colleagues that the knowledge of these old ones is still available to Indian and non-Indian communities. Spier wrote many ethnographies on tribes in the Southwest, especially Yuman tribes. *Havasupai Ethnography* is his best work.

The Havasupai Alphabet

Vowels

Havasupai has five short vowels and five long vowels. The short vowels are represented by one letter; the long vowels are represented by two identical letters. Vowels may also occur in diphthongs, which are short or long vowels followed by the letter "w" or "y".

Short vowels

The letters for Havasupai vowels are given about the same pronunciation as in Spanish.

a *'ha*, 'water'. The Havasupai *a* is pronounced as the *a* in English f*a*ther.

e *he*, 'dress'. As in K*a*te, or more like the Spanish p*e*so.

i *ilwi*, 'snake'. As in k*ee*p.

o *oba*, 'no'. As in p*o*ke.

u *gud*, 'already'. As in h*u*la.

Long vowels

The long vowels are pronounced like the short vowels, but are drawn out a little longer.

aa *'haa*, 'cottonwood tree'.

ee *beemg*, 'to be out of'. Remember, this is still like the *a* in K*a*te or the *e* in Spanish p*e*so, NOT like the *ee* spelling in English.

ii *mdiig*, 'beans'.

oo *joovg*, 'to fight'. Remember, this is still like the *o* in p*o*ke, but held out longer. It is NOT like the *oo* spelling in English.

uu *uuva*, 'tobacco'.

Consonants

b *bees*, 'money'. As in *b*oy, s*p*it.

ch *chaw*, 'material'. As in *ch*ild.

d *duvg*, 'thin'. As in *d*ime.

f *'fu*, 'coyote willow'. As in *f*ine.

g *gaya*, 'dog'. As in *g*ain.

h *haneya*, 'bucket'. As in *h*ave.

j *jnpug*, 'ant'. As in *j*ail.

k *kandemavya*, 'Christmas'. As in *k*ite.

kw *kwa*, 'knife'. As in *qu*ail.

l *'lava*, 'prickly pear'. As in *l*ike.

m *muuso*, 'cat'. As in *m*ouse.

n *niis*, 'spider'. As in *n*ice.

ñ *ñgwaay*, 'shirt'. As in ca*ny*on.

ꞥ *haꞥgja*, 'handkerchief'. As in si*ng*.

p *pu*, 'gun'. As in *p*un.

q *qsaq*, 'crow'. Like *k*, but with tongue touching farther back in throat.

s *suwmaj*, 'watermelon'. As in *s*ail.

ŧ *ŧiyaj*, 'corn'. Somewhat like English *t* as in s*t*ick, but with tongue touching teeth.

t *taagg*, 'to tie shoelaces'. As in *t*ail.

th *thbal*, 'peach'. As in *th*anks.

v *vdav'ij*, 'thunder'. As in *v*an.

w *wagsi*, 'cow'. As in *w*et.

y *yaas*, 'turkey'. As in *y*es.

' *'mhlu'u*, 'pipe'. Glottal stop; occurs in English as break between two vowels in words like "uh-uh".

Havasupai Music

Leanne Hinton

Forming a large part of the Havasupai section is a group of songs—some of them short songs of the sort found inside long tales, and some of them very long narrative songs. The long narrative songs, in particular, are quite characteristic of Havasupai music, but not commonly found in very many other North American tribes—or at least, not often transcribed. The songs are astounding works of art that deserve an honored place in the literature of the world.

Yet, if it is difficult to transcribe and translate tales, it is almost doubly so with songs. The language in songs is drastically different from spoken language, both in sound and grammar. And rhythm and melody, two things very difficult to transmit in writing, form a very important part of songs. The transcription system used for Western music is difficult to apply to the music of other traditions, for that notation system is based on many assumptions about music that do not hold in other cultures. Furthermore, no notation system adequately portrays voice quality or subtle variations in tonality, rhythm and speed.

In an effort to communicate something about the melody of these songs, they have been transcribed with a slightly modified Western notational system. When two notes are tied, , it means that in some verses they are separate notes (i.e. sung to separate syllables), while in other verses they are sung to a single syllable. When a note is tied to a second note with a straight line, 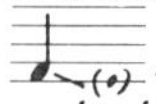, it means that the singer glides from the first note to the second. The lack of a stem on a note means that it is not accorded any time value. An x instead of an oval, 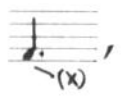, means that the note's tonality is inexact.

The voice quality of Havasupai singing is relaxed—not piercing or pulsating as it is in some areas in North America, such as the Plains. While many types of Havasupai songs have a strong beat, the ones transcribed here are loose in rhythm. They are sung without any instrumental accompaniment. They were not traditionally sung for any ceremony, nor even in public—but rather were always sung, rather quietly, in the singer's home or some other informal setting. Medicine songs are usually sung during curing sessions, to the accompaniment of a rattle, but the two medicine songs here were more often sung without a rattle.

All these songs can be thought of as partially improvised—that is, although the content and the melody are set, how the content is put into words within the song varies somewhat from performance to performance. Thus the singer needs more than just a good memory. He must be knowledgeable enough about the rules of singing to be able to compose his song as he goes along. A part of his composition process also involves making changes in the words—adding syllables, changing the vowels, sometimes mutating the consonants to improve the flow of sound. Transliterations of each line of song into a spoken counterpart are provided so that the Havasupai reader can recognize what is being said, and also so that any reader can study the difference between the sung and spoken words. In some songs, the text is correlated rhythmically with the melody through the use of accent marks (´).

Versions of all of these songs except the White Horse Song will be published by Gunther Narr (Hinton, in press). An English version of the Medicine Song was previously published in *Alcheringa* (Hanna and Hinton, 1971). ◇

Medicine Song

Dan Hanna, Singer

Dan Hanna learned this song from Mark Hanna, a shaman. Although it is a medicine song, it is not necessarily sung by a medicine man. It can be sung by someone who is ill and wants to cure himself. Many people had these personal medicine songs in the old days, and some people still do. Like the medicine man's songs, a personal medicine song is received through a dream from a spirit. The song goes into rich description of Havasu Canyon. At the end, the song refers to some boulders which lie in a certain place, which, when one lies down on them, absorb sickness. The word *bay gjama*, which is translated as "an illness," is more correctly either an illness or an accident, and really refers to a straying from the rightful road, the development of a disharmony with nature—which is what illness is defined to be.

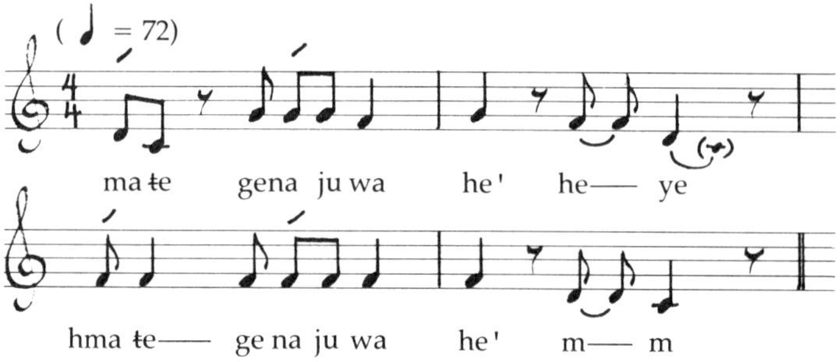

Singing		*Translation*	*Speaking*
Máŧe genájuwa	he' heye	The land we were given	('maŧ gnaajva)
Hmáte genájuwa	he' mm	The land we were given	
Vá geyóvuwa	he' heye	It is right here	(va gyova)
Vá geyóvuwa	he' heye	It is right here	
'Áwe yuhwáŧiga	he' heye	Red rock	('wii hwaŧga)
'Áwe yuhwáŧiga	he' heyem	Red rock	

Ñá oséemega	he' heye	Streaked with brown	(ñaa seemga)
Ñá oséemega	he' heye	Streaked with brown	
Ñá om gyájvga	he' heye	Shooting up high	(ñvgyajvga)
Ñá om vgyájevega	he' hemm	Shooting up high	
'áwam sigávoga	he' heye	All around our home	('wa sgavoga)
'wámje sigávoga	he' heyem	All around our home	
Wé yiwáthuga	he' heye	Red rock	('wii hwaɫega)
Wé yiwáthiga	he' heye	Red rock	
Ñá om mgyávoga	he' mm	Shooting up high	(nvgyajvga)
Thá giyóhuwa	he' heye	It is right here	(tha gyova)
Ñévo ñibúvguge	he' heye	Down at the source	(ñvu ñbuvgge)
Hábag ñiyújuwa	he' heye	A spring will always be there	(haabag nyuj)
Ñá guwíjuvuwo	he' heyem	It is ours	(na gwiijva)
Ñá guwíjuwo	he' mm	It is ours	
Hé ñiyúmowe	he' heye	Since a long time ago	(ga vuñyum)
Gávo ńyúmowe	he' heye	Since a long time ago	
'Máɫe ñuwíjuwa	he' heye	In the land that is ours	('mat ñwiijva)
Ñévo ñiɫúvume	he' heye	Moving right down the center	
Só 'ugwáthuga	he' heye	Bright blue-green	(suuwgwatga)
Vám jimísevga	he' hemm	There moves a line	
Ñó 'iyúhuwa	he' heye	This is what I'm thinking	(ña yuha)
Ñá 'iyúhuwa	he' heyem	This is what I'm thinking	
'Á giyúyuwo	he' heye	At the edge of the water	(ham s'ivɨvga)
Hámes'e'ívɨevga	he' heye	Cattails appear	
'áme si'ívɨevga	he' heye	Cattails appear	(suuwgwaɫga)
Só'ogwátuwa	he' heyem	Bright blue-green	
'Ám buwámbuga	he' heye	All around the water	(ham vwamvga)
Ñá 'iyúwuwa	he' heye	This is what I'm thinking	(ña yuha)
'Á gejúyiwo	he' heyem	At the edge of the water	(ha gyuuyo)
'Á 'amálega	he' heyem	Water foam forming	(ha 'malga)

'Á 'amálega	he' heyem	Water foam forming	
'Á gejúyiwo	he' heyem	At the edge of the water	
Gwáyyve gwáyvuga	he' heye	Swirl, swirling	(thgwayv thgwayvga)
Gwáyve gwáyvuga	he' heyem	Swirl, swirling	
'Á gejúyiwo	he' heyem	At the edge of the water	(ha gyuuyo)
'Á gejúyiwo	he' heyem	At the edge of the water	
Má gwanóvjiga	he' heye	Silt layers forming	('maɬ gwanvjga)
Mát gwanóvjiga	he' eyem	Silt layers forming	
'Á gejúyiwo	he' heye	At the edge of the water	(sgwin sgwinga)
Máthgwinath-gwínega	he' heye	Ripple, rippling	
Máthgwinath-gwínega	he' heye	Ripple, rippling	(ña yuha)
Ñá iyúwawa	he' mm	This is what I'm thinking	
Ñá 'iyúhuwa	he' heya	This is what I'm thinking	(ha gbadga)
Háge 'abádiga	he' heye	Water-walking beetles	
Ágeyabádiga	he' heyem	Water-walking beetles	(ha javme)
Há ñijáwome	he' heyem	On top of the water	
Ñévo jiháyviga	he' heye	Spreading out	(ñvu jhayvga)
Ñá iyíwuwa	he' heyem	This is what I'm thinking	(ña yuha)
'Ámesegwáthuga	he' heye	Water grasses growing	(hamsgwathga)
Hámesegwáthega	he' heye	Water grasses growing	
Shó'ogwáthuga	he' heye	Bright blue-green	(suuwgwaɬga)
Shó'ogwáthuga	he' heyem	Bright blue-green	
Há ñiyálowe	he' heye	Under the water	(ha ñyaala)
Há ñiyálowe	he' heye	Under the water	
Mágnognóvoga	he' heye	Wave, waving	(gnov gnovga)
Mágnognóvoga	he' heye	Wave, waving	
Ñá'iyúhuwa	he' heye	This is what I'm thinking	(ña yuha)
Ñá'iyúhuwa	he'hmm	This is what I'm thinking	

Há ñiyálowe	he' heye	Under the water	(ha ñyaala)
Há jwáiga	he' heye	Water pebbles	(ha jwayga)
Ñévo jiqvújega	he' heye	Tiny little ones	(ñvu jqayvjga)
Géjijávuwa	he' heye	Spreading out over them	(gjjavva)
Vóñijávume	he' heye	Spreading out over them	
Há'eñihájiva	he' heye	Our drinking water	(ha ñhajva)
'Á jimhévgowa	he' heyem	The water is gliding	(ha jmhevga)
Máte megɫávoge	he' heye	Toward the north	('mat mgɫavge)
'Ó ɫeyávoga	he' heye	On in that direction	(vu ɫyavge)
Thá thelávuma	he' heyem	And then it is gone	(tha thlavm)
Ña 'iyúhuwa	he' heye	This is what I'm thinking	(ña yuha)
Ña 'iyúhuwa	he' heyem	This is what I'm thinking	
Thág ño'evó'oga	he' heye	Here we arrive	(thag ñ'voga)
Thág ño'evó'oga	he' heyem	Here we arrive	
Báyovgijámoha	he' heye	An illness	(bay gjama)
Báyogijámoha	he' heye	An illness	
Thá vuwámuga	he' heye	I sit down	(thag vwamg)
Thá vuwámuga	he' heyem	I sit down	
Gwéwe 'eswáduga	he' heye	I sing myself a song	(gwe 'swaadga)
Gwéwe 'eswáduga	he' heyem	I sing myself a song	
Ñá 'iyúhuwa	he' heye	This is what I'm thinking	(ña yuha)
Ña 'iyúhuwa	he' heye	This is what I'm thinking	
'Ágwe simájuwa	he' heye	A medicine spirit	(gwe smaaje)
'Ágwe simájuwa	he' mm	A medicine spirit	
Bá qetheyévuwa	he' heye	A shaman	('ba gthiyeva)
Bá qetheyévuwa	he' heye	A shaman	
Vá'aluwíñuga	he' heye	I am the same as him	(vlwiivga)
Vá'aluwíñuga	he'hmm	I am the same as him	
Báyo gijámuha	he' heye	An illness	(bay gjama)
Báyo gijámuga	he' heye	An illness	

Há buwámuga	he' heye	I sit down	(thag vwamg)
Há buwámuga	he' hmm	I sit down	
'Ágwe weswáduga	he' heye	I sing myself a song	(gwe 'swaadga)
'Ágwe weswáduga	he' heye	I sing myself a song	
'Ágwe 'asíñiga	he' heyem	The things I have named	(gwe 'siiñga)
'Agwe 'asiñiga	he' heyem	The things I have named	
'Atɨe nemáguga	he' heye	I leave them behind	('ɨnmagga)
'Atɨenemáguga	he' heye	I leave them behind	
Nó 'iyúhuwa	he' heye	This is what I'm thinking	(ña yuha)
Nó 'iyúhuwa	he' mm	This is what I'm thinking	
Thág ño'ovóga	he' heye	There we arrive	(thag ñ'vóga)
Thág ño'ovóga	he' heye	There we arrive	
Thám jovibájuga	he' heyem	We are leaving the canyon	(tham jo jbajga)
Thám jo wibájuga	he' heye	We are leaving the canyon	
Máłoódwova	he' heye	Out on the rim	('mat ɨ'odva)
Mátoódwova	he' mm	Out on the rim	
Gwé ñihátowa	he' heye	Horses that are mine	(gwe ñhat)
Gwé ñihátowa	he' heye	Horses that are mine	
Ñó 'uwávowo	he' heye	The place where they roam	(ñowavo)
Ño'uwávowo	he' heyem	The place where they roam	
Ñwá 'ajóqowa	he' heyem	Is there at the junipers	(ñwa 'joq)
Jóqa havíɨega	he' heyem	Where the junipers are straight	('joq hviɨga)
Ñabiñáboga	he' heye	And low and low	(ñab ñabga)
Vú 'ayóhowa	he' heye	They are right here	(vu gyoha)
Gwé ñihátove	he' heye	Horses that are mine	(gwe ñhaɨ)
Thám jejebúvuvga	he' heye	Are gathered right there.	(tham jjbugvga)
Ñó 'iyúhuwa	he' heye	This is what I'm thinking	(ña yuha)
Ñó 'iyúhuwa	he' heyem	This is what I'm thinking	
Thág ño'evówoga	he' heye	Here we arrive	(thag ñ'voga)
Thág ño'evówoga	he' heyem	Here we arrive	

Yá hawíniga	he' heye	We swing back	(siihwinga)
Yá hawíniga	he' hmm	We swing back	
'Áwe gewéyiwo	he' heye	Descending the rocks again	('wii gweeyi)
'Áwe gewéyiwo	he' heyem	Descending the rocks again	
'Áwe gethíltewa	he' heye	White rock	('wii gthiltva)
Ña'usémuga	he' heye	Streaked with brown	(ñaa seemga)
'Ó ñibóvuvga	he' heyem	Down at the source	(vu ñbuvvga)
Hábav ñiyújuwa	he' heyem	A spring will always be there	(haabag ñyuj)
'Ágwe ñigethá- łemwa	he' heye	The spring that heals	(gwe ñgthaajme)
Ñá geyóhuwa	he' heye	It is right there	(ñgyoha)
Gá geyóhowa	he' heyem	It is right there	(gwe ñhała)
Gwé'e ñiháłowa	he' heye	Horses that are mine	
Úniháj̇uve	he' heye	They drink the water	(vu ñhajva)
Gá geyóhowa	he' hemm	That is right there	(ga gyoha)
'Áwe gethílłega	he' heye	White rock	('wii gthilłga)
Ñá vusémuga	he' heyem	Streaked with brown	(ñaa seemga)
Ñam gyávuga	he' heye	Shooting up high	(ñvgyávga)
Thá thiyóvuwa	he' heye	It is right there	(tha gyova)
Ñívu vetóvume	he' heyem	Moving down the center	(ñvu vtuvme)
Gwé'e ñihátuwa	he'mm	Horses that are mine	(gwe ñhata)
Ñóviñájuwo	he' heye	There is their trail	(ññáaje)
Ñóviñájuwo	he' heye	There is their trail	
'Ágwe gethávuga	he' heye	The color of dust	(gwe gthavga)
'Ágwe gethávuga	he' heyem	The color of dust	
Ó eye'óyvuga	he' heye	Zig-zagging	(vu łs'uuyvga)
Májyo yi'úyvuga	he' heye	Zig-zagging	
Vógse vuwávuga	he' heyem	It leads to the source	(buge vwavga)
Vógse vuwávuga	he' heyem	It leads to the source	

Thágе yóvuwa	he' heye	It is right here	(vá gyóva)
Ñó 'iyúhuwa	he' heye	This is what I'm thinking	(ñá 'yúha)
Ág ño'uvówuga	he' heye	Here we arrive	(thag ñyovga)
Jégamímowa	he'mm	Down in the canyon	(jgmimo)
'Áwe ñihwáłoga	he' heye	Red rocks	('wii hwałog)
Jé gamímoga	he' eye	Down in the canyon	
Vú giyóvume	he' heyem	They are right here	(vu gyovme)
Amqe ghmimoga	hm' hmm	Down in the canyon	
'Áse yehwáłega	he' heye	Red rocks	
Míñabeñáboga	he' heye	Low and low	(vñab ñabga)
Ó giyóvume	he' heye	They are right here	
Ñáj ivóguwa	he' heyem	Here I walk	(ñaj voga)
'Á'iyámoga	he' heye	I go alone	('yaamga)
Ñá'ji yúwuga	he' heyem	This is what I'm thinking	(ñaj yuhga)
'Áwe huhwáłega	he' heyem	Red rocks	('wii hwałga)
Ñá 'usémega	he' heyem	Streaked with brown	(ñaa seemga)
Ñá em 'ugyávuga	he' heye	Shooting up high	(ñvgyajvga)
Vú giyówuwa	he' heye	It is right here	(vu gyova)
Ñóm ñibóvuge	he'mm	Down at the source	(nvu vbuvge)
'Áwe yihwáłega	he'eche	Red rocks	('wii hwałga)
Óhwináloga	he' heye	Boulders they are	(onalga)
Thá vuséemuga	he'mm	Streaked with brown	(tha vseemga)
Thá vuséemuga	he' heye	Streaked with brown	
Thági yóthuwa	he'eye	They are right here	(tha gyova)
'Áwovethátevemo	he' heye	Where my illness is absorbed	(vthatvmo)
Ágiyóhuwa	he' heye	It is right here	
Yá 'iyíñuwa	he' heye	This is what I will	(ya 'yiiñu)
Yá 'iyíñuwa	he' heye	This is what I will	

The White Horse Song

Dan Hanna, Singer

This song, one of Mark Hanna's medicine songs, depicts the thoughts of a medicine man during a curing session. It begins with the medicine man at home asleep, suddenly knowing telepathically that someone is coming for him. He places his shoes by his pillow so that he can be ready to leap up quickly if necessary. The visitor claims that his relative is almost dead already—"They are starting to mourn, gathered around him." Nevertheless, he is persuaded to go to the sick man, and he has his white horse saddled for him. At first he goes slowly, even though at his slowest speed the white horse moves so quickly that the shaman is able to catch jackrabbits. As he goes along, he sends out his spirit to see what the situation is at the sick man's house. The spirit comes back and says that it is really true that the sick man is almost dead. Hearing that, the shaman whips his horse into a run and arrives almost immediately at the man's bedside. The shaman experiences a moment of self-doubt, crying "What can I possibly do for him?" But he draws four lines radiating from the man's head, and sends his spirit inside. All night he sits with him, and when dawn arrives, the man is miraculously healed. This song came to Mark Hanna in a dream, and he taught it to Dan when the latter was living with him. Dan reported that often Mark would sit up in bed in the middle of the night, singing a song that had just come to him in a dream.

Singing	*Translation*	*Speaking*
Íbá ñevájuweé	A visitor	('Baa ñvajva)
Íba'á ñevájuweé	A visitor	
Íbá ñevájuweé	A visitor	
Íba'á ñevájuweé	A visitor	
Íbá ñevájuweé	A visitor	
Íbá ñevájuweé	A visitor	
Íba'á ñevájuweé	A visitor	
Íba'á ñevájuweé	A visitor	
Gá thé ñiyúweé	Someone there is coming	(Ga the ñyuwa)
Ñéwa'á ñetámeé	Right about now	(Nwa ñtam)
Gá thé ñiyúweéga	Someone there is coming	
Ñéwa'á ñetámeé	Right about now	
Gá thé ñiyúweéga	Someone there is coming	
Ñéwa'á ñetámeé	Right about now	
Gá thé ñiyúweéga	Someone there is coming	
Ñéwa'á ñetámeé	Right about now	
Ñá'á maháñowá	My shoes	(ña mahño)
Gavéya ñáji yógaá	I take them	(ñaj yoga)
Ñá'á sibóboó	At my pillow	(ña sbugvo)
Geñája héjowógaá	I place them	(ñaj jwoga)
Gá thági yágeé	I lie there	(ga thag yaga)
Gá thahági yágeé	I lie there	
Gá thahági yágeé	I lie there	
Gá thahági yágeé	I lie there	
Ñá thé 'iyúthig	I stay there	(ñaj the 'yuthga)
Ñá thé 'iyúthmm	I stay there	(ñaj the 'yuthm)
Ñá'á gamáthuwíl	Into my awareness	(ña gmathwl)
Gá jávuwáhaáh	He will enter	(gaj vwahga)
Gá thijá viyútheé	That is what I think	(ga thii vyuthga)
Gá thijá viyútheé	That is what I think	
Gá thijá viyútheé	That is what I think	
Gá thijaá viyúthmḿ	That is what I think. Then:	(ga thii vyuthm)

Báwa héje óboó	"The man cannot move	('baawj heja 'obg)
Gebáwa héje óbom	The man cannot move	
Báwa héje óboó	The man cannot move	
Gebáwa héje óbom	The man cannot move"	
Gá yáha ítheyém	So he said, but	(ga ya ithm)
Geñája háya óboó	I said, "He's not so sick"	(ñaj haya oboo)
Geñája háya óboó	I said, "He's not so sick"	
Geñája háya óbomm	I said, "He's not so sick"	
Gá vú ñe'éveé	He heard what I told him	(ga vu ñ'evga)
Gá va'ú ñe'éveé	He heard what I told him	
Gá va'ú ñe'éveé	He heard what I told him	
Gá va'ú ñe'évemm	He heard what I told him, but:	
Báwij héje óboó	"The sick man cannot move	
Báwij héje óboó	"The sick man cannot move	
Báwij héje óboó	"The sick man cannot move	
Báwij héje óbmm	"The sick man cannot move.	
Hwáy vtégalúmeé	They are starting to mourn	(hway tglumga)
Hañéva'ú sigávahéh	Gathered all around him	(ñevu sgavga)
Hwáy vtégalúmeé	They are starting to mourn	
Hañéva'úsigávehéh	Gathered all around him."	
Gá yáva'ímeé	That is what he said	(ga yava'ime)
Geñá á yéveé	And I heard him	(ña yeevga)
Geña á yéveé	I heard him	
Geña á yéveé	I heard him.	
Máh ñó viyóme	"If that is true	(mah ñu vyum)
Máayógegmímoó	I'm ready to go.	(Mayuggmimo)
Máh ñó viyóme	If that is true	
Máyógegmímoó	I'm ready to go"	
Yává'i'ímeé	That is what I said	(yava'ime)
Gá va'ú ñi'éveé	And he heard me	(ga vu v'evga)
Gá va'ú ñi'éveé	He heard me	
Gá va'ú ñi'éveé	He heard me	
Ólo gáñimsávaá	My white horse	(olo gñmsava)
Ólo gáñimsávaá	My white horse	

Geñá'á ñehátaá	My pet	(gña ñihata)
Ñigáva óñe'ógaá	They get him	(va ñyoga)
Ñéevóñe éjeé	They bring him to me	(ñivu ñ'ejga)
Mathága 'ávawámeé	I mount him	(thag 'vwamga)
Gethága 'ávawámeé	I mount him	
Gethága 'áva wámḿ	I mount him	

Ñéwága wágeém	Slowly, slowly	(ñwag wagm)
Mathága 'ámawógaá	I start him at a walk	(thag 'amoga)
Ñéwága wágeém	Slowly, slowly	
Mathága 'ámawógaá	I start him at a walk	
Ñája wáma gúlaá	On my way, jackrabbits	(ñaj wam gula)
Jawógaá mamáyeé	I pick them up	(jwoga)
Ñája wáma gúlaá	On my way, jackrabbits	
Jawóga mámáyeé	I pick them up	

Havé ñe'áji yútheé	I do that until	(ñaj yuthg)
Havé ñe'áji yútheé	I do that until	
Hmáta véla wíleé	I'm about halfway there	(hmata vlwivog)
Vgñáá yégaá	So I think	(ña yig)
Gebáwa 'ájiyámaá	I send out my spirit	('bawa 'jyaam)
Genhéwa áña dám	To go ahead now	
Báw'áji yámaá	I send out my spirit	
Genhéwa áña dám	To go ahead now	

Báw'á jiyámaá	I send out my spirit	
Genhéwa áña dám	To go ahead now	
Báw'áji yámaá	I send out my spirit	
Genhéwa áña dám	To go ahead now	
Vígág tewáyaá	A little later	(vgag twaya)
Gañívú tópeé'	Not very long	(ñvu t'oba)
Gihágm gévagáweé	He comes back here	(hag vag)
Gihágm gévagáweé	He comes back here	

Báwij hé 'opoḿ	"The sick man	('bawij obom)
Gováy yáji íjoó	Is truly almost gone	(vavyum ijog mi'i)
Hwáya tégalúmeé	They are mourning	(hway tglumga)
Geñéva ósagáveé	Gathered all around him	(Ñevo sgavga)
Gováy'áñe íjoó	He is truly almost gone	

Gováy'áñe íjoó	He is truly almost gone	
Gováy'áñe íjoó	He is truly almost gone	
Gováy'áñe íjoó	He is truly almost gone."	
Gá yáve'ímeé	So he tells me	(yav'im)
Geñá áye'éveé	And I hear him	(ña 'evoga)
Hálthíg gwáya	Very fast	(halthig gwaya)
Ñéwa'ája dámamḿ	I start to go	(ñwa damga)
Thága 'éja náleé	I arrive there	(thag jnalmga)
Gethága 'éja náleé	I arrive there	
Thága 'éja náleé	I arrive there	
Gethága 'éja náleé	I arrive there	
Báwé ñe'óboó	The sick man	('baa ñ'obo)
Váyáñemíjoó	Is truly almost gone	(vavyum ijogmi'i)
Gáva'áñewíteé	What can I possibly do?	(gavawite)
Hngáva'áyewíhaá	What can I possibly do?	
Má yóge míjoó	I see it is really true	(ma yug mijo)
Gamáyóge míjoó	I see it is really true	
Máyóge míjoó	I see it is really true	
Gamáyóge míjoó	I see it is really true	
Gává awíteé	"What can I possibly do?	
Hngáva áyewíhaá	What can I possibly do?	
Máyóge míjoó	I see it is really true	
Gemáyóge míjoó	I see it is really true"	
Gá ñá a'ígaá	This I say	(ñaj 'iga)
Gá ñá a'ígaá	This I say	
Gá ñá a'ígaá	This I say	
Gá ñá a'ígaá	This I say	
Hábágiyágwaá	Here where the man lies	(hag 'baa yagga)
Hñéva ó sabóboó	I am by his pillow	(ñvu sbugvu)
Há bági yágwaá	Here where the man lies	
Hñéva ó sabóboó	I am by his pillow	
Mátwa'él waqídií	On the ground, straight lines	(matl waqidi)
Gahóbáwóó	Four of them	(hoba)
Ghám ña'ája tídií	Here I draw them	(ham ñaj tidga)
Gehám ña'ája tídií	Here I draw them	

Hám ñe'ája tídií	Here I draw them	
Gehám ñe'ája tídií	Here I draw them	
Hébá giyágwa	Here where the man lies	('baa gyagva)
Ñéva'ó go'óyoó	At the top of his head	(ñva g'oym)
Báwa 'ájiyámaá	I send my spirit	('baawa 'hyaama)
Geñéwája dámaá	He is already inside him	(ñwaj dam)
Báwa 'ájiyámaá	I send my spirit	
Geñéwája dámaá	He is already inside him	

Hábá giyágwaá	The man lying there	('baa gyagwa)
Héya ó ñiyógaá	Is still the same	(yav ñiyuga)
Gá ñámathávaá	When the dawn	(ñmthava)
Ñé tégabáyaá	Is approaching	(ŧgbayvm)
Níbágiyágweé	The man lying there	
Nívú ñimáneé	Begins to get up	(ñvu ñmanga)
Gávavóñiyówa	Over his face	(gav ñyuwa)
Gájájahájeé	He passes his hand	(jijhajga)

Gávóñiyówaá	Over his face	
Gájájahájeé	He passes his hand	
Gávóñiyówaá	Over his face	
Gájájahájeé	He passes his hand	
'Ágwé 'amáhaá	"Something to eat	(gwe 'mah)
Geñé wája támaá	I want it now	(. . . tam)
Ágwé 'amáhaá	Something to eat	
Geñéwája támaá	I want it now"	

Háwa'á hathíhaá	"Water to drink,	(ha thiha)
Geñéwa'ájatámaá	"I want it now.	(. . . tam)
Háwa'á hathíhaá	Water to drink,	
Geñéwa'ájatámaá	I want it now."	
Gáyá viyúgaá	That is all there is	(gavayug)
Ñigáyávayúmeé	That is all there is	(gavayum)
Gavé ñiyáji 'ígaá	That is all I'll say	(gava ñaj 'ig)
Gáyóga'ímaá	That is what I'm here for	(gayug 'imo)

Tháyáhayúmeé	That is all	(tha yaviyum)
Geñáji yúgi 'íma'	That is what I'm here for	

Maŧwidiŧa

Dan Hanna, Singer

This is a sung version of the story "Mađwiđa" printed in the Hualapai section. This song tells only how Meriwitica Canyon came to be abandoned. It does not tell about the subsequent migrations to different parts of the Southwest. In this moving rendition, not all the details of the story are told—they do not need to be, for the traditional audience knows the story well. The goal of a performance is not to inform the audience of details they already know but rather to present the story in a dramatic and aesthetic manner. Alternatively, just a few verses of the song are sometimes sung in a situation where tempers are getting out of hand, to remind people of the terrible thing that once happened as a result of loss of temper. I witnessed a singing of this sort at a Parent-Teacher Association meeting once, where people were getting angry at each other over some trivial matter. One woman simply got up, sang a few verses of this song quietly, and then sat down again.

In this version, Dan Hanna sings the song as an objective narration, in third person, until close to the end, when Waqeyasima is alone in the canyon. Then he switches to Waqeyasima's own viewpoint and sings in first person for the rest of the performance.

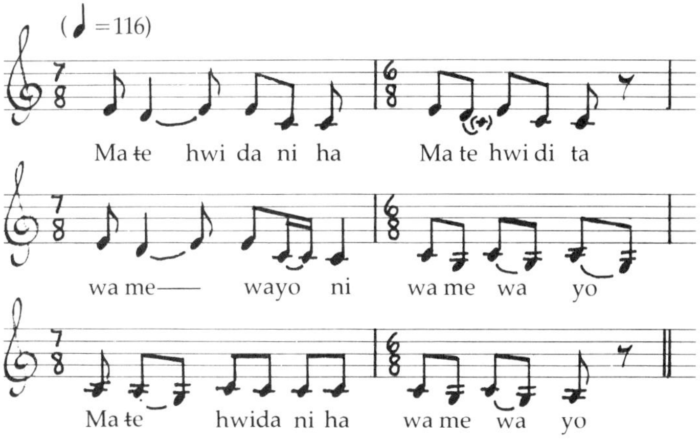

Singing	*Translation*	*Speaking*
Maɨehwidañiha	Meriwitica	('maɨhwidɨa)
Maɨehwidita	Meriwitica	
Wa mewayoñi	We lived there	(wamyo)
Wa mewayo	We lived there	
Maɨehwedañiha	Meriwitica	
Wa mewayo	We lived there	
Wame hemañoñiha	There the children	(wam hmaño)
Wame dayega	There they played	(wam dayga)
Thag wenowedne	So they did	(thag vnuwja)
Thag wenowedne	So they did	
Thag wenowejha	So they did	
Thag wanowajem	So they did	
Maɨe nayaha	Clay	('maɨ naya)
Maɨ wanayawaj	Clay	
Gore goreñe	Little round balls	(gore gore)
Thag wanowage	So they did	
Voje ɨemevegña	They shot them at each other	(vu jɨimvga)
Thag wanowaɨa	So they did, until	(thag vnuwɨa)
Man geɨeyeveje	The Boy Who Cries Easy	(hman gɨyevj)
Ɨay ɨay wa	"Tay, tay!"	(ɨay ɨay)
Yaño'imeñe	So he said	(yav'ime)
Yaño'imewe	So he said	
Yaño'imeña	So he said	
Yaño 'ime'm	So he said	
Qemewedema	Old lady	(qmwidma)
Qemewedema	Old lady	
Wayegejebaweje	Who Loses Her Temper Easy	(way gjbawij)
Thag wedadega	She got up	(thag vdadga)
Ɨegeɨuwaña	Her cane	(ɨgɨuwa)
Voñe yogewa	She picked it up	(vu ñyoga)
Hwisi hwisigye	Swish, swishing	(hwis hwisga)
Hwisi hwisiga	Swish, swishing	

Ŧeŧgehwisweñeha	She chased them all	(ŧŧgwiijvga)
Ŧeŧgehwisweñeha	She chased them all	
Yeneyamegye	And they ran this way	(vye ñyaamga)
Eneyamega	And they ran that way	

Ya ñeyogaña	So it was	(ya vyuga)
Thag wanowoga	She kept on	(thag vnowga)
Mwejemeŧamahña	"Do it now!	(mwijm ŧam)
Weje ŧamawa	Do it now!	
Ga meyoyeña	Why is it that	(ga myuy)
Jejewaqave	You scatter away?"	(jjwaaqve)

Ya ñeemeve	So she said	(yav'ime)
Ya ñeimevem	So she said. And then	(yav'imm)
Qemewedema	An old lady	(qmwidma)
Haqemewedema	An old lady	
Bogemawena	Wears-A-Navajo-Necklace	(buguma)
Thag wadadaga	She got up:	(thag vdadga)

Ga meyojeñeha	"Why is it	(ga myuj)
Vo meyoyega	That you are this way?	(vu myuyga)
Thag mowanogañeha	You keep on	(thag mvnuwga)
Mowanomawe	And you keep on!	(mvnuwme)
Waveeyogaña	Being this way	(vavyuga)
Wañayogo'm	Being this way	

Maŧe boyveñeha	It is shameful	(maŧ buuyvga)
Maŧe boyvega	It is shameful	
Vo ñeyomene	So it is	(vu ñyume)
Vu ñeyomowe	So it is."	
Ya ñoitheme	So she said, but	(ya ñ'iga)
Ga ñe'evaha	They did not listen	(gag ñ'eva)

Vu ŧeobañeha	They did not	(vu ŧ'oba)
Vu teobeme	They did not	
Vu ñeogañeha	When she saw that	(vu ñ'uga)
Vu ña'ugawa	When she saw it	
No ñeŧamaha	She started in too	(ñu ñŧamga)
No ñeŧamagem	She started in too	

Thag wenowenyeha	And they kept on	(thag vnuw)
Thag wenowega	And they kept on	
Yejwegoveñeha	They were locked together	(gjvgoova)
Thag wanowaga	They kept on	
Ya ñeyogaña	This is how it was	(yavyuga)
Ya ñayoga'm	This is how it was	
Gejenajwañha	Berating each other	(gjgnaajva)
Gejenajwaga	Berating each other	
Vamowejeñha	"Do it!"	(va mwija)
Vo ñomeyega	"Say it!"	(va m'iga)
Ma mowevaña	"Your vagina	(ma muwevnu)
Vo weñaga	It is black!	(vu vnaaga)
Ya ñeyomañeha	So it is!"	(yavyume)
Ya ñe'ejega	So they said	(ya ñ'ijga)
Gejenajweñeha	Berating each other	
Thag wanowega	They kept on	
Yume ñewoganeha	When she saw this	(yum ñ'uga)
Yom ña'ogwa'm	When she saw it	
Qemewedamaha	An old lady	(qmwidma)
Jajgethivahaj	Named Jajgethiva	(jajgthivahaj)
Tha ñeyoɫiñeha	Entered in too	(tha ñyuutñe)
Tha ñeyuuɫega	Entered in too	
Jetheweganeha	She reprimanded them	(jthwega)
Vo gamolethe	As a leader would, but	(vu gmultho)
Ya ñe'evañeha	They would not listen	(ya ñ'evah)
Vu ɫu'obeme	They would not	(vu ɫ'obame)
Ya ñeyogaveha	When she saw this	(ya v'uga)
Ya ñavuga	When she saw this	
Tha jevuwavña	She went in herself	(tha jvwwava)
Vu ñathamaga	She started in	(vu ñtamga)
Thag venowemña	And they kept on	(thag vnuwme)
Thag wenowome	And they kept on	
Ya ñe ugaveha	When he saw this	(ya ñ'uga)

Ya ño'ugawa	When he saw this	
Ya ñeyon̵ogave	When he saw this	
Ya ñavogo'm	When he saw this	

Ba gemolvañiha	A chief	('baa gmulva)
Ba gamolvowa	A chief	
Mu ñemeyaniha	Mountain-Sheep-Skin	('muu ñmiya)
Vo ñemeyawa	His-Skin	(vu ñmiya)
Mu ñethawañeha	Mountain-Sheep-Baby	('muu ñthawa)
Mo ñameyawa	Mountain-Sheep-Skin	

Jage dabañiha	Wears-It-On-His-Back	(jag daba)
Thag wadadaga	He got up	(thag vdadga)
Qewa qewa ñeha	"Qey! Qey!"	(qey qey)
Ya ño'igawa	So he said	(ya ñ'iga)
Ba jetheweganeha	He reprimanded them	(bajthwega)
Ba jewege'm	He reprimanded them	

Ba gegogañeha	He blocked them	(ba ggoga)
Hełegyegewa	He pushed them away	(łgyega)
Vu gemolehña	As a leader would	(vu gmola)
Bu ña'obaga	But he failed	(vu ñ'obga)
Ya ñeyomevhe	When he saw this	(ya v'uga)
Ya ño'ugo'm	When he saw it	

Thag wedadeñeha	He got up	(thag vdadga)
Thag wadadaga	He got up	
Ba ñemulvañiha	A chief	('baa gmulva)
Ba ñemulvewa	A chief	
Emanałwaña	Wrapped-in-Yucca-	('mnał)
Vo gałedvuwa	Fibers	(vu głidva)

Gaje sivañiha	He who was so named	(gaj siiva)
Thag wadadaga	He got up	
Qaya qewañiha	"Qey! Qey!"	(qey qey)
Ya ño'igawa	So he cried	(ya n'iga)
Ga meyujaña	"Why is it that you	(ga myuja)
Thag muwanuwoga	Keep on this way?	(thag mvnuwga)

Vu meyumañiha	You being this way	(vu myume)
Vu meyujeme	You being this way	
Maɫe boyveneha	It is shameful	('maaɫ buyva)
Maɫe buyvega	It is shameful."	
Ya ñe eyetheme	So he said, but	(ya ñ'igatho)
Ga ñe'evaha	They did not listen	(gag ñ'evaha)
Vu ɫe obañiha	They did not	(vu ɫ'oba)
Vu ɫa'obaga	They did not	
Thag wenogañiha	And they kept on	(thag vnuwga)
Thag wanome	And they kept on	
Yeñeyavegwe	They hit each other this way	(vye ñ'avga)
Veñe'avega	They hit each other that way	
Thag wenowañiha	And they kept on	
Vo ñe uguwa	When he saw this	(vu ñ'uga)
Thal jeguwagañiha	He went in himself	(thal jvwaaga)
Baweyevega	He joined right in	(bayeevga)
Ya ñeyogañeha	So he did	(ya ñyuga)
Thag wanogo'm	And they kept on	
Ya ñemogavha	When they saw this	(ya ñ'uga)
Yañamogava	When they saw this	
Ba ñejavañeha	The Big Chief	('baa ñjava)
Ba gajawawa	The Big Chief	
Wa geyasimaha	Waqeyasima	('wa gyasmha)
Vo genavajem	They told him	(vu gnaavjm)
Thal vedadñiha	He got up	(thag vdada)
Thal vadadaga	He got up	
Qeyam qeywañiha	"Qey, Qey!"	(qey qey)
Ya ña'igawa	So he said	(ya ñ'iga)
Mathwen ɫuneyalehe	Into the soil he thrust his hand	('maɫm ɫniil)
Matña vo ɫanelega	Into the soil he thrust his hand	
Qwaqeɫe gwawahñe	An elk antler	(qwaqɫe gwa)
Thal neyomagam	He pulled it out	(thal nyomgm)
Thal neyomagam	He pulled it out	
Ya ñawigwewa	So he did	(ya ñwiga)

Thag ñeꞥawjeheha	He jumped around	(thag vnawja)
Jeyemavaga	He waved it about	(jyimaavga)
Qeya qeywañeha	"Qey, qey!"	(qey qey)
Ya ño igewa	So he said	(ya ñ'iga)
Thag wenogañeha	And he kept on	(thag vnuwga)
Thag wanogowa	And he kept on	
Baseyemiꞥyeha	And he went toward them	(ba syeem)
Vo ñeyamem'm	He went	(vu ñyaamme)
Vo ñemugañeha	When he saw what was happening	(vu ñ'iga)
Vu ñemugawa	When he saw it	
'Owinalwañeha	Boulders	(onal)
Vu gawajuwa	That were there	(vu gwaja)
Vu łesłohgim	He stabbed them	(vu łsłohga)
Salem salega	And they burst into pieces	(salvsalga)
Ya ñowemeñeha	So he did	(ya ñwime)
Vu ña'uguwa	When they saw this	(vu ñ'iga)
Jejewaaqevege	They scattered away	(jijwaaqvga)
Jejewaqave	They scattered away	
Yeneyamegwehe	They ran this way	(vye ñyaamga)
Yeñeyamethem	They ran that way	(vye ñyaamthem)
'Uhiwageñeha	Two of them	(hwaga)
Husetovoga	He stabbed with the antler	(stohvga)
Vu ñe'uleꞥye	He strung them like beads	(vu ñ'ul)
Magel jemaga	And threw them behind him	(magl łamga)
Vul hemulgemyeha	Three of them	(vul hmuga)
Vu sa'onaga	He impaled	(vu s'onga)
Magel jameñeha	And threw them behind him	
Magel jamega	And threw them behind him	
Jeyemaveña	He waved the antler about	(jyimaava)
Qeya qeyawa	"Qey, Qey!"	(qey qey)
Yaño iꞥega	So he said	(ya ñ'iga)
Thag wanogawum	And he kept on	(thag vnuwga)

Seyehwideña	He whirled around	(siihwida)
Seyehwidiga	He whirled around	
Yañeyothema	So he did and	(ya ñyuthm)
Jejewaqave	They scattered away	(jjwaaqva)
Vu ñeyamegwe	They ran this way	(vu ñyaamga)
Eyeyamaga	They ran that way	(vye ñyaamga)

Thame bemeehe	Then they were gone	(tham beemm)
ya ñe'uguwa	When he saw that	(vu ñ'uga)
Thag wenugañeha	He kept on	(thag vnuwga)
Thag wanugawa	He kept on	
Myumemetamawa	"Act that way now!	(myujm łam)
Meyujemełamwa	Act that way now!	

Ga meyogañeha	Why are you	(ga myuga)
Vu meyujeye	Behaving this way?	(vu myuje)
Ga meyogaña	Why are you	
Vu meyujeye	Behaving this way?"	
Ya ñomegañeha	So he said	(ya ñ'iga)
Thag wanogawa	And he kept on	

Thevewayvañeha	All remained quiet	(thwaayvga)
Thevewaguwam	Quiet	
Yamgethowayvañeha	Quiet	
Them yagethewavega	Quiet	
Vutheyomewetheñe	So it was	(vu ñyume)
Thag ñeyomowe	So it was	(thag ñyume)

Ya ñenogahaña	When he saw this	(ya ñ'uga)
Ya ñe'ogowam	When he saw this	
Vu ñevomegña	He went home	(vu ñvoga)
Vo ñevomega	he went home	
'Oweyavoñeha	To his cave	(way havo)
Vo ñawagawa	And there he stayed	(vu ñwaga)

Ga ñewagañeha	He did not sit down	(gag ñwaga)
Vo ñeyuthega	He did not	(vu ñyuthig)
Gag ñeyagegñha	Nor did he lie down	(gag ñyagga)

Vu ñasmajwa	To sleep	(vu ñsmaaja)
Ñaje ewełe	Not I	(ñaj iłe)
Veñaja ’iłewem	Not I	

Ñemethavañha	Dawn	(ñmthava)
Vu ñeyuwume	When it came	(vu ñyuwme)
Wa ’eyagehñe	I stayed here	(vag ’yaga)
Naje yutheme	So I did, but	(ñaj yuthme)
Gag ñeyaghña	I did not lie down	(gag ñyagha)
Vu ñesmajwa	To sleep	(vu ñsmaajwa)

Mañajeulvemeñha	At night	(náa łqebme)
Velewiyiva	At midnight	(vlwiiva)
Wañeyajajñeha	At night	
Veleweyeve	At midnight	
Hwa ’yavamega	I kept watch for them	(hwa ’yavmga)
Ñaje yutheme	So I did	(ñaj yutheme)

Gag ñeyageñehe	I did not lie down	(gag ñyaga)
Vu ñesmaajwa	To sleep	(vu ñsmaaja)
Veñaje ełewe	I did not	(ñaj iłe)
Veñaje ’iłewe	I did not	
Wame ’eñawehñe	The sun	(’ñaa)
Vu ñadobeme	When it set	(vu ñaa dobme)

Hwa e yaveghñe	I kept watch for them	(hwa ’yavmga)
Ñaje yutheme	So I did	(ñaj yuthme)
Gag ñeyageñhe	I did not lie down	(gag ñyaga)
Vu ñesmajwa	To sleep	(vu ñsmaaja)
Ñaje hełee	I did not	(ñaj iłe)
Veñaja ’itewe	I did not	

Gwejełiyajihña	Something terrible	(gwe ij łiyaje)
Gwejełiyuwa	Something terrible	
Vu ñeyawañiha	Has come here	(vu ñiyawa)
Vu ñeyawove	Has come here	
Vu ñeyuwemehe	So it has	(vu ñyume)
Ñaje ’iguwa	So I say	(naj ’iga)

Yogo imahña	So I say	(yu g′ime)
Yogo imawem	So I say	
Ya veyumewe	So it is	(ya viyume)
Veñaje ega	So I say	(ñaj ′iga)
Ya mohaꞥewahe	You hear this!	(ya m′eva)
Ya mamevaha	You hear this!	

Wolf's Boy

Sinyella, Narrator

First transcription by Leslie Spier

Hatagwilahaj guda 'bayŧg
Thag ñwevga hawil withg wa ñwevig
"Ña lwa beemg
'Sitaŧhg vag wathm hana ŧ'obga
Bqi 'lwevm vag wag gwe ñwidm 'mahga
'Siŧathg vag wathg gweñwidg 'sbo ŧ'obg
'Yaamg Sasa Vasuwha vjaya 'siŧm 'yo
    'yaamg 'yug
Sasa vasuwha ñwaha vamg
Bqi 'siŧathm 'yog 'lwehga
Bqihj obga yama yi ŧ'obg
Ee m'obg mimo me 'vomhg 'yu"
Haŧgwilahaj bogg yug
Haŧgwilaha ñiñawaha ñvag
Gavyum sasa vsuwha vjayahj 'ña gag ña hana ŧ'obg
        'imo 'i
Wa siivg vag wag
Ha wayvj vag yum
halgŧaba val jwag
"Halgŧaba 'havl mawah
Ŧwaya ŧ'obŧg mya'beh
    'baa ñmvlwiihg wig 'i
'Siŧa smaam 'vahg 'yu"

Long ago Wolf was a man.
He was living at Mountain Camp.
"A wife I lack.
Being alone is not good.
If I had a wife she would cook things for me to eat.
Here I am alone. I don't know how to cook.
I went to get one of Bluebird's daughters,
    I went.
I came to Bluebird's house.
One of the women I wanted to take for a wife,
The woman refused, she wouldn't go.
All right, if you want to refuse, I'll go home."
Wolf went home.
When Wolf got home,
"Why don't Bluebird's daughters like me?"
He sat thinking about it.
A pool here—
He put an abalone shell in it.
"Abalone Shell, stay there.
Soon you will be alive,
    like a man.
After one sleep, I will return."
When Wolf came back, came back to the pool,

Haŧgwil vamg ha waya vamg
halgŧaba ug
Qejm 'baa ñvlwiig
Uthm yuyg hang val wag
"Halgŧaba 'jwowj mhana mniwg myu
Ŧwaya ŧ'obiŧg 'ña 'baava mvlwi mñiwg myu
Sasa Vasuwa vjayahg maj myaamhg myu.
Haŧagwila yog thag jwog jthuulg bay maaŧva
va'hanog
Wiv jyog thavaŧim val jwog ŧ'omg
Gthadhj yaamg
Hmaña yoga
Babg bogg 'wahg vag
Ñvam haŧagwilahaj ug
Gthadhj ig
"Ña homevju"
Haŧagwilahj gwawg
"Oba gthad mhomevjuŧa ŧuyvju
'Na'a Haŧagwilava homevju
Ma gthadñj maj mjthulg mya'hana"
Haŧagwila gwawg
"'Ña homevj yaamg Sasa Vasuwha vjayaha 'siŧm
yomhgwi
Yomm va wag ŧyaj ŧaag smgwinm 'maja
Mah myaama Sasavasuw vjayaha myug
'Ña'lwa' mi"
Halgŧaba 'bayg 'ahanga
Haŧagwila home Kaume'e
"Mah myaama
Sasa Vasuwha ñwaha mvama
Mvamg m'uh
Sasa Vasuwha vjehj ma Kaumen ñm'hanogtho
'ña luwa 'mihg mi'"
Vamm ñ'ugtho bqihj Kaumeñ ñm'ugtho
Ee 'ñm'hanogtho yaamhg'"

he looked at the abalone shell.
It looked a little like a man.
When he looked, it appeared to be good in there.
"Abalone that I placed there, you are progressing
well.
Soon you will be just like a man, like me.
To Bluebird's daughters you will go."
Wolf took it out and washed it well all over the body.
He placed it inside a rock hole and closed it up.
Coyote went.
He took the child.
Carrying it on his back, he arrived at the house.
When he arrived, Wolf saw him.
Coyote said,
"This is my son."
Wolf spoke.
"No, Coyote, this is not your son, not at all.
Me, Wolf, he is my son.
You, Coyote, you wash him well."
Wolf spoke.
"My son is going to Bluebird to fetch one of his
daughters.
He'll fetch her and she will stay here grinding corn
and making corn mush for us to eat.
Now go, get one of Bluebird's daughters,
'Marry me,' say."
The abalone shell was a real man.
Wolf's son was Kaume.
"Now go.
Go to Bluebird's house.
Go there and look.
If Bluebird's daughter likes you, Kaume,
You say, 'My wife.'
When you arrive, when she sees you, when the
woman sees you, Kaume,

Baquuyavj hwagg yaamja Kaume lwavja
"'Baava 'hanjog 'yu 'hangyu
'yaamjhg'yu"
Hatagwila homevj Sasa Vasuwha vjaya hwagm yug
Sasa Vasuwhj gwaawg
"Mah 'baavj Kaumeñm mtnmagovg tnmagovg
Mmadja
Mah baa tethg baya mahgi 'yaamg 'yug"
Kaumehj 'sitthg mtavg tyavg yaamg yug'i
Kaumeva nmagjga yaajmga yaamg vyuwe ñadobvga
stulg
Sasa Vasuwhj hamg
"'Baa gtewa 'ña ñwiiwj Wi Hlawa hobaja togavgg
the yuwjg"
Kaumewij gavayug evg yugyumoyu
The yuwthg Kaumewa nmagjg the yuwg
Kaumewij yuwa tamgyu
Wi hlawa hobaja tgavgg yuwi tamgyu
Kaumewij yuwig baghavog tamgwi
Swadg
"Gtnmagvjij
Baa hmilaj mvyaamga
Yavmijg myuta ga myujg myu
Ña jgavj mvyaamga myuta gavayug myu
'Ña Kaumevj 'yaamg 'ha gwemava 'gnaavm
'Bamgvgawjo gjvgawva gnaava
Gbeh yaamg yug Sasa Vasuwha ñwaha 'vamg 'yug
Baquuya hwagm Sasa Vasuwa vjaya yuwg
'Gwe naja gavhogwi"
"Qwaqa gavg
Nohvg Sasa Vasuwa homaya vjaya 'ñaatqebm
Sasa Vasuwha vjaya Kaumehj bamadga
"'Qwaqa 'gwe baya 'ñaja bamada
"Sasa Vasuwha 'gwe gwenaja qwaqa mgavg
mtojva"

She'll say 'Yes, it is fine with me to go.'"
Two women went to marry Kaume.
"We like this man. Good,
let us go with him."
Wolf's son took both of Bluebird's daughters.
Bluebird spoke.
"Okay, our men will run races with Kaume.
You men will win.
Come on, all of the men, everyone, let's go."
Kaume alone went toward the north.
They left Kaume behind, going and going toward
the west.
Bluebird watched.
"All you men, my relatives, go four times around
Moon Mountain and come back."
Kaume felt a change in himself.
He was coming but they were ahead of Kaume, he
was coming,
Now he was coming along.
Four times around Moon Mountain he went, and
now he was coming back again.
Kaume was coming back, and now he caught up
with them.
He sang,
"Racers,
'Brother-in-law, keep running!'
You aren't saying that any more.
My cousins, why aren't you running?
I, Kaume, I'll go. 'Water and food!' I'll tell them.
When I meet them, I'll tell them.
I'll go play ball when I arrive at Bluebird's house.
Bluebird's two daughters I will get.
I'll bet Navajo blankets."
He bet buckskins.
He played the Hide-the-ball game with Bluebird's

Ɨojva ɨamthg withg Kaumehj baya bamaɨg
Sasa Vasuwhj gnaavg 'ig
"Mdudva mah myuja
Kaumeñj gavauɨvg gwimowi"
Baya bamaɨg Kaumehj bamaɨg
Kaumehj Sasavasuwha vjaya hwagm yug
vomgyu
Ñiyaamm baquuyavj baya 'ɨega yaajmñga
Sasa Vasuwhj gwaaw'ig'i
"'Baa gɨewa 'ña wiiwj mah myaajm
Mghavg mɨgwaja"
Kaumeha gyathg gag jnala ɨ'obg
Baquuyva hbida baya bagjmwajjgwi
Kaumehj swaadg
"Baya 'baya 'hanovj 'yuɨe
Haɨagwilahj baya'baya 'hana ñyoovavj 'yute
Gag yuɨg ya 'ɨuvg 'majayga 'thuñvm
Mɨgwanja myuɨa 'uummi i'i
Mvojma 'mnmagjm 'yaahg 'yu
Vgag 'yuɨg 'gyaga 'jamhg wihg wig'iɨa
Baya bañgmwajg bañwidhg'wi."
Tu ɨgwang 'ɨek buuyg
Wigwitg 'ñaahj dobigyu
'Yuuhj 'bayaɨg thag vag vathm
Kaumehj "Obg 'ig ig
Ga myuhg mvag myumomyu
Yuɨg mɨgwanjhmi"
'Yuuhj gwaaw'ig
"Ba'gyahg 'yu"
Ɨuya vvɨeya myujg
Sasa Vasuwha homaya 'yuuha gyathg vam tmuyga
Qasaq "Kah kah kah gwe myujñg myu
Ñmyujthm myuɨg 'baa mnehjjhgwi
Bagyahg yug" i'i
Miyavg yuwg bagyagwi

sons and daughters that night.
Kaume won Bluebird's daughters.
"Buckskins, everything, I won from them.
Bluebird, put up your stakes—blankets, buckskins—
for Shinney."
Playing shinney now, Kaume won everything.
Bluebird said:
"Come on, play the Hoop and Pole game.
Let's see how Kaume does at that."
He won everything, Kaume won everything.
Kaume took Bluebird's two daughters
and went home.
As they were going, all the women went too.
Bluebird spoke:
"All my men, come on, you go,
Catch up with him and kill him!"
They shot at Kaume but they did not drop him.
They only kept killing all the women.
Kaume sang:
"I am not a real human being.
Wolf made me not a real human being.
I do not thirst nor hunger nor weaken.
You can never kill me.
You go home and leave me alone, and I will go.
If you don't, I will shoot and I will drop you every
time.
I will kill all of you, I will finish you all!"
He killed them, many died.
He did this until the sun set.
Owl, who was human, arrived.
Kaume said "No, no!
Why did you come here?
Perhaps they will kill you!"
Owl spoke:
"I am going to shoot them."

Sasa Vasuw homaya qasaq gyag hehjga
'Ñaa bodggyu 'ñaa ɫqebgyu
Kaumehj gwaaw i'ig
"'Baa 'Yuu maɫahaya 'maɫ ñaaja gsumaavj
yum mig miñ
Vswava miwa 'ñaa ɫqeba
Kaumehj 'yuuhm baquuyavj hwaga yaamg
Haɫagwilaha ñwaha ñvamg
Baquuya hwaga waha vamgyu
Baquuya hwagm waha bagmimgwi
"Ñahamidj mahangyu
Baquuya hwagm myug mvam hangyu 'adyegyu
Ɫiyaj ɫag smgwinjma mag hangyu" ig'i'i
"Qwaqa ñig nehg hagyeg vag vminva" 'ig'ig
"Qwaqa maɫ mt'olm 'maja"
Haɫagwilahj "Lwa 'bemg 'yu
Ɫu 'siɫathg 'yu
Kaumewij baquuya hwagm mwijg
'Siɫm 'm'eh
'Siɫthg vag wathm 'hana ɫ'obga
Gwe ñiñg wal yig yu 'ig'i
Kaumehj gwaawg ɫ'obg
Vgag bqiva 'siɫm ñ'eg wal yi ɫ'obg
Kaumehj waya 'layg vgyaamgyu
Vgag vah ɫ'obga smaamg smaamg smaamgyu
Ñvag 'siɫa ñasmaag Haɫagwilahj gwaaw 'ig
"Homewj vɫ'obgyu
Yaamg 'ñaj 'haɫagwilovj 'yaamg 'amjg ham"
Kaume'e yuwoha msiig ñyaamg
Yutm kaume 'muu ɫiwgyu
Haɫagwilahj yuɫg ug vmadjiwg
Gwava yilhlu yilhluyig wiwimg
"Mah Kaume'e vomja
"Gamyug vag m'aamjg myumo myu
'Hana ɫ'obg 'yu

He just kept fluffing his feathers.
Bluebird's sons shot at Owl and grazed him.
Crow said "Caw, caw, caw! What are you doing!
If that is how you behave, the men will kill you!
I will shoot them."
He came from the air shooting them.
Bluebird's sons shot Crow and killed him.
The sun had set and it got a little dark.
Kaume spoke:
"Owl Man, you are a shaman of the wind and black
sand,
so you said.
Tear some off and make it dark."
Kaume, with Owl and the two women, went on.
He arrived at Wolf's house,
With the two women he arrived at the house,
He brought the two women to the house.
"My relatives, you did well.
Two women you took and came, it is good, I am
happy.
Corn to grind, mush to eat, it is good," he said.
"Deer to hunt, to carry it on the back, to bring it
here," he said.
"You cook the venison, and we will eat it."
Wolf said, "I have no wife.
I am entirely alone.
Kaume, you have two women.
Give me one.
Being alone is not good.
I'd like something to make love to," he said.
Kaume did not speak.
He did not want to give a woman to him.
Kaume felt angry over it, and ran away.
He did not return for many sleeps.
After one sleep, Wolf spoke:

Mah 'vomja
Vomjg waha
"Ña 'luwa 'hangyu"
Baquuyaj "Kaume'e vag mwam 'hana." ◇

(It is probable that Sinyella did not finish telling the full story. In all other versions, Kaume goes back to join the mountain sheep again and again, until he turns irrevocably into a mountain sheep, and never comes home again.)

"My son does not return.
I go, I, Wolf, I go, I will go look around."
Kaume's tracks he followed along.
Meanwhile, Kaume became a mountain sheep.
Wolf saw him and seized him.
He pulled off his horns and cast them away.
"Come on Kaume, let's go home."
"What's the matter with you, wandering around
here?
I don't like it.
Come on, let's go home."
They reached the house.
"My wife, it is all right."
The women said, "Kaume, you stay here with us." ◇

Songs of Wolf's Boy

Dan Hanna, Singer

Havasupai stories almost always have songs as an integral part to them. Sinyella must have sung songs as part of his version, but they were recorded only in spoken form by Spier. The songs below were recorded by Dan Hanna to go with a version of Wolf's Son very similar to the one told by Sinyella.

Wolf's Song

As Wolf stirs the abalone shell in the water to make a little boy out of it, he sings this song. Dan Hanna sang it twice through, and had a different meter both times. Therefore, both verses have been transcribed musically.

Singing	*Translation*	*Speaking*
Ñé´'ehávolé	In this water	(ñhavle)
Ñévő´ 'ugwévejé	There is something	(ñvu gwevje)
Ñéyő´gegyúme'ú	It seems to be there	(ñyug gyumo)
Ñésó´ gwáte'á	Dark green	(vsuuw gwała)
Ñédá´ve dávemé	Swirling, swirling	(ñvu dav davme)
Yő´gedéñe'á	I'd like to take it and play with it	
'íyő´ge déñe'á	I'd like to take it and play with it	
Héyő´gedéñe'á	I'd like to take it and play with it	
'Éyő´ge déñe'á´	I'd like to take it and play with it	
Ñévő´ hávalé'é	In this water	(ñvu 'havle)
Ñévő´ 'gwévéje'é	There is something	
Ñéyő´gegyúmu'ú'ú	It seems to be there	
Ñésú´ gwáta'á'á	Dark green	
Ñédá´vedávemé'é	Swirling, swirling	
'Íyő´gedéñe'á'á	I'd like to take it and play with it	
'Íyő´ge déñe'á'á	I'd like to take it and play with it	
Íyő´ge déñe'á'á	I'd like to take it and play with it	
'Íyő´ge déñe'á'á	I'd like to take it and play with it	
Héyő´ge déñe'á'á	I'd like to take it and play with it	

Miracle Boy's First Song

In this version of Wolf's Son, the name "Kaume" does not appear. Wolf's Son is called "Miracle Boy," instead. In this version, Wolf instructs Coyote to travel with Miracle Boy to Bluebird's house. But Coyote, as usual, forgets his orders and just runs around in circles chasing lizards. Wolf has told Miracle Boy to sit on a certain rock and smoke wild tobacco, after which he should catch the scent of women. He should follow that scent until he reaches Bluebird's house. Miracle Boy sings this song during his journey.

Singing	*Translation*	*Speaking*
Háŧegwíli'á´	Wolf	(haŧgwila)
Ñá negúde'á´	My father	(ña nguda)
Háŧegwí´li'wá´	Wolf	
Heñá negúde'á´	My father	
Heñá negúde'á´	My father	
Heñá negó´dem´	My father	
Getháde ñé'wó´	Brother Coyote	(gthad ñiyo)
Getháde ñé'wó´	Brother Coyote	
Getháde ñé´yuwó´	Brother Coyote	
Jimóñíguwá´	Should lead me, he said	(jmoñ 'iga)
Móñíguwá´	Should lead me, he said	
Mó'oñí´muwé´	Should lead me, he said	
Áhuwágegá´	Go along with me	(ahwagga)
Áhuwágegá´	Go along with me	
Ŧó vó´huwá´	Just walk along	(ŧu vwaga)
Yá ñi'íw wá´	So he told you	(ya ñ'iw)
Veya ñi iuwom´	So he told you	
Méŧeñú´vehá´	So you should do	(mŧñuva)

Ña′méŧe′óbemé′	But you aren′t doing it	(ña mŧ′obme)
Yúge ′ímewó′	So it seems	(yu g′imo)
Yúge ′í′mowuḿ	So it seems	
Ŧáyethílewá′	Lizards	(ŧathila)
Úmeñégewá′	You are hunting them	(vu mñega)
Vág me′á′mjemé′	You go about doing that	(vag m′amje)
Hayúge′ímuwó′	So it seems	
Yúge′ímuwó′	So it seems	
Yúge′í′moweḿ	So it seems	
Ŧoñómiyúguwá′	That's just how you are	(ŧu ñumyuga)
Ŧáyethílewá′	Lizards	
Vó meñé′guwá′	You are hunting them	
Havág me′ámjihá′	You go about doing that	
Yúm ′iyúmu′wú′	So you seem to do	(myumyumo)
Meyúmuyú′muwó′	So you seem to do	
′Iñáji yámugá′	I go on alone	(ñaj yaamga)
Ñáji yúthugá′	I do that, but	(ñaj yuthga)
Ñáji yó′thugaḿ	I do that, but	
Gáva ′ayúhuwá′	What will happen	(gav ′yuha)
Yógigyúmuwó′	I don′t know	(yug gyumo)
Yógigyú′ḿ′	I don′t know	
′eñá ′eláye′wá′	A lone trail	(′ña ′laya)
Wú ñeqéjevé′	A doubtful one	(vu ñqejva)
Ñethám ñiyá′gemé′	Lies that way	(ntham ñyagme)
Hathám agúñuguwá′	I′ll follow it	(tham ′gñuga)
Yáñi′íyuwá′	As he told me	(ya ñ′iw)
Yáj ñiyú′huwá′	This is the one	(yaj ñyuha)
Ñevú lumáŧemé′	So it seems	(nvu lmaŧme)
Vámigiñúguwá′	I′ll follow it along	
Ñáji yá′mehá′	I′ll go along	(ñaj yaamha)
Hayígiyúmuwó′	So I guess	(yig yumo)

Iyígiyúmuwú´	So I guess	(yig yumo)
Yígiyú´m ḿ	So I guess	
Awíɫage'ódejá´	A rock pile	('wii ɫg'odja)
Thág uwáhagé´	A place to sit	(thag waga)
Mé vuwá´guwá´	"You sit there	(mvwaga)
Ha'úvegedáva'wá´	Wild tobacco	('uuv gdava)
Wúmejáguwá´	You smoke it	(vu mjaaga)
Wú meyú´huwá´	You do that" (my father said)	(Vu myuha)
Ḥeñáyo'óyuguwá	So I do	(ñaj 'yuga)
Ñáji yúthumé´	So I do, but	(ñaj yuthme)
Ñáji yú´themé´	So I do, but	
Baqí haleɫesáyevé´	The women's odor	(bqi halɫsaayva)
Sugévugwáhowá´	Does not reveal itself	(sgi vgwaha)
Wá ɫ'ó´bemeḿ	It does not	(va ɫ'obme)
Heñáji yúguwá´	I wait here	(ñaj yuga)
Yúgi'ímuwá´	So it seems	(yug 'imo)
Hñá ni'í´guwá´	He said to me (it would come)	(ña ñ'iga)
Háɫegwíle'á´	Wolf	
Ña negúdehá´	My father	
'Úñé'guweḿ	So he said	
Yá ñi'íjethó´	So he said, but	(ya ñ'ijtho)
Haɫúyiñi'íu'mé´	He was wrong. But then	(ɫuy ñ'iwum)
Baqí haleɫesá´yevé´	The women's odor	
'Úvegwáguwá´	Reveals itself	
Váme máguwá´	Penetrates me	(vam maga)
Yá ñu'í´muwé´	As he said	(ya ñ'ime)
Heyéyeqemúyngemé´	I turn away	('qmuyngme)
Geyéyeqemúyngemé´	I turn away	
Mágol honó´gowá´	But it continues behind me	(magl nuwga)
Hayúge'ímuwá´	So it does	(yug 'imo)
Hayúge'ímuweḿ	So it does	
Yóge'í´muwá´	So it does	

Miracle Boy's Second Song

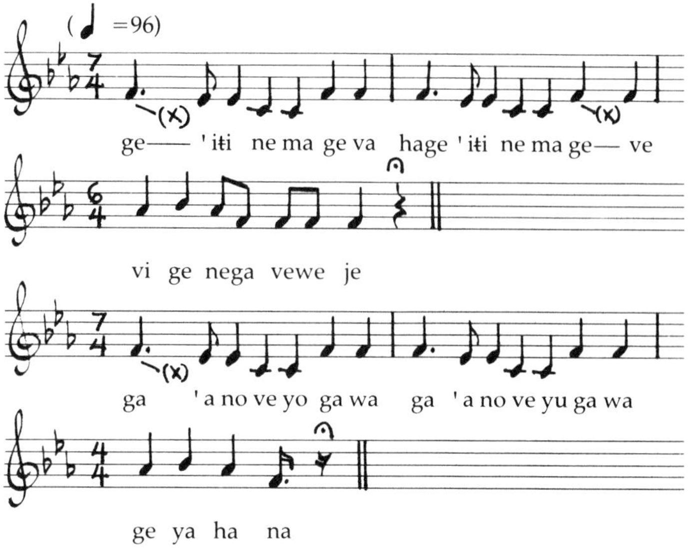

In this song, Miracle Boy is taunting the racers as he passes them by. The tune is very unusual, being a mirror image of the usual Havasupai melodic contour. This breakage of the rules of melodic form adds to the humorous, taunting quality of the song.

The last line of the verse varies in length. It can be as long as six beats or as short as four beats. The first and second verses are both transcribed musically to show the variation in the length of the last line.

Singing	*Translation*	*Speaking*
Gé´´iŧínémágévá	Racers I have left behind	(gŧnmagva)
Hagé´´ iŧínémágévá	Racers I have left behind	
Vígé ñégavéwejé´	They are left behind somewhere	(vge ñgbeeja)
Gá´´añóvéyógáwá´	What can have happened?	(ga ñuvyuga)
Gá´´añóvéyúgáwá´	What can have happened?	
Géyéháñá	They are moving camp	(giiyhan)
Ñé´´ewámeláyeñó	They are angry	(ñwamlayñu)
Ñé´´evélewígaŧá	So it seems	(ñvlwiga)
Ñéñó simídevé	They are just quarreling	(ññu smidva)
Gá´´evó ñeyúméwé	Such a thing	(gag vu ñyum)
Gá´´evóñéyúméwé	Such a thing	
Ñévó meyújiyé	Has surely never been before!	(ñvu myuja)
Ñé´´evómeyójeyé	Never been	
Ñé´´evómeyójeyé	Never been	
'Éñá gégénó	"My younger brother,	(ña ggino)

Gá´´añá 'ahawágén̶éḿ	Keep up with me!"	(ña ahwagme)
Gá´´añá nejáwéjé	"My uncle,	(ña njawaje)
Mívíyámá	Keep running!"	(mvyaama)
Gá´´eyávé 'ígáwá´	They don't say that any more	(ga yav'iga)
Já´´ejmíhewílívi´	To urge each other on	(jjmwiilvga)
Ñívó helemátwemé	So it seems	(ñivu hlmaɫme)
Gá´´iyógé'émáwá´	So it does	(ga yug imme)
Gá´ eyógé 'ímé'ḿ	So it does	
Ñíñájé yámugá	But I, here I go!	(viñaj yaamga)
Há´ 'egéjuwegáwevá	Back at the starting point	(Ha gjvgaawva)
Gwé´ geɨéseyúmevá	They'll learn the rules	(gwe gɨsyuwmva)
'Íñájé genávehá	And I'll instruct them	(ñaj gnaavha)
'Á´ 'ayíge yúmá'á´	So I will	('yiig yume)
'Á´ 'ayíge yúmán̶á'	So I will	

Miracle Boy's Farewell Song

In all complete versions of the story of Wolf's Boy, the boy turns into a mountain sheep and stays that way forever. This is Miracle Boy's song as he perceives himself turning into a mountain sheep.

Musically, this song has two very similar melodic phrases, varying only in the second measure of the phrase where one variant has one note that is higher than in the second variant. The phrase with the higher note occurs at the beginning of new ideas in the text; there are a varying number of the phrases with the lower note in between. The text has been laid out so that all phrases with the higher note are left-justified, while all phrases with the lower note are indented. A few verses are transcribed musically in the same manner below.

Singing	*Translation*	*Speaking*
Hátegwílihá	Wolf	(hałgwila)
Meñá nagúdahá	My father	(ña nguda)
Ñigáva ígiwá	He said something	(gava iga)
Yúgugímowó	So it seems	(yug g'imo)
Neyúgugímowó	So it seems	
Hñáje yúguwá	So here I am	(ñaj yuga)
Hvága'ámjigeḿ	I'm wandering around	(vag 'amjgm)
Móñe yágewó	Where the mountain sheep sleep	('muu ñyago)
Ñemóñe yágejó	Where the mountain sheep sleep	
Vú geyówowám	This place	(vu gyowa)
Hałáłañójwegá	I keep on doing this	(ŧŧñujvga)
Nivége 'ámjigá	I'm wandering around	
Ñeyúgu'ímiwó	So it seems	(yug 'imo)
Yúgu'ímiwom	So it seems	
Ñá gomáŧwejé	My body	(ña gmaaŧvje)
Ñigávayúyehá	It feels so strange	(ñgavayuyeha)
Ñeyúgugímowó	So it seems	
Thúla thúlamé	It tingle, tingles	(thul thulme)
Hathúlathúlameḿ	It tingle, tingles	
Váge 'ámjigá	I'm wandering around	
Hayúge'ímewó	So it seems	
Yúga'ímowoḿ	So it seems	
Ñá gomáŧvejé	My body	
Ñigávayúyehá	It feels so strange	
Ñeyúgugímowó	So it seems	
Hthúlathúlomé	It tingle, tingles	
Váge 'ámjigá	I'm wandering around	
'Amúñe yágawó	Where the mountain sheep sleep	
Vúge yówogé	This place	
Hałáłañójvegeḿ	I keep on doing this	
Ñá gasálvowó	My hands	(ña gsalva)
Ñigávayúyuhá	They feel so strange	
Hayúgugyúmuwó	So it seems	
Yúgugyúmuwoḿ	So it seems	
'Añá gɫgánamé	Darkly shaping	('ñaa gɫganme)
Hayúgu'ímuwóm	So it seems	

Ñá gewáwawó	My hair	(ña gwawa)
Yathqwíyathqwíyegá	Is spiraling	(ya thqwiy
Hathqwíyathqwíyegá	Is spiraling	thqwiyga)
Heñáj 'agwáyahá	I have horns	(ñaj gwa)
Qóya'awíjiwó	My women	(bquuya 'wiija)
Ha ñeqáseqéjewój	The youngest one	(ñqejqejje)
Madíga ła'ólowá	Boiled beans	(mdiiga ł'ola)
Ha ñá ño'émowé	She gives them to me	(ña ñ'em)
Ñájo mágowá	I eat them	(ñaj 'maga)
Meñájo 'yíłigá	So I imagined	(ñaj 'yiitga)
Ha łúya 'ayúwugá	But I was wrong	(łuy 'yuga)
Na łúya 'ayúwagem̃	But I was wrong	
Súłegewájawó	Cactus blossoms	(suła gwajo)
Hmbáda yómegá	I ŧake the tips	(bad yomga)
Jájasgwíligá	I pick them off with my teeth	(jjsgwilga)
Meñáji yúwugá	That's what I do	(ñaj yuga)
'Ayúgu'ímuwum̃	So it seems	
Qúya awíjiwó	My women	
Hañégałáywós	The oldest one	(ñgłayje)
Hamłé ła'ólowá	Boiled pumpkin	(hmłe ł'ola)
Vú ñu'émuwé	She gives it to me	
'Iñáj 'emáguwá	I eat it	
Heñáj oyíłigá	So I imagined	
Hałúya 'ayúwugá	But I was wrong	
Łúya 'ayúwugem̃	But I was wrong	
Hálebáyiwá	Grass	(halbaya)
Havú guwájvuwó	Where it grows	(vu gwajvo)
Báde yómogá	I take the tips	
Heñáje májegá	I eat them	
Heñáje eyúwugá	So I do	
Yúgu'ímewó	So it seems	
Haqúya wíjiwó	My women	
Haqúya wíjiwo	My women	
Gáve'íguwá	He said something about them	(gav'iga)
Vú ñedávagá	It hurts me	(vu ñdavga)
Ñevú ñeyújemé	So it does	
'Eyúgayúyuwó	I feel so strange	

The Farewell Song

Henry Hanna, Singer

Henry Hanna learned this song from his sister's husband, Kit Jones, who was a medicine man and a singer. There are, or were, many Havasupai farewell songs. This one is very old, composed by a man named Heart-Horn. He lived long ago, and no one knows when he died or where he is buried or whether he had any relatives. This song, as the content demonstrates, is sung by old people bemoaning loss of health and saying goodbye to past wealth and to the land that they once roamed. Henry Hanna himself was in his eighties at the time he sang this song, and had recently had a serious operation which had left him very weak.

Singing	*Translation*	*Speaking*
'Eñawamebeyo	These are my thoughts	(ñwam be)
Hañewamebeyo	These are my thoughts	
Hañewamebeyo	These are my thoughts	
Han̵a	Han̵a	
Hañawameñaje	These are my thoughts	
Hagudeba ejawem	Long ago I was a runner	(guda davoga)
Hen̵e	Hen̵e	
Veñaje yude	So I was	(ñaj yuŧe)
Hña eveyamo	Where I used to run	(vyaama)
Viyagme geyovem	Those places	(vyag gyovme)
Heje	Heje	
Heveyaj me'eve	You hear me	(myaj m'eva)
Guwamejemagem	Forget about me	(wam jmagega)
Hen̵e	Hen̵e	
Heñawameñaje	These are my thoughts	
Hgudaba 'edawee	Long ago I was a runner	
Heveñaje yoŧem	So I was	
han̵em	Han̵em	
Ñaja 'ibave	I was proud	(naj 'jbaavga)
Heveñaye yogam	So I was	(ñaj yuga)
Han̵m	Han̵a	
'Agwe ba'e dayaha	An old man	('gwe baa 'ŧayga)
Haña heŧe 'obege j	I never would	(ñaj ŧ'obga)
Yuwegeyuwam	I would not be	(yugyum)
Han̵a	Han̵a	
Hveña deyega	So I believed	(ñaje yiga)
Heyejaye bagam	I was proud	
Han̵a	Han̵a	
Hveñaje yujitho	So I would always be	(ñaj yujtho)
Ñiŧuya 'eyuwe	But I was wrong	(ñtuya 'yu)
Hŧuya 'eyuwe	I was wrong	
Hen̵e	Hen̵e	
Hamaŧe amo	Those places I used to roam	(mat 'amo)

Hamaŧe genawam	Those places that I point to	(mat gnaava)
Haꞥa	Haꞥa	

'Ewiwdehemeve	Rocky High Hill	('wii ŧŧhhmiga)
Gawame gewajvee	That place there	(gwam gwajva)
Heveyaj me'evem	You hear me	(vyaj m'eva)
Heꞥe	Heꞥe	
'uwamejemage	Forget about me	(wam jmagga)
'uwamejemagm	Forget about me	
Haꞥa	Haꞥa	

'eñaye veyamo	Where I used to run	(ñaj vyaamo)
Veyagmegeyove	That place there	
Veyaj me'evem	You hear me	
haꞥa	Haꞥa	
Huwamejemage	Forget about me	
Huwamejemagem	Forget about me	
Haꞥa	Haꞥa	

Hbaqeydisbayva	Dripping Spring	(Ha gŧsbayva)
Ñaeje abemo	Where I bent to drink	(ñaj 'j'abmga)
Hiyagme geyovem	That place there	
Hejem	Hejem	
Meveyaj me'eve	You hear me	
Uwamejemagem	Forget about me	
Heꞥe	Heꞥe	

Gawe newaja	Rock Sitting There	('wii ñwaja)
Ña'egegamemom'	The Stumbling Place	(ñaj 'ggammo)
Viyagme gewave	That place there	
Hajem	Hajem	
Hveyajme'eve	You hear me	
Uwamejemagem	Forget about me	
Heꞥe	Heꞥe	

Ga'eñeyagam	Where the Log Lay	('ii ñyaga)
'Esegewalemo	That I Went Across	(sgwalmo)
Viyagme geyagwem	That place there	
Heje	Heje	

Heveyaj mi'ivi	You hear me	
Uwamejemagvem	Forget about me	
Heꞥe	Heꞥe	

Vawelewaja	Where the tree stands	('ii wila waja)
Mña ełemeñemo	Where I passed by	(łmiñmo)
Viyagme gewavem	That place there	
Heje	Heje	
Hveyaj mi'ivi	You hear me	
Uwamejemagem	Forget about me	
Heꞥem	Heꞥem	

Gwee ñeyujive	So I would always be	(gwe ñyujve)
Veñaje yuga	So I believed	(ñaj yuga)
'Amałe 'amo	The land that I roamed	(mał 'amo)
hoꞥo	Hoꞥo	
'Amałegenawa	The place that I point to	(mał gnaava)
Wewołesemevem	Where the rocks are straight	('wii łsmiiva)
Heꞥe	Heꞥe	

Hveyam gewajve	Those rocks there	(vyam gwajva)
m'iviliwivi	I thought I would be like you	(m'vlwiiva)
'Ayu iyithem	So I believed	('yithm)
Haꞥa	Haꞥa	
Geja 'ibavi	I was proud	
Veñaje yujithem	So I was	
Haꞥa	Haꞥa	

'Łuya 'iyuwe	But I was wrong	
Veñaje yumo	So I was	
'Ewaye gemole	It saddens me so	('way gmola)
Heꞥe	Heꞥe	
Vłuya 'eyuga	I was wrong	
Hveña iyime	In what I believed	(ña 'yim)
Heꞥe	Heꞥe	

Hgoda ba 'edawe	Long ago I was a runner	(gud baa 'dava)
Haveñaje yutga	So I was	(ñaj yułga)
'ma'ul ñithawve	A little antelope	('m'ul ñthawa)

Heje	Heje	
Hegeythawidadami	It jumped up	(thag vdadme)
Hthagwa yemajwam	And ran away	(waymaja)
Haꞥa	Haꞥa	
Hveñaje eve	And I went with him	(ñaj 'ivm)
Hgwajegwiyuwa	Right beside him	(gwajge)
Hveñaje'egam	So I did	(ñaj 'iga)
Haꞥa	Haꞥa	
Habuvuve lagega	I pulled out my bow	(hbuva lagga)
Hethage yegwithe	I took him	(thag gwithga)
Heꞥe	Heꞥe	
Geñaje eyuga	So I was	
Ñigavuha 'eyuwa	I was that way	(gava'yu)
'Adave gehwiya	I took him so fast	(dava gwi)
Haꞥm	Haꞥm	
Gayegeyujitho	So I would always be	
Hƚuya eyuwem	But I was wrong	
Heꞥe	Heꞥe	
Gaguledawa	Jackrabbit	(gula)
Hdedahahelogove	Cottontail	(hlo)
Gethag we dademem	One would jump up	
Haꞥa	Haꞥa	
Hthag wayemajwa	And run away	
Hveñaji'ivem	And I went with him	
Heꞥe	Heꞥe	
Veqwajehegwiyuwa	Right beside him	
Veñaje yoga	So I was	
Thage yegwethe	I took him	
Heꞥe	Heꞥe	
Ñaj ñeha'evuga	So I did	
Heja e bagvem	I was proud	
Heꞥe	Heꞥe	
Hveñaje yujitho	So I would always be	
Vƚuya 'eyuwe	But I was wrong	

Hłuya 'eyuwem	I was wrong	
Heꞥe	Heꞥe	
Hveya ñimivi	A bobcat	(vya ñmiyva)
Gathag vedade	It jumped up	
Heꞥe	Heꞥe	
Ñawa veñaje	And I too	(vñaje)
Thagweyemajwa	It ran away	
Veñaje 'ivem	And I went with him	
Haꞥa	Haꞥa	
Gñevo ñimiwa	That bobcat	
'agegeyale	With a black belly	('ñaa gyaala)
Heꞥe	Heꞥe	
Gveñajiyuve	So I was	
Veñajiyułiga	So I would always be	
Nigwaje gwiyuwa	I was right beside him	
'Iga	Iga	
Hveñaji'avuga	I hit him	
Ñajgeyegwithem	I took him	
Heꞥe	Heꞥe	
Geveña'iwiga	So I did	(vñaj 'iwga)
'Eja'ibave	I was proud	('jbaavga)
Veñaje yujithem	So I would always be	
Haꞥa	Haꞥa	
Hełoya 'eyuve	But I was wrong	
'Ña'e eyambom	Where I used to roam	(ñaj yaamom)
Haꞥa	Haꞥa	
Veyag me geyove	This place	(vyag mgyova)
Viyaj me'eve	Listen to me	(vyaj m'eva)
Wamejemagem	Forget about me	(wam jmagega)
Heꞥe	Heꞥe	
Hamhate'amo m	Place I used to roam	(mał 'amom)
Małe genawem	Place I used to go	(mał gnawom)
Haꞥa	Haꞥa	
Halege gwavuva	Gegwava Spring	(hal ggwavva)

'Aŧeŧegavo	Where I inserted prayer sticks	('ŧŧgavo)
Ñaje j'abmo	Where I bent down to drink	(ñaj j'abmo)
Han̵a	Han̵a	
Viyag me geyove	This place	
Hveyaj me'evam	Listen to me	
Han̵a	Han̵a	

Guwamejemage	Forget about me	
'Uwamejemage	Forget about me	
Haŧuya e yuwem	I was wrong	(ŧuya 'yum)
Han̵a	Han̵a	
Jithgwila ewiwje	My many hides	(jthgwila wiiwje)
'ajoqa 'ewage	On two cedar trees	('joq wag)
Hen̵e	Hen̵e	

Gjoqa yemogume	On three cedars	(joq hmuga)
'Ñaja e ugam	I see this	(ñaja 'uga)
Heja 'ebave	And I am proud	
Hen̵e	Hen̵e	
'Agwe ñesaya	Suet	(gwe ñsaya)
Hveña 'ewewim	That belongs to me	(na wiiwom)
Haja	Haja	

Agwe eñaja	Navajo rugs	(gwe 'ñaaja)
hegavo ñegaja	Small ones	(vu ñqeja)
Huwage hemugume	Two or three of them	(hwaga hmugme)
Hen̵e	Hen̵e	
'Ñaj ñiha euvgam	I see them	
Heja ebave	And I am proud	
Hen̵e	Hen̵e	

Veñaje yujigho	So I would always be	
Hŧuya eyuwe	But I was wrong	
Bŧuya eyuwe	I was wrong	
Hen̵e	Hen̵e	
Hveya me'evuga	Listen to me	
Huwamejebave	Forget about me	
Hen̵e'	Hen̵e'	

Origin Tale

Earl Paya, Narrator

Transcribed and translated by the staff of the Havasupai Bilingual Education Program

Vya, vya havsuwv gud dava gthad gnaavɨg, va siijvjuh iijg, ijm m'eevjñmyuje, maa oobjgtho, ñaj ɨu qejm baa gɨay gwe gnaavjaha evg qejm 'sbomyujg, ñuvyum, gnaavm m'eevjah.

Guda, Guda jyugɨg ij, vam hmañ gyaamhj gwem ɨgwaadjmwijm, "marijuana", ñum ɨgwaadjmwijg, ñuvñyujvj bqivj gud ñahmiivñ gyuthg, wilpuyvg wilpuyvm, gwe gayuja ɨiym ñyahaanjohgyuh'yu yig wasiivñ gyuthg, uuva ɨiy gyujgi uuva, uuva ɨiyha.

Yum, hwayvj hag yom, hwayve ijg, "water pocket" ijj thag yom hag, hag wawg gyujg. Hag wawg gyujm, baya hmuujg we yaajmg siɨthg hag wam, yaamg yomjahg yujɨm, ham yayug hnawg ñ'iimg, haahj ñuvyug jbaagaha, hajyuɨ uuv ɨiyha uuv ɨiym, uuv uuvm buydavmyujgyu, uuv ɨiym, uuvñ vaam hmañ ɨɨgwaadvmwijg, ɨu qajvjyuyiɨ ñuñyug uuv ɨiym, wijm hal ñyug hnawg ñ'imm, ham'om yuɨ hahj yavyug, mlulvmluulvig, mlulvmluulvig, ijg, "like boiling," ñuvyum, ham ha ñyugmyuɨ havyug, "Jack in the Beanstalk" vlwii

Long ago the Havasupai told what they called Coyote stories. Have you heard them, or not? If not, I will tell a little of what I know.

Long, long ago, in the beginning, there was a lady who wished she was married, but the men hated her. She wanted to turn into something really good, so the men would like her. She thought about turning into tobacco, like the marijuana young people today smoke. So she turned into tobacco.

She lived there at the "water pocket." Then everyone else moved away and she was there alone. When they came back to get her, she jumped into the water and the water started flowing out. It turned her into a tobacco plant. Nowadays everyone likes tobacco, both the young and old. After she jumped in, the water kept bubbling and boiling, and the plant kept growing just like "Jack in the Beanstalk." The people climbed on the leaves up to the sky, but I don't know exactly what happened. One branch really grew out and they slept there. But the

gwadve, "Jack in the Beanstalk" vlwiig, hajyuŧ ŧu hwalvg yavyugg yuwa. Havyugm, ghmuujahjyuŧ miyaahl jbgaamjñ gavyugyuh'yu, gag sboodavgiŧ ŧu miyaahl jgbaajyiŧ ha gwe hwal hayug, jgbaam, "leaves" thag yum, hag yayug qejm vŧeg hag hayug sihyalvm smaajmyuj, smaajmyujthm, haahjyuŧ yavyuwg yuwgyuwña, yuwgyuwg, baa ŧgwiivg baa ŧgwiivg, yavyug maŧ ñwaavo bay dav baa nmaag, bay yavwig, bay yavwig, haahj bay ham yavyug vyaa'a, guda maŧhj kay hlmaŧgyu, gud ñyum, baa ŧgwiivñ, haahj baa ŧgwiivg, yavyug yuwg yuwg yuwg yuwgme, ŧu vhmii'ig, ŧu maŧ gwe ñwaavo bay ŧŧmaadm, smaag yayuwg, yayuwg yayuwga, gwehj gjbaañme, gwe, gwe hwalja 'm'iijg "Jack in the Beanstalk" ñlwiiñha, miyaahl yaamm, hayumg smaajmyujg, smaajmyujŧg, ham'om yuŧ we'e "sky, sky" iijg ña uumg, miyaaha ijñg ñajvj hal ña ñyumjg, ham jbaamjm, jbaamjah mi ga yuj gyu'hyu, gag ñu gnaav bay jwiida ŧa'oobm ijgi, ŧu ham ñjbaamjm, haahj iŧ ham'om iŧ "sky" mij "sky", haahj iŧ ham yayug yayumiŧe ñumyuŧ ñuvyuhim ñ'uujg, ŧujv maŧv maŧ miyaahl ñvlwiivjg, sboojga, sboojga, msii, msii yoovjg, gwevl jwojgwijg wi thvliivl, wii'i, gwe thvliivl jwojg, gwe bay dav "seal"g, glwijm, yuŧg, "Ga ña yujg baa ñwaam, baa gavñwiijgtho, maa ñmyabeehꞥyu," iijg, ñuvwijg, hal msii ñjudjg, gwe maahyii ha thiihyii, gwe gawiihyii bay dav hal yawig "seal"g, ñwijg, gthyeevah, mig, gthyeevah haj seeh ihyii, hal ya wiiyaha "air", "'Air' hal ya wiiymiŧe ya myabeehꞥyu," ig. Hal ña wiiyah ñvwiŧm, haahj bay baa wide mii ña uumg, gavwiigwiha. Baajah baa ñwiidm, gkuuva miijg, gkuuve gag haygu siivyom sig sbo ŧ'uumg, ŧu gkuuva, haj yiŧe ha miyaahgiŧ, miyaahj gavyum miijaha ham yayug, "ceiling" ñlwig, ham yayug

water kept coming and coming, forcing them to go up, covering the land where they used to live. In those days the land probably looked different.

Still the water kept coming, forcing them to go up higher. They kept climbing and climbing, and the plant kept growing. And they continued to sleep there. Finally they were halfway to the sky, and still they were climbing. I don't know if they made it out or not, because the old people never told how that part ended. But the water kept coming almost to that certain spot where they were. They knew it was coming, so they got a girl, and they put her in something with a hole in it, and they sealed it. "Whatever happens to us, you're the one that will be alive," they told her. They put food and water in with her, and the medicine man blew in air for her to breathe. He said, "The air is for you to breathe so that you can live."

Probably the water finished them all off, I don't really know, but then, when there was no one left, a bird, a flicker, was clinging to the sky, like to the "ceiling" (I don't know what the sky looked like in those days). The water was rising and was going to get him, and he was crying "Gwiig! Gwiig!" He

yavyuñe mi gayugyuh'yu, gag sboojña ŧ'ob ñaj. Ñuvyum, hag ñuvyug tog vtog hag ŧbeevmm, haahj ham yayug yayuwg yayuwg yayuwg, ñuvyum vab ham'om gkuuhj iŧg, "Gwiig! Gwiig!" v'iim miija, ham'om vyohim ñ'uuga, haahj yohim ñ'uug, ham'om vavñyum ham'om haahj ŧu magl yayuwg, yuwg yuwg yuwg, yuwg yuwg, ŧu magl voog ham'om. Ha ñyugm wa msiihj gwevl judjgwiigi, hajiŧ ñyuñha haa jaahg aamj, ge gayu gyuh'yu, ŧu yag yayug aamjg, aamjg, aamjg, yuŧg, ham'om haahj bay ham'om duuva duuvg ham'om vayug duuv'm, duuvñ'me, vye'e gag maŧm m'uuꞥ msboojña mdava mŧ'oobm ye Wiqdwiisa iijgi, Wambodjwogohve, "Grand Canyon", we Qmwidm Ñwaa iijg, Ha Thaaw Gyoh gwaajg, Ha Thaaw Gyoh gwaajg, Qmwidm Ñwaa iijm, haj ga gyujg giŧe "land"aha "land" giŧe hahj hag ham'om bay duuva. Ii jmiim, thag yaagŧga, haahj waamjg, haahj waamjm eevg sboog ñyujg, ham'om ŧu ŧ'iinm ñ'eevg, gudm gnaavjm ñ'im m'eevog, mŧthhwaalgg yamwig, vam mjbaahꞥyu iijiym, gnaavjom myujg, ñwig ham jbaaha. Jbaaŧm hag gyu gyujgi. Ñyug hag oyaavj haandavg hag yoye migayum hal ñhal wah, ñhal wagiŧ ñha Qmwidm Ñwaa iija.

Gyume hag hmañ baa gjaaŧa hwagm yoovahii wasiiviyg, ñum ñyujg, ñaahj v'al iga ñaahj v'al iga, ñaa jbaamyujg ñjvyum . . . oob yaj yafogyu, qejm jaama iijaŧ'wi wa, wa gkuuve mij ñhaj miyaahl waamñahiŧm, hal hahj waamm hajiŧ gwam eevah gwam eevm ñaa ñŧqib, ña uum ñaa ñdobe mi gañyum gwam mijm eevg, eevŧg thaj bqihj msiihj yaamg uuŧm, "Maaj gamuñ yabeeñga?" "Jo hahv ñwaamahg iŧm, ha miyaah ŧbeevg hag glyug glyuŧm, ham'om, vam'om ñgmaagme miij, 'When its all disappear. Gone.' Ññyum, vag yabeeg aamjñ

thought the water was going to get him, but then, in the end the water went back. It kept going down.

The girl that had been put in something, she was in the same kind of situation, just floating around on top of the water. She didn't know where she was. She was just floating. Then finally, the water kept going down and down, till it came to Red Butte, and Grand View Point, at Grand Canyon. They say she landed near those places, in that piece of wood, when the water dried up. She lay there in that piece of wood, listening to see if she was still floating. When she heard it was quiet, she picked a hole through the wood to get out as they had told her before. When she got out, she found she was near a cave, so she lived there. That place came to be known as "the old lady's house."

And then she wanted to conceive two big strong sons. You know how the sun comes up . . . but wait, I'm getting ahead of myself. Remember the flicker that almost was washed away by the flood? He lived too. She heard him calling every night and every evening, and finally she went to see. She asked him, "How did you stay alive?" The flicker said, "I clung to the sky, and then when the water was gone, I was wandering around, wondering where that fire came from. Then I saw that you were the one that was building the fire."

ge oo ɫujg gwe ga wiij gwihwi, imyujɫm, maaj vag oo mɫum haagmyujig." ñ'iigyum hag gj'uujve.

Gj'uujvg ham hwagg hag bayɫg, ɫu hmaañ gawig baa yoovg gwalayig yig wasiivg, msiihje ig iɫe, ñaahj ham v'aal igmyujm, ha haamg iɫe,bada ɫobjuyiɫe, yaamg iɫ, thag gyaañvmyujg qyaañmyujg, ham ñaa jbaam ñ'igm, imyujm, ha ñaahm ñinvg gyu iijaha ñaahm ñinva, ñug iɫ wemaaj iiv voogmyujg ñug iɫ ha baqvj ñyum jaq jaq imyujogñ, ñyuym ñuvyuj, ñuvyujmiɫ ñyuyaha yuyiɫ gag ñha gnaavg ñhe ijm, sboh ɫ'ob'yiɫ, ɫu ñyujmiɫ, yuygyu iijm, eeviym myuj hag qyaañvmyuj ñyug ha hmañ hwagm baa yoov ñuvyugyu. Ñaj vaam sbo'yumagñ, gwe ga iij gwe gnaavjahj ɫu vaam ñuvyug, msiij ɫu ñug waɫg ɫu qwadv thawv. Yujiɫ gayujj wim sbovmyuj ñvag ñuvyum, ñvam bay qejm ɫñuuvjg, msiiñ.

Haj hmañ ñwig, baa gjaaɫa hwagm yoova, ña vlwiya, yoovm. Ñthag ɫwaɫg, ya Havsuw, Havsuw uujaha gwe ñeg ñug ɫwamyujg gwe gayug ñug ɫwamyujg, ñuj ñva uujg, qmwidma jgwiijha, ge be, ge be ɫha haana yoojaha, ham ɫu, maɫki iijg, ña uumg 'mvalv, ɫu gwe gayuja, baa yoovjg, ham "bow and arrow" wijmwiijg, ham baa yoovjg, wijmwiijɫg, ñvajyuɫ yal ɫu kayjg mɫha iijg, val yal Havsuwvl yom uujg, jgwiijthm, oobog, "Gag gbada ɫobv, gag gbada ɫobl ɫhavjom gwevj yom gag hal myaam m'uuñ myoojahgi ɫu ńu mmɫhaajñj ñuj haanyiɫ ñyumijm gag baa ñu ñ'ig gwalayiɫ ɫ'ob-'yu, iiyiɫ wajmagvm, ñhal yogyum, Wii Ggaaba iijm hal yogyu, Wii Ggaaba Wii Ggaaba iijm hal yog gag bada ɫ'ob, wii ɫu magl voog voog'ig, baaj baa gɫwiidahj hal yoomih, gag ñuñyuj gwalayi ɫ'ob'yu, ɫu hmañ mhaang, baa mgjaaɫa baa ñwiiyg, gag ñumyug mbiijm baa ñ'uu gwala'yi ɫ'ob'yu." Iiyiɫe,

So that's how they met and lived together. Later on she decided she wanted children. Remember I started to tell about the sun coming up? Well, I don't like to tell this part, but she went to see the sun. Also there was a spring nearby. So she went back and forth daily from the spring to the sun, and that's how she conceived two strong boys. I really don't know, but that's how they say she conceived those boys. Nowadays the girls do the same kind of thing, having babies out of wedlock, but you can tell who the father is.

Anyway, she had two boys, who were big and strong like me. They were wandering around hunting or just roaming around, and they discovered this place which is now called Supai. They asked the old woman where they could get some reeds to make arrows. In those days, people used Apache Plume and Ash to make bows and arrows for hunting, but they wanted their arrows to be different, made from the reeds that grow down here. They asked the old lady, but she told them no. "It's bad for you to go down where those plants are growing. It's OK to make arrows, but use the plants around here. Don't go down there." But they really wished for those plants.

Then she went on and explained to them. "That place is called Wii Ggaaba (Where the rocks come together). It's a bad place to go because it kills people. The rocks go back and forth, coming together

ñva Havsuwvjum, Havsuwvjum, ha Wii Ggaaba ijg, guda yoovg Baagiyoovahj ñva nmaaga, jyugɨg 'm'iijɨg, jyugɨg.

Hmañj, "Mah yaamjg, gwe ñeehj'yum," ñ'ig ɨu yegɨg he ɨyuwg, va ɨu jgnaag vaj ɨu jgnaagjg, vye g'oodva gagyujñg bayga, Ɨovgyovge mi ña uumg yag gagyujmyiɨ bay g'uujah yag wiiñ vayug, ɨu magl voog vooghg gag bada ɨ'obm, guda uujiyiɨa, "Mah! Baa mgvyaamdav ñyum miñ, maaj myafoovm myaamg, hal, wal, ɨha mqaawmg, vogmg mggeeg myugmdavg vam jgbaavga hmaɨe?" ñ'ithm, "Ee'e yuhi'yu, ee'e, ñaj yuhi'yu." m'iijg gjqejahve mi ña oobg, gɨayve mi gañgyuj, "Ee'e ɨu magl voom iyam ggeem 'yumadav hal qawqaawa ɨu vogah'ih, ggeeg vam jgbaav hmaɨe," miijɨm. Ye Kogɨlaba iijogiñ ñu yaag ga gyujg'imo ɨha ñug guda yomyujm gwe qejolwiɨg uuymyujñ, ñug Andrew wawoñ gagujñgyumo, ñug gwe ñuvyujj ñug yovolm uumyuj'yuj.

Ñuvyugiɨ hagyuja, "Mah ɨu ahwagɨg yujih'yu. Ahwagɨa yujih'yu, ahwagɨg buyahyiɨ haangyu," miija, siɨga, siɨg ya ii ithm iɨ siɨthg iɨe, "Mah, yag gwe iijgyaɨjo'wim, iijgyaɨjg, ñum vam sahkeejoh'wi ñywaajohm miija "on the shoulders" ña ywaajohm sahkeejg ɨobeemg, hal qaawjg, ña wijgtho vogjih'yum. Wiihj voogahñg, voogyiɨ yag yayug ɨgeevg, ɨgeevg, tham'om ɨu vag ñyuj ih hmaaɨgyuñ yiijgiɨ, ñyugiɨ, wavsiivg iijgyaɨgiɨ ñwig, vam nalg vam yaamja, ye yuwjgyug, ye'e Wii Gwal Qthyaañe ijg ve wam m'uujm myujg msbojɲyu. Ve ɨyaavgja mi gavyujg, ham naalg ɨha qaawg ñwiidjg, vab voomjg, gagyujg ñvooje mi gañyujm wa wiihj voog'ig ham yayugiɨ, ɨu wii, wiihj vag jiig'ig, vag ɨɨgofg ham'om ñva Wii Ggaaba iijg Havsuwa igsiijg vaam ña oob, ya ig

and crushing the people who go there. I'd hate to see you two strong boys killed that way."

That place called Wii Ggaaba is Supai. Long ago, in the beginning, the Creator left it that way.

Even though the old woman told them not to go, they decided to go anyway, telling her they were going hunting early the next day. Instead of going hunting, they headed straight for the Canyon. Maybe they went to where we call Topacoba or Hualapai Hilltop or somewhere along up that way. They sat up there watching the rocks go back and forth, as they had seen before.

One of the boys said to the other, "You said you are a fast runner, so you go first. Go down there to where those plants are growing, grab some, and run back as quickly as you can. Do you think you can do it?"

The other one said, "Yes, I can do it, when the rocks open up. I'll run fast, grab some plants and come right back. I can probably make it back up," he said. (I remember I used to see those plants growing somewhere near "Kogɨlaba," and near Andrew's.)

The boys were there on the cliff, and one of them said, "We'll both go. Even if we both die, it's OK." But the other one said, "We should cut a piece of log and put it across our shoulders. Then when the rocks go apart we can run down and grab some plants, and come back. When the rocks come together again, the log will keep it open." So they cut the log and went down. The place where they did it is near here. It's called "Wii Gwal Qthyaañe"—you've probably seen it—that's where they say they came down.

They went down into the canyon and got some of that plant. They were on their way back when the

gwe ggnaavñj qejm gyul wijahŧe, ga wijg qaj davm gd'udg wijogwi, qajm vŧewjogwiwg maŧj ŧeg hanaŧe, gwaawg haanm val wayoñŧe iijogi, iijiyiŧ iijm'iijm m'eevm myujñ ñaj ñuva iiñ gwadv'yu, qejm vŧeewjog, gyuljog, jgyaŧjgwiwg, hanm val maŧj vŧem val Wii Ggaaba iijaŧe, ñug iija ñva Havsuwa igsiijvj, gud gthadgnaavŧg, Wii Ggaaba iijvj, vaj vayumg yaamg. Ñvwwimjg, he ñwijg ŧu gudm ŧu ŧslaagmga. Ñvoomjg he vav wij'wiñ ijg ijyiŧ qmwidma gnaavjom, ŧu miiha, ŧu miihŧm wiijmyuŧ ñuñyumg, hag baa gjaaŧahj ha yumjg yujŧg, hañyumjgiŧe, havñyumjga, ham'om ŧu chwayl yaamjñah, bquyñ msiiñ jujmyujm, ñyug ñuvyujm, ŧu chwayl yaamjm, hal hwagŧm baa jnehjyiŧa, siŧg hmañ yooviyg, yavwijiym, haj hmañ hag vog vaag 'Grandmother' wiih ñ'uug, moda iwg, moda, ña moda uug, ge wag gyuhiyu. Yig, yiŧg, hag ñ'uug, ham'om hag ŧv'oog giŧe qmwidmahj ye ñaa dobo yaam gyujgi, qmwidmahj "Ñaa dobo yaamg, gwe, gwe haana gwe gayuuj gag ñaj wiiña ŧ'oobo'we. Ŧu qejm, ŧu gwe qlyaayvo, gag haandava iŧ ŧu gavyuuja wiiyñ ye wañih'yu ñaa dobo, yugtho, maaj ña awa m'iijaha, 'Grandson', ña awa maaj myaamññiŧ ñaa j'aalo, ñaa j'aalo 'east' myaamñ, he yiŧ gwe ghaanajiŧ yuwaha, gwe ghaana maañ mwiiñha ñyugiŧ gag, gag buyña ŧ'obaha, ŧu yabeejaha, yuŧg, maa ña m'uu gwalñmigtho, ya myuwa, ñaahm myuwa, 'rain' miwo, ña uumg gwe yaj ñmjjnalah, gweñ mmaawahñ 'yig gweñ mmawo yiŧg ñaj maañ ñ'uug gwalñyig ñaj ñmyaamg, ñu wiiñh'wi, hanbaje, 'rain' iiwñog, 'rain' iwoh, gwe vam jjnalg ya wiiyjg ya maŧme, maŧme, iijg, iijg yoovjujgi guda.

Gud ñaa gthad gnaavja, gthad gnaavja ñaa ñwig yoovjm, ñaj qmwidm, qmwidm wawo ña

canyon started to come together, but it suddenly stopped because of the log across their shoulders. So that's why Havasu Canyon is called Wii Ggaaba, "Where the rocks come together."

Today, whenever anyone tells this story they always think the twins should have used a bigger longer log, so this place would have been bigger and wider and longer. I myself think that way.

When the boys told the old woman what they had done, she just cried and cried.

The boys grew older and they went away to find wives, but they got into a war over the women, and they were both killed. But before they died, one of them had a son. The young boy grew up and wanted to see his grandmother, but he didn't know where she lived. He was told he should go toward the setting sun, where his grandmother lived. There he saw his grandmother. She recognized him and called him "my grandson." She said he couldn't stay because she was poor and didn't have anything, and that he would live in the east where all the good things come from. She would live in the west, where all the useless things come from. "We won't die," she said, "We'll live forever. When you want to see me, come with the sun, or the rain, or in the harvest of nuts and crops. And if I want to see you, I'll do the same, in the rain, or snow or in the harvest." And still today the old lady and the boy live on.

The place where the old lady lived, and where the sun lived, are over there near Flagstaff. I have

uuga, wa 'ñaa, qmwidmahj ñaahm ñinvgyu'g, ha ñaa ñowah gag gwe uuv sbova ɨ'obm msbojñmyujmiɨ "Flagstaff" yaag Wii Hagnbaajg ha yaag, hag ñaa ñwawo hag yo gwadm miija. Nva gwe ñgnaavj davahj, ñvaj vayuujm baajñ bay ɨsboojg, gwe gnaavjñ ñ'iijm'iijm, ñaj Havsuw gwe gnaavjñ ñgnaavm, ñahaanm iijogi, iijmyujm, ya qejm baa gɨayj va ñ'iig ña ñgnaavjoh, m'iijm eevmyuj'yu gwe wa Panmita iijg, Panmita, Package Coffee, Jack Payaj ñva gwe ñgjnaavjm m'iijm eevg, va baya 'sbo'yu. Va yug vam v'oogyu. Mah!

Ñvaj ɨu gweñ "Bible" ñlwigyumagiñ, ya gwe gnaavja ɨu "Bible" ñlwig, gwe gthad gnaavjg ijgi, ñvaj vayuyg ñlwig, va ñyum va qejm ña 'sbog, ɨu wasiivmyuj'yu ñaj, ñyum, ɨowiig, kay tem gnaavahyiiyiɨ, ɨu qejm ɨu 'guudog gnaavahg'imahg. Mah!◇

seen them myself. Not many have seen them, but the ruins are still there.

This story is true. It has been passed on to me by the old people. Panamiɨa, Package Coffee, and Jack Paya, they used to tell this story.

The whole story is very long. It's a lot like the Bible. There's a lot more, but I've told you a little of it. That's all. That's the end.◇

Bibliography

Coues, Elliott. 1900. On the trail of a Spanish pioneer. *American Explorers*, Series 3. (Translation from Spanish of the diary of Father Garces.)

Hanna, Dan, and Hinton, Leanne. 1971. Havasupai medicine song. *Alcheringa: Ethnopoetics*, no. 3, pp. 68–75.

Hinton, Leanne. In press. *Havasupai songs: A linguistic perspective.* Tübingen, German Federal Republic: Gunter Narr.

Spier, Leslie. 1924. *Havasupai (Yuman) texts. International Journal of American Linguistics* (*IJAL*) 3: 109–16.

———. 1928. Havasupai ethnography. *Anthropological Papers of the American Museum of Natural History* 29: 83–292.

Credits

Wolf's boy. Adapted from Spier, Leslie, 1924. *Havasupai (Yuman) texts. IJAL* 3: 109–16.

Photo credits: pp. 99, 100, 146, and 154—Victor Masayesva.

ALAN SHATERIAN, PAMELA MUNRO,
and MARTHA B. KENDALL, *Editors*

The Yavapai

The Yavapai at Prescott

Violet Mitchell

The Yavapai at Prescott are one of four subtribes which comprise the Yavapai tribe. The eastern Yavapai live in the Camp Verde–Clarkdale area; the southern Yavapai reside at Fort McDowell. The western Yavapai, who formerly lived near Arlington, have been absorbed into the other Yavapai groups. The elderly members of the western Yavapai still maintain their identity with that subtribe.

The Yavapai believe that their origins are near Sedona. Before the coming of the white man, the Yavapai land base ranged from the San Francisco Peaks to the area of present-day Williams and Ashfork, to north of the Santa Maria and Bill Williams River. Today this area constitutes central and west-central Arizona.

From the beginning of Anglo encroachment on Yavapai territory, the interlopers confused the Yavapai with the Apaches. In 1871, when General Crook ordered all Apaches onto a reservation in Middle Verde, the people actually interned were Yavapai.

The federal government's decision in 1874 forcibly to place the Yavapai at San Carlos with the Apaches resulted in one of the most tragic periods in Yavapai history. The Yavapai were made to walk approximately 180 miles over rugged terrain, crossing rivers and sustaining themselves on natural food substances. The walk not only demoralized the spirit of the Yavapai but brought death to many. Of the approximately 1,500 Yavapai who began the journey, only 200 remained alive to return to their homeland in the 1880s. The rest had succumbed to the hardships of the march, to captivity and disease.

When the Prescott Yavapai returned, they began to work along with people in Prescott to obtain lands for a reservation. In 1935, the Department of Interior deeded 75 acres for a reservation north of Prescott. In 1956, an additional 1,300 acres were added to the reservation.

Presently there are 109 enrolled tribal members. Seventy-six tribal members live on the reservation. Thirteen speak Yavapai fluently.

The Prescott-Yavapai community is governed by a Board of Directors elected by tribal members for two-year terms.

The Yavapai at Fort McDowell

Pat Mariella and Sigrid Khera

Many of the Yavapai and Tonto Apache returnees from San Carlos settled near the abandoned military post at Fort Verde, and in 1907 the Bureau of Indian Affairs (BIA) established an Indian day school there. In 1910, 40 of these acres were suitable for farming; most Yavapai living there continued working for wages.

In 1912, there were many Yavapai and Tonto Apaches working in the copper mines and at the smelter at Clarkdale, 18 miles northwest of Camp Verde, and the BIA opened a day school there. After World War I, the power of the mine unions was broken; and the number of Indian miners increased (Spicer, 1962:257).

In 1914 and 1916, an additional 448 acres with water rights were set aside for the Yavapai 8 miles west of Camp Verde at Middle Verde. This place was more suitable for farming, and many people from Camp Verde moved to Middle Verde.

The slowdown, and finally closure of the mines in Central Arizona during the 1930s and 1940s greatly affected the Yavapai workers. Consequently, more people returned to the reservations, and farming and cattle-raising activities were expanded. However, off-reservation employment still provided most of the earned income into the 1980s.

A tribal project, designed to provide greater local employment opportunities for reservation members, is a tourist center complex associated with the neighboring Montezuma Castle National Monument (a prehistoric cliff-dwelling site).

In 1969, 60 acres near the former mining community of Clarkdale were established as reservation land for the Yavapai and Tonto Apaches who had been living there while working for the mines. A housing program sponsored by the Department of Housing and Urban Development helped to provide new homes. Camp Verde, Middle Verde and Clarkdale all combine to elect one council under an Indian Reorganization Act constitution.

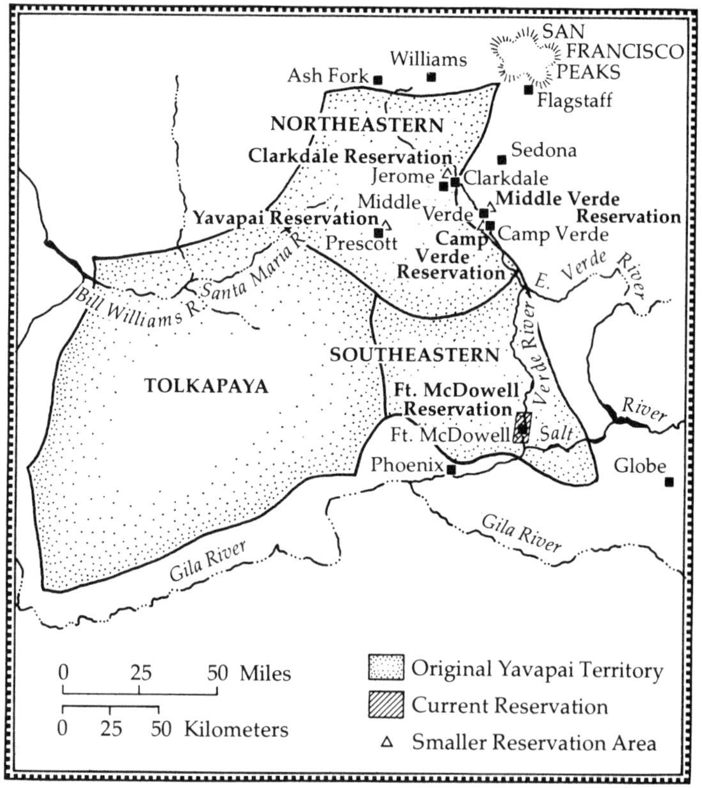

The Yavapai at Camp Verde, Middle Verde, and Clarkdale

Pat Mariella and Sigrid Khera

In the 1880s and 1890s the Indian Agents at the San Carlos Reservation allowed many Yavapai to return to their homelands. Several families tried to settle at the abandoned military post at Fort McDowell. However, after the closing of the military post and the rejection of the Indian School idea, Anglo and Mexican squatters, some of them land speculators, occupied most of the arable land. Yavapai delegations went to Washington, D.C., to ask for exclusive use of the land.

Eventually, the non-Indian settlers were bought out by the federal government, and the entire reservation was turned over to the Yavapai living at McDowell in 1903. The Yavapai farmers labored constantly to develop and maintain their irrigation system which was periodically washed out by flooding of the Verde River.

In 1906 the Bureau of Indian Affairs recommended that no more funds be spent on the irrigation system of Fort McDowell. Instead, it was proposed to relocate the Fort McDowell Yavapai onto the neighboring Salt River Pima-Maricopa Reservation where it was hoped the farmers could take water from the Salt River Project's Arizona Canal.

The federal government was never able to settle the legal problems involving the transfer of water rights to the new location, and the Fort McDowell community members did not agree that it was in their best interests to move to land without water rights. The Fort McDowell Yavapai were able to avoid this relocation over the next thirty years by political activities on their part with the assistance of Dr. Carlos Montezuma. Dr. Montezuma was a Yavapai who had been captured as a child and raised in Anglo society; he recontacted his relatives at McDowell and contributed his resources in the effort to secure a permanent irrigation system for the Fort McDowell Reservation.

The Fort McDowell farmers continued to resist removal, but as irrigation labor costs continued to rise, many community members turned to other ways to make a living. Many Yavapai sought out wage labor in mines, ranches, and farms. Cattle ranching on the reservation was also developed.

A major issue that faced the Fort McDowell community since the 1950s was the proposed Orme Dam, a feature of the Central Arizona Project that would have flooded the Reservation. The Fort McDowell community opposed Orme Dam, and in the fall of 1981 Secretary of Interior James Watt rejected Orme and selected an alternative site for a dam. ◇

The Contributors

Molly Fasthorse, who was about 70 years old in 1982, is one of the last speakers of Tolkapaya Yavapai. She was raised on the Fort McDowell Reservation but lived for much of her adult life in Los Angeles. Upon her recent retirement, she returned to Fort McDowell. She is a resourceful and exciting teacher, equally adept at translating, explaining fine semantic distinctions, and telling stories. She remembers many old tales and reads much ethnography and Indian lore.

Martha Kendall began working with Yavapai speakers on the grammatical structure of their language in the summer of 1969. In 1972 she received her Ph.D. in anthropological linguistics from Indiana University, where she subsequently became associate professor. She has worked with speakers of Hualapai and Havasupai, in addition to her work on Yavapai dialects of the Verde Valley and Oak Creek Canyon areas.

Sigrid Khera is a professional anthropologist who has worked for over ten years with the Yavapai of the Fort McDowell Indian community. She has her Ph.D. from the University of Vienna. She has collaborated with John Williams (see below) on a forthcoming book on Yavapai history. Since 1982 she has been a Visiting Professor at the University of Alaska in Fairbanks, where she also works for the Fairbanks Native Association.

Patricia Mariella, a research specialist with the Intertribal Council of Arizona, has worked on several historical and economic research projects with the Fort McDowell Indian community. She has a Ph.D. in social anthropology from Arizona State University.

Grace Jimulla Mitchell (1903–75), Msi Ktnyi·va, was born in Pinyon Heights on the present site of the Yavapai-Prescott Reservation. She was the daughter of Sam and Viola Jimulla, both Yavapai chiefs, eminent leaders of their people, and revered members of the Anglo community as well. Msi Ktnyi·va succeeded her mother as chief in 1965, a position for which she had been given meticulous instruction.

In the decade from 1965 to 1975 Grace Mitchell worked with Alan Shaterian whenever he could come to Arizona. It was her wish that the Yavapai language be taught to the children and that her knowledge of the language and Yavapai institutions be preserved. She lived to see a preliminary version of a Yavapai dictionary (1974) and the publication of the *Yavapai Alphabet Book* (1975), which marked the beginning of Yavapai language instruction on the reservation near Prescott.

Grace Mitchell's devotion to the study of Yavapai was not her only contribution to American Indian linguistics. She aided the study of Yuman languages in general when in 1975, together with her husband Don Mitchell and her sister Lucy Miller, in the company of linguists, ethnographers, and others, she represented her people on the occasion of an historic meeting between two Native American groups which had been separated for over two centuries. Although she was quite ill at the time, she realized the significance of establishing the exact relationship between the Northern Yuman languages (Havasupai, Hualapai, and her own Yavapai) to Paipai, a Yuman language of Baja California. Today, thanks to her willingness to make this journey, the designation Pai Languages has entered the Americanist vocabulary and an important prehistorical connection has been reconstructed.

Violet Mitchell is the granddaughter of Grace Mitchell (see above). She is serving as a research assistant for the Intertribal Council of Arizona in Phoenix. She has a bachelor's degree in social work from Arizona State University.

Pamela Munro. See Mojave section.

Alan Shaterian has his undergraduate degree in Russian and German, and completed his Ph.D. in linguistics at the University of California at Berkeley. He first began work on Yavapai in 1965, when he went to Arizona to do a dialect survey of Yavapai, which at that time had received little attention. By the following year he had chosen the northeastern dialect in Prescott as the focus of his work on Yavapai. Since that first year, Shaterian has made many field trips to Arizona, continuing to learn the language. In the summers of 1975 and 1976 he was asked to give Yavapai language courses at the Yavapai-Prescott reservation. Alan Shaterian has also worked on several other Yuman languages. He himself is trilingual in English, Norwegian and German. He teaches courses in English and German and also serves as the dialect coach for the American Conservatory Theatre.

Effie Starr and Mabel Dogka are cousins, and both are native speakers of Verde Valley Yavapai. Mrs. Starr has made her home among the Prescott Yavapai-Apaches for the past forty years; Mrs. Dogka resides at the Middle Verde Reservation. In telling the story "Coyote Marries His Daughter," Mrs. Starr was aided by her cousin, who commented both on the story line and on the forms of words chosen to construct the text. Both women use their mother tongue almost exclusively when they are together, though Mrs. Dogka probably speaks Yavapai more frequently in the course of her everyday life.

John Williams, born sometime around 1904, was raised by his grandmother, who had lived most of her life before the white men invaded Arizona. He never went to school, and so had a very special education, which resulted in an especially profound knowledge of traditional Yavapai culture. In his later years, he gained much recognition. He won an award from the Indian Historian Press, by whom he was named the Indian Historian of the year. In 1983 the State of Arizona presented him with the Spirit of Arizona award. John Williams also collaborated with Sigrid Khera on a book of Yavapai history. He was one of the original and major opponents to the Orme Dam project at Fort McDowell and was instrumental in helping the Yavapai win their battle against the dam. His home for most of his life was Fort McDowell, where he died in July 1983.

The Yavapai Alphabet

Northeastern Yavapai

Vowels

Northeastern Yavapai has five vowel qualities: a, e, i, o, and u; these show three degrees of length: short, half-long, and long. Half-long vowels are written with a raised dot: a·, e·, i·, o·, u·; long vowels are written with a colon: a:, e:, i:, o:, u:.

Stress

Three degrees of distinctive stress (accent) are written V́, V̀, V for primary, secondary, and weak. Stress is largely, although not entirely, predictable.

Pitch

Vowels occurring with primary stress show two distinctive pitches or tones. The two pitches may be characterized as high and falling and are marked as V̄ and V̂, respectively, when pitch can be distinguished. Because of sentence-stress, rhythm, and tempo found in connected speech or narratives, however, the distinction is usually obscured and therefore rarely marked.

Consonants

c	*càscá·sa*, 'pinyon jay'. As in English ques*ti*on, or Spanish mu*ch*o. Somewhere between English *ch* and *j*.
ch	*'chúra*, 'year'. As in English *ch*in.
hc	*hcá·*, 'Milky Way'. Like *c*, but with a soft, short "h" sound in front of it.
h	*hàmté*, 'squash (n.)'. Much like *h* in English, but a little harsher (a fricative).
hw	*hwát*, 'blood'. As in English *wh*at.
k	*kómvi*, 'ball'. As in s*k*i or Spanish *q*ue.
kh	*'khó*, 'pinenut'. As in English *k*ey.
hk	*hké·*, 'carry across'. Like *k*, but preceded by a short, soft *h* sound.
ky	*kyá·*, 'shoot'. As in English s*k*ewer.
khy	*skhyéva*, 'cross (n.)'. Like English *c*ute.
hky	*shkyá·ti*, 'ax'. Like *ky*, but preceded by a soft, short *h* sound.
kw	*kwáwa*, 'mother's father'. As in English s*qu*id, or Spanish *cu*ervo.
khw	*'khwá*, 'metal; knife'. As in English *qu*id.
l	*léqi*, 'squash (v.)'. As in English si*ll*y, or Spanish *l*atino.
hl	*hlí*, 'milk (v.)'. Like *l*, but voiceless; like an *h* but with the tongue held in *l* position.
ly	*qlyé·*, 'dislike (v.)'. As in English mi*lli*on.
m	*mí*, 'foot'. As in English *m*e, or Spanish *m*esa.
hm	*hmí*, 'tall'. This *m* sound is voiceless; the sound made when air is blown out through the nose lightly.
n	*'ná·la*, 'mesquite tree'. As in English te*n*th, with tongue touching teeth.

hn	*'hná:l*, 'gourd rattle'. The *n* sound is voiceless, the sound made when air is blown out through the nose lightly.
ny	*hànyá*, 'frog'. As in ca*ny*on.
hny	*hnyáqa*, 'beaver'. This *ny* sound is voiceless, the sound made when air is blown out through the nose lightly.
p	*pí*, 'die'. As in English s*p*ot. Somewhere between English *p* and *b*.
ph	*yàphí*, 'chin, jaw'. As in English *p*ot.
hp	*hpú*, 'stagnant, gun'. Like *p*, but preceded by a soft, short *h* sound.
q	*vqí*, 'woman'. Somewhat like English *k*, but said with back of tongue farther back in the throat.
qw	*nqwá*, 'crane'. Like *q*, but with lips rounded. Somewhat like English *kw*, but said with back of tongue farther back in the throat.
r	*rú·yi*, 'hot'. Yavapai *r* is an alveolar tap or trill, like Spanish pe*r*o/pe*rr*o.
hr	*hrú·yi*, 'remove clothing'. Like *r*, but voiceless.
s	*'síti*, 'one'. As in English *s*ink.
sy	*msye·*, 'fear (v.)'. As in English *sh*e.
t	*tá:*, 'grind'. As in English s*t*op (but tongue touches teeth).
th	*'thá*, 'reed, cane'. As in English *t*op (but tongue touches teeth).
ht	*hté'*, 'prickly pear cactus'. Like *t*, but with soft *h* sound preceding.
θ	*θrápi*, 'five'. As in *th*in.
v	*váka*, 'awl'. As in Spanish ca*b*o, *v*aca; a *v* said between the lips.
hv	*néhvi*, 'kill oneself'. Like English *f* except said between the lips.
y	*'yá·s*, 'turkey'. As in *y*es.
w	*h·wá:l*, 'pine'. As in *w*et.
'	*''ó*, 'fire'. Glottal stop. The stop between the two "ohs" in "Oh-oh!"
·	raised dot after a consonant marks syllable breaks where the spelling would otherwise be ambiguous.

Tolkapaya Yavapai

An orthography has been developed for Tolkapaya Yavapai by Pamela Munro and Molly Fasthorse that is slightly different from the one developed for Northeastern Yavapai by Shaterian. Many symbols used for Northeastern Yavapai do not show up in Tolkapaya. Stress is not written in Tolkapaya. Long vowels are represented by double letters (aa, ee, ii, oo, uu) rather than a letter followed by a raised dot or a colon. Only long and short vowels are distinguished, not half-long vowels. The following consonants also differ in the way they are written:

Northeastern	*Tolkapaya*
c	ch
θ	th
sy	sh

Texts

Grace Jimulla Mitchell, Narrator

Transcribed and edited by Alan Shaterian

Sayings, Injunctions, and Fragments of Tales

'Pá:vc hák wák k·wá:wk, yáv 'íkm: Mi·wá·yl mnh·mérvka, wà'sí·va 'hána. Yàpéye· twá·yk yúcah.

Pà·tá·ya mtn·yú·cnyu 'é·vm kvkwí·ka. Nyúv ny·yú·kθò·, píra m'hánk m'á·mcaha. Pa·mttopá·yk m'á·mcka. Vké' wàm'nyácah 'úmaha, 'cmrávaha, mmcá:yaha, mtopé·va mhná:qaha.

Pa·mnh·mé·rvk mspó·vk. Nyma'úmkθò·, vké· 'pá:vc wám 'á·mca 'úmaha. Tú· nyúm 'á·mcaha. Yúm yá mí·ha, "Yá mspó'. Yák 'wányk 'wárkm." M'sítθk tú· nyúk mttyú·paha.

Vké' 'cwàhávcah 'úmcm. Mnh·mé·rvk mspóvka. Nyma'úmkθò·, vké' wám 'á·mcaah 'úmaha. Nyúm 'ám·caha. Yúm yá mí·ha, "Yák 'wányk 'wárkm. Mspó'." M'sítθk mttyú·paha.

'Kwé· mkcí:cvah ma'úmi. Nyú 'kwè·qlyé·vc yúm. Tú· nyúl msqá·mmcaha.

A man was sitting there talking and said this: Be kind in your heart and mind and live a long life.

Mind your old parents and you will be a good person. Help them in whatever they do. Then they will never forget you, when you are sick, hungry, or if you need help.

If you are not a good person, nobody will visit you or think of you. They will just pass by. When they do that you will say, "You know I am here!" But you will just roam around by yourself.

Do not be stingy. Be a good person. If you are not, people will not visit you. They will just wander past. Then you will say, "Realize that I am here!" But you will just be by yourself.

Do not steal. That is not good. People will just push you away.

Ké· pà'tá·yk myú·va ma'úmi. Myútk mnyhmí·vaha. Má·t hi·pú·yvkm, mpápk pà·lá·wl m'á·mcme·.

'Lwì·yúwc, lwì·yúwc nyúk nyúm ny'á·mk ny·yúwkθò·, cá:vm mkmàlmá·lk mk·hké·ka. Mmpára mθú·lva ma'úmaha.

Hi·pác msyáyaha 'úmcm. 'Khó·, yá:mle·, nya'pà:vmí: (nya'pá:vle·). Nyú myúkθò·, pír myàpé·ha. Nymθáv'ìktk mánckm. Nyùvyúk pír wà'sí·cca, 'hánk. Wà'sí·va 'hánm wàmsí·vaha. Msmáca mswálkθò·, pà·c·hwá c·hmnálaha.

'Cúrka mmá:k, yúm yúk nmá:qmi ma'úmi. Ké· pà·c·hwá·vc c·hmnálaha. Cúrka mnmá·qa ma'úmi.

Hmány ksmácò', hmányhmé· ksmácò·. Nùvlwí·θm msmá:.

Mmáni. Nyá·m tkwí·lkm. 'Nyá:hnyc mck·wárkm.

Mhnyó·mi. Hlàyákkm. Mvyá·mi. 'Í: mcmnpévk, m'óyka.

'Khó·, mmánk, mhnyó·mi. Mvyá·mi vtwáym 'ìmk myá·mi. Mwílvk, mvó·ki. Vké' myá·mè·'?

'Khó·, 'hàvcú·la m'nú·km. Vláhmnyc 'hána ''ík.

'Sé:, 'íckm. Cká·va, hmá:rc csí·tvk, 'sé:, 'íckm.

Pà·múlvc hák wátk, 'crávkm. Yútk k·wá:wokm, "Tyác mhwálka ná' mtmárckθò·. Nyà'i·wá·ya cá:vk. Nymákθò·, páya pa·m'é:cnyka. Mθpí:rvaha. Nyùnyú yàpéye· pa·'é:k yúccm."

Do not look upon older people (of the opposite sex). You may find yourself married to one of them. Then (in years to come) carrying around an old person is a shame.

Snake tracks must be rubbed out. If you do this your legs will not be weak.

Do not be afraid of the night. Grandson, come over here. If you come to me, you will be alive. Get up early in the morning, and you will have a good mind. When you sleep too much, the enemy will find you.

Do not eat and pound too many walnuts. The enemy will find you because you are not paying attention, pounding walnuts.

Sleep, little baby. Sleep, little baby boy. You are going to go to sleep.

Get up. It is early in the morning. The sun is laughing at you.

Step lively. It is the new moon. Run. Get some wood and bring it back.

Grandson, get up and exercise. Run, go far. Hurry, come back. Where did you go?

Grandson, I am going to blow all over your body. Then you will be refreshed and healthy.

Buzzard! Indians call their cousins this when they are together. They call each other buzzard.

An important person dwelling there became sick. Then he spoke, "When you bury me, plant corn on my heart. When it is ripe, give some to everyone. It gives you life."

Kó·lá, kúrm 'yá:mkm, vtwá·y 'ìm 'yá:mk. 'Hàktlákva 'há:mkm. Vyé:kk wícm. Nyúv 'ík hanyó·mk 'ínyka, máta 'há:mkm. 'Màt·θí:wa 'há:mkm, 'ík. 'Wì·kcása 'há:mkm, 'ík. 'Wì·k'nyáca 'há:mkm, 'ík. 'Wì·kvté·wa 'há:mkm, 'ík. K·hàvsúa Yó:có· K·hlé·va 'há:mkm, 'ík. H·wà·lkyány·yánya 'há:mkm 'ík. 'Nyá:vm, màtk'á·mvc nyúv yúca mólckm. ◇

Grandma, I went for a long time and a long distance. I saw Toozigoot. I go farther every day. When I do this I will see the land. I saw Camp Verde. I saw Four Peaks. I saw Black Mountain. I saw Granite Mountain. I saw Turquoise Mine. I saw Mingus Mountain. Today they have the same names. ◇

Place names mentioned above

'Hàktlákva, 'crooked water'. Tuzigoot is an English spelling of an Apache word also meaning 'crooked water.'

'Màt·θí:wa, 'salt land'.

'Wì·kcása, 'smooth cliffs'.

'Wì·k'nyáca, 'black mountain,' as in the English name.

'Wì·kvté·wa, 'great mountain'.

K·hàvsúa Yó:cò· K·hlé·va, 'the cliff where one gets turquoise'.

H·wà·lkyány·yánya, 'pine on top of the flat'.

Contest with the Wind

'Rá:yk, ttkwílvk, tkávkm. Pà·lá·wk nyhák yúckny. Skàrk'á·mca nyhák pá·yé·vk. Kwè·nypáya wí·nyk wárkm. Va'wí·rvkm, pàkwírvm, kwè·kyácck, vyá·mk, vyá·mk, vrí·t 'ìmck, ckwí·θk. Tú· kwè·-nypáya pa·hpínkm.

Màt·háyc nyhák vskwí:tk, 'ík, "'Sítθi pí·cvk wárkm: nyhá' má:m 'h·wákk yú·ca ''íkm. Q·wá:wca ''hrúyk wínyk. ''Ú·ca 'nú·km, kàvyú·cc 'kyú·lràvk. Ny·yú·k·hò·, nyúc pa·tkwí·lah hí·km."

Màt·háyc nywí· q·wáwa hrúyk, wím. Mákl vhrúyvi 'ímk. Yá:mk 'kúrm hovó·mk, yúnyk. Nyhák mákl vó·kik, q·wáwa mákl nyvál . . . nyhál tpé·vi, 'íkik. Skàrk'á·mcc q·wáwa hrúynyik wárk. Yá:mk,

There was a game. They played all kinds of games. Many people were there. Skàrk'á·mca was with them. He took part in every game: bow and arrow, shooting, running, jumping, and wrestling. He won every game.

Màt·háya (the wind) was standing there and said, "There is one more game to be played with me. We undo our hair and see whose is the longer. That person will win."

Màt·háya undid his hair first. The hair rolled backward, down so far, and then rolled back to the back of his head, in place again. Skark'a·mca undid his hair, too; and it rolled a long distance, a long way

kúrm yá:mk, Màt·háya, nyhá' q·wáwa hovó·mò·. Nyhá tkwí:lmk nyú:km yá:mk. Nyhák mákl vó·kik, yúnyk. Nyvlwí·nyk wárk, mák·ha q·wáwk 'tpé·vi, yúk yúnyk.

Nyhá' nyá:kwàhm páya 'íck 'ínyk, "Nyúc 'sítθk, qyátk hi·vó·km!" 'íck. ◇

past the place where Màt·háya's hair had reached. So his hair was longer. Then it rolled back to the back of his head in place.

That day all the people said, "He is the champion of them all." ◇

How to Weave a Basket

K'ú· 'pú·vahk 'nú·km. Pm'á 'yá:k, cpák wínyka kwí:rka, kcθpá:lk wínyka. 'Trú·va. Nyrú·vkθò·, 't'ólahk 'nú·km. T'ólk wítm nyuvlwí·kθò·, 'o'álk. 'Skwá:nahk 'nú·km. 'Skwá:nk, 'trú·vim. Nyrú·vkθò·, 'c'pák wíik 'nú·km. Nyhám 'háθk wínyka. 'Pú·vah 'nú·ha, 'ccvlwí:k cckwácahk 'nú·km.

Hlá:ka 'yá·ik 'nú·km. Hlá:ka yó:k, kyú·lk, 'nyá:k, 'hánk yúca yó:k. 'c'páhk 'nú·km. 'Kácok ccvlwí:k wínyk. 'Kcrkó·k wínyka. K'ú· 'pú·vahk 'nú·km.

Cmí·i 'yáhk 'nú·km. 'Há· 'yá·k, 'vhú· yá·k, pm'á yá·ik 'nú·km. 'kmí:k wínyka. 'Háθk wínyk, 'kcθpá:lahk 'nú·k. Yúok, k'ú· 'pú·vah 'nú·km.

Hlá:ka 'yó·k. Nyhám 'pú·vah 'pú·kahk 'nú·km. Púkahl 'cyúwk. Nyθác θpí:rvk, hi·kwíθk. Yúm vté:mk tltllá 'ìk. Cá:vk kmsávm 'pú·vik wínyk. Cmí·im hál 'tθcú·rk wínyk. Wík 'pú·vahk 'nú·km.

'Wík 'tnyú·rk wínyk. Wík ny'wí:rkθò·, kv'ómahk nyhám, hlá:ka 'pú·vk wínyk, 'cká:mka. Wík ny'tká:vkθò·, nyhám nyuvlwí·θah 'nú·km. Hlá:k·hc θpí:rvk. Nyhác hi·kwí·θahk nú·km. ◇

I'm going to weave a basket. I'll gather mulberry shoots, split them and roll them, and then tie them together. Then I'll dry them. When they're dried, I'll boil them. I'll boil them until they're ready. Then I take them out. I'll peel them. I peel them and dry them, too. When they're dried, I'll split them, too. Then I'll scrape it. I'll arrange them to size so that they are ready for weaving.

I'll gather devil's claws, too. I'll get devil's claws which are long, black, and good. When they're ready in small bunches, I'll tie them in small bundles. Then I'll weave a basket.

I'll gather long shoots, gather cottonwood and willow. I'll gather mulberry, too. I'll bring them home. Then I'll scrape them. Then I'll tie them in bunches. After doing this, I'll weave a basket.

I'll get devil's claws. With them I'll weave at the base. They will come up from the base. Devil's claws strengthen and hold it fast as it spreads out. On top I'll weave with white ones, too. I stick the long shoots in it. Then I weave.

Then I put in designs. When I have finished this, I weave the edge with the devil's claws as the last thing. When I have reached the point where I began, I will have finished. Devil's claw is strong; it will hold fast. ◇

From the Story of Quail

Wì·kvtè·púkahk, nyhák 'pá:vc nywé·vkm. Vqí wí:vck. Bcèqécc yú:yik. Pà·kθára pa·nywé:vk, hák wák. Yú·tm vqìwí:θàc pík. Pà·kθára pa·ttopá·yk. 'Cnwí:rk, 'wá:h hi·hánk, pa·vwé·wok, hák wányik. Ctáθàc yá:mk, kwè·nyé·k yá:mk, kwè·máca hí:, nyé·k yá:mk. Tú· vyé·k kwícahm nywík. Kwè·máva kmí:k, wím wíck. Pà·kθarc 'wá·h tú· wányk. Nyhák kwè·máva kmí:θà' hi·hánk ccvlwí:k. Tt'ó·lk kàvwík, hák wányk.

Nywí:itm, vqìhmányahc hi·pé:k hák wák, 'ú·tm. Hló qwáqk ho·nú·tmè·, sálm hwátt pám. Yútm vh-wítv'ìwk. Vqìhmányθà mθíla máqv'ìwk. "Kúra mkcahtú·vk myú·km. 'Ú, hwátc nyú mpáckm," ík. 'Ím vqìhmányθàc 'ík, "Má:c nyhwátm máqma, kàvyúk nyúv yúha." Kθárθàc c·h'wírk, 'ínyka, "Mkcahtú·vk myú·k ''í·ma. Vyá kwè·máva vké· mθó: kàmwínya ma'úmah mnú·ma. Hopàcsmá:ràvk 'núkm, ma'úmmè·. Nyhám hopáck smá:ha, nyθám, 'hàmθpú·yk, mtθámvk wínyk. Nyhám píra nyvá kwè·θó· mmányah 'núkm. 'Há mθí: mí:kθò·, 'thá:vm 'há mθí:. 'Há:nc myák myá:nyk, púknyùl púlmkθò., myàvnymí·vk pá·hma mí·vc myúcm mlwíha," ík. Yúm c·h'wírm ny'é·vk, vqìhmányθàc hi·wá·yl tú· mòlèvyí·k, hák wák. Pa·yé:vk hák wák.

Hák wátk, hopàcnysmá:m nyhám nùvyúk, "hàθpú·yk, tθámvk yúnyk, nyhák, pa·yé:vk wányk. Yútk wàsí:vk, hák wátk, "Nyúl 'yá·mah 'yí·km. Ké' 'hánaha mú·km." Yí·k yúnyk. Kθàrnyháta, 'Sàv-kctú·lva mólk, nyθá vk·wá·wk, "Nyúl 'yá:mah 'nú·km. Nyùvyú yí·t, má:c tú· vák pa·myé·vi, nyvák mwányi. 'Nyá' ctányu mvwé·. Má:c h·wákk kàmyúk nyvák myú·. Nyác píra 'yá·maha núkm."

Nywá:cθà nmákk. Vó:k vám 'á·mk. Hù·váka knyàk·hké·va nyvám, kckmí:hm nyvámka. Nyhák

At the foot of Granite Mountain lived a person with his wife and small daughter. Then his wife died. Coyote helped them with housework and cooked for them. Father goes out every day for food. He brings the food home. Coyote stays home and prepares the food that is brought home. He boils it and stays there.

He was again preparing food, and the girl was nearby watching him. He cut the rabbit open, and blood was on his hand. He shook his hand, and the blood splattered between her legs. "You have already menstruated (this is the menarche), and there is blood on you." The young girl says, "You are the one who splashed the blood on me, and it is not what you say." Coyote insisted and said, "You have your menarche, and you cannot eat meat for four days and nights. After the four days and nights, bathe and cleanse yourself. Then you will eat meat. When you drink water, use a straw so that the water will not wet the corners of your mouth. Otherwise hair will grow there just like on a man." He insisted that this had happened to her. She could not protest and felt very sad and stayed with them for a long time.

After the four days and nights, she took her bath, ate her meat, and stayed there with them. Then she began to think, "I will go away. It is not right." Her dog's name was White Rolypoly. She talked to him and said, "I will go away. You stay here with them. Stay with my father and look after him. I will go alone."

She left their home and traveled until she came to Mosquito Ford. She was thirsty and stopped there to drink water. She was drinking water. Then she

yàkrú·vm pík. 'Há θí:k. 'Há θí:k hák. Yútm 'é: vtm kθárc 'há' cqwálk ho·nú·kk. Yútk wàvsívk, "Nyá nyhát·hc 'í· yí·k." Yá:mk 'ú·tm. Sàvkctú·lvθàc yú·k. "'A'ú:mk. Má:c tú· 'wá· myákk. Nyhá, nyá' ctáha mvwé·. Nyhá má:c h·wákk m'á·mci, ''ík ''yú. Kàmyúmràvk mc·h'wírk vá myúwè·? Yú:va mvómah myí·km. Yí·t 'hán twànypú·vo 'núkm. 'Ì·cé·qa θéql, 'há ttmná:rm. Yàkrú·vm nympíkθò·, nyú 'sítm mhrú·yk, mθí: mwíci. Yúk yúnyk." Nyθák tvyó:k.

Yúha nyθá vqìhmányθàc kyú·ck yá:mk. Màtq'-qwárm yá:mk. Wì·k'ámvha hák ckpámk. Nyhá mákk. Nálmik yá:mk. Nyθá, mát, Wì·pùk'pá:vc nyθál ckà·mm hál vá:mk. Nyhá vá:mtm, hèvtqípny vá·t. Yútm nyhák, qmwí·rmc hák wám. Nyhá vá:mk. Yútm 'ík 'ínyka, "Mwílvi, vyál vyúrmiki. Pà·hmí·nyc vám, vám yúcnyθk, qlyépi cqyátkm. M'ú·kθò·, tú· wàmyá:caha," 'íkny. Yúm vqìhmány-θàc 'wá:l vyúri 'ìmk. Yúnyka 'wák tvkói nyhá vs'ámk. Tvkó·k wínyk.

Wí·ha, nyhá vhi·pá ny'ìmm. Pà·kθárθàc vá·ik yúnyk, "Vyák 'pá:vc—vqìhmányc—vyák 'á·mck. Yúm ''ú·km. Vké kàmwí'? Vké vyá·vk kàmwík mt·hó·tè·'? Yú yí·t 'wá:lk mì'síh 'núkm," ík ínyk. Q'qwári v'ál 'ìmk. Nyθé wá:lk, mì'sík yúθm. Yúwc vké· kwáck yá·mah 'úmk nyθá'. 'Wá: píra tká:vkm ny'ú·k. Hál vo·ki, 'ík. Vó·kik yúnyk yú·ha. Nyhá Pà·nykθárc 'ìk 'ínyk. Qmwí·rmθà vk·wá·wk, "'Npí·, nyác 'lwé· ''í· 'í·θmè·. Kàvyú myúk mt·hó·tè·, mt·hó·twè·'?" 'ík 'ík. ◇

heard a dog lapping water. Then she thought, "It must be my dog." She went to see it, and it was White Rolypoly. "I said, 'No, you stay and take care of my father and stay with him.' But you are stubborn. Will you go back? I will prepare water for you. I will put water in grape leaves and tie them up. Take off one and drink the water each time." And then they separated.

The young girl continued her journey. She went to the prairie, then climbed the mountain, and went down. Then she went to the valley and found the Verde Valley Yavapai. At dusk she got to where an old woman lived. The old woman said, "Hurry and get inside. There are men here, but they are no good. If they see you, they will attack you." The young girl went inside. Then she closed the curtain of the door.

That evening Coyote came and said, "I see the young girl's tracks outside. What did you do with her? I will look again for her tracks outside." Then he went outside. He found the tracks. They did not lead anywhere but around the house. He came inside again. Coyote said, "My Auntie, I want to marry her. Why do you hide her from me?" ◇

Eagle

Hmànyhmé·θàc, pà·vtá·ya 'ímk, pà·kyú·lkm. Kó·l·θàc'è· wí·wok. Kwè·'ó·ni yó:vok. Kwè·qwárk h·wáva káca 'ó·nhí· yó:vokm. 'Pàkwírva yó:vok wárk wí·wok. 'Kwè·'cpá·ya né·hhí· wí·wok. Yó:vk wárkm. Yúk nyhá' hi·kó·k nyhé· 'á:mck, 'kwè·nyé·tk, 'ú·k, 'kwè·'cpá·yθàwc yúci yí·θè· ccí·vm h·wákk. Ccí·vk yúom ny'úk, wà'sí:vk. Yútk vó·kk nyvá:k, Kó·l·θà cckwí·k 'ínyk, "Nyà'cí·tahc-pè·?" 'íkyu.

Yútm Kó·l·θàc kná:vok, "Mcí·taθàc, kwè·yác yá:k, Wí·pù·ke· 'á:mctm, 'sá:vc né·hkm." Yúm hmá-nyθàc 'kwè·nyé·k nyhé ny'á:mcka, wà·'sí:vka, "'Sá:ha 'né·hah nú·km. Nywítk páya pà·nykmwá·-cah, 'ík yú·k 'í," wà·sí:vi.

Yú·k Kó·la kwá·θàc vá:tk, kná:vok 'ínyk, "'Sá:ha né·hk wàl'í:km. Mí:vk kè· pà·né·hi 'úmaha, ''í·ka." Yúm Kó·l·θàc topé·k 'ínyk, "'É', nymwí· yú·ha. Qwákt·hmàva nyhé' yákaha mné·hk, mnú·na myó·k. Mwínyka, hwáta hál, hwáta myó·ik, nyhál mkcθpá:lk, myú·rka. Nyhé Wí·pù·ke· m'á·mcny, nyhák mccí·θà né·hkny. Nyhé m'á·mci," 'ík kná:vok. Yúm nywík wínyk.

Kó·l·θàc 'ík 'ínyka, "Mvá:mka pà·nykotú·. 'Mto-pé·nye!' mím. Nyhác mát m·hwá·lm, hál myá:mmò·, mí:ha," 'ík. "Pà·nywé: mvá:mkm. 'Mtopé·!' mí·m. Nyhác yá:mk yúnyk. Qwákt·hmáva k·yákaha nyhá . . . há vá:mk yúnyk. Nyhác hi·wá·ya 'ú:k. Nyhá nymí·ya nyhám mscó·wok, nyhám khwá·vm mvqámò·, mí·ha. nyhák ccvwí·yò·."

Yúm nyhá·k pà·nykotú·θàc, "'É'," 'ík 'ínyk. Yúm nyhá nywí·k hwálok, màt·hwálok. Yúm nyhál yú·rmk 'ínyk, yá:mk. 'Khwá-wì·'qsá·h, 'khwá yó:va, nyhá hi·kó·k 'ínyk. Hál yá:mk yúnyk. Yá·l hál nyvá:mk, nyhá 'kwè·hi·kó·θàc nyháq, hi·wá·ym vqám. Yúm nyhák qwákt·hmàvc nyhák vqvó· 'ík

The Boy had grown to be tall. Grandmother showed him how to make things. She made a trap for him to trap little animals around there. She also made arrows for him. She showed him how to kill animals. She did this for him, too. And he carried that (the bow and arrow) there wandering around, hunting. He saw that young animals are together with a mother. Having seen the mother there, he thought about this. And after he had returned home, he asked Grandmother, "What about my mother?"

Then Grandmother told him, "Your mother was gathering seeds, wandering around at the foot of Granite Mountain (?). An eagle killed her." When the Boy was out hunting, having wandered out there, he thought, "I'm going to kill that eagle. In time it will just kill all of us."

Grandmother was coming, and he said to her, "I want to kill that eagle. I don't want it to kill again." Then Grandmother, helping, said, "All right, do it. It will be so. Kill the bull lying there and take his stomach. Get the blood that is in there, too. Tie the blood up in there and get in it yourself. Go to the foot of the mountain, there where it killed your mother. Go there." She told him this, and he did it.

Then Grandmother said, "Go to Gopher. Say 'Help me!' to him. He will dig in the earth for you where you have to go. Then go to Mouse. Say 'Help me!' to him, too. He will go there to where the bull is lying. He'll see the heart. He'll scrape the fur away from where you'll stab him. He'll have it ready for you."

And so Gopher said, "Yes." He dug under the

yúnyk. Mátva tú· sqná·nka nyhák hunú·tk. Tú· nyhák v'ó·mk. Nyhák pík, yákk. Yúm nyhák c'á·lkk yúnyk, nyhá qwáktθàk yó:vok. Nyhá mnú·na ho'álk, hwáta yó·ik, nyhál kcθpá:lk. Wík wínyk. Yú·rk yúnyk, yá:mk.

Nyhá màt·hwáca kwá·θà yá:mk yúnyk. Nyhák svó·vk, hák yútm. 'Sá·θàc vá:k yúnyk, nyhák któ:hi, mátk wílm. Nyhák vyák. 'Ítm píkyù yí·k yúnyk. Nyhák vkvná·wk. Wí· myá·h wá·mk, nywá· wá·mk. Nywá: wá·mk wínyk, nyhá 'sáθà·wk, nyhál yúm, nyhál wílmk. "'Wá, mθó·ci!" 'ík. Wík wínyk, 'kwál pú·pú·'iim. Yúk nyhá nmákk, c'álmk, 'cnyé·ìk yá·mk wárkm.

'Sáθà:waθàc, "Hmá, 'θó·ca!" 'ík. Vhíny'ìkk myúcθk, msyá·yk. Nyhá pà·hák·k·yákah vlí·wk myú·cm, msyá·yk mákl vlwé·vi, 'ícm yúck. Vhínyi 'íck wárkm. Vc·húym 'ícm. Nyhá msyá·yk mákl vwé·vi, 'ícm yúck. Tú· hák wà·yó·k. Yútm ccí·cθàc vá:k 'ínyk, "Kàvyú vyám 'kwè·mθó·ca, nyà'kmí·wa mθó·cah ma'úmk? Tú· vák 'wàmyó·," 'ík. "'Msyá·ykm. Káv 'ík 'ímò," 'ím 'ícme·. 'Ím hák yá:mk yúnyk, ccí·cθàc nywí·ik wárk, któ·h wím tkwál 'hwátc kwál pú·pú·'ìim wárm. "'Wá, mθó·ci!" 'ík yúnyk. 'Cnyé· vró·p'ik wárk.

Hmànyhmé·θàc nyhám-pè· vrá:rk yúnyk. Nyθák nyvrá·rmk yúnyk, nyhá csà'θá·wa pà·cckwí·k, "Mccí·θàc vó·kk, káv k·yúcm yú·rkm myúce, káv k·yúck wá myúci?" 'Ím kná:vcm. Nyθák 'sàθá·wθa pà·kmwá·ck, k'í:la pà·tlú·mk. Yúk vsvó:k, nyhák wátm nyhák kθá:wθàc vá:m. Nyhák nywí·ik wárk yúnyk. Nyhák né·hk, nyhál màtk'í:la wílmik.

Yúk 'ínyk yútk 'ú:tm, vké· káv k·yúcm nálah 'úmah má·tk. Yúm nyhák tú· vnyá:nyk nyhák wárk. 'Màtpá·ya 'há:mk. Pà·kàvyúcc ké· 'á:mcm há:mk. "Mtopé·ci!" 'íh 'ík yúθm. 'Úmk tú· k·yó:vk. Nyhák wátm màrmárm há:mè·, màtpúkahl há:mè·tm

earth. Then the Boy went in, carrying an agate knife, which he had made. After he had gotten in there underneath, he stabbed the bull with the knife he had been carrying. The bull growled and was ploughing up the ground. Then he came to his end. He died and lay there. Then the Boy came out and butchered the bull. He took out the stomach, the blood, too, which he tied up in the stomach. Then he stepped into it and went on.

He went to a hillock. There he waited. The eagle came, kicked him, and threw him to the ground. He lay there. The eagle thought he was dead. She picked him up and carried him to a high mountain, to her lair. When she got there, she threw him down in front of the eaglets and said, "All right now, eat!" She kicked him, and blood spurted out. Then she left, going out to hunt again.

The eaglets said, "Okay, let's eat!" But the Boy moved and kept moving, and they were afraid. The person lying there was twitching. The eaglets moved away. He kept making a short whistle. They just sat there, afraid. Then the eagle arrived. "Why haven't you eaten the food I brought you? You're just sitting there." They answered, "We're afraid. He keeps saying something." Then the mother went and did the same thing again: she kicked him, and the blood spurted out again. "All right now, eat!" she said. Then she went down again to hunt.

Then the Boy, for his part, got up from there and asked the baby birds, "When your mother comes, which way does she come into the lair?" They told him. He killed the eaglets and threw them down the cliff. Then he sat there waiting until their mother came. He did the same thing: he killed her and threw her down the cliff.

nyhál, Qampànyqaqmwí·rmc 'á:mcc, kwè·yác nywé· hál 'á:mcm, há:mk. Yúk nyhé· vcá:r 'ìmk, "'Nkhó:, myúwke!" 'ím. Nyhé· vcá:r'ìk 'ínyk, "'É', 'yá:ma, 'yá:mk. 'Ny·yúmah nú·km," 'ík. Ckpákkny.

Ckpákk yúnyk, yútk vá: yúnyk. "'Khó·θò·va, nyvál kwè·qlyé· msyé·va qyáta wàyá·wa nyvál wàyó·km. Kwé·θ ká mík nyvál myú·?" 'Ím 'ík. 'Ím kná:vok 'ínyk. Kwè·mákl kyúw 'páya kná:vok, 'ínyk 'ím. "'É', 'Khó·, 'nytopé·h 'nú·km. Yú·va qθák 'yúskva, nyvá mq·wáwa 'sítm, mscó·k wínyk. M'é:, mkθpá:lk, 'yúskk 'ínyk. Yúm nyvál mwám 'tná·lma, 'í·km," 'ík. "'Tná·lma 'í·tvk, ké myú, myúnye ntó· ké· ké hàlmtí·sa ma'úmka. Myúnye tú· ms'ámka, yúk kwé· h·wàyá·tvca'ì." 'Ím "'É'," 'íkk. "'É'," 'ítk.

Màttú:vk nyvó:mcka, tú· twá·yràvm pé·mk hokwák, ny'é·vk, Nyhá yú·θa vkwá:k, v'íwk, súrk yúnyk. Yútm nyhá qθáq k·yúskθàc vkyátvk. Yúm páya nyhák, nyhál páya v'úw'ìmk. 'Màtpúkmàk, nyhák 'vqót 'ímcm. Qapànyqaqmwí·rmθàc nyhák páya mqwánk, nyhák yó·k 'ík. Yúm Qapànyqaqmwí·rmc 'ík, "'Khó·, nyvá vyúca yúk. 'Íh, nyùvyú ma'úmi. ''Íkyu 'sí:tkm c·h'wírk myúm-pè·, vák tú· vám v'ómk, vák 'yó·k 'yú," 'íkyù.

Yúm Hmànyhmé·θàc 'ík, "'Nkó·, vké· nymí· ma'úmi. Nyác ny'hánah 'nú·km," 'ík yúnyk. Má:t·h·c cyá:k káca nyθám k·yákha yó:k. Mà:tθpíla nyhá cmàrmá·rk wínyk. Nyθá cyá:ka tθcú:rk wínyk. Wík wínyk. "M'ú·, Nkó·! Yáv wík ny'hánahk ''íma. Mvrá·re!" 'ím. Vrá·rk. Nyhák yúci. 'Ícm. ◇

Then he saw that there seemed to be no way to go down. He just sat down there. He looked over all the land. He looked around to see if there was somebody to whom he could say, "Help!" There was no one. After sitting there awhile, he looked again and saw Old Lady Bat, who was wandering at the foot of the mountain. He called to her, "Grandmother, come here!" She said, "All right, I'll come. I'm coming. I'm going to get you (down)." She climbed up.

She climbed up and got there. "Grandson, here there are many dangerous things dwelling here. Why are you here?" And he told her everything from the beginning. "All right," she said. "I'm going to help you. I'll carry you in the basket on my back. Give me one of your hairs. I'll tie it to the basket, and I'll carry you on my back. I'll get you down. I'll take you down, but don't open your eyes. Just shut your eyes, or we will get hurt." "All right," he said. "All right."

When they had gotten halfway down, he felt it had been a long time. He opened his eyes and looked around. And then the basket broke away. And everything down there made a great crashing noise. Down toward the bottom they hit the ground. Old Lady Bat was in pieces, lying down there. The Old Lady Bat said, "Grandson, we are in a bad state. That's why I said, 'Don't (open your eyes).' And then you had to insist on doing it. Here I am. This is the end of me."

Then the Boy said, "Grandmother, don't cry. I'm going to make you better." He took the small bones and pieces of skin lying there. He rubbed the skin. Then he put the bones through it. "Look, Grandmother. This is the way I said I was going to make you better." She stood up. And there they were, it has been told. ◇

Coyote Marries His Daughter

Effie Starr and Mabel Dogka, Narrators

Transcribed by Martha B. Kendall

Tolkapayk kθaraqwarac nyuwe:km
Vqi wi:yc hma:nya la:wm wi:y
Hma:nya khwa:kaha vca:yc yucm 'sitθk pe: hme:ye: tuwik pe: tu qac 'rava
Kθaraqwarac 'ic'ravk 'ic'ravk yunyek nyihak ya:km hla la:wm
'Pa:cc yuok kθaraqwarah 'u:cm
Tu vqeya:ph 'imi
Kθaraqwaraθac 'ik 'pih 'nukm
Ny'pikm minyek 'i'i: hak mpa:k mwinyeka vtwa:yh mimk mwi:ck mwi:me:
'Nya:'pikθo nyiha ca:k mwi:cm mwici
Nyul we mya:mck mwinyek mvo:ck 'o'o:ha mtkwatci yit ke nyivak myuch m'umi
'O'o:ha mtkwatckθo tu mwivk mvo:ch m'i 'wa: mvo:ch m'i
'Pa'vce 'nya:vrop'iwo yuok va:h nuk va:k 'nya: 'vca:yanyu lwe:h 'ika
'Kwal hwa:km qmwirma wi:ynyu 'e:h nukm
'Nya:c 'pikθo pa'hmi pa:mtopek hma:nyavh pa:mwe:yh nukm
Maramaram ny'im kθaraqwarac pioh 'i:vii

Coyote lived in the south.
His wife had many children.
Two of the children were daughters, one was a son, and the others were all very little ones.
Coyote was sick, very sick, and he lay there many months.
People watched him.
He just kept getting worse.
Coyote said, "I'm going to die.
When I'm dead, you come and put wood there and set a fire.
When I'm dead, put me on top of it.
Go away when you've set fire to the wood.

When you set the fire, go away, go home.

A man will come from the west to marry my daughters.
He will give two skins to my old woman.
When I die, this man will help you; he'll help care for those children for you."
After awhile Coyote pretended to die.

Yum 'o'o: 'kwe:θac cckwa:ck ckwa θa ca:k nyihak
'Kwal hwa:km nyiθa ma:ta pirckm
Pa'hmi 'sitk nyiθak yuk yunyek nyiθak yum
Tuwik vo:cmi
Viya pa'hmi 'sitk hak yutk nyiθak ya:mnye:k wari
Kθaraqwaraθac hamtm pa pe:mi pa pe:mi nyiham vqotk 'imk
'Kwal hwa:km hikok nyul 'kwe: nya:vrop'iwo ya:mm
'Cura 'sitm vo:kk va:k paca:θa va:k yuok
Qmwirma wi:yθa hma:nyaθa wi:θa pa:'u:k tu 'pa hkayc yuoh 'i:vi
Yum ke spo:cnyeh 'umk wari
Tu pima yicm
Pa:kna:vk 'inyek vca:ya 'sitm 'lwe:h 'nukm

'Ik 'inyek vqeha cici:ha 'kwe: 'kwal hwa:km 'e:kny
Θawa kpaya lwe:kny
'Cura 'sitm kθaraqwaraθac vce nywi:ym hwa:km θak payi
Maramara ny'imm kθaraqwaraθac pahmilam hwa:kk 'pe:mi ne:hh 'ika
Pahmila yem hme:vc yum
Kθaraqwaraθac miltah ne:hk yum milta 'sitk vkak hwilk yunyek 'wi: yal yurk 'im

Kθaraqwara khma:nyac 'wi: yal vyurnym kθaraqwaraθac pe: 'wi: ca:k ya:kk ckwark kwa:wm
Kθaraqwara khma:nyac 'mihyava kθaraqwara yu: vhamh 'itm kwa:wk yunyek ckwark
Yum khma:nyac 'kwe: yo:va 'kyula qyatm kwerikweri 'u:k 'ik 'inyek
'Nya: 'θalac yuh ma:tkm
Nyuc hwilk hwilk 'inyek 'ik ma:c yem mvceha mlwe:km
Kθaraqwaraθac v'ork 'inyek tkwi:vk 'i:k 'inyek 'kwe:

Then they put him on top of the firewood there.
They wrapped his body in two skins.
One man stayed there, stayed there.
The others walked away.
That man who was there left too.
When Coyote looked around, they were all gone, all gone from there, so he got down.
He took the two skins and went off to the west.
After a year, he came back to his family.
He saw his old woman and his children, but he pretended to be a stranger.
They didn't know him.
They thought he was dead.
He told them, "I'm going to marry one of those daughters."
Saying that, he gave the two skins to the mother.
He married the elder daughter.
A year went by and Coyote lived there together with his daughter.
After awhile, Coyote and his brother-in-law went out to hunt.
His brother-in-law was his son.
Coyote killed a ground squirrel, and another ground squirrel ran out of somewhere and got under a rock.
While Coyote's Child got under the rock, Coyote lay on top of it, laughing and talking.

Coyote's Child got to looking up at Coyote's face while he was talking and laughing.
Then Coyote's Child saw a very long tooth on one side (of his mouth), and he thought,
"He could be my father."
He ran away crying, "You married your own daughter!"
Coyote jumped down and gave chase saying,

kav yum pe: 'pahmila 'ik 'inyeka yem 'vceha 'lwe:km 'ikm
'Kuraθa ma: mθala pik 'ickm
''e:vkm
Yutk kavmyuk pe: vce lwe: kavm'i

Ke 'nya:'vce 'umc yum
Ke ma: 'nya: 'hme: 'wi:yha 'umk wark 'ikm
Nyiva kθaraqwara khma:nyac vo:mk yunyek cici:ha kna:vk nyiva pa'hmivc 'nya: 'θalac yum
Yo:vc 'kyula ''u:km
Maramaram kθaraqwaraθac vo:kk va:k 'wa:k va:kk
Ke kwe:θa 'ih 'umi
Qmwirmaθa θawaθac kna:vk pa'hmiθa ma: mθalac yum
Ma: mhwaki nyuc yo:v 'kyulam 'u:k 'ikm
Yuha mre:yk mwinyeka mwim
Ckwarme: yo:v m'u:h mnukm
Mθalaθac smalka maka nya: klapak yum
Nyiθa m'u:
Θawaθac pa'hmi wi:yθa temckwartm yo:va 'u:k
Yum qowawa cθultk nya: klapak smalka maka 'u:k

Cici:θa knavk 'nya: 'θalac yuokm
'Ne:hca 'ikm
Yum qmwirmaθac θawam hwa:kk kθaraqwaraθa ne:hckny◇

"What's this?, my brother-in-law, you're saying that I married my own daughter?
They say that your father died a long time ago.
That's what I hear.
So what do you mean he (your father) married his daughter?
She's not my daughter.
And as for you, you're not my son either."
Hearing that, Coyote's Child ran and told his mother "That man is my father.
I saw his long tooth."
After awhile, Coyote came back.
He didn't mention anything.
His old woman told her daughter, "That man is your father.
Your brother said he saw his long tooth.
So, you play with him.
When he laughs, you'll see his tooth.
Your father had a black spot behind his ear.
You look for that."
The daughter made him laugh and saw his tooth.
Then she washed his hair and saw the black spot behind his ear.
She told her mother, "It's my father all right!
Let's kill him."
Then the old woman and her child killed Coyote.◇

The Great Wrestling Match

Molly Fasthorse, Narrator

Transcribed by Pamela Munro

'Kurtha 'chpayche lawk vam hwaavm yuchtme,
tkavk 'ichka, "Pathpirvkyuchche
pathpirvqyatkyuchche 'yoochme
pachkwiithvh yiikyum," 'ichk'm.
Twik 'ichka, "Panykpitvche pathpirvqyatkyum.
Nythache kavyuchme hwakk pachkviithv yimo,"
'ichk'm.
'Sitek 'ichka, "Panyktharche pathpirvnyqyatchyum.
Pavyamchyum.
Nythache hwakka chkwithvchh yimo," 'ichk'm.
Yuchka chkwithk vak unu Panykpitvch Panyktharm
hwakka pachkwiithvk.
Panyktharche qyatka hak unuk: Panykpitva maka
kvwekvk yuthk vwari.
Vwarme, Panyktharche mank yunyk miiva matraka,
nyhak vyak 'imtme vlwithkyum.

"Panykpitvche patkwilkwiwkwum," 'ichi.
"Panyktharche Panykthara payevhche mshayvk,"
'ichk'm, "mshayvk.
'Nyachchpe 'kwe nya'kavcha paya 'yoochhk
'unuk'yum."

Long ago, when all the animals used to roam
around, they gathered together and said,
"We will get a strong person, a very strong
person, who will wrestle."
Some said, "Turtle is very strong.
He will get someone to wrestle with him," they said.

The others said, "Coyote is a very strong one too.
He's a runner.
He may wrestle," they said.
Now the fight was on, Turtle wrestling with Coyote.

Coyote was trying with all his might: he tried to turn
Turtle on his back.
After trying that, Coyote fell down and dragged his
feet on the ground, and when he lay down
that showed [that he had lost].
"Turtle has won," they said.
"Coyote and those on Coyote's side are angry," they
said, "they are angry.
Those of us [who bet on Turtle] are going to get the
full amount of our bet."

Panyktharvch 'ichka, "Kavyuka 'nyachche 'kwe kavchk 'wark'yuny.
Pamikavyukupe 'kwe nya'kava 'yoochha 'umha?" 'ik.
Nytha chawvk hak unutka, tu paya 'kurm yamchka tswakvk 'kurm yamchka.
Nyuvyumnya'hanme 'chpayche nythampe tnwahvka 'hanchha 'umkyum.
Tu mshayvi. ◇

[The supporters of] Coyote said, "Well, we bet something too.
Why on earth don't we get what we bet?"

Then they got in a fight, and then all of them went off and scattered.
That's why the animals haven't been good friends since then.
They are just hostile. ◇

The White People Meet the Yavapai

John Williams, Narrator

Transcribed by Sigrid Khera

Over there in that cave on the Salt River these people, my people, died in there. That was the *first* time the white people meet the Yavapai, and they kill them all in there. There was only one girl that came out of this shooting in the cave. Only one. That girl jumped off the bluff and she got out. The rest of them, they killed them. This was up in the Salt River Canyon.

My mother's two brothers and one sister died at that killing. And my grandmother's brother and two sisters died in there. My grandfather died in that place. All my relatives died in there. That is why I don't like to talk about it. But anyways.

When the white people come, lots of Yavapai get killed. This here is our home. But when the white people come, they take it away from us. They start mining out of these big rocks. We know nothing about these things. White people come here and they get gold, they get silver, they get copper, they get iron, they get lead out of these rocks. If the white people would not kill the Indians, it would be all right. But they kill them, kill them, and I don't know why they do that.

Before the white people live here, we have no trouble at all. At that time we all stay together, not like now, all separate. Now there are few of us left and that is why we are scattered out. Each family group when they stayed some place they had a chief, a *mayora*. The chief tells the people how to get along and how to get things. And when we kill a deer or some other animal, we all eat it together. Anything we get, we eat it all together.

In summer we stay in the wikiup. It stays cool. In wintertime the Yavapai went back to the mountains to the caves. There they built a fire and it kept them warm. A whole bunch of them stayed at one place. People stayed together like quails. That is why the soldiers killed all of them in one place.

People stayed together in the cave at the Salt River, and they sent a boy to some other people at Saddle Mountain. The chief sent him to tell the others to come and share deer meat. But the army scouts got this boy, and he showed them the cave. Otherwise the soldiers would not have found it. The soldiers went up to the cave and they could shoot right into it.

When the soldiers got that boy, some Yavapai were up on a mountain and they watched it. They knew now the boy is going to show the soldiers where they live. So they tell the chief in the cave, "They are going to get us. Let's get out of here." That chief was my grandmother's father. He was the best medicine man and he knew everything. He knows what is going to be. So he tells them, "If I go out, they don't let me go. They look for me and kill me wherever I go. So I'm not going to go out. I'm going to stay right here. Right here. Rest of you, if you want to go out, go out. They are not going to forget us. They are going to do the same thing to us all the time."

Lots of people stayed with him. My grandfather stayed there with him. My grandmother tried to get him out. "No," he said, "you go ahead and go." My grandfather stayed in there and he died in that cave. My grandmother's daughter and two boys died with him. She wants to take them out, but they don't want to go. The father is there, and that's why the kids don't want to go out. My mother was a baby then, so my grandmother took her out. And she took out some of her sister's children. Two boys and one girl. The older children of her sister stayed behind.

A bunch of people went out from the cave before the soldiers came. Women with babies, boys and girls. When they left, my grandmother's father said to them, "You go out. Maybe you save a few days. But maybe they kill you over there, when they kill another bunch of our people."

My grandmother and the others went out from the cave to go to Saddle Mountain. When they go over the hill they hear the shooting, pang, pang, pang. They know what happened. But they never did go back after that.

The soldiers didn't really come up to the cave. They were right across the cave. It is open all the way and the people can go no place. The soldiers shoot them down, shoot them down, shoot them down. Kill them all. One girl jumped out, off the cliff and got saved. That's only one. But she was not in good shape. She must have hit the rocks. She broke her hip. And that is the only one that got out of there.

In 1923 we went with Carl Montezuma to get the bones from the cave. In that cave, on the wall, it looked like oil sprayed on. Down on the floor it looked like oil. There is that 'oil' all over. It is the blood. When the bullets hit the bodies, the blood got scattered all around. Looks awful. We found many bones. Lots of little bones also. When we bring the bones, Montezuma is standing there crying. And we all start crying right there. We see that blood on the wall. It is too bad for us. It is here that all our people died. For nothing. And when I got back to Prescott and told my grandmother, my grandmother sure cried. ◇

Bibliography

Gifford, E. W. 1936. Northeastern and Western Yavapai. University of California Publications in Archaeology and Ethnology 34: 247–354.

Hardy, Heather. 1979. Tolkapaya syntax: aspect, modality, and adverbial modification in a Yavapai dialect. Ph.D. dissertation, University of California, Los Angeles.

Kendall, Martha B. 1976. *Selected problems in Yavapai syntax: the Verde Valley dialect*. New York: Garland.

———. 1979. Wolf and coyote: an upland Yuman text. *Amerindia* 4: 127–47.

———. 1980. Coyote marries his daughter. In *Coyote stories II* (International Journal of American Linguistics: Native American Texts Series [*IJAL: NATS*], Monograph 6), ed. M. B. Kendall, pp. 129–33. Chicago: University of Chicago Press.

Kendall, Martha B., and Sloane, Emily-Sue. Skara K'a:mca: The Lofty Wanderer (Yavapai). In *Yuman texts* (*IJAL-NATS* 1:3), ed. Margaret Langdon, pp. 68–83. Chicago: University of Chicago Press.

Munro, Pamela. 1978. Molly Fasthorse's Story of the Great Wrestling Match (Tolkapaya Yavapai). In *Coyote stories* (*IJAL-NATS*, Monograph 1), ed. William Bright, pp. 149–54. Chicago: University of Chicago Press.

Shaterian, Alan, 1983. Yavapai phonology and dictionary. Ph.D. dissertation, University of California, Berkeley.

Spicer, Edward H., 1962. *Cycles of conquest*. Tucson: University of Arizona Press.

Notes, Acknowledgments, and Credits

Coyote marries his daughter. From Kendall, Martha B., 1980. Coyote marries his daughter. In *Coyote stories II* (*IJAL-NATS*, Monograph No. 6), ed. Martha B. Kendall, pp. 129–33. Chicago: University of Chicago Press.

The story of the great wrestling match. From Munro, Pamela, 1978. Molly Fasthorse's story of the great wrestling match. In *Coyote stories* (*IJAL-NATS*, Monograph No. 1), ed. William Bright, pp. 149–54. Chicago: University of Chicago Press.

Texts, by Grace Jimulla Mitchell. These appear in the same order in which she recorded them on magnetic tape in the winter of 1966. The translations are, for the most part, Mrs. Mitchell's own.

Photo credits: pp. 163, 164, and 172—Victor Masayesva; p. 188—courtesy of Pat Mariella (photographer unknown).

MAURICIO J. MIXCO, *Editor*

The Paipai

No one really knows how long the Paipai have been in northern Baja California (Mexico). Because their language has a close kinship with the Pai languages of Arizona (such as Yavapai, Hualapai, and Havasupai), it is assumed to be of relatively recent northern origin among the Yuman-speaking communities of the peninsula.

There may once have been some small linguistic variation in the extensive territory once inhabited by the Paipai from the Colorado River delta and the shores of the Gulf of California to the Pacific beaches. In modern times Paipai continues to be spoken in two indigenous communities: at San Isidoro in the Valle de la Trinidad (where there are only a few families), and at Santa Catarina, a larger community near the site of the former mission by that name. The place should more properly be called by its Paipai name, *xaktvxol* (churning water), after the stream that winds its way among the huge boulders, passing through the communal cornfields and gardens in the bottomlands at San Miguel, crossing the plain in a southwesterly flow down a canyon, and emptying into the Pacific near the coastal town of San Vicente.

The Paipai community at *xaktvxol* is composed of more than three hundred members whose homes are scattered along the arroyo by that name. Other families live on ranches in the San Felipe Desert several thousand feet below the green Santa Catarina plateau.

For many generations (if not centuries) there have been strong kinship ties between the Paipai and the neighboring Yuman-speaking communities. There is still a small *k*ʷ*ʔaL* nucleus (of Diegueño speech) in a part of Santa Catarina known as Escondido (Hidden), as well as a Kiliwa-speaking family on the upper reaches of *xaktvxol*.

The Paipai consider themselves to be ethnically distinct from the Spanish-speaking Mexicans of the region and maintain a great pride in the dignity of their culture. Native-speaking educators are encouraging them to preserve their linguistic and cultural heritage as a patrimony for future generations.

Los Paipai

Nadie sabe desde cuando han estado los paipai en la Baja California Norte. Por su parentesco cercano con los idiomas *Pai* de Arizona (así como son: el yavapai, hualapai, y el havasupai [javasupai]), se les supone de orígen norteño relativamente recién entre las comunidades yumanas de la península.

Es posible que hubo alguna pequeña variación lingüística regional en el extenso territorio paipai que abarcaba desde el delta del Río Colorado y las orillas del Golfo de California hasta las playas del Pacífico. En la época moderna el idioma paipai se sigue hablando en dos comunidades indígenas: la de San Isidoro en el Valle de la Trinidad (en donde habitan apenas unas cuantas familias) y en la mayor de Santa Catarina en el lugar en donde existió una misión dominica del mismo nombre, incendiada en 1840.

Este lugar mas propiamente se debe de llamar en paipai *xaktvxol*, que significa "agua caudalosa" por el arroyo que pasa entre los grandes peñascos, pasando por las milpas de la comunidad en el vallecito de San Miguel atravesando la llanura hacia el poniente por un cañon para desembocar en el Oceano Pacífico cerca del pueblo de San Vicente.

La comunidad paipai de *xaktvxol* actualmente está compuesta de mas de 300 personas cuyos hogares se encuentran disperos por las orillas del arroyo.

Por generaciones (si no siglos) han habido lazos de parentesco entre los paipai y otras comunidades circunvecinas. Junto con los paipai y aparentemente con los mismos privilegios comunitarios existe un pequeño núcleo *k^wʔaL* de idioma tipai (Kumyay-Diegueño) en un lugar llamado Escondido.

Los indígenas paipai se consideran étnicamente distintos de los mexicanos hispano-parlantes de la región. Preservan un gran orgullo en la dignidad de su cultura autóctona y junto con los promotores-educadores indígenas estan tratando de fomentar una misión de rescate cultural y lingüística como patrimonio legado a las generaciones futuras.

The Contributors

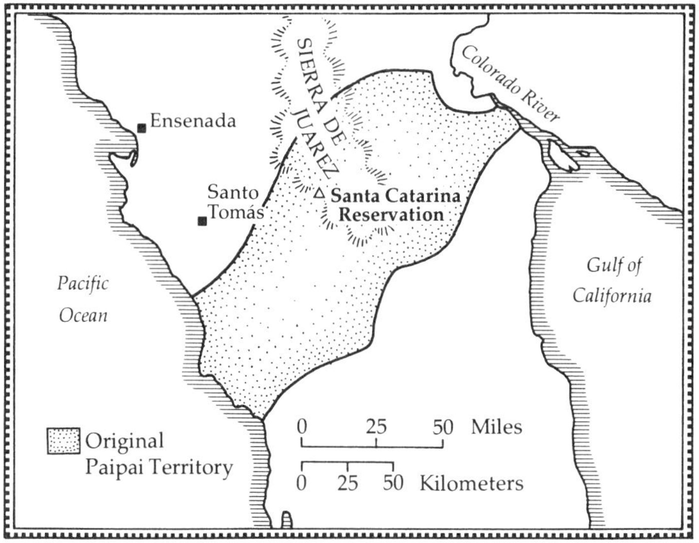

Mauricio J. Mixco was born in El Salvador (Central America) of Native American and Hispanic ancestry. In Pipil, an Aztecan dialect, Mixco means "Place in the Clouds"; it is the name of a Mayan kingdom, now a small village near Guatemala City, which came by its Uto-Aztecan name under the Toltecs who swept into Central America as conquerors from Mexico in the ninth century A.D. Mauricio Mixco's abiding interest in his Native American roots has led to a specialization in the native languages of the Americas. His doctoral research on the Kiliwa language began in Baja California in 1966 and culminated in a dissertation in the form of a grammar of Kiliwa. He received his Ph.D. in linguistics from the University of California at Berkeley in 1971, and his studies of the Paipai language began in 1975. Since 1973 he has served on the faculty of the University of Utah in the Department of Languages and the Interdisciplinary Linguistics Program.

Rufino Ochurte: "They shot all the men and boys . . . including my father and three brothers . . . I ran into the bush and stayed three days and escaped. It was a horrible thing—we weren't soldiers, how could there be war?" (Owen, 1963). These are the words of the author of the texts presented here, a man at ease in Spanish, Paipai, and Kiliwa, and in the cultures they express. Rufino Ochurte died in 1977, having reached an age of over eighty years. He died at Santa Catalina, only a few kilometers from the spot where he had witnessed the tragic events of a June morning many decades before when the forces of Porfírio Díaz and a small band of frightened Indians had lived out one of the many bloody scenes of the drama of the Mexican Revolution (Blaisdell, 1962).

Until recently, life in Baja California has always been hard. War, famine, and disease have all dwelt in the land. For generations the interior of this arid peninsula has been isolated from the world not just geographically but culturally as well. Rufino Ochurte's generation has seen the transition from a life led at a walking pace in utter simplicity, as it had been lived virtually unchanged for centuries, into the age of the automobile, speeding down paved highways, of men flying to the moon to leave their footprints in its dust as if it were just another desert. Rufino refused to believe that this sacrilege had actually been committed, but he delighted in the effortlessly smooth flow of the highway as it passed under the wheels like a river. This was his image as he would say *yii*, "it comes."

It takes an extraordinary spirit to go beyond mere survival to the wellspring of wisdom. Rufino's whimsical sense of humor bore witness to this achievement. In one narration, describing a nineteenth-century treaty signed with the typically elaborate flourish of the Mexican signature, an old Kiliwa headman is handed the document only to ask sarcastically, "Where am I going to put this?" "You see, he had no pockets, being naked," explains Rufino (*The Burning of Santa Catalina*; Mixco, 1983).

In mind and body Rufino was a man of infinite grace, a privileged person endowed with many talents; indefatigable in work, a singer, storyteller, and dancer. He laughed and sang in the face of the loneliness he doubtless felt at having outlived the friends of his youth who had dwindled in number through the years, and with them the fires of the memories of the land and people as they had been.

Not one to leave this life with a whimper, there is a note of defiance in these words recorded by Rufino some years before his death, "There were people in these mountains, to the East (*ʔnyuu-m*), to the West, (*t-k*^{w}*-nyaa-m*) from this place they reached to the South (*xwiy-m*). All the way to land's end (*ʔ-mat=h-wat-uʔ-nyaa-q*). Nothing but pagans (*ipaa=s-xʔil-k*^{w}*-mat* 'unwashed people', 'unbaptized'). There were no foreigners (*t-k*^{w}*-smaay-u* 'unknown ones') . . . The way they lived is still present. The places they pit-roasted and ate are still there. Their water jars are there (still). Their mountains are there (still). [But] these people are finished (now). They are dying out. They were in the valley (*ʔ-mat=x-uʔ-saa-w-y* 'Clear land') . . . further on there are no people . . . only these remain; there are no Indians left. But their deeds are there and (the places) where they dwelt are still there. The people's dwellings, the places they cooked, the holes blackened, they are there. Their broken pots are strewn over the land, here and there *metates*, *manos*, and *tepetates* (bedrock mortars) . . . Now the foreigners have been filling up this land . . . I am the only elder left, a Kiliwa elder; I am called Rufino Ochurte. . . . I say there are no foreign deeds, only what we did. . . . (*Creation of People and Customs*; Mixco, 1983) . . . Those peoples' deeds . . . (the people) who spoke about those things are not heard any longer. This will surely be the end (of all that). . . . Those who continue beyond will surely say the same (about me) when I've donned my crest of stars. . . . I have been speaking on this the first day of June (1969), the sun is yonder in the West as I speak. This day might be the last I speak. I don't know, (only) God knows; day after tomorrow, if you're still about, I may tell you (some more). I may still be speaking" (*My Crest of Stars*; Mixco, 1983).

Los Colaboradores

Mauricio J. Mixco nació en la República de El Salvador de ascendencia ibero-indígena. Su nombre en pipil (nahuat) significa "lugar en las nubes"; fue el nombre de un reino maya, actualmente una aldea en los alrededores de la capital de Guatemala; su nombre yuto-azteca asciende a la época de las conquistas toltecas del noveno siglo de nuestra era.

Mixco se ha interesado en sus raices indígenas desde muy jóven, cosa que lo llevó a especializarse en el estudio de los idiomas indígenos de las Americas. Comenzó sus investigaciones doctorales sobre el idioma kiliwa de Baja California en 1966; recibió el Ph.D. en lingüística de la Universidad de California en Berkeley. Su tésis doctoral fue una gramática del kiliwa. Desde 1975 ha estado estudiando el idioma paipai, en lo cual tiene proyectos de más estudio. Desde 1969 hasta 1973 Mixco fue profesor de español y portugúes en la Universidad Estatal de Idaho; desde 1973 ha enseñado lenguas y lingüística en la Universidad de Utah.

Rufino Ochurte: "Mataron a todos los hombres y muchachos . . . A mi papá, a mis tres hermanos . . . me metí corriendo en el monte y me quedé allí tres días y asi me escapé. Fue algo terrible—no eramos soldados ¿cómo podía haber guerra?" (Owen 1963; traducción, M. Mixco). Estas son las palabras del autor de los textos presentados aquí. Un hombre que hablaba el español, el paipai, y el kiliwa con igual facilidad, sintiéndose igualmente a gusto en las tres culturas representadas por estas lenguas. Rufino Ochurte murió en el 1977, habiendo alcanzado mas de los ochenta años. Murió en Santa Catarina a unos cuantos kilómetros del lugar donde había presenciado, hace décadas, los trágicos acontecimientos de una mañana del mes de Junio cuando las fuerzas porfiristas y un pequeño grupo de indígenas vivieron una de las muchas escenas sangrientes de la revolución (Blaisdell, 1962).

Hasta hace poco, la vida en la Baja California siempre ha sido difícil. La guerra, la hambruna, y la enfermedad, todas han habitado en esta tierra. Por generaciones, el interior de esta árida península ha estado aislada del mundo, no solo geográficamente sino en su idiosincracia cultural. La generación de Rufino Ochurte ha vivido la transición de la vida a pie a la vida en automóbil, pasando veloz por las carreteras, alzanzando a dejar el hombre sus huellas en la luna como si fuera otro desierto mas. Rufino nunca creyó que este sacrilegio hubiera sucedido, pero le encantaba ver el fluir del camino bajo las llantas del vehículo. Decía, "*yii* 'viene'," hablando de este movimiento en que parece que el mundo se mueve y no uno.

Es preciso un alma extraordinaria para ir mas allá de la sobrevivencia hasta los manantiales de la sabiduría. De ésto daba testigo el gran sentido de humor de Rufino. En una de sus narraciones, en la que se describe un acta firmada con una rúbrica típicamente mexicana, un viejo general kiliwa dijo, tomando el documento, "y donde voy a meter esto? Pues no tenía bolsas, estaba desnudo," explicaba Rufino con una mirada maliciosa (*The Burning of Santa Catarina*, Mixco, 1983). Rufino fue un hombre de infinita gracia tanto en su espíritu como en su físico, una persona privilegiada, de muchos talentos; incansable en el trabajo, como cantador, como narrador, y como bailador. Reía y cantaba enfrentando la soledad que indubablemente sentía viéndose sin sus viejos amigos que año por año iban desapareciendo y que se llevaban consigo las llamas de los recuerdos del país y del pueblo indígena.

Pero Rufino no era de los que se "rajan," se percibe su desafío in las siguientes palabras que fueron grabadas unos años antes de su muerte, "Habia gente en esta sierra, al Este (*ʔnyuu-m*), al Poniente (*t-k*^{w}*-nyaa-m*) de aquí llegaban hasta al Sur (*xwiy-m*) hasta el fin de la tierra (*ʔ-mat=h-wat-uʔ-nyaa-q*). Puros paisanos (*ʔipaa=sxʔil=kw-mat*) . . . . Todavía está la manera en que vivían. Los lugares donde tatemaban allí estan. Pero ya se acabaron. Se van muriendo todos. Vivían en el valle (*ʔ-mat=x-uʔ-saa-w-y*) . . . mas allá no alcanza la gente . . . solo éstos quedan. Ya no hay indígenas. Pero sus hechos estan allí y (los lugares) donde cocinaban, los hoyos enegrecidos, allí estan. Sus ollas rotas estan desparramados por la tierra, los metates, las manos, y los tepetates . . . . Ahora la tierra se está llenando de puros extranjeros . . . soy el único que queda, de los mayores kiliwa, soy Rufino Ochurte . . . No hay hechos extranjeros solo lo nuestro . . . (*Creation of People and Customs;* Mixco, 1983) . . . . Los hechos de la gente . . . los que dijeron esas cosas ya no se oyen, los que siguen, seguramente dirán lo mismo de mí cuando me haya puesto mi sombrero de estrellas . . . . He estado hablando este día, el primero de Junio (1969), allá está el sol en el Poniente. Éste podría ser el último en que hable yo. No se, (solo) Dios sabe; pasado mañana, si todavía andas por aquí tal vez te diré (mas). Todavía estaré hablando" (*My Crest of Stars;* Mixco, 1983).

The Paipai Alphabet

Benito Peralta with Mauricio J. Mixco

This is the Paipai spelling system as we know it today. It will have to be modified as the need arises.

Vowels

The vowels are like those of Spanish; an English counterpart is offered as an approximation.

a *xa*, 'water'. As in w*a*ter.
e *sʔel*, 'salty'. As in b*e*ll.
i *ʔiwíl*, 'vegetation'. As in m*ea*l.
o *xlo*, 'cottontail'. As in sl*ow*.
u *mulc*, 'names'. As in p*oo*l.

Long vowels

These are held for a longer time during pronunciation.

aa *vcaay*, 'daughters'.
ee *krxee*, 'lizard (variety)'.
ii *cvsii*, 'liver'.
oo *cvsoo*, 'rib'.
uu *muul*, 'name'.

Diphthongs

These are vowels followed by *y* or *w*.

ay *xay*, 'wet'.
aay *cmwaay*, 'Mormon Tea (*Ephedra*)'.
aw *paráw*, 'fast'.
aaw *paṣuraaw*, 'gallop'.
ey *mcṣey*, 'fearful (plural)'.
eey *xṣeey*, 'dark horse'.
ew *xukyew*, 'carry'.
iy *tvṣkwiy*, 'stand (several)'.
iw *tliw*, 'nudge'.
oy *svoy*, 'light (weight)'.
ooy *svooy*, 'light weight (plural)'.
ow *qwow*, 'head hair'.
uy *ṣklpuy*, 'carry under the arm'.
uuy *ruuy*, 'hot'.
uw *yuw*, 'come'.

Consonants

The consonants are grouped according to their type and their position in the mouth.

Note that *c* is used for *ch*, that *x* is somewhat like a "harsh" *h*, while *h* is "softer"; *ny* stands for *ñ*. Neither *ṣ* nor *q* exists in English or Spanish; the first is distinguished from an *s* in that there is a slight whistling sound from the contact of the tip of the tongue with the area just behind the teeth, while *q* is distinct from *k* in that it is pronounced by contacting a point deeper in the throat (the soft palate). Capital *L* is used for a voiceless *l*; no sound is heard coming from the vocal cords. This sound is rare.

p *pa*, 'bullet'.
t *kitú*, 'gopher'.
c *cicí*, 'mother'.

k *kkikṣ*, 'crawl'.
kw *kwas*, 'brown'.
q *qpay*, 'head'.
qw *qwas*, 'yellow'.
ʔ *ʔoʔó*, 'fire'.
v *vmas*, 'twenty'.
s *ckos*, 'small'.
ṣ *ṣal*, 'hand/arm'.
x *xlpú*, 'net'.
xw *xwat*, 'red'.
h *ha*, 'that, the'.
m *mu*, 'sheep'.
n *vnun*, 'belly'.
ny *nyac*, 'black'.
l *xla*, 'moon'.
ly *lyeeyt*, 'garter snake'.
L *nyeL*, 'friend'.
rr *ksarr*, 'coyote'.
r *paráw*, 'fast'.
w *wa*, 'house'.
y *yo*, 'tooth'.

Ortografía Paipai

Benito Peralta con Mauricio J. Mixco

Esta es la ortografía Paipai según nuestros conocimientos actuales. Se tendrá que ir modificando de acuerdo con la necesidad de mejorar este primer alfabeto.

Vocales breves

Se pronuncian con el mismo valor de las del español.

a *xa*, 'agua'.
e *sʔel*, 'salado'.
i *ʔiwíl*, 'rama, vegetación'.
o *xlo*, 'conejo'.
u *mulc*, 'nombres'.

Vocales largas

Se detienen por mas tiempo.

aa *vcaay*, 'hijas'.
ee *krxee*, 'tipo de cachora'.
ii *cvsii*, 'higado'.
oo *cvsoo*, 'costilla'.
uu *muul*, 'nombre'.

Diptongos

Estos son grupos de vocales seguidos de *y* o *w*.

ay *xay*, 'mojado'.
aay *cmwaay*, 'canutillo'.
aw *paráw*, 'rápido'.
aaw *paṣuraaw*, 'galopar'.
ey *mcṣey*, 'temerosos'.
eey *xṣeey*, 'caballo retinto'.
ew *xukyew*, 'cargar'.
iy *tvṣkwiy*, 'de pie (varios)'.
iw *tliw*, 'empujoncito'.

oy *svoy*, 'liviano (de peso)'.
ooy *svooy*, 'livianos'.
ow *qwow*, 'cabello'.
uy *ṣklpuy*, 'cargar debajo del brazo'.
uuy *ruuy*, 'caliente'.
uw *yuw*, 'venir'.

Consonantes

Los consonantes se agrupan aquí por el tipo de sonido de acuerdo con la posición en la boca.

Nótese que se emplea la letra *c* por la *ch* y que la *x* equivale a un *j* aspera, la *h* como una *j* leve, la *ny* es la *ñ*. Ni la *ṣ* ni la *q* existen en el español; la *ṣ* se distingue de la *s* por su pequeño silbido causado por la punta de la lengua en leve contacto con la zona detrás de los dientes. La *q* se distingue de una *k* siendo el contacto mas interno (con el velo). El símbolo de la *L* mayúscula indentifica una *l* "sorda," o sea sin voz. Se usa muy poco ésta última.

p *pa*, 'bala'.
t *kitú*, 'topo'.
c *cicí*, 'mamá'.
k *kkikṣ*, 'deslizarse'.
kw *kwas*, 'café'.
q *qpay*, 'cabeza'.
qw *qwas*, 'amarillo'.
ʔ *ʔoʔó*, 'lumbre'.
v *vmas*, 'veinte'.
s *ckos*, 'pequeño'.
ṣ *ṣal*, 'mano/brazo'.
x *xlpú*, 'red'.
xw *xwat*, 'rojo'.
h *ha*, 'ese, el'.
m *mu*, 'borrego'.
n *vnun*, 'panza'.
ny *nyac*, 'negro'.
l *xla*, 'luna'.
ly *lyeeyt*, 'vibora sorda'.
L *nyeL*, 'amigo'.
rr *ksarr*, 'coyote'.
r *paráw*, 'rápido'.
w *wa*, 'casa'.
y *yo*, 'diente'.

The War of Revenge

Rufino Ochurte, Narrator

mat tayl kwa ipayu nyweevc wak mvṣi txwak. yak wak, yak wak, yak wam. ṣit kuha, xmany wikuk; tiv kwak xkay. txwakv kyom yuk.

nyamṣitm kwi ˀuwk; sak yak ˀim ˀap paxmi. xkay wat kuha sam kxkye, micav kxkye. yukwev cˀiny micav nalm ˀev. maa, yukwevc ˀmicav nalk ˀi, ckkwik xkayha. yumkuk cut vyawk. pem yukweuli mkak nal tem. hak wakunuk nmak. maa, kavˀik ˀiwe ˀik waṣiv, waṣiv yak wak. cpaak nyuk sam yaam huuk. heh! yavˀik ˀit ya ˀˀik

El ser subterráneo estaba casado con dos mujeres. Ahí estaba. Una de ellas tenía un niño; la otra estaba embarazada. Las dos eran suyas.

Un día lo estaba espulgando una esposa, el hombre estaba echado boca abajo. La otra esposa pasó por ahí, le pasó por encima de la pierna. El hombre sintió que algo le cayó en la pierna. "Bueno, ¿que me caería en la pierna?" le preguntó a la otra. Se limpió la pierna. "No fue nada, no cayó nada." Así está, lo dejó. "Bueno, ¿como sería?" Estuvo pensando. Salió, allí iba. "¡Ijij!

The Being under the Earth had two wives. There he was. One of the wives had a child, the other was expecting. They were both his.

One day one of his wives was delousing him; the man lay face down. The other wife passed over his leg. The man felt something fall on his leg. "Well, what was that I felt drop on my leg?" he asked the other wife. He cleaned his leg. "It was nothing, nothing dropped." There he was, he left it. "Well, I wonder how it happened?" He

yusm. wak ˀuw, cxwat wam, cxwat nyuk nalm yuk; ruv kwamuk. hih! yuvyukulim ˀiso nycpuyk ˀyiw kmyik. vaam kwakuha; xot nyˀik kavnyuk mvṣihac vook. vook yiwk yok, wak; maa, kavaˀyuh kwak ˀyuw. mvṣi kwik vmak ˀim kwik nymtyiw nymtyiw.

mat kakyom yuha, naal yec kwartuyu ˀikukwac, sak vaak. sak ˀam kxav naal cxul sak ˀam yiwm ˀuwk. mlek nyuk cpak ṣyeek vaam, ṣal kyom nymay kpun cwom vqam maat ṣwitu ˀik, ˀˀi lavlavm qwow cxancu yuvyuc. nymay kpun cwow vqam, cxwat vkwiskwis ˀim. yok xwiṣ, mya kwek xkyevm xwiṣm. nya xwat cwok xumey wit, mnwiy knymatp ukwacyac mvṣi naxcyom nyˀsac ṣpoovkum. mnwiyknymatp nax pay vook yaam vaam ṣe wak wak wam yu.

xkay nyvony, vok yu, maa nykin yiwm ˀuw, vaa temuku? hem, vaa tem kyokut yukvohac, xla nya ṣit matm ˀˀit, hih! paavc nax txotm yuwkum

Así me suponía." Vió una mancha de sangre, le habia caido una gotita de sangre, estaba seca. "¡Ijij!" dijó así, "pero como que me engañó." Llegó, ahí estaba, al rato se fue la mujer. Al mucho rato de haberse ido, estaba ahí, "bueno, ¿y que voy a hacer?" Se fue siguiendo a la mujer, se fue detrás de ella.

En un lugar "donde aparece la semilla del mesquite", como le dicen, ahí llegó. Ahí andaba, la alcanzó, estaba comiendo mesquite, lo vió llegar. Se le acercó sonriendo, llegó acercándosele. La tomó del brazo, la apuñaló en el pecho con el palito rascador, un palito labrado para arreglar el cabello, uno de esos. El pecho le apuñaló, la sangre le hirbió. Lo agarró el palito y lo aventó al otro lado del cielo. Creó el anillo de sangre del sol, cuando matan a una mujer taraisa aparece así. Mató a la mujer taraisa y se fue, allá estaba.

La otra esposa también se fue, venía preguntando, "bueno, ¿no ha visto a mi hermana llegar?" "No, no llegó," le respondían. "Ya tiene como un mes, ijij! alguien la mató

was thinking. She left, there she went. "Ah hah, just as I suspected." He saw a blood stain; a little drop of blood had fallen on him, it had dried. "Ah hah!" he said that, "But, she really deceived me!" He arrived, there he was, after a little while, the woman left. A long time after he'd left, he thought, "So, what am I going to do?" He took off after the woman, pursuing her.

He got to a place known as "Where-the-Mesquite-Seed-Shows." There he was, he caught up with her; she was eating mesquite, watching him approach. He approached smiling. He grabbed her by the arm, stabbed her in the breast with a head-scratcher, one of those carved sticks. He stabbed her breast; the blood boiled out. He took the stick and flung it to the other end of heaven. He created the Sun's Blood Ring (a patch of rainbow in the clouds); when a Taraiso woman is killed, it appears. He killed the Taraiso woman and left; there he was.

The other wife also left, asking everyone, "Well, haven't you seen my sister arrive?" "No, no, she hasn't arrived," they answered. "She's been

ˀi. maat kunaavu paa tay cwakik, yavˀik ukwak ˀacma. heehee! kṣyec wamyuk xemcum vaak, chaaypkukwak vṣkwim ṣutatk ṣxlak chaayp vnamaan ˀitk mxalyaam temtk. knaav, maa nya ˀeevkulik yute, paavc yiw kulimyut. vṣkwik pay chaayp ˀam kyuwkpaq ˀicm kyakyaˀ cak ciik paaqcum vpaqpaq ˀim ˀˀeevm ˀˀit mat xa kṣye yak yak yac nyum cpakulik vaˀnyaw ˀˀevk ˀit. heehee, paytkwek chaayp. hee hee! vaam yuwkulim yute, cṣa kxokmaac, ˀicm yamyak. cṣa xvṣu yuvyuc miulik nycpak ˀim ˀˀite. paavc nyiw ˀim ˀˀite ˀik. ˀaaa, paxmi nyapay ˀyuw maat yoov aaq, huh huh! uyaym cpakm, haa cxwarkwakukwak patayvc wakik. cxumey maat yoov, kwit paa waa kxkyek, kmṣrayc vcharchaar ˀikukwak. nykyook nyaˀpay yowhac yowhac yowm yuwha.

y la escondió." Avisó a la tribu. Así dijo. "Eje, je!" Había un sabio hechicero lo mandaron a llamar, se paró a rezar apoyandose en su bastón, sin demorar mucho. Dijo, "bueno, parece que oí venir a alguien." Siguió parado llamando a los espiritus; hay una hierba que le dicen garbanzillo, oyó que pasaron eso, lejos se oyó el tronido de las semillas. "¡Eje, je!" volvió a rezar. "¡Eje, je! parece que viene, gritó el pájaro que come piñón." Uno de esos pájaros azules gritó, "¡ya viene saliendo!" Dijo, "ya viene la persona, el alma." Aah, el hombre se hizo tecolote, gritó, "¡ju, ju!" Salió por la puerta, echó muchos alaridos la multitud de gente. Se convirtió en un ser poderoso. Pasó por un pueblo el jefe, echando gritos. Cuando se calló, quedó en silencio por mucho tiempo.

gone almost a month; ah hah! Someone has killed her and hidden her." She told the tribe. She said thus. Hah! There was a sage witch, they sent for him; he leaned on his staff and prayed without a moment's pause. He said, "It seems like I can hear someone approaching." He went on standing there calling the spirits; there is a bush called *garbanzillo*, he heard a footfall on this seed; at a distance he could hear the popping of the seeds. "Ah hah," he went back to praying. "Ah hah, she seems to be coming!" cried the Pinyon Jay. One of those blue jays cried out, "She's coming out!" It said, "The person is coming, the spirit!" Aah, the shaman turned into an owl, it cried out, "Hoo! hoo!" He flew out the door, the people all raised an uproar. He was transformed into a power being. The shaman flew over a village crying out. When he fell silent, it was quiet for a long time.

wa mvṣi ktiv kvac kwahcuha watk pay sov xme saw. heh! myaav kyak saw kwiw. yuvyuk yak nyaam xwak nyxmuk paac picv tem kyak ˀik knaav, maa myaav kyak kwartuykut. ˀeev

La mujer embarazada que vino ahí se alivió. ¡Ejej! parió un dios. Ahí estaba, a los dos o tres días, no falta quien venga a avisar. "Bueno, ha nacido un dios." Estuvo escuchando, el mar, los ani-

The pregnant woman bore a child. Ah hah! She gave birth to a god. Two or three days later someone came to tell of it. "A god has been born." He (the father of the child) was listen-

yak yakm xaxsil cpay nyak wac kˀam payt ˀrˀuy ṣwarkukwam. mat kyak tvxac kik yak wak. mkakukwam cxumey yok ˀyiw ˀim kˀam ya ˀev ku nypaym yak. cṣa payt maa, nyxan paavc kwartuym ˀiw kˀim ˀik yak. pay yiw muh! yam ˀˀuw.

nyumyiw cpayt twir nyiw tuula, malka pay cpayt nya kuwac twir. mi vqam vwal vaa. yuvyum vaak waak ˀwa vtnal ˀik vwaak. yumyuc xmehac sak ˀam xaam cṣavṣu ˀicm yakm xvcul reek nyam we nal. see vaak yok, myiw myiw mtaav ˀwak ˀyut. miiv nywi tyiw xvcul yiw yaak kvwak. pay yov xvyeny. heh! mtaav ˀwak ˀyume. pay maat cyumk xmehac vok yam vaam. cciha kunavu, maa nytaav cˀik, vaa nyukwakwak ˀim ˀite. heh! yuvyuc wi tpay mˀam myuma. xmany nyaktuy yuvyuc mṣpo tem mˀam myuma. nyˀis minikimolukwak mˀacme.

pay xme tkwek nyyaamik yaam vaam. yok xvyeny, pay kweha ˀeek malka, cpay twir

males que hay, todos cantaban felices. Por todo el mundo se oía. A donde empieza, viene el poderoso; escuchó, entonces todos los pajaros cantaron. Dijo "es cierto que nació alguien." "Ahi va, ¡baj! voy a ver."

Viene matando animales, lagartijas, ratas, toda clase de animal que hay, mata. Los trae colgando de las patas ensartadas con palitos. Y de ahí vino, se sentó a cierta distancia de la casa. Divisó al niño que andaba soplando una bejiga de águila como le llaman, soplando jugando, caía allá, allá iba. Iba y lo agarró, "ven, ven, soy tu padre." Volvió a hacer lo mismo, sopló, vino se paró cerquita. Entonces lo agarró el padre. "Jij! soy tu padre." Entonces se juntaron; el niño se fue, llegó. Le contó a su mama, "bueno, me dice que es mi papá, ahí esta diciendo." "Ijij! de eso no tienes." "Hijo natural, eso no conoces tu." "No mas te dicen eso burlándose de tí."

Volvió el niño. Lo agarró en brazos; le dió los animales que había cazado. Todo lo que traía se

ing: the sea, the animals, all sang joyfully. It could be heard all over the world. The powerful one goes to the source of this sound; he listened to all the birds and said, "It's true someone has been born! There it goes, I'm going to see."

He came along killing animals, lizards, rats, he killed every kind of animal. He carried them dangling from a stick piercing their legs. He arrived and sat at some distance from the house. He spied the child who was going about playing with an eagle's bladder, blowing it; it would fall yonder, yonder he'd run. He'd grab it; "Come, come, I am your father." The child did it again; he blew and came very close. The father grabbed him. "Hey, I am your father!" They were together; the child left, he got home. The child told his mother, "Hey, there's someone out there who says he's my father." "You don't have any such thing! You illegitimate child, you have nothing of the kind! He's mocking you!"

The child returned. The father cradled him in his arms, giving him all the game he

kmimha ˀeek pay yok waam kmimk ˀeek. cciha, pay yok ˀˀismaq cyumk cyumk xltuk unuk unuk. nytmaack xway ṣyax kwil kwil xnmehac tkweek, nyvaamik vaam. ˀik mwaamha kavwi mwamha. heh! kur ṣilkunukwit. kavwik ṣileˀ. ˀoˀoxwatl poqkwit. xway ṣyax kwil kwilm ˀucpack wit tmaac. nywim mso wicm-wikwe. pem kwit, payncak xanu ṣil kwirm so ˀmwic. ˀick-yum yuvyum nyuk cmiik ṣil nyusow mwic.

lo dió. La mamá entonces juntó basura y lo chamuscó. Cuando lo había chamuscado, el niñito regresó a su padre. Le preguntó, "lo que llevaste ¿que hizo con eso?" "Ijij! ya lo está asando." "¿Como lo asó?" "Lo echó en las llamas." "Lo sacó chamuscado, lo coció." "Cuando lo ha hecho así, ¿tu te lo has comido?" "No, lo haciá bien, bién asada me la como yo." "Lo puso allí, lo ha tatemado, así como yo."

had hunted. He gave him everything he had. The mother gathered kindling and scorched it; the child came back to his father. He asked, "What did she do with what you took her?" "Ah, she's roasting it." "How did she roast it?" "She flung it in the flames! She pulled it out all scorched, it was cooked." "So when she's cooked like that, you've eaten it?" "No, she does it right for me, I eat well roasted meat! She places it there, pit roasts it, that's how I eat."

tkwek nyyaami, tkwek vaay. mci yukwe kavwikunu. maa, kwe ksiv unyak unuk wit kavwik unyaa ˀˀoxwatl nye unyakwit. yuvwim, mmakmwicm mwamhe. pemkwit, ˀˀo tum ˀici xanm, ˀiciha yook umunyaak pay cak xanu. tmaacm maamwit tyelm, winm.

Volvió, se fue de vuelta. "¿Que está haciendo tu mamá?" "Bueno, esta tostando pamita;" "¿como la tuesta?" "En la llama la metió para tostarla." "¿Así lo hecho para que tu lo comas?" "No, de ninguna manera, atizaba con buena braza, toma la braza entonces bien la tostaba." "Bien tostada, así la he comido yo; molida, con agua."

He left and returned. "What's your mother doing?" "Well, she's parching Tansy Mustard seeds." "And how is she parching them?" "She placed them in the hot flame." "Has she done it that way for you to eat?" "No, no way, she just made embers, she takes them and uses them for parching. Well parched, that's how I eat Tansy; the powder mixed with water!"

tkwek yaami xme vaamkuk. nytyelkunuk, tkwek vaak. kavwi. hee hee! ksiv nytyelkunuk wit. kavwik tyeleˀ. tkyel nyukcwokwit ṣalha. nywim, mmaa mwiceˀ. pemkwite, ṣal pay cak

Volvió el niño. "¡Está moliendo otra vez!", dijo. '¿Como?" "¡Ejé, je! está moliendo la pamita." "¿Como la está moliendo?" "Hizo un "chapulín" con la mano." "¿Asi lo ha hecho, cuando tu lo comes?" "No,

The child returned. "She's grinding again" "How?" "Ah hah, she's grinding the Tansy Mustard." "How is she grinding them?" "She has her fist clenched into an obscene ges-

xanu, xvca yikwis tyel yuvwim, ʔmaam ʔwic ʔwit. xanku.

tkwek nyvay kyaam, yaam vaam. sakwak ksiv siik xmany vaam kunaavu nyeʔnkweevc ʔam mnax hikʔit kyam mirmirulik wim ʔʔite. yel pi ṣvtik kyat kyet wim ʔʔite. ʔwe vxe ṣxlak kyat kyet wim ʔʔite. xta ckyet cwok kya ksolm ukxavk wim ʔʔite. mnax mak ʔʔite.

maa, vaam kwak yak nyanyxav ṣma sakyak vcqwar ʔik xanu kul tuk ʔaam paa tay cwak ʔaam. heh! nyeʔwan cta, myaam kul tuk nyaʔ nyam tem myute. eh heh! ʔʔev ʔyak ṣek ʔyute. xot ʔim yuvyuw tem kwilv rav ʔaam. yeh nyeʔwan cta nyam kul nyaʔ tuc tem myute. hih! ʔʔev ʔyaks ʔyute. yuvyuwk kxkyekuwahac kxkyekuwahac nya cpakyiw mya xvṣu kxkyem.

payt vaʔnyaw, paytk ʔam ʔeev. cpaak matkyak ʔuwt, vli ʔik. eh! paavc kakʔam tem. pay xmany wa nyok pap pay yuvyum nyvok hyam. knax ʔiku-

pone la mano con cuidado; toma la piedra para moler, asi la molía para comer yo." Está bien.

Vino de vuelta, llegó. Ahí estaba, se tomó la pamita, llegó el niño y le contó al papá, "mi tío dijo que te quería matar; tiene muy buena puntería. Estiró una hebra de mescal, le disparó y la trozó. Colgó a un ratoncito de la cola, le disparó y lo trozó ¡Te va a matar!"

Bueno, ahí estaba, se acostó, durmió; a la madrugada iban a atizar liebres mucha gente. "¡Je! papá de mi sobrino ¡vamos a atizar liebres!" "¡Eje! les estoy escuchando, sigo acostado." Al rato pasaban mas "¡Je! papá de mi sobrino, ¿porqué no vas a quemar liebres?" "¡Jij! pero todavía sigo acostado." Así iban pasando, y pasando. Salió el sol, atravesó el cielo azul.

Desaparecieron todos, oyó; todos se fueron. Salió, miró para todos lados, estaba en silencio. "Eh! no hay nadie." Entonces tomó al niño amanche; así se fue. El que lo

ture!" "She's done it like that for you, then?" "No, she folds her hand properly around the pestle, that's how I eat it." "All right."

The child came again. He had drunk the Tansy Mustard; the child told the father, "My uncle says he wants to kill you, he is a real marksman! He once stretched out a single thread of agave fiber and sundered it with one shot! He hung up a tiny mouse by the tail, shot at it and severed it! He'll kill you!"

Well, the father fell asleep [having gone into his wife's house]; at dawn the next day many people were leaving camp to burn out the underbrush to hunt jackrabbits. "Hah, Nephew's Father, let's go burn out the jackrabbits!" "Ah hah, I'm listening, but I'm still in bed [with your kinswoman.] Later some more came by. "Hey! Father of my Nephew, why don't you come burn out jackrabbits!" "Hah, but I'm still in bed!" And so many more came by, the sun rose, climbing into the blue sky.

All had disappeared, he listeṇed, they were all gone. He emerged, looked all around; it was quiet "Hah, no one's about." He placed the child on

kwahac ṣvok nyukwak. yumyuk kˀuhac unukuk, paavc xmany kciicvk waam kwite. eh heh! pay nyxpu yook vṣkwik, kyaaa. cxwat nalukyohak cwok kyaaak tkwan sal xwil. pay nyam xmanyha cyawhikunu. pem yukwe mltat pil ˀuculik sak vṣkwim myiw myiw ˀikukwacm. pem, myaav yaam waˀṣit. wa ccmakv ntmak.

iba a matar le estaba esperando ahí. Así es, los que estaban viendo, gritaron, "¡se robó al niño el hombre!" Eje! luego tomó su arco, se paró, disparó. Le pegó donde le había caido la sangre; ahí lo tumbó. Luego llegaron, unas personas querían agarrar al niño. No; parecía una biznaga ardiente, ahí se paró; "ven, ven," le decían. "No"; subía mas arriba. No le pudieron hacer nada.

his back and left. The one who was going to kill him was waiting for him there. So it was those who were watching him shouted, "The man has stolen the child!" Ah hah! He took his bow then, standing, he released his shot. He hit him where the blood had dripped; there and then he toppled him! The people arrived then; they wanted to seize the little boy. It was not to be, he looked like a blazing barrel cactus; he stood there; "Come, come," they called to him. "No!" he answered, and rose ever higher. They could do nothing with him.

nyvooc vweq ˀim, xmehac nal mim ktox qpay ktox. vkwalk ˀik, man pay vyaaw kyok nypapik kos ulmityum. ˀpap tem mtmak mpap, ˀeev tem ultiyum.

Cuando se fueron, quedó silencio, el niño bajó. Le pateó la pierna, le pateó la cabeza al papá. Se levantó de repente, lo agarró rápido y lo puso amanche, "no me pongas para enfrente." "Ponme volteado," no hizo caso lo puso de frente.

When they had gone, all was silent; the child descended and kicked his father's leg, his head. He immediately got to his feet, grabbed the child and placed him on his back; "Don't set me facing forward," said the boy. "Set me backward"; but he paid no attention, he kept him facing forward.

heh paavc man kyam kut, haha! man kyamkut. eh heh! nyxpu yok yaam. kkyemu kaˀṣit kakyemu kyaak kaˀṣit cwok kaˀṣitk cwok kyaa. tkwan sakxwil. maa pit pay ooh kavyucvcu. vaam, yoov, vxawa kyaat kwir; slmak kyet kxwalk, kaam xmeha

"¡Jij! se levantó y se fue el hombre ¡ja,ja!¡se fue!" "¡Jej!"; agarró el arco y se fue. Se paró donde mismo y tiró, le pegó donde mismo, donde mismo le pegó. Ahí lo dejó tumbado. "Bueno, ¿este no sabe morir o que?" Llegó, lo descuartizó, le trozó las tripas, lo acabó completa-

"Heh! The man arose and took off, hey, he's gone!" Heh! The shaman took his bow and took off. He stood in the same spot and released his arrow, he struck him in the same place as before. There he toppled him. "Well, what is this, doesn't he

cyaw hikunum. pem myaavu-wam, myiw myiw ʔihukwacm. pem ʔikukwacm wacmak ʔik pay nal. cyaw ckmik, mikukwak kwartem xan. maa, cam pik, ka-vyukʔiny, yel nyulwam mʔem mak. yel ʔecm, maa, ʔiwayl xa kxan ʔulnyeek, laqm, yel xu-mey, yel lxac, yel xvṣiw xumey. hitha yo tem, xotm; maa, ksiv nyulwam, mwinm siik ʔik, ksiv ucpac win ʔecm siik. ʔiway lxa yakl nye, ʔutm ksiv lxac xumey. vliw ʔik wak xot ʔim pay wac-mak ʔik pay kyook. kaam raay kwakunu.

mente, le arrancaron la paleta; llegaron, quisieron agarrar al niño. "No," se puso mas arriba, "ven, ven," le decían. "No," les con-testaba; al fin bajó.

Lo agarraron y lo trajeron, es-taba llorando muchísimo. "Bueno, pueda ser que tenga hambre; el mescal que hay ahí, dénselo a comer." Le dieron mescal, comió; el estómago lo sintió amargo, lo vo-mitó, creó mescal amargo, el mescal verde creó. "¡Carajo!" no lo tomó, al rato lo comió. "Hay pamita ahí, di-suélvansela para que tome"; sacaron la pamita y le dieron de tomar. Del estomago amargo la echó y creó la pamita amarga. Estuvo buen rato quieto y luego se calló, estuvo quieto. Lo estuvieron acariciando.

know how to die, then?" He came up to the dead man and tore him limb from limb, hack-ing his guts, he killed him com-pletely; they tore his shoulder blade off; they had arrived; they wanted to seize the child. "No," he said and rose above them; "Come, come," they called to him. "No," he answered; but in the end he did come down. They took hold of him and brought him along; he was weeping bitterly. "Perhaps he's hungry; give him some mescal we have then." They gave him the mescal, he ate some; his stomach turned bitter, he vom-ited it up; he created bitter agave, green mescal, he created. "Damn!"; he didn't eat, later he ate. "There's some Tansy Mus-tard there, stir some up for him to drink"; they brought out the Tansy Mustard and gave him some to drink. He spewed it up from his bitter stomach creating Bitter Tansy (or Peppergrass). He remained quiet for some time, he fell silent, he was still. They fondled him.

nyam ṣitm mkam xavmuk ʔamtk tṣmay kwakunu. mi kvkyet nyaam nyiw paa tay kway. pem, mkam cpamuc yak tem. yukwe wiparr paycʔam

Un dia desapareció; lo andu-vieron buscando. Andaban cor-tando huellas por aquí y por allá una multitud de gente. No, no ha-llaron por donde salió. "Esa per-

One day he disappeared, they went searching for him. A great number went looking here and there for his tracks. They couldn't find his trail. "Where

kuk, mkam yu kavyukum ˀik, tṣmay kunuk. tnyaavtk cyuwm, maat mikwakukwak, ṣitk cpaak yaam nyuk sak vṣkwik, ˀiwil cyom sak vṣkwik, ˀeev. paa ṣwarkulik, ˀiwilhal ukwak. vaa knaav, maa paavc ˀiwilhal ṣwarkulik ukwam yute, vkapk ˀik; kaam cˀuw. heh! sal vṣkwikukwak ˀyiw cyaw cak mik raaykwakunu ˀam yakˀam yak ˀam cˀuw yook wir ṣˀam cpaa tem hˀik. mi xwakt ṣit weevkwak, weevkwak mi xwakt kṣceha caav ckwak ˀam. wik cˀuw, cˀuw uman; cˀuws, mkal wa tem. kur kam xavmuk; yaam kyohac, nyam ṣit xwak vaam yuc, yaam kyok xlaˀ ṣit maatm tkwek vaak.

sona poderosa ¿por donde se iría?" Lo anduvieron buscando. En la mañana se juntaron llorando mucho. Salió uno, se puso a cierta distancia; eschuchaba. Parecía que alguien cantaba. Llegó a contar, "bueno parece que alguien está cantando ahí entre las ramas." Fueron y la rodearon. Jij! ahí estaba cantando, lo agarraron y se lo trajeron acariciándolo; lo agarraron y lo encerraron para que no se saliera. Lo metieron debajo de una olla embrocada con dos hombres sentados de ambos lados deteniéndola con los pies. Levantaron para ver; miraron, pero no estaba. Ya había desaparecido. Así se iba, por uno o dos días, luego llegaba; asi va y viene; como al mes, volvió.

did that power person go?"; they could not find him. The next morning they gathered together weeping. Someone went out of camp a little ways; he listened there in the bush. It sounded like someone was singing out in the bush. He came to report, "Hey, it sounds like someone is singing out there in the bush." They went and surrounded him. "Hah! There he was, singing; they took hold of him and brought him back, fondling him. They took and locked him up so he couldn't escape. They turned a large pot over on him, with two men holding it down on either side with their feet.

They lifted it up to look; they looked, but he was gone! He had disappeared. And so he would take off, for one or two days, then come home; so he had gone; about a month later he returned.

ˀickspoc nyul wak; maa, yac yuvwik ˀam paa viny kwir hicˀam kute pavcnyu wirhik ˀam kum ˀˀite. yuvyum yuw kuso, ksar ˀim kyak, macc yukwe nax nyaso kwil miv; mnax mˀeec yukyus heh heh! ksar kcwic nyaam nyiw mat kvtec nxkyek; xwak, xmuk nyum.

Había un sabio ahí. "Bueno, este va andar así hasta que acabe con todos nosotros, va a acabar con todos," dijo. "Si así es, estos que les dicen "coyotes", ustedes que dicen, ¿'qué mataré para comer'? "dénmelo muerto." je, je! los coyotes lo persiguieron para allá para acá, atravesaron el mundo dos o tres

There was a shaman there, "Well, this child is going to finish us off, he'll kill us all." "If that is the case, you who are called 'coyotes,' you who say, 'what am I going to kill to eat?' bring him to me dead." Ha ha! the coyotes chased him this way and that, they went around the

xwakul ʔam xmuk xkay nyum nytvlwiiv nyam yak nckyo hik xanu. mak kyam mtksa nytṣtox nyam xuum. heh! nynaxclmaat-kumyik. mat mtxak yukwe kavyuc xumeycum, vṣkwik nyulyev vṣkwim; kavwik wic par tem. kwak pa wac peku-kwak, patkskwaykukwak pa matc kwam. vooc tyiw ʔiny, kaav, pem kut paa kavyuc kav-wik wiparr temaat. kavʔwik wic parr tem.

ooh, xyiw nyuk yakc yukwe winy naxkulmikwiculik, mnax mʔec. xyiw kcwickunu, kaʔṣitu-liw vṣkwimu kaʔṣite, vṣkwim kavyuk wicpar tem. vṣkwikukwak pawacpekukwak, yuvʔi patks-wayukwak paa matckwam. vooc tyiw kaav; pem! ʔit, pa kavyuc, kavwik wi parr tematm yut.

ʔkwi ʔim kʔam, mac yukwe-winy nyaʔnax kwil myik, mnax mʔeew. heh! ʔkwi kcwickwa-kunu. matsak yak ukxyek xwak, xmuk wim. xmsil yunyxaym. yucv maa, yac nynax temaat ʔiwk ʔim yaamk ʔam kaʔṣithai vṣkwimu kaʔṣithai ulyev sai vṣkwim. rruy cʔop. vṣkwik nyʔiku-kwak, pa wac pek patkswa-yukwak pa mat ckwam. vooc

veces. De ambos lados iban; un tercer coyote ya iba emparejando-sele; ya le mordía el que iba atrás. Ya le rozaba los talones con el hocico. "Jij! parece que me van a matar." Algo creó para el norte, ahí se metió, se paró no le pudieron hacer nada. Los regañó mucho, los puso en ridículo. Se regresaron, di-ciendo, "no, no hay quien le haga nada. No le pudimos hacer nada."

"Ooh, allí está el viento siempre con ganas de matar algo, dénmelo muerto." Los vientos empezaron a corretearlo; fue igual, se paró en el mismo lugar. No pudieron hacer nada. Estuvo parado hablando, re-gañándolos; así dijo, los puso en ridículo. Se regresaron diciendo, "no, nadie le puede hacer nada."

"Nube que anda, tu dices, '¿que cosa mataré?' mátamelo." Ijij! las nubes lo corretearon. Cruzaron las tierras dos, tres veces. Le corrían los mocos y las lágrimas. "Bueno, como que me van a matar"; llegó, se paró allá mismo, se metió allá mismo. Estaba calientito. Empezó a hablar, a regañarlos; los puso en ridículo. Llegaron diciendo, "bueno, no se puede; nadie puede

world two or three times. They ran on either side of him; a third coyote was catching up to him; he was snapping at his heels. His muzzle was brushing his heels. "Heh! It looks like they're going to kill me!" He created something up north and got inside it, he stood there; they could do nothing to him. He scolded them, he ridiculed them. They returned saying, "There's no one who can do anything to him. We could do nothing to him."

"Ooh, there's the wind, always wanting to kill someone; bring him to me dead." The winds began to pursue him. He stood for some time, scolding them; he mocked them. They too came back saying, "No, no one can do anything to him."

"You, cloud who goes about, you say, 'What am I going to kill?' You kill him for me!" They crossed the lands, twice, three times. Tears and snot streamed from him. "Hey, it looks like they're going to kill me"; he arrived and stood at the same place. It was nice and warm. He began to speak, scolding them, he mocked them. They returned

kaav; maa, pemkut pa kavyuc, kavwik wi parr temaat kut. heh! heh!, maa, yac yavwikunut nynaxl mat pay lukuv paxmi.

yaam ʔam kuha, panyuweevc yakm, vaam. sak wak ʔam kwaq saw cnkaṣ, yuvyuc nax kmiik soom wic. paac yos paʔe tem, miiv nyyamik yom kaam ccmoor soockunu, maa paa kavyuc cvkwal cxumey. vaakuh paavc nyʔe nyulitem, kwaq mi ṣik vqnuṣ ʔik ʔamtk, ʔev sev wak timṣ uyaawa kʔaksot. paavc ʔṣe yuk, ntpac. nywik pay nmak, wam yaam.

hacerle nada." "Je,je! estos me van a matar"; huyó el hombre.

Se fue; llegó a un poblado. Ahí estaba; había de esos venaditos; mató uno, se lo comió.

Había gente, pero no les daba de comer. Después lo hizo otra vez, comiendo; "bueno, ¿que clase de gente es ésta tan mesquina?" No les dió nada; andaba siguiendo la huella, escuchó de allá; brincó, cayó encima de la cueva y se sumió ésta. La gente se convirtió en auras. Asi los dejó, se fue para allá.

saying, "Well, it can't be done; no one can do anything to him." "Heh, heh!, these will certainly kill me"; the man fled.

He left, he came to a village. There he was, there were fawns there; he killed one and ate it. There were people but he would not give them anything to eat. Once more he did the same, eating in front of them; "What kind of person is this? He's so stingy!" He didn't give them anything; he was following a trail, he listened; jumped, falling on top of the cave, which collapsed. The people turned into vultures. He left them like that.

vaam pir nyaʔluk taama nyyikuk, yaam mat kavyuc, xac yaam maat tvaavuhak nyiʔsak vṣkwim. mim mat cxan maa ʔcwi vte hʔik ʔam yute. ʔevsum mat yak yak nymṣiwvultyev ʔiw ʔa pemultyevk ʔiwk ʔim yik. tkwek nyumyiw yiwk yiwk yiw; maa matnyak xaama ʔit xamso pemultyev xuw nyuyk yiwk yiw kʔor cpak. matnyak xaam vaak sak vwaak; paa, pac kul ktuk nway xiL xanu wakunuk paa xaak wak wak mik ukwak xiL xanu. yunyxay kʔuw tayo xac nyuk yakum ʔit, xwak ulʔut.

"Ahora si voy a huir mas lejos," dijo. Se fue a una tierra desconocida, allí donde se juntan las aguas y se paró allí. Arregló la tierra con los pies," bueno quiero hacer una cosa grave." Quedó vacilando, la tierra apestaba todavía, "no," dijo. Volvió, se vino y se vino, se vino; "bueno, voy a divisar para el norte," dijo. Divisó, no había nada todavia, venía y venía hasta la lumbre. Miró hacia el norte; llegó, se sentó; allí la gente andaba atizando liebres; hubieron muchos, divisó la gente, se puso a llorar. Le corrían muchas lágrimas. Allí está

"Now I shall really run far away," he said; he went off to an unknown land, where the seas come together; he stopped there. He prepared the ground with his feet, "Well, I'd like to do an important deed." He remained hesitating; the earth still reeked; he said, "No." He turned back, coming, coming, coming. "Well, I am going to look northward," he said; he looked, there was nothing yet; he came and came up to the flame. He looked northward; (when) he arrived, he sat down;

ukwak nykyok, nalk nyumyiw nyuwac wam yuk vaak. nmooc sakwak ˀvaak ˀyut, paavc vaak yut. hih! mnˀ-kiˀmool mukwak mit; vaak mukwak mim loomk ukwak. hem, yumi tem; mvraar mkrˀet, mtwaṣ mˀev. ˀeheh! ˀik, pay raar krˀet twaṣ mitknsaak twaṣ. nyaˀxan, paa mvaak myiwh mim maa, xa ˀaw mwi kamyu. pem yut xa ˀic wis tpay; xa ˀic ˀev tpay yak wak yum. xac nyuk yooso, yukwe kavyucc nyuk yakm paa kavyuc txipe tem. upukuhak ˀuwsum npoo ṣutathac sakyak yok nyuṣutat xamat cwam yook nytcaq. pay xavm yaam xamsm sakyakm ˀiw. vmṣev ˀik; maa, xa mwi sinyhˀik ˀˀam ˀyut. heh! xmany kavyuc yuvny hˀik yak tem ˀyum. yaam kyuc kyaam pay xvcul wa ṣiv uxiny. xa mwi msiny ˀik ˀˀamk ˀˀite. pay ya xal vyoo ˀik. xa yaal nyuyoom, vraar caav wam cpaq ˀaav ckyat wir. xa cxwatultyev kweyum pay paraw vkmim nmo wa,

todavía; el agua corriendo en dos chorros.

Calló, venía bajando; llegó a una casa. Allí estaba la abuelita. "Ha venido alguien, he venido." "¡Jiji!. Te estas burlando de mi," dijo la anciana, "llegaste pero estoy ciega!" "¡No, no digas eso!" "¡levántate en pinganillas y tiéntame!" "Ejé!" dijo, se puso en pinganillas y lo tocó; le tocó el talón. "¡Es verdad, has llegado!" "Bueno, ¿no tienes agua?" "No, nunca he tenido eso, agua; ni siquiera he oido la palabra agua." "Hay agua allí, pero hay una cosa allí; nadie se le arrima." Vió el rinconcito; allí estaba el bastón del abuelo, lo agarró y se apoyó en él, agarró una olla y se la encajó en el cinto. Entonces entró para allá, fue y divisó—era cierto. Era horroroso. "Bueno, quiero tu agua; por eso he venido." "¡Jij! ¡no estoy para que ningún chamaco me diga eso!" Llegó, siguió, entonces sopló, le quitó el pensamiento. "Digo que quiero tomar donde tu tomas" Luego el animal bajó la boca al agua. Cuando se acercó al agua, brincó encima de él; le pegó; lo hizo pedazos a garrotazos. El agua

the people there were burning out the jackrabbits. There were many people, he spied them and began to weep. His tears streamed down. It is that way still, the water falling in two streams.

He fell silent, he was coming down; he came to a house. His grandmother lived there. "Someone's come, I've come!" he called. "Heh! you're mocking me," said the old lady; "you've come but I'm blind!" "No, really, rise up on your tip toes and touch me!" "Eh heh," she said, rising on her tip toes; she (barely) touched his heel. "It's true, you've really come." "Well now, do you have any water?" "No, I've never had any of that, water; I've not even heard the word, 'water.'" "There's water there, but there's something there, no one comes near it." He looked into the bend of the house, there stood his grandfather's staff; he took it and leaned on it; he took a pot and slipped it under his belt. He headed yonder, he looked and saw it—sure enough! It was horrible: "Well now, I'd like your water, that's why I've come." "Heh! I'm not going to let any kid talk to me like that!"

yook kmi nyulxwil. xal vaˀnyaw ˀim salcpak yiw xarṣi. maa, mat yavyuk yokuw ˀikuwk. myum mvok pay pqic vook yaam. sakwak cpayt xumeykunuk; cxwat wam ˀutm unuk.

quedó ensangrentada; así es que corrió para abajo, agarró a la abuelita que estaba ahí. Esta desapareció en el agua, salió de ahí con los ojos abiertos "¡Pero, así es el mundo!" exclamó. "¡Andale, vete!" Entonces la viejita se fue. Allí estaba, estuvo creándo todas las enfermedades; tirando la sangre.

He drew near, he blew at it taking hold of his mind. "I said I'd like to drink where you drink!" The animal lowered its mouth to the water. When he drew near the water, the other jumped on top of him; striking him, he hacked him to bits with the staff. The water turned red with blood; he ran down the canyon and took hold of his grandmother. She disappeared in the water, she emerged with her eyes opened wide. "So that's how the world is!" she exclaimed. "Go, now, go home!" The old lady left. He stood there flinging water, creating every kind of disease.

nywir xa nyyook yaam vaam yak, sak yak yakm ktnyaavhm. yel xwat xav tyaam wik vwi ˀyu tem. pqi vwaak miwi nyaˀpay nyum vcip ˀim. mnwiknymatp wick mikukwak nyumvcip ˀim yook taxm. maa, sakwam nytvyul xani, kvyul vaˀkur ˀim.

Cuando acabó, agarró el agua, se fue; llegó, se acostó allí de noche, Se pintó con mescal rojo completamente. La viejita se sentó a llorar toda la noche, amaneció llorando Por los taraiso lloraba hasta el amanecer, echándoles maldiciones. Bueno, ahí estaban los zapatos, se los puso.

When he had finished, he took the water and left; he got there and lay down at night. He painted his whole face with red mescal dye. The little old lady sat weeping all night long; she was still crying at dawn. She was weeping because of the Taraiso, casting curses on them. Well, there were the sandals, he put them on.

kṣit yak. vxnyaav nyˀik. kamyuuli pa ˀic wiv xlyec nyukwa nyuyuw mˀuwme. ˀih, kavaˀyuk ˀˀuwhmuw paavc ˀˀaam kos txpeulitem ˀˀam ˀyute, myiw ˀik nyuvwam. qwoow tṣkyat tṣkyat. vaam mnyxpu

Uno se presentó, se paró allí. "¿Como está? Por allí hay una fiesta, ¿la has visto?" "¿Ej? como voy a ver eso? Soy gente, no me he arrimado del todo, aquí ando," le dijo, "a ver" y lo sentó. Le trozó los cabellos. "Ahora, agarra tu arma, ve

Someone came. "What's up? There's a feast over yonder; have you seen it?" "Eh? How am I going to have seen that? I am a person, I haven't even come close!" "Let's see," he said to him and made him sit down.

myook wak mwam, xwaamyuwc nyukmikpakm, ˀˀuwk yuso. nyxpu yook sak vwam xwa yuuc, yapk; ṣit, xwakm yak vwak. ah hah! yuvyulmaatm ˀˀit. myaam mˀuwk, mvaam myuso mimak mxav myuso mkkaav mˀevcm xnalhaˀ kavwikunuk mˀek, kavyuhcum ˀit. pem kut, yukwe kwar tpay kavwik nyˀecw hucyoo tem. hem kut mnwiknymatp ˀickṣpo sal yak. yukwevc kakyom kaṣpom tem ˀit, nyˀe pem xvcum yus myuk mˀuw,nyˀaam vaam yaak yam himak tyam. paxmi txiwin xanu, vaam xaav himak yak yak xiL xanu. muh! mˀec xac ˀˀev ˀiway xan xan hikyawa ˀik. mnwiknymatp ˀickṣpo sal yak, pem kut yukwe ṣpoov tpaycut pema. heh! ˀivˀil ˀikˀit ˀik ˀevm xvcul waṣivuxiny. himak yak yak, paxmi vakur ˀim, nykkaavi mˀecm xac ˀiway xan hˀik ˀit. eh he! xan mˀec mˀik yus vkap mika, yukwe ṣpov yoo tem ˀˀit ˀiultyev; paxmi xac himak yak yak yok. pac vkap ˀik xanu mkam kavyuhic yo tem. pa mi vntuk salxkyevm ˀuwk, paxmi sam vxkyev ˀim; yok wam kwit ˀik. kcwic nyam ṣxwir yakm yapk vraar, qwow tnanc, kur hickaayvc wakuk

allá, capeate; salta así para verte yo." Agarró su arco, se sentó allá, brincó capeandose; uno, dos saltos se sentó aquí. "¡Aja! así mero," dijo "Vete a ver; cuando llegues, entra bailando, pídeles a ver el bule, a ver si de alguna manera te lo dan. "Pueda ser," dijo. "No, es un poderoso el hechicero no me lo va a dar de ninguna manera, no." Allí estabá el sabio de los taraiso. "No hay nada que se le pase, todo lo sabe, no me lo va a dar pero ve a ver ahora. De aquí para allá iba bailando. El hombre bailaba de un lado al otro; entró bailando muchísmo. "Muj! dénme la sonaja para sonarla y quedar contento yo." Allí estaba el sabio de los taraiso, dijo que no, "es cosa que no se sabe." "¡Ijij! ya sabía que iba a decir eso," sopló y le quitó el pensamiento. Andaba bailando mucho el hombre, al rato pidíó otra vez diciéndoles, "dénmela para sonarla y quedar contento." "¡Eje! bueno, dásela, pero rodeenlo, no sabes lo que puede suceder," decía aún, el hombre la sonó y bailó. Estaba rodeado; ni por donde hacerle. Vío un portillo; por allí salió rapidísimo, "¡se lo llevó!" dijo. Lo corretearon; había un cerco y lo brincó; lo agarraron del cabello. Ya estaba preparado, se zafó. En dos saltos se

He cut his hair. "Now grab your weapon and go over there, come dodging this way, so I can see you." He took his bow, sat over yonder; he leapt, dodging this way and that; one, two leaps, and sat here directly in front of him. "Ah hah! Just right!" he said. "Go see now, when you get there approach them dancing, ask them to see the rattle, let's see if they'll give it to you." "Maybe," he said. "No, the shaman is a person of power; he won't give it to me under any circumstances." The Taraiso lineage shaman was there. "Nothing escapes him, he knows everything, he won't give it to me." "But go see now"; he danced away toward the feast. The man danced from side to side; he entered, dancing furiously. "Whew! Let me have the rattle so I can enjoy myself!" The Taraiso shaman was there; he said not to. "One never knows," he said. "Eh heh! I knew he was going to say that!" The god blew and took his mind away. The man was dancing wildly; a moment later he asked once more saying, "Let me play it so I can enjoy myself!" "Eh heh! All right give it to him, but

vcperq ʔik. yapk xwak se vwam, paxmi kkyek tkwek ʔkmiik wite yook xac ʔev.

heh! maa, paavc reelmaatm wicukum xan kuwkum pay sakyak, yakm yukm yuwha pay nyʔi myaam mik. myaav kyak vaak kwakut mihvcum, vaam myaavkyak vaak kwakut ʔik nyuvmkwaaw hukwam yek ʔite. kwaawuli tem pay kkyek tkwek. paa myaav kyak vaa ʔumukwawkukwak nyayek ʔʔiso kwawuli temkute. heh! heh! . . . ah! myaam myus, vaakukwak, mvși naxvya wașiv ʔim ʔʔite mixvcute. yaam nyvaami myaav kyak vaa tnyaavm nyumukwakukwak mvși mnaxha wașiv ʔim ʔʔite. heh! paa tpay mun supac naxk ʔamhac mʔamheʔ; maa, mnyam mcʔuwcum ʔik nyaʔxanukwak o kavyukukwak yum yuso.

paró allá, allí se devolvió, "la traje," dijo.

"¡Ijij! bueno pués, uno se puede divertir con ésto bien"; entonces allí estaba, y dijo, "vete para allá." "Diles que vino el dios, que allí está"; llegó y les, dijo, "vino el dios allá está; amaneció hablando de ustedes." No dijo nada entonces, se regresó, vino. "El-Del-Cielo llegó, y habló contra ustedes hasta el amanecer, pero no contestó nada. "¡Ijejé! aah, si vas dí, 'se acordó de la mujer que mató.'" "Vino dios y amaneció hablando contra ustedes se acordó de la mujer que mató." "¡Ijij! no es gente; ha de ser el que andaba muriéndose del frío; bueno vayan a verlo a ver si es cierto lo que dice o no."

surround him; you don't know what might happen," he insisted; the man shook the rattle and danced. He was surrounded; no way out. He saw a small slit, slipped through like a flash. "He's taken it!" exclaimed (the shaman). They chased after him; he leapt over a barricade; they seized him by the hair, but it had already been prepared; he slipped away. In two leaps he landed yonder, he turned the rattle over. "I got it," he said.

"Eh heh, all right now, this is really enjoyable"; he said, "Go back." "Tell them that the god has come, that he is there"; he went and told them, "The god has come; he's been ranting about you all night." They didn't answer; he returned. "The 'One-From-The-Sky' has come, and has railed against you into the dawn"; there was no answer. "Ah hah hah! If you go, say, 'He has remembered the woman he killed.'" "The god has come and it dawned on him railing against you, he recalled the woman he had killed." "Eh heh! That's no human being, it must be the one who was freezing to death; so go see if it's true."

paa xwak nyiw kaav nykaavhikukwakm ʔev myaav kyak sak yak nymnypihik, nyyamkakur vaam temaat. sa xaʔpay cʔuw, nkwek nkaam knav. kavyuwe, pem kut yukweuli cʔuw tem. yuvyul ʔik ʔʔite pay vaak ckwim, nytkwek ʔik ʔik.

xwayhik ʔit, vaam knaav xwayhik ʔit. heh! nyeulik tek mʔamheʔ maatcumk tyamkyok. pa kwac yuk vyiw ʔitem, nyeulik tekuku xway ʔik mʔamhe. pay xankuwkm vwak myaav kyak kwaawac yoov, pay kwir hpu yoov, qlyayyaʔ xwakna, xpuk mat yaal xwa knam. cmyul nyac ckas kyaknyu xwa knam. mat yaal yiw cpak vyiw ʔitem. ʔuwk hiway vlsa ʔim pay uya kʔak sot unuk. nycwir mtkwek nyaʔxankut mik mknav. nyaami paxmi. pay kur xway nyxan pay nymnmanchik ʔit. xankukumʔik pay paac yumkunuk xiL xanu myaav kyak paa wic ṣvlwik cwok yeryeru.

myaavkyak paavc tekwil, kyook tyaam ṣxwir cmik maat nkyahik, mtʔinc ʔik, nyvntusm mvṣkwick. vraar myaav yak

Dos hombres fueron, llegaron, los oyó; ahí estaba el dios moribundo, no alcanza este día. Eso no mas vieron, regresaron, y llegaron a contar. "¿Que pasó?" "no, nada, no vimos nada." "Ya sabia eso," dijo, entonces vino y preguntó, se arrendó.

"Va a haber guerra"; llegó y dijo que iba a haber guerra. "Ijij! han de haber muchos reunidos como nosotros." Había una gran multitud, han de haber muchos como nosotros para hacer guerra. Luego dijo, "bueno"; se sentó dios; hizo el pedernal, formó arcos; llamó primero de guerreros a los mexicanos, bajo la tierra llamó a a la guerra. A las hormigas negras, a esas chiquitas, las llamó. Salieron de la tierra muchas. Cuando les vío, le dieron asco, sumió la cuevita con una patada. Cuando acabó, le dijo al hombre, "ve otra vez y avísales." Fue otra vez el hombre. "Ya está listo, ya van a empezar," dijo. "Bueno, entonces juntó a la gente; muchísimos, la gente del dios; los puso en el puro medio a los enemigos.

La gente de dios eran muchos mas. Formaron una hilera; cuando ya se iban a disparar dijo, "estense quietos un momentito." Voló al

Two men went, they arrived, he heard them, there was the god, on his deathbed; he couldn't live through to the end of that day. That's all they saw, they came back and reported that. "What happened?" "Nothing, we didn't see anything." "I knew it," he said; he came, asked and went back.

"There will be a war," he arrived and said there would be a war. "Eh heh! They must be as many as we are." There was a great multitude, "There must be as many as us for war." Then he said, "All right"; the god sat down; he made arrowheads, shaped bows; first he called under the earth for warriors. The small black ants, he called. Many came out of the ground. When he saw them all, he was repelled and kicked their anthill in. When he was done, he told the man, "Go once again, to tell them." The man went again. "He's ready, he's about to start," he said. "All right," Then he gathered the people together, an immense horde, god's people; he surrounded the foe.

The people of god outnumbered the others. They formed a row; when they were about to shoot, he said, "Be still for a

piim, payt ˀik yak twiru hivya payt xumey wir vaampira mwick. kyam ṣit, paa kyatetkwan xwil curcur ˀim nyamhac nyamhac paawir ˀik ˀit tnyyiwk yakm. nykakwacm, maa, mtyuc xpir nypicvkute mnkwevi, mckaavi. hem kute, mun supac nax kˀam pem, nyulum mwircum paytm twir cwir. mnwiknymatp ˀickṣpo ṣiṣ, vraar, tnyaavm cpam. mya kskyehik yaamm kxav, qpay ˀaav kyet mat kwekum ukxav xa vaˀnyaw ˀim. maat xpir xal nal sacˀam, maat nyaˀxwaym cpak xmṣi kṣkul ˀim kˀamnyu ˀim ˀˀit. mat xwaym cpak kur qwinyckuk tṣpeev yaam yuvyuk cpak ˀamkum ˀˀit. paa wac twir kwir pa mat kyak paaulikakˀam tem.

cielo acostado, hablando de todo lo que usaría para matarlos, lo creó todo, "ahora sí." Un jarazo tumbaba al enemigo diezmándolos, acabaron a los que venían. Al fin le dijeron, "bueno, solo quedan tus puros parientes; tus tios, tus primos." "No," dijo el que había sufrido del frío; "no, terminen con todos." Solo quedaba el hechicero de los taraiso; voló de noche. Iba a cruzar el cielo; dios lo alcanzó, le trozó la cabeza de un garrotazo, siguió para el sur, se perdió de vista. El cuerpo cayó al golfo; ese es el cometa que anda cuando va a haber guerra. Sale cuando hay guerra, se ladea porque; no está firme la cabeza. Acabó con todos los habitantes de la tierra, no quedó nadie.

moment." He flew into the sky and lay there naming all the things he would use to kill them; he created them all. "All right, now!" One arrow would kill many enemies, decimating them; they were slain. Toward the end they said to him, "All right, only your closest kin are left, your uncles and cousins." "No," said the one who had suffered the cold, "No, kill them all off." Only the Taraiso shaman was left; he flew into the night. He was going to cross the sky; the god caught up with him and hacked his head off with his club; the head flew into the South and disappeared. The body fell into the Gulf; the head is the comet that appears when there's going to be war. It comes out when there's a war, it wags back and forth because it is not firm. He finished off all the earth's inhabitants, no one was left.

vlii ˀi, kavyucicwam, ˀickṣpo cxumey cˀam sac ṣkulnac vntum kwartuy. mat yak yak yac xvṣu lip ˀik yuvyus. pac man ˀikukwak ˀam ṣit xwak manso paytek paawa panywir nyaˀpaym.

Quedó silencio; había alguien, un sabio, ese apareció. Esta tierra se tiñó de verde, asi fue. Unas cuantas gentes se levantaron; uno o dos pero aumentó la raza.

All was silent; there was somebody there, a sage, he appeared. The earth turned green, so it was. A few people arose; one or two, but from them the human race began again.

aah, pay luk yum yaam yaam kˀam mat kavyuc mkak

Aah, se fue huyendo llegó a un lugar desconocido, donde había tri-

Aah, he fled; he came to an unknown land, he arrived at a

yom ʔnpe yaku ʔicucyom vaam. vṣkwik sak nyvaam cicihac kxav ʔmayva lsik wir ṣalk cci kuwik ʔamkuw. maa, yac kavnya hikuwkum ʔik kaʔṣitk nax ʔmayhac sak ʔut, ʔnpe yumkuk npe xumey nmak.

vlo ʔik wam yaam kyuc wi nyukwe nyukm tkwil vṣkwik. mat yak yak ya ʔuwm, wi kʔam kyat yaam myiw. maa, kavyukuw ʔuwk vṣkwik; maa, yukwe kavyuk wi kparr nyeuli ʔam kuwkum ʔik ʔuk vṣkwik vṣkwitk nyaʔpay. maa, hwil knymatp ʔam yuw nysaʔac myum yuwk yum waṣiv pay ʔmaat tkwek kaṣitulik, xkaym yak tem pay kyuc vmak ʔim. heh, sac wiwkum kyuc wam yaam yaam kʔam yam kʔam kuwha mat mkak yom yuwha, mskwa cscmicu ʔicuc yoom yak sak vaam.

xaxsil nyul qam kyakm yuk, sak mim matcaʔxaankunuk. wir yavʔwim wam nukwas xa nynal cpayt yal waac paavc soo hivcut ʔik wa ṣivv. yoov kwir pay nmak kyuc yaam mat mkakk yomk wem, xakkwac.

nyiʔsak paavcc yakm vaam, sakwak paamiceev cpayt wicm sook ʔiny sakwak unuk. tiyp

gal llegó. Se paró allí, alcanzó a la mamá; le ordeñó la teta, la leche le quedó en la mano; andaba persiguiendo a la madre. "Bueno, ¿que me irá a decir esta?" allí mismo la mató. La leche cayó, se creó el trigo, la dejó.

Desapareció, iba por allá le dio vuelta al cerro *Nyukwa*, ahí se paró. Vió todo el mundo, iban pasando pedazos del cerro. "Bueno, ¿cómo está ésto? pues, debe de haber otro como yo de poderoso," dijo. "Bueno, ha de ser duende el que está haciendo ésto," pensó; entonces volvió la tierra a ser como debe ser; no cambió, siguió igual. "¡Je!, ese es el que hizo"; siguío caminando.

En un lugar cerca del mar estuvo arreglando la tierra. "Aquí voy a hacer ésto así, cuando baje la marea va a quedar aquí para que coma la gente," pensó. Hizo todo, entonces lo dejó; se fue. Llegó a un lugar desconocido, al último aguaje.

Había habitantes ahí, estuvo con ellos, hacía algo y comían. Andaban pescando con una de esas

wheat field. He stood there, caught his mother, milking her breast, the milk lay in his hand; he pursued his mother. "So what's she going to say to me?"; he killed her then and there; the milk fell and created a wheat field; he left.

He disappeared, he skirted *Nyukwa* mountain, and stopped. He looked at the land, broken earth came flowing past. "What's this? There must be another power being like me about," he said. "It must be a genie who is doing this," he thought. He changed the earth back to how it should be, it was as before. "Heh! He's the one who did it!" He kept walking.

At a place near the sea he remained fixing the earth. "I'm going to fix this so that when the tide goes out this will remain for people to eat," he thought. He did it all, then left it; he left and got to an unknown land, the last water hole.

There were people there, he stayed with them. He would make something and they'd eat.

ucpaac wakunucum ukwak. mltat tatha sac yuvyucham. tiyp ucpaack unucm wicu ʔuwk. ʔmu kwavc yakm ʔikok pay yoovkunuk wir ṣitm ʔek. yook nyukcvok ncpaackunuk kwartem xanu unuk. nyuwik nyumyuw hyuwm yuha, kyethivcut ʔik ʔiwayl waṣiv kyak ukyak. nyucpaac raavm kyet, kal vaʔnyaw ʔim. sakwak wacmak xkay cyok ucpackunuc paʔuwk wakunuk. ṣithulwaku kavwikunuk ʔṣitm yook. maa, ʔmukwa ʔʔeha nyiʔsaʔ kkyet kʔamka ucpaccut ʔik waṣiv. uyiw hucpac ukyoov vnun titʔuwk. sal wam uk. maa, yukwe cuny yak wak ʔi us yuvyucvcu. xkay, nykwihac sakwak ʔik, kavyuwehik, ʔʔe ya nyʔwi yanyʔwi mʔek mʔek yanyʔwivcut. nyumkkamwik myoy ʔiv ckwikukwaac vaam kavaac nyuc nyʔem wit ʔi knaav payt yuvwik paa kwic ntpacm. aah, sam xpir panywitaam wakunuk yuvyuwkwaku.

nyam ṣitm yuw, nyec maknyul vaak cwi xkayv ʔnmakwit. mnyaam mcʔuw xaʔil ʔac ʔo yukwec nyul wam, mkmicm

espinas de biznaga. Vió que así pescaban. Cargaba un cuerno de borrego; lo arregló y se lo dió a uno. Agarró y empezó a sacar pescados, muchísimos. Pensó dios en su corazón que se iba a trozar la cuerda de pescar. Cuando sacó el pescado, se trozó; el pescado desapareció en el mar. Ahí estaba otro sin nada, lo estaba jalando, los estaba viendo dios. Había uno, quien sabe como le hacía; pescó uno. "Bueno, al que le dí el cuerno de borrego lo sacará," pensó dios. Trajo y lo sacó, le rajó la panza y vió. Allí estaba. "Bueno," ¿qué está aquí?" dijo. El otro, el dueño, estaba allí y dijo "¿que cosa? No, este es mío, dámelo, dámelo, ¡es mío éste!" Cuando lo pidió le dijeron, "agarralo"; ahora le preguntaron; "el que llegó ahorita me lo dio," contó; les dió a todos igual. Ahora sí, les trató mas; así estaba haciendo.

Un día dijo, "llegué al otro lado, hice una cosa allí." "Vayan a ver si hay pescados o otra cosa allí" "Tráiganlas para comer." Iji! fueron

They were fishing, with one of those barrel cactus thorns. He observed that that was the way they fished. He had a mountain sheep horn; he fixed it (made a new hook) and gave it to one of the people. He began to pull many fish out. God thought in his heart that the line was going to break. When he pulled the fish out, the line broke; the fish disappeared into the sea. Another man who didn't have anything was there, pulling the fish out; he was watching them, god. There was one who fished one out, who knows how. "All right, the one I gave the sheep horn to will fish it out," thought the god. He pulled it out, split the fish's belly and looked inside. There he was. "So what's this?" he said. The other man, the owner of the hook said, "What? No, that's mine, give it back, give it here, it's mine!" When he asked for it, they said to him, "Take it." Then they asked about it. "The newcomer gave it to me just now," he told them; he gave them all hooks. Now they could all do it.

One day he said, "I was over there and made something." "Go see if there are any fish or something there. Bring them so

soocck. hah! maknyam cʔuws, heh sakwakuw ʔooyok yuk vyuw ʔi tem. twir cakmik sooc-kwakunu wak ʔam paykyuc.

nyumyaam kʔam xaknʔoor ṣxwir. mvṣiy xmuk yom xaam xaknʔoor ṣxwir; xmany cnkoṣ yuwk. xaknʔooru ṣa xwir xma-nya ṣmacyuk cnkʔoṣ. paraw xal yoom kʔam. cxa kyok, xmany kyiw nyeʔcmoor nyeʔcmoor mcnyiwk wakukwak. yam vaam ṣit sakwak vxe nyvṣap vxe ṣpuk sakyak, cʔuwkyok. spay ʔicm yak ṣilkunuk ṣit; ṣilkunuk nymunuk mwir myuso, kway nvṣap ʔicmyakm nyul micmik miʔexvcut ʔik waṣivk yak. ṣilk-unuk nycwir yuvyucl ckwak ʔeec mat kavyuhe smit kakyul ʔicm yak, sam tnilm, ṣit loq kmi lipkunu paxmi. nycṣkwak, pay uyoov man vwaak vamṣev ʔik. cʔuw sakyok yukwe kavyucvc vaakum ʔicukʔim. nyukyoy xwak nyaʔpay vrar tpay; kcxwil maat yoov. cṣa ṣiṣ yok kyuc wam yaam panyweev yakm sakyakm sak vaam.

y vieron pero, ijí! había mucho in-comparable cantidad. Mataron, los trajeron y estuvieron comiendo.

Siguió dios por la playa, por la orilla. Divisó a tres mujeres que es-taban a la orilla del mar; se hizo niño chico. Y siguió por la orilla del mar, un niño perdido. Iba co-rriendo. Lo estuvieron divisando, "me hallé un chamaquito," andaba mesquineándose. Llegó; había una mujer vestida de blanco, se le acostó como almohada en la folda; se le quedaron mirando. Estaban azando almejas. "Cuando las acabes de azar, hay una clase de mateado, pongan las almejas allí," dijo en su pensamiento. Cuando acabaron de azar se las dieron en un de esas. Muy lejos habia ixtle largo; metió para allá la mano, arrancó uno y se lo trajo y estuvo chupando la carne el hombre. Cuando se llenó, lueguito se le-vantó que daba miedo. Lo vieron, "¿que cosa vino?" dijeron. Dos de ellas se levantaron, se hicieron gaviotas. Agarró un pájaro y siguió; llegó a una ranchería.

we can eat." Eh heh! They went and saw; wow!, there were a lot of fish, an immense amount. They killed them, brought them home and ate them.

The god wandered along the shore. He spied three women near the seashore; he turned himself into a little boy. He continued along the beach, a little lost boy. He went running along. They were looking at him; "I've found a little boy," she was anxious to have him. He drew near; one of the women was dressed in white, he cradled his head on her; they stared at him. They were roasting shellfish. "When you've done roasting them, there's a type of bunch grass, place the shells there," he said to them in thought. When they were done, they gave him some on some of the grass. At a great distance there were some long agave fibers; he reached way over, snapped one off and sat there swallowing the meat. When he'd had enough, he sprang up quite suddenly. They saw and asked, "What is this?" Two of them arose and became seagulls. He caught one bird and went on, coming to a village.

xempik, nyuk samyam ṣutatm sak cṣkyak. xa sak ucpac. qwow loq kwik, sak cwok skwin. yiw, vaa; heh! maa, xacpac nyukyookum, myaam xa myiw mkmim siiv. mvṣic yaam xaha vaam. neel nyek lwi sak wak; ckyok. kaʔṣit-hak nax. paxmi sakyakyak xoot ʔim vaa tpay, kavykuwko waṣ-ivk yak yakt waṣiv. heh! maa, nyec yavaʔwik ʔʔuw sak cpaak vlwiceʔik. vaam, kurr yaw sa-kwam vaam, ṣal, mi, ktox. xwat yam ʔut kwalk man, kaam kyok pamicev sakwak tiyp sook ʔam haa. mi kavyul haa mikwal ka-vyul. kur temtk ṣit vaam yel twapuk wak makcaav. yel xwat xav, vaamm ʔuwk. heh! paxmi yel twapuk yuw ʔam maak caav. nyec ya sʔel, ya nymṣiw yak yak nyʔev pem, kavyuku-kuwkoʔyik. tiyp ṣilkunuk wir, unuk nywir ʔek. paakvaac tiyp msook ʔicsʔel winy ulcmik ʔe tpuy. paxmi sook nycaav, xa sik, caav xacpac nyuk yom myaam. si sak yak, sikunuk, kavyunytem.

Tenía sed, fue allá y con su bas-tón clavándolo. Sacó agua Se arrancó un pelo lo puso allí en-redado. Llegó, "¡Ijij!" dijo, "bueno, hay un aguaje allí, ve, trae agua para que tomen." Fue una señora al agua. Había una víbora; en cuanto agarraba el agua; la mordió. Inmediatamente la mató. Estaba acostado el hombre allí, al rato pensó, "¿cómo es que no ha lle-gado, que pasaría?" pensó "¡Ijij! bueno yo hice ésto," arrancó rápido. Llegó, hacía bastante que había muerto; allí estaba; le pateó la pierna. Le salió sangre de la boca. Se levantó rápido; llegaron, estuvieron comiendo pescado con ellos. Se calzó el zapato, los hua-raches. Al poco rato llegó uno, llevaba mescal de provisión; se lo comió todo. Se pintó con el mescal rojo, miró. "¡Ijij! el hombre traía mescal de lonche y se lo comió todo." "Yo estaba con una gran hambre que me apestaba la boca y no me dió. Azó pescado, cuando acabó le dio. "Cómete el pescado," le echó cosa salada de brujería en el pescado. El hombre se lo comió, tomó agua, "hay un aguaje allí, ve a tomar." Estuvo tomando no pudo mas.

He was thirsty; he took his staff and pierced the ground. He drew water out. He pulled one of his hairs out and coiled it on the ground. He came and said, "Hey, there's a water hole there; go fetch some water so that you can drink." A woman went. As she went to draw water, a viper bit her! It killed her immediately! The man lay there; after a while he thought, "Why hasn't she returned, what's happened?" "Eh heh, I did this"; he ran off. He came, she'd been dead quite a while; there she lay; he kicked her leg. Blood spurted out of her mouth. She sprang up, then went home and ate fish. He pulled on his sandals. Some time later a man arrived with some agave in his pack; he ate it all. He painted himself with red agave dye. "This man had agave and ate it all." "I was starving, my mouth stank from hunger." He roasted some fish; when he was done he gave the man some. "Eat this fish"; he had cast a salt spell on the fish. The man ate it, he drank water. "Go to the water hole to drink." He drank until he couldn't hold anymore.

paxmi paynyvo, vok yiw. mkak vaak sak paxmi maat tckay, maat xikwilx. mat sˀel kyak paytm yok sak poq. siv cyakm paavc maam wic siv cyakm. nyˀam kuw paxmi nya-yek nyukyekukwam tiyp vte ˀam, vtevcyak mˀecm. ˀcim hikyute. yuvyukyakm, ucpack ˀec. maat cxankunuk. nywir nyanykyek, tnyavtk nyaˀpay myaa ṣpecuvc yakm yok; myaa ṣpek pay myaa ckpaa, va kaxkax ˀik kˀorham cpam . . .◇

Se fue el hombre. Llegó no se a donde. Se convirtió en no se que cosa el hombre, se revolcó en la tierra salada, echó todo allí. Había una clase de sal que la gente comía. Así andaba, mañana o pasado mañana, agárrenme un pescado. Quiere bajar los espíritus. Así de grande se lo pescaron; se lo dieron. Acabó de arreglarse. A la mañana siguiente, tomó una escalera; la recargó en el cielo, y subió al cielo tronándole los pasos subió a la cumbre del cielo . . .◇

The man left. He went I don't know where. The man turned into I don't know what, he rolled about on the salt bed vomiting it all up there. There was a type of salt that people used. And so he lived there; "Catch me a fish, one of these." He wanted to call down the spirits. They caught one this big and gave it to him. He was finished getting ready (for a trip). The next morning, he took a ladder, leaned it on the sky and climbed up to heaven, his footsteps thundering as he climbed to the top of the sky. . . .◇

Bibliography

Blaisdell, Lowell A. 1962. *The desert revolution, Baja California, 1911*. Madison: University of Wisconsin Press.

Hinton, Thomas B., and Owen, Roger C. 1957. Some surviving Yuman groups in northern Baja California. *America Indigena* 17: 87–102.

Mixco, Mauricio J. 1977. Documentos en Paipai (Yumano), con comentario. *Tlalocan* 7: 205–26.

———. 1983. Kiliwa texts: "When I have donned my crest of stars." University of Utah Anthropological Papers 107.

———. Forthcoming. *A grammar of Kiliwa*. Salt Lake City: University of Utah Press.

———. Forthcoming. *Kiliwa dictionary*. Salt Lake City: University of Utah Press.

Notes, Acknowledgments, and Credits

I am grateful to Rufino Ochurte for having shared his cultural memories with me and for his permission to publish the materials he entrusted to me; this permission has been posthumously ratified by his closest kin, his brother's children—Ceferina, Trinidad, Cruz, and Teodoro Ochurte. I thank all of the above for their kindness. I should like to express special thanks to Trinidad Ochurte and Benito Peralta for their assistance in the translation and grammatical analysis of the Kiliwa and Paipai materials, respectively. I am particularly grateful to the latter gentlemen and their households for the hospitality they have extended to me through the years I have been visiting Baja California. I also thank the authorities of Santa Catarina for their kind cooperation.

The work which has contributed to this publication was initially funded by grants from the Survey of California and Other Indian Languages of the University of California, Berkeley, Department of Linguistics; subsequently by The American Philosophical Society's Phillips Fund and by the University of Utah Faculty Research and Career and Development Committees. The latter also authorized two quarters of sabbatical leave, while the former granted me a David P. Gardner Faculty Fellowship. I gratefully acknowledge this indispensable support.—*Mauricio Mixco.*

Photo credits: pp. 191 and 192—Victor Masayesva; p. 201—photographer unknown.

Notas, Reconocimientos, y Créditos

Le agradezco al difunto Rufino Ochurte la manera en que compartió conmigo sus memorias. Además le agradezco el permiso de publicar el material del cual me dejó encargado; este permiso ha sido ratificado por sus parientes mas cercanos, los hijos de su hermano—Ceferina, Trinidad, Cruz, y Teodoro Ochurte. A todos les debo un voto de gracias. Quisiera agradecer en forma muy especial la colaboración de Trinidad Ochurte y de Benito Peralta en la traducción y el análisis de estos materiales en kiliwa y en paipai, respectivamente. Agradezco además la hospitalidad de estos caballeros y de sus familias en haberme hospedado a través de los años, siempre recibiéndome como a un amigo en su hogar. A la communidad indígena de Santa Catarina le agradezco la autorización de publicar este texto en paipai.

Mi trabajo ha sido sufragado por becas de la Universidad de California en Berkeley, por el Philips Fund de la American Philosophical Society y por el comité de investigaciones de la facultad por medio del sabático que facilitó esta Universidad. —*Mauricio J. Mixco.*

Créditos por fotographías: pp. 191 and 192—Victor Masayesva; p. 201—fotografo desconocido.

DIEGUEÑO
Literature

LEANNE HINTON and MARGARET LANGDON,
Editors

The Diegueños

The term Diegueño is meant to designate the Indians who were under the jurisdiction of the Mission San Diego de Alcala, in Southern California, and has been extended to include other people speaking dialects of the same language. Some people have differentiated the northern dialects of Diegueño from the southern dialects by referring to them as 'Iipay and Tipay, respectively—words for "people." The term "Kumeyaay" is also used by some Diegueños to refer to themselves.

Diegueño is the westernmost language of the Yuman linguistic family, geographically centered around the present location of San Diego, California. Diegueño territory comprises all of San Diego County south of 33°15′ latitude, most of Imperial County south of the same line exclusive of the easternmost section along the Colorado River, and the adjacent areas of Northern Baja California down to about 60 miles south of the Mexican border.

There are many communities, each one characterized by its own dialect. From north to south, the present communities are Mesa Grande, San Pasqual, Santa Isabel, Inaja, Barona, Baron Long, Jamul, Cuyapaipe, Manzanita, Campo (all north of the border), and south of the border San José, Neji, Ha'a, San José de la Zorra, and La Huerta. A number of Diegueño speakers also live in the Paipai community of Santa Catarina.

Traditionally, there were many more permanent settlements than these; probably each valley had one. People would make treks from their villages to other locations to gather foods not available in their village territories. Every family, then, had resources in the valleys, the mountains, and the coast. They were extremely flexible in their adaptations. The Diegueños of the deserts and the eastern mountain regions, where appropriate summer moisture was available, had irrigated fields of corn, beans, and squash. Beyond that, all Diegueños practiced the burning of expanses of land to encourage the growth of beneficial plants. They broadcast semi-domesticated grass seeds over the hills and planted a variety of other wild species, including the oak. It is worth noting that several species tended by the Diegueños became extinct when they were forced to cease their plant husbandry (Shipek, 1977).

The Diegueños, along with the Cocopahs, live on both sides of the border between the United States and Mexico. Because of this artificial political division, they have had very different recent histories (see Shipek, 1978). ◇

The Contributors

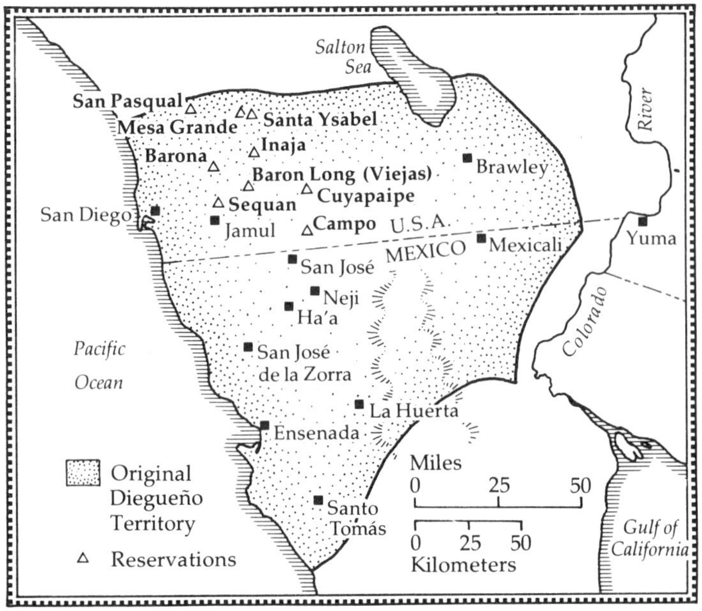

Rebecca Alto was a native of the Santa Ysabel Reservation who moved into Southern Diegueño (Kumeyaay) territory as a young adult. She worked with Alfred S. Hayes in 1953, but died long before the story she authored was ever transcribed. Little is known about her life; that she was a knowledgeable and extremely talented storyteller is attested by the tale reprinted here.

Ted Couro, born in 1889, was the son of a former Captain of the Mesa Grande Indian Band. He was educated at Perris Indian School and later at the Sherman Institute. In his youth he was a professional baseball player, violinist, rancher, and organizer of the Progressive American Indians, a precursor of the Mission Indian Federation. In 1917 he married Lillie Damron, and soon after became a minister in the Nazarene Church. For many years he was a minister in Yuma, for the Quechans. He worked in an aircraft factory during World War II. After retirement from his ministry, he and his wife returned to Escondido, where he became well known as a lecturer, artist, musician, and teacher—as well as a champion horseshoe player. An eloquent speaker of the Diegueño language and extremely knowledgeable about traditional Indian ways, he spent a great deal of time in his later years working with anthropologists and linguists to record the language, culture, and history of his people. He died in 1975.

Christina Hutcheson was Ted Couro's first cousin and an eloquent speaker of the Mesa Grande dialect. She was born in 1880 and, like Ted Couro, was educated at the Perris Indian School and the Sherman Institute. Later she received training as a nurse. She lived most of her life in San Diego. Until her death in 1973, she stayed very well informed about Indian affairs and maintained a precise and unfailing memory for genealogy, historical events, and other aspects of Diegueño tradition. She co-authored a dictionary of the Mesa Grande language with Ted Couro, which came out just before her death.

Margaret Langdon received her Ph.D. from the University of California at Berkeley in 1966, and has since been a professor of linguistics at the University of California at San Diego. She has been studying Yuman languages since 1963. Besides numerous scholarly works, she has helped some Diegueño speakers develop materials useful to their communities, such as a dictionary of the Mesa Grande dialect and a practical grammar, "Let's Talk 'Iipay

Aa." She has also dedicated much time to assisting native speakers of Diegueño in teaching their language to interested members of their communities.

Alejandrina Murillo Melendres was born and raised in the Diegueño community of La Huerta, Baja California. She remembers her childhood as a time of severe economic deprivation. When no other food was available, her grandmother would send her out to gather the "Indian Cherry," which gave nourishment but also caused severe stomachache. When the ranchers began to come into the area, so that wage labor became possible, the quality of life began to improve. Alejandrina Melendres was married for many years to Alberto Murillo, and they lived most of the time in La Huerta. When Alberto died in 1970, she began to spend much of her time in Ojos Negros, living with her son Ishmael and his family. Unceasingly energetic, she travels often to San Diego to visit with relatives there, and in her town has developed a small business in clothing sales. A native speaker of the La Huerta dialect of Diegueño, she knows many delightful folktales, two of which have been reproduced here.

The Diegueño Alphabet

Vowels

Diegueño has five short vowels and four long vowels. The short vowels are represented by one letter; the long vowels are represented by two identical letters. Vowels may also occur in diphthongs, which are short or long vowels followed by the letter "w" or "y".

Short vowels

a *mat*, 'self'. This vowel can vary between the vowel sounds of n*o*t and b*u*t; it is most often like the *a* in Spanish names like M*a*r*í*a, Tiju*a*n*a*.

e *'emat*, 'land'. This is an indistinct vowel which is never accented and never long. It is the same sound as Quechan ə. It is like the *e* in English brok*e*n, or the *a* in sof*a*.

i *'ewik*, 'west'. *i* is like the vowel in English p*i*n, t*i*p.

o *wetoch*, 'they hit him'. This sound is very rare in Diegueño. It is like *o* in Spanish 'b*o*nit*o*'.

u *hemuk*, 'three'. This is like the vowel in English p*u*t or f*oo*t.

Long vowels

aa *paataat*, 'his father'. This is pronounced like *a*, but held out longer. It is like the vowel in English f*a*ther.

ii *wii*, 'he said'. This sound is exactly between that of the vowels in English b*ee* and b*ay*.

oo *'etoo*, 'I hit him'. As in the vowel of English l*aw*. There are not many words with this sound in Diegueño.

uu *'emuu*, 'wild sheep'. This has a sound between the *o* of d*o* and that of *o*pen.

Diphthongs

ay *matetay*, 'mountain'. *ay* is like the *e* in m*e*t plus the *i* in b*i*t.

aw *yuupaw*, 'he is ahead'. *aw* is like the diphthong in English n*ow*, but a little shorter. There are very few words with the sound *aw*.

iy *'ekwiy*, 'rain'. *iy* is somewhat like the *y* sound in English prett*y*.

iw *weyiw*, 'he comes'. Diegueño *iw* is like the *i* in English p*i*t followed by the *u* of p*u*t.

uy *wemuy*, 'he skins it'. Diegueño *uy* is like the *u* in English p*u*t followed by the *i* of p*i*t.

uw *wenuw*, 'he runs'. Diegueño *uw* is like the diphthong in English m*ow*, but shorter.

aay *'emaay*, 'high'. The sequence *aay* is like the italicized portion of English b*y*.

aaw *umaaw*, 'no'. Diegueño *aaw* is like the *ow* in English c*ow*.

iiy *'ekwiiy*, 'clouds'. Diegueño *iiy* is more like s*ay* than b*ee*.

iiw *'apesiiw*, 'very much'. *iiw* is like the vowel of s*ay* followed by the vowel of p*u*t.

uuy *paachuuy*, 'her husband'. *uuy* is like the vowel of s*o* followed by that of p*i*t.

uuw *mewuuw*, 'you see it'. *uuw* is like t*oe*, m*ow*.

Consonants

is not actually a sound, it is a catch in the throat which stops the sound before it or gives a sharp beginning to the sound after it. Linguists call it a glottal stop. It is what separates the two parts of the exclamation Oh-oh!, which in our spelling would be written 'O'oo.

ch *chaap*, 'short person'. Sounds like the *ch* in *ch*ur*ch*, *ch*ip, *ch*ocolate.

h *hemaa*, 'sleeps.' This is a sound that does not exist in English. It is a rather harsh sound pronounced far back in the mouth. It is the sound that in German is spelled *ch*, as in Bu*ch*, 'book,' and in Spanish is spelled *j* as in ca*j*on, 'big box,' fri*j*oles, 'beans.'

hw *'ehwatt*, 'red'. This sound is *h* followed by *w* but pronounced quickly, somewhat like English *why*, *wh*ich, but harsher. It is more like *ju* in Spanish, as in Ti*ju*ana.

k *kum*!, 'look!' This sound is somewhat like English *k* as in *k*ick.

kw *kwilkwil*, 'dangling'. Like English *qu*ick.

l *li'*!, 'well!' Like English *l*, as in *l*ight.

ll *llapellap*, 'flat'. This is a very unusual sound which has no English equivalent. It is somewhat hissing, and somewhat slurping; to make it right you have to combine the hissing quality of a sound like *s* (as in *S*am) with the pronunciation of *l* (as in *l*aw). One nice trick is to try pronouncing words like *sl*ip, *sl*ap as if the *sl* were one sound. Listen to someone doing it and keep trying. One clue: the tip of the tongue touches the inside of the mouth above the upper teeth.

lly *'emally*, 'century plant'. This is another difficult one. It sounds very much like *ll*. It combines the hissing quality of *sh* (as in *sh*arp) with the pronunciation of *ly* (as in wil*l y*ou). The trick is to pronounce *sh* and *ly* together as one sound. There are no words like that in English, but it is easy enough to make some up. Try *shly*im, *shly*up pronouncing the *sh* and *ly* together. Listen to someone do it and try again. Watch the position of the tongue; the tip of the tongue is down below the bottom teeth; the rest of the tongue is humped to touch the roof of the mouth.

ly *lyask*, 'light'. Diegueño *ly* is almost like the same combination of letters in wil*l y*ou or the *lli* in mi*lli*on. It is a single sound; the position of the tongue when making it is exactly like when making the *lly* sound but with no hissing.

m *metaat*, 'your father'. As in *m*other.

n *nemas*, 'raccoon'. This is not quite the sound of English *n* (as in *n*ow), but more like the Spanish *n* in Tijua*n*a. To make this sound correctly, aim for an *n*, but put the tip of your tongue against the very edge of the upper teeth. If you look in a mirror while doing it, the tip of your tongue will show between your teeth.

nn *nnemii*, 'he is mad'. This is somewhat more like the English *n* sound of *n*ow, ta*n*. The tip of the tongue touches the inside of the mouth just above the upper teeth.

ny *nyemii*, 'wildcat'. This is like the same combination of letters in ca*ny*on. It is a very common sound in Spanish, where it is spelled *ñ*, as in ma*ñ*ana, 'tomorrow.'

p *pilpil*, 'flickers'. As in *p*in.

q *'aq*, 'my bone'. Like *k*, but pronounced farther back in the throat. It is more like the *k*'s of coo*k* than like those of *k*ick. The *q* sound is fairly rare.

r *weraaw*, 'hot'. Diegueño *r* is very close to English *r* as in *r*ight.

rr *werraaw*, 'sharp'. Diegueño *rr* is like the trilled *r* of Spanish, as in pe*rr*o.

s *sekap*, 'half'. As in *s*ip.

sh *sha'ii*, 'buzzard'. Diegueño *sh* is somewhat like English *sh* in *sh*ip, but the tip of the tongue is held higher and tighter to produce a somewhat whistling sound.

t *tetepach*, 'he takes it out'. Diegueño *t* is different from English *t* in the same way that *n* is different from English *n*. In other words, try to make a *t*-like sound, but put the tip of your tongue against the very edge of the upper teeth. The tip of the tongue will show slightly between the teeth. It is like the Spanish *t* sound in *T*ijuana.

tt *wettuk*, 'he jumps'. Diegueño *tt* is much more like English *t* in *t*wo, *t*ie, pa*t*. The tip of the tongue touches the inside of the mouth above the upper teeth.

v *'ematvu*, 'the ground'. Diegueño *v* is a sound intermediate between the *v* of *v*ine, de*v*il, and the *w* of *w*e. Try for the sound of *v* but put your lower lip close to your upper lip instead of touching the upper teeth. It is the sound that *b* and *v* have in Spanish in such words as pue*b*lo, *v*i*v*ir. This sound is found in Diegueño only in endings that are attached to words when making sentences. In these words, the accent always comes on the syllable directly before the *v*.

w *wenak*, 'he sits'. As in *w*ine.

y *yaas*, 'he breathes'. As in *y*es.

– is not a sound at all, and is used only in the very few cases where words require a sequence of letters for which there could be more than one interpretation.

The Flute Player

Ted Couro, Narrator

Transcribed by Margaret Langdon

Tewaaches 'iikwich 'ehinch. Pechaay 'ehin tenarr. Peyapch 'emtaarvi nyechewayp tenyeway.

Kupilly 'ehin siny 'elymaamvech yip tewaa, maaykaam umarrch yip. 'Iikwich 'ehin maay tewaach, aakily 'uuch helul wii chuuhiim tewaa.

Puuch helulem yip, nyaapum umannch waam. Matetay wekull, 'ewily wekull, aachanp puwkch weyiwk nyewaa paas. Paataly ukenaa: "'Enyaach 'eyips maapch aahiishem 'eyip, 'enuw ta'aach 'aakuuhaph 'emaaw. 'Epuwkch peyii 'epaa ta'waa."

Nyaapum nyametenyaallyem nyiyuyech yip. Kupilly nyaamat aakilyem yip, aahiish, helulem yip tewaas.

Kupilly 'ehin waam, peyaach waak hemay tewam, weyuuwh wiich waam. 'Enyaaklly kuuyumch waam, waam tewam tewam 'ekur. Tewaach kupilly 'ehin yipches, aakilyem yip tewaas.

Once there was a man. He had a daughter. These people lived in the valley.

One day, the girl heard something, she got up early in the morning and heard it. It seemed like a man somewhere playing that thing they call a flute.

She heard him play it, then she got up and went on her way. She climbed a mountain, she climbed a rock, then got off and came back to her home. She told her father: "I heard somebody, I heard him play, I ran but couldn't catch up. So I turned around and here I am."

Then in the morning, again she heard it. The whole day she heard the music, the playing, the flute, she kept hearing it.

Finally one day she left, this girl went looking for him, determined to get him. She headed east, kept on going a long way. Finally one day she heard it, she heard the playing.

Tewaach pams. 'Iikwich 'ehin tewaach, 'ewily 'ehin emak wenakch helul tewaas. 'Enyaak nyayaaypem helulvu, helulvech waam 'ewikem. Puu yipkeh siny 'elymaamvech. Nyayipch nyaapum akewiich waam.

Nya-aakuuhapch nyaapum ii wayches 'iikwichvu. 'Iikwich nyii waayplly warh umaaw, nyii ewuuwlly warh umaaw, siny 'elymaamvu. Puy ii way tenamvem, nyaapum kenaapches 'iikwichvech: "'Enyaach peyaa heluls siny 'ehemaych." Nyaapum siny 'elymaamvech wiis: "Ee-een nyuk nyemeyuuws, 'enyaach 'ekurk 'eyiws, 'enyaa hemukem 'enuw 'eyiws. Pily peyii 'epaas. 'Enyaach nyaamlly 'ar, 'eyiws. Nya-aam maak 'etaat nya'taly mewuuwh." Nyaapum 'elymaam 'iikwichvech wiiches: "Nyii 'aahlly 'arh 'emaaw, 'ekurch apesiiw." Wii tenamvem waamches emiy akewiich waam, naam, naam, naam, tenamch nekemich, paataly paataat nyewaa nekemich.

Kupilly 'ehin 'iikwich 'elymaamvech 'ehaavu ewuuw tewaas, llehup tewaam, 'ehaa tuuyaq. Puuch nyaewuuw tewaach wettuk, wehap 'ehaavi. Nyawehap puy ukuwaayi tewaa, 'ehaa kuwaayi nyewaayp, nyii chepakh umaaw.

'Elymaam siny wenuwch wehap paataat ukenaa. Paataat waach achepachlly war, llyepuuwar, wecham. Wecham nyaapum maaykally puwk waach ewuuw. 'Iikwichvech tewaach 'ehaa ukuwaay wenak tewaa. Puy kenaam tenam, nyii chepakh umaaw. Nyuully tewaa.

Nyatewaam nyaapum siny 'elymaamvech wehápechi. Nyawehapch waam puully nyechewayp, mat weyum, nyechewayp, 'ehaa ukuwaay tenyeway.

Puy tenyewayem, nyaapum 'enyaach 'eyiwks. ◇

She had gotten there. There was a man sitting behind a rock, playing the flute. When the east wind blew on the flute the sound of it went west. That must have been what the girl had been hearing. She listened and then followed it.

When she reached him, she spoke to the man. But he didn't want to talk, he didn't want to look at the girl. She kept on talking to him, so then the man finally spoke: "I play this flute to find a woman." Then the girl said: "Well, you've already got me now, I've come a long way, for three days I've come running. Now I've got here. I want to take you with me, that's why I came. When I take you, you'll meet my mother and father." Then the young man said: "I don't want to go, it's too far." She kept on talking and finally he went with her and followed her, they went until they got there, they reached her mother and father's house.

One day the young man sat looking at the water—there was a hole there with water in it. He kept looking at the water and jumped into it. He went inside the water, he lived inside the water, and didn't come out.

The girl ran in to tell her father. The father went and wanted to get him out, but couldn't, had to leave him. He left him, and then in the morning he returned and came to look. The man was still there inside the water. They kept calling him, but he didn't come out. He stayed right there.

At last, then the girl went in too. She went in and now they live right there, they're married, they live together inside the water.

They're still there, so I came away. ◇

The Story of Eagle's Nest

Rebecca Alto, Narrator

Recorded by Alfred S. Hayes

Transcribed by Margaret Langdon

Translated by Christina Hutcheson and Margaret Langdon

This text was recorded on audiotape in 1953 in San Diego County. It reflects the Santa Ysabel dialect of Diegueño, with some elements of more southerly dialects, since Mrs. Alto moved south as a young adult. A copy of this tape was filed with the archives of the Survey of California and Other Indian Languages at the University of California at Berkeley, then headed by Professor Mary Haas. Margaret Langdon was given permission to copy this tape when she began fieldwork in the Diegueño speech area in 1963. Mrs. Alto had died before Professor Langdon began her fieldwork, and the chances of transcribing the tape seemed remote. But Christina Hutcheson, a speaker of the Mesa Grande dialect, expressed a desire to hear it, and after listening to the story a couple of times, she expressed a willingness to help Professor Langdon transcribe and translate it. A number of details of form and content, and biographical details about Mrs. Alto, came from Lillie Couro. This text was originally published in slightly different form (Langdon 1976).

The Story of Eagle's Nest shares with many other Yuman stories, not only the character of Coyote, but the relation of events responsible for certain local topographical features or otherwise associated with them. In this case, the major landmark is the mountain peak called Eagle's Nest located on the Los Coyotes Indian Reservation, a few miles east of Warner Springs, in the vicinity of the Santa Ysabel Indian Reservation.

'Enyaach 'aaknach hemiiym 'eyip ta'yuuw nya'ehemii, 'ehmiiy nyii 'uuyaawh maaws. 'Enya'taat tewaam . . . nyip 'uuch 'ich wii chuuhiia pily, Ben Paavl, nyipch peyii 'uuch San Saveel Ranch, Makintaarrvech; yip tenyeway. Nyahiichuur, nya'ekwiy nyaweyuum, weyiwch paas. "Bween, kurak, nyipily mekenaap, makenaam 'eyiplly 'ars. 'Umpees pa'waaches." "Hoo." Weyuuw 'umpeesvu, 'umpeesvu nyaweyuuwch: "'Uuch 'akenaak meyiplly mara?" "'Uuch, puy makenaak, Hattepaa

I heard a lot of stories when I was growing up, I heard a lot of them but I don't remember them. My father was there and . . . what's his name now . . . Ben Pablo, and that guy here, hm . . . from Santa Ysabel Ranch, that MacIntyre; they were listening. When it was cold, or when it rained, he would come by. "Well, old man, you tell a story now, I want to hear you tell about it. Here is a dollar." "OK" [said the old man]. He grabbed the dollar, and when he had it: "What do you want me to tell?" [he said].

Anepuuvu mekenaapm 'eyiplly 'ar." "Hoo, 'ehan." Nyaapum iichaa nyatewaa: "'Ehans, nyipily 'ekenaap meyiph, Hattepaa Nepuuvu."

Hattepaa Nepuuvech—'emat puu nyii chuuhiih maaws—kenaap 'iikwich 'ehin tewaas. Tenyeway, 'iipay hemiiy peyii pa'nyeways, pu'yuuk may 'ewaa 'ehiin 'ehiin wechuwh umaaw nyewaykeh. 'Ewaa 'ehinkm wechuw kweyaqvu mewuuw kwa'maay. . . . 'Ich wii chuuhiia? Hiiwaatt nyipm annakch eyuwis. Aannakch, 'ewaa 'ikuuuuum wechuw eyuwis. Nyatenyewayyyyych, 'iikwiich siinych weyuum, pu'yuuk tenyewaykeh. Nyechewayp nyaamatch 'ewaa nyakwa'hinvi.

Nyam puuch tewaayikeh, Hattepaa Nepuuvech, nyim aayaayp. Nyatenyewayyyyych, kupilly nyaamat may'kally pemannch, wesuw, 'uuchuch nyawepaym, peenooooolvech, trreeg, posoooool, sha'wiiiiivech, wemach weyuu. Nyatenyewayk naamkeh wenyaay, nyawim puuch haakaayk pa'yuuwch waach eyuwis. Nyawaamches nyuk pu'yuukeh Hattepaa wiim, shuuhuuph 'uu nya'arvu weyuuwk, ewiikeh. Nyaewiich nya'waykm nyawaach nya'arvi aayullpch paam. Nyapaam nyaapum hemaa 'uuchuchvu weyuuwk, tepaakeh. Tenayyyyykm nyaneyiwkm, puuch wemannch nyaemiiy weyiwkeh. 'Ekum nyanaakm, nyaapum weyiwkeh wenuwk yaas uullyuup wepilly 'ehar sar wii nesoom. Kunyay kunachvech 'ehmaall, hellyaaw, kunyaaw, 'uuchuch nya'kwar, 'uuchuch nya-aamuuch acheyiwkeh. Nyanekemich, puy wellyully wesuw weyuukeh. Tenyeway pehemachkeh. Kupilly nyaamatvu pa'wipvu. Naa neyiw wenyay neyiw, nyaapum Hattepaa 'ehinkm nyawaak, nya'ari aayullpkeh. Nya-aayullp puwk nyaneyiwk, siinyvu suunaly weyiwkeh tewam 'enyaa wehapkeh.

"Well, now you tell a story, I want to hear you tell about that Coyote." "Well, OK." Then when he had thought about it, he said: "Good, now I'll tell about him so you'll hear it, about that Coyote, that is."

About that Coyote—he didn't say where this was—he just told about this man being there. There were a lot of people here then, just as there are now, but they didn't have separate houses to live in. They made only one like the one you see up there. . . . What do you call it? They take this thatching brush and tie it up. When it is tied, they make a big house out of it, so he said. At that time, the men and the women got married, that's how they were. They all lived together in a single house.

So he was there too, that Coyote, together with them. They were there, and every morning they'd get up early, they'd eat, whatever there was, pinole, wheat, posole, acorn mush, they ate it. They stayed around and then went hunting, and he went along but staying on the side. So he went, he was already meant to be that way Coyote, he'd steal or grab anything, that's what he'd do. He did that and afterwards he'd go somewhere and hide away. He'd stay away and then sleep and he'd get up and come home with them. If they had come a long way, then he would come running, breathing hard, bathed in sweat, running all over him in streaks. Those who had been on the hunt had caught ground squirrels, cottontails, jackrabbits, anything, whatever they had killed they had brought with them. When they got back, they cooked that there and ate it. Then they went to bed. Every day they would do that. They came and went always hunting, and then Coyote would go by himself, always hiding somewhere. He'd hide and come back, he'd play with the women until the sun went down. In the evening

Nyatenaym nyapuwk waak nya'arvi aayullpkeh, nyaemiiy weyiwkeh.

Nyaewup tenamch: "'Ooooo, 'iikwich peyaach wellich apesiiw, 'ema'wipllya?" wiich yuuchaap, hemiiiiiych yuuchaap tenyewaykeh. "'Achemuchvek, ucheyuuwpvek. . . ." Nyaapum 'ihpaavech hekwany tuuyuuwch—matetay 'emaay mu'yuukm—pully achkehaapk achemuchh wiik tenamkeh. Uchewayp, pu'yupek uchewayp, uchewayp nyatenam nya'ekurrrrr, nyaapum: "Maapech wehaph hetuuhllya?" wipch. Nyatenam puu wiikm: "'Emaawhches, 'emehehaay . . .welliches." Pa'wipech ii wehaallp tenamem: "Hoo, 'ehanches," wiich eyuu: "'ehaphs," wii.

Nyatenyewayyyyych. . . 'ich wii chuuhiis, 'e-en, chuuhiich 'iipay aam 'uuch yaqm 'uuch ewiich, yukwip chikoot wechuw . . . haa, wekwip chikoot wechuw pa'wii. Nyatenyeway kupillyvu chekenaakeh: "Nyaapum kupillyvu, maak mehaph, meyips." 'Ekur muuyuuk tuuyuuwkm wih, 'uuna mii dos mii mu'yum, maaykallllly naam. "Hoo" nyawiim, mat wemiiiii weyuu nyatenam puy nyanetewaatt naamches. Nyanaam nyatenaach puully nekemichm 'enyaach nyachepakm puu 'emaaaaay nyawaam puully nekemichm tenyewayh ewupch. Nyaapum puu . . . 'uuch . . . hekwanyvech 'elyiimis tenyewaych eyuus, 'uuchvech 'ihpaavech. Ewup tenyewaych: "'Ehan, pily mehaph."

Puy wechuw yukwip wechuwvu, chikoot wechuwvech 'equll perewiih umaawkeh. Nyaapum puwk marway 'iikwiichvech wenyay nyanaak puu wechuw wenyiipkeh. 'Uuchuch tuunnak acheyiwkeh. Nyawenyayk puu tepally tenamkeh tenam, nyanetewaattch etuuvi tuunnak; nyanewatt—matetayvech mu'yuuk pawanemi—puuk wekull

he'd go back somewhere and hide, then come home with [the hunters].

They were watching him: "Oh, that man is very bad, what shall we do with him?" they thought, a lot of them were thinking. "But if we kill him, if they [his relatives] find out about it. . . ." At the time the eagle was having its young—how high in the mountain I don't know—but they would put him in there intending to kill him. They talked, they talked like that, and went on talking about it for a long time: "Who should go in there and get them [the eaglets]?" they said. They asked Coyote but he'd say: "No, I won't, I'm afraid . . . it's bad." But they kept saying it and bothering him until finally: "OK, all right," he said: "I'll go in," he said.

When they were there . . . what is it called, yeah, the Indian name for something that they do, that they twist to make rope . . . yeah, twist and make rope like that. And then they set the day: "Then on that day, you go in, you hear." I don't know how far he said it was, one or two miles maybe, but they started early in the morning. When he said: "OK," they cried and carried on and when they had finished there they started out; I don't know how high the sun was after they had left and got there but when they reached that place they looked things over. At that time those . . . well . . . babies were very small, those eaglets. They looked the place over and [said]: "Good, now in you go."

But what they had made by twisting, the rope they made was not long enough. Then the rest of the men went hunting and made some more and put it on themselves like a belt. They tied it up and brought it with them. They hunted and knotted the pieces together, and when they were finished, they tied them around their waist; when it was finished—

wenak eyuwis. Nyaapum 'ehinvech 'emaayk wekull eyuwii. Puuch 'ily kwa'qullm . . . puu puuyuuk kwa'maayvech sarrrrr 'ewilyvech, nyawechankm iinuypek puy puuyuuk aahwaark chekatthvu puy nyii warh umaawch. Puu chikoot kurwiivu 'ilyvem pa'wiich aanally naach eyuuch, 'uuch 'ewilyvi aahwaarp warh umaawch, pa'wiich eyuus. Nyatenaaaaachem, puuch ewuuw. "Mewuuwvu" wiich eyuu. "'Ehan tepa'aasvech." Puully 'emaayvi kuwachvech peyii kwe-yuuwvech chikootvu kurwiivu, aahwaar aanally naakeh. Nyatenaaaaach nyatenaach . . . nyapuully nyapamk 'ewily uuhaavu—muuyuuk 'allk pu'yuuk llehup muuyuuk—tenyewaykeh, 'ihpaa hekwanyvech. Nyapamk puy nyawenakm 'uu nyamu'yuukm, kwa'maay kuwachvech nyawiim nyaapum: "Wenak sah wii." Nyawaamem aakatt eyuus. "Aaaaa . . . wekatt ekatt ekatt" nyawiich mat wemiich eyuus. Tiiwaar tetellah wiikeh, maay wekattkeh tiiaakatt. Puy mat wemii weyuuw tenam, nyanetewaattch neyiwkeh.

Nyiphutt 'emelyays panemaawvech matt paatalyvech . . . panemaaw wiikeha? Panemaaw wiich—puy tewaayikeh—puuch haylly puu tiinyewillkeh warh umaawch: "Warvech tiiwarvu maachmuch pema'wiih namches," wiibes. Nyawehwaall nyatenamkm: "Hoo, 'ehanches," wiis, wehaphvu. Puy achkehaap puully nyaaakatt wechaamkeh, kuwaayvelly 'ihpaa nyewaavelly. Nyaapum puuk hekwany 'esalyem nyii lemis-h umaaw tiinyeway eyuwiis. Nyatenyewayyyyychem, mechheyay yuuhuy. Kupilly puully nyawehapchem

there is a mountain there though I don't know what it's like [on the other side]—one of them climbed up and just sat there. Then another one climbed up [in a different spot]. With a long stick . . . the cliff was so high and steep, that when it [the rope] came down there maybe it would somehow get worn and break and he didn't want that. This rope-like thing they went and moved it like that with the stick because they didn't want it to wear out on the rock, that's what they did. As they kept doing that, [the one up on the mountain] was watching. "Do you see how it is?" [someone asked from below]. "It's going all right," [he said]. The man up on the mountain was holding the rope-like thing, but it was wearing out and they kept moving it. They kept that up . . . then he got down to the cave—I don't know how wide the hole was—but they were there, the eagle babies. When he got down there and landed or something, the one who was on top then said: "He's landed plop." Then he went and cut [the rope]. "Aaaah . . . it broke, it broke, it broke," they all began to cry. But they had been lying, they just said that, about where it broke, [actually] they had cut it. Then they started to cry, and when they were through, they came away.

I don't know which one it was, his father's mother or his mother, did he say his father's mother? . . . He said his father's mother—she was there too—she hadn't wanted them to deny it: "All they want to do is kill you, that's what they are going to do," she had said. But they had kept pestering him so that finally: "OK, very well," he had said, he would go in. When they had taken him in there, they had cut the rope and left him there, inside the eagle's house. At that time the little ones were just beginning [to grow feathers], they didn't have feath-

sekaann 'ekurlly penak eyuwis. Hewak tenyeway. Nyatenyewaym nyakutnayvi, 'ihpaavech nyapaach mehayaayi. Nyaweyiwch 'ekurlly wenak. Pu'yupa tewapech nyahunnm pamch eyuus. Pambes nyii helyiipayh umaaw eyuwii; mehehaay. Nyamehehaay puy nyatewaach nyatewaach nyamaaykallym waamch eyuwiis. 'Ihpaavech wenyaych nyawaam, pa'wiich 'uuchuch nya'kwarvu aawatt eyuwiis, hellyaaw, kunyaaw, 'ephar, 'uuchuch aawattk ateyiw wesuwhvu hekwanyvu.

Nyatewaach kupilly mu'yummmmm nyatewaam, kunychiiwaayp eyuwiis. Nyakunychiiwaayp puy nyimaayaayp tetenyewaykeh. Nyatenyewaykm kupilly 'ehin, 'ekwak 'ehin aamuuch akemich eyuwiis; 'ihpaavech 'ekwak toorr 'iikuuuuu aamuuch. Nya-akemichch puuch aamally 'ekwakvu, 'uuch lemisvu uusuur eyuwiis, 'ihpaavech. "Haa, 'ema'wiik ta'waak 'esaawh 'eyuuh?" nyuk nyiiwar tewaa. 'Ehaa wesiihlly war mu'yuuk. Nyatewaach nyaapum puy 'ewilyvek—llapellap mu'yuuk tuuyaqm—puy nyaweyuuwch, ewiich 'ewily 'ehinklly aahwaar. Pa'wip tenam werraaw ma'alkm nyaapum ewiik uusaak, shetekattkeh 'ekwakvu. Emaatvu nyashetekattch, nyaapum weyuuwch ewiich uusuur, pa'wii tewaas, 'enyaa chepakvi 'ewilyvi chekwaapm uusaaykeh. Nyasaaykm, nyaapum puu wesaawkeh. Wesaaw tepu'yupk tetewaakeh. 'Iiwaar 'iiwaar 'ihpaavech tekunyewaypch eyuwiis, kwaaykuuvech. Nyahunnchem hekwanyvu hetuuch nyachehwilychem, nyaapum puuch nyawi-nym, Hattepaavech. Yewirewirvu uurur mat aapitt eyuwiis, mat aapittch puy hemaayikeh, pu'yuuk tewaakeh.

ers yet. They were there afraid of him at first. On the day he arrived they stayed way ahead far away from him and just sat there. There were two of them. They stayed like that and in the evening, when the eagle came home she was afraid of him too. She came and sat far away from him. She just stayed there that way till it got dark. She was there but not too close; she was afraid. She was afraid of him and just stayed there, and in the morning she left. The eagle would leave to hunt, and what she did was to kill anything she found, cottontails, jackrabbits, brush rabbits, and bring them home to feed her little ones.

After he had been there I don't know how many days, they became friendly. They kept each other company. One day when they were there, she killed a deer and brought it home; the eagle killed a big buck. When she brought the deer, she swept it in, tore off its hide in strips, the eagle [did that]. "Well, how am I going to eat that?" [thought Coyote, for] he was already hungry. He needed water to drink, but how? He sat there and then—there was a sort of flat rock lying there—he grabbed it and what he did then was to scrape it onto another rock. That's what he did until it got kind of sharp and then he used it to stab the deer, to chop it up. When he had cut up the whole body, what he did was to take [the meat] and tear it in strips, that's what he did, and he laid it out on the rock in the sunshine to dry. When it dried, he would eat it. He ate it and so it went. After a while the eagle became friendly, the big one that is. At night she gathered the little ones [around her] and cuddled them, then he would do that too, Coyote. He'd stretch the wings into a circle to cover himself up, he'd cover himself up and go to sleep too, and that's how things went.

Haylly kunykuuyvech, kupilly nyaamat kuny-kuuy pam weyiws. "Meyaqa?" Nyawim: "Haa," wiicheyuus. Tewam pu'yupk tewam 'ekurkeh. Nyatuuyaq puu wesaaw 'ekwak sayvu. Nyate-waaaaach maaaaas nyanyaakurm kunykuuy nyapamch. "Meyaqa?" wiich eyuus. "Meyaqa, 'elyich?" "Haa, peyii 'eyaqch 'eyis. Kaam!" wiich eyuus. "'Uuch mema'wiih peyii mekekeway te-mamchmeyu? Nyuk 'emat nyimichlly 'ekuuyumh. Nya'aak peyaally nyachuurapmkeh eyuuh. Keskwiiy tiikaam!" wiich. "Ma'yum mat 'ewuuwh teke-muwh," wiis. Kunykuuyvech puy wemii tewaas, waamch eyuus.

Nyam puully kunyewayvech tenyeway tuuyaq-keh nyuk aamuuch wiik, 'elyeyaawpk, wenyayk, wesuwk, wemaak, hemaak tuuyaqkeh. Tuuyaqm pa'wiim tiiewuuwk tewaakeh. 'Ekwak aawatt ateyiwvu. Nyuk wekwiirp tewaak tiiwees nyaamaat nyaamat paamkeh. Melayh nyuk pam tewaakeh. Ewuuw nyatewaach, kupilly 'ehin iichaach eyuus. "Aamuuch akemichm 'ewuuwch, 'ekwakvech 'iikuuch wenihches. 'Enyaavu ma'wiik nyachpachh umaawhkeh? Nyachpachh. . . ," wiich eyuus. Iichaach: "Nyachpachs, mu'yuuk umaaw? Nyeyih nyaaahkeh. Nyawiich maaykally wemannch, pu'yuuch . . . 'ihpaavech yullp tepaach mat uunipm eyuuch puy kekewayh tepaach waamh. "Nyipily peyii nesoomhkeh," wiis. "'Emat nyiimichlly 'ekuuyum 'aamh. Nyachpachh umaawvek, 'emat kuwaay nya'arvi nyaarapmkm, puully 'emelaym nesoomh. Maas 'ehanhches," wiis, iichaa tewaach eyuwiis.

Meanwhile the old woman, every day the old woman would come by. "Are you there?" [she'd say]. Then: "Yes," he'd say. She kept doing that for a long time. So he lay there and all he ate was some dry deer meat. For a long time more the old woman would come. "Are you there?" she'd say. "Are you there, grandson?" "Yes, I'm here. But go away!" he said. "What do you expect to do here going back and forth all the time? Already I am headed for another land (i.e., I am dying). When I go they'll throw me off in here. Give up and be on your way!" he said. "We will never see each other again," he said. The old woman just cried there, and then she left.

Now the people who lived there assumed that they had already killed him, they were pleased, they hunted, ate meat, ate mush, and slept. They were doing all that and she [the old woman] kept watch-ing them. They killed some deer and brought them home. But he [Coyote] was already so thin that all that was left of his body was bones. He was near death already. She went to see him and one day he had an idea. "I saw how she [the eagle] killed a deer and brought it home, a big deer and heavy. Why couldn't she take *me* up? She might be able to take me out . . . ," he said. He thought: "She could take me out, why not? She could carry me on her back and take me away." He said that and early in the morning she got up, that's what she did . . . the eagle got ready to go shaking herself and pacing back and forth there before leaving. "Now this will be the last time," he said. "I'll be heading for an-other land. If she can't take me out, if she can't drop me on the ground somewhere, I'll die right there and that will be the end. It'll be better that way," he said, that's what he was thinking.

Tewaam puy 'ihpaavech mat uunipm wirewir 'uuch uukwiiw weyuuwk tewaam, puuch nyuk mewallk uy wiik tuuyaqkeh. Mewall nyayuuhan nyatuuyaqm, nyaapum 'ihpaavech tewaa waamhch weyutt. Mat yuuhan nyim waam yur wiich iipukm a-aamch, peyaam aasequpch, weyuuwkeh. Nyawe-yuuwchem wenih ma'alch eyuwiis. Nyawemanch rurrrrr nyawiich, kuwaaaaayvelly pam nyemily eyuwiis. Nyaapum puwk 'alypaayem pu'yupch 'emaaylly kuuyum. Nyatuuyuuw puu matetayvu nyaaaaa nyapurhch tepur wiich, 'alypaaaaayem 'ematlly nyawaach, hil hil hil—'ewilych ewaach eyuu, 'ewily 'ihpaa 'aanaakvech. Nyaaaaa 'emati emilyvi tekehiil eyuwiis. 'Ewilyvu pamch, nyapamk puy aarapmkeh.

Puy nyaaashukpm 'ihpaavech puy wenak nyatewaak, nyaapum weman waamkeh wenyayk. Nyawaamkm puuch peyii tuuyaqkeh. Puy tuuyaqm kunykuuyvech nyatuuyiwch puy nyapaach, puu wiich: "Meyaqa, 'ellyit meyaqa?" 'Uyyyyy wiich eyuuwiis, umaaw, puy wemiik tewaakeh, kunykuuy wenakkeh. "Puy tewaak mu'yuuk wiik chepaah, wiikm mu'yuukm 'ihpaavech achepach may may aarapm pa'yaqkeh. Haa. . . ," puy iichaakeh, 'ewilyvu. Nyawaa nyatewaach, 'ewilyvi nyapamch, pu'yuuk, nyaapum puwk wamp kaakap tepaa puuk tuuyaq. Tiipatt tuuyaqvu nyii uuyaawh umaaw; nyaumaawch nyaapum: "Meyaqa, 'uuch muuyaaw? Piipaach, piipaaches," wiim, tii'uyches. Nyuk enyally nyaamatvech saay, nyuk 'ehaa wesiich, we-suwh umaaw nyatuuyaqkeh. Nyarewiikm nyaapum nyawaak 'uu mu'yuuch uumannm temewall kwile-kwil aashukp. Aashukpchem puy 'ehaavech, hemal, sha'wii peenoolvech taawaah. . . . Puy 'ehaavu

There the eagle was shaking herself, stretching her wings and reaching out, and he was so weak altogether. He was so exceedingly weak lying there, and then the eagle was ready to go and got startled. He was all set to go with her and he grabbed wildly, threw his arms around her neck and hugged her like this, and held on. He held on tight but he was rather heavy for her. She flew out and swept down, and almost went under. But then, very slowly, she turned back like that and started upward. When she was about over the top of the mountain, very slowly she went for the ground, barely moving—there was a rock there, where she would always sit. Her feet were so low that they dragged on the ground. She reached the rock, and when she had reached it, she dropped him there.

When he had fallen off and the eagle had sat a while, then she flew off and went hunting. After she left, he just lay there. He lay there and when the old woman came and reached that place [above the eagle's nest], she said to him: "Are you there, grand-son, are you there?" There was no answer, nothing, and she started to cry, the old woman just sitting there. [She thought:] "Maybe he tried to get out, and somehow the eagle brought him out and dropped him and he is just lying somewhere. Yes . . . ," and she remembered there, about the rock. She left and when she reached the rock, some-how, then she turned around and circled the rock and there he lay. She didn't know if he was alive, she didn't, but then: "Are you there? do you know me? Here I am, here I am," she said, but there was no answer. Already his throat was all dried out, he had had no water to drink, nothing to eat lying there. He was like that, and she went and tried to

stikm winykm wesiikeh. Nyawinykm nyawesiikm-bes puuk yulk chepam waaches. Ma'wip tenam etuuvech tuupitt tuuyuuws. Nyaumaawchem puy winy wesaaw tepuuyuyiches etuuch 'esuwvu. Nyatewaaaach nyatenayhm nyawaahchem, kunykuuyvu wiich: "Nyipily nyamaak 'uuch pemaayiwh millychis 'ekwaa . . . 'uuchvu . . . pehmaavu." Tekwaach nyaapum wiim kechamkeh 'uuchvu esaawvu.

Nyaapum kunykuuy waamch nyaapum maaykally emiy pehmaavu wehill nyatepaach aayiwch akemichm chuuhwar tewam tuupittkehbes, wiich nyii 'iiwalph umaaw. Nyaapum puy pa'wiis, winykm wesaaw, stikm wesaaw tetuuyaqkeh. Nyuully wecham. Nyam nyam kunykuuy pane-maawvu: "Maach pily nyamaam nyamepam, makechuukwich maaym maamchmeyu, maayvu maach, 'esuwvu 'emaavu mewiikeh. Tii'arvech 'a-aach puully 'aatuqmches ukuwaay. Nyii meke-naaph umaaw. Mekenaap meyuuvek, machmuchh."

Nyawiikm kunykuuy nyawaam nyam akechuu-kwich: "Mema'wiih nyuk kumlay kunsoom . . . maamhchmeyu?" "'Ema'wiik 'emeyuuh 'emaaw? Puully tuuyaqk nyanesoombes pa'wiik puully 'etop 'emat tuuyaq. 'Etrravahaarrvu ewaaches." Pa'wipk nyatepaak, tepaak tuuyaq, 'iiwaarm sepirvu. Nyasepir nyaapum pu'yuukeh, may wamp sepir puyyyyy weyuuwh umaaw, tesepirvu. Nyatewaa tewaa nya'ekur sepir yuuhanvu, nyaapum 'aly-paayem kech-kewaay wamp, 'ekurm waa, puwk

lift him up or something, but he was so weak and limp that he fell back. He fell back, but she had carried some water with her, also some greens, acorn mush, pinole. . . . She gave him a little water to drink. She gave it to him and he drank it, but it slipped right through him. Somehow his stomach couldn't hold it. When that didn't work, she gave him something hard to eat, but his stomach was too slick for the food. Then in the evening when she was going to leave, he said to the old woman: "Now when you go, bring me some of the white man's braided . . . sinew." She heard him, then he said for her to leave something behind for him to eat.

Then the old woman left and in the morning she barbecued the sinew and brought it with her to him and he ate it and chewed on it and it tightened him up, but still he couldn't talk clearly. But then she did this, she gave him something to eat, a little bit to eat while he lay there. She stayed right there. By and by he told the old woman, his father's mother: "Now when you go and get back home, they are going to ask you where you went, where you were, and what you did with the hard and soft food. [Tell them:] All I wanted was to take it there and throw it down to the bottom [of the cliff]. Don't tell them anything. If you do tell them, they will kill you."

He said that and then the old woman went home and they did ask her: "What are you up to now that he is already dead and gone . . . what are you going for?" "Why shouldn't I? He was there and he is gone now, but all I do is to take it up there and throw it on the ground. That's my job." She did that and she got there, she got there and he lay there, but after a while he got stronger. He became strong enough to try to walk, but not strong enough to stay standing. So he stayed there a long time more and he got

tewaa. Nyatewaach nyaapum wiikeh: "Nyasepir nyipily 'eyuuhan," kunykuuy panemaawvu: "Pily nyamaak 'uuch pemaayiwh." 'Uuch . . . palachaa 'eyip nyachuuhii tewaa, 'emelyay . . . 'ehkat. "Nyip maayiwh, nyaapum 'uuch 'uuchuch heyully lemisvu metaayiws." wii. "Puu 'uuch 'epal 'echuwh, 'ewihvu. Nyaapum helyepay peyaa 'uuchvech 'ephiivech, metaayiwhs." Kunykuuy nyawaam taayiwvu pehmaavech 'uuch 'epalm aannakvu, nyip 'epal—'ech wii chuuhii—'ehkat . . . chikoot wechuwvu nyip aayiwkm ewiikeh. 'Ehkat ewiikm nyipm ma'wiik . . . wekwip chikoot wechuw, 'uuch 'aatim aarrapkeh tewaas. Tewaak 'ekurrrrr nyaapesiiwk newattkeh.

Newatt nyaapum kunykuuyvu ukenaa kuwaayklly, kuwaayklly 'uuchuch mu'yuu tuuyuuwvu mu'yuuk, 'ihpaavu mehehaayvu mechheyayvu kenaap. Puy 'iiwaarp kunychiiwaayp tetewaaches. Kenaap 'ekwak taay wesuwvu. Nyaapum puuk 'ihpaa hekwaanyvech nyahetemii 'uuch puu . . . 'uuch iiwirewirvu, puuch umaawvu, puuch umaaw. Hachekwiik uumannch naamch llyepechewar. Puu wetookeh yiiwirewirvu, puully nyatuuyaqches. Hachekwiik setepir uumannch naams, nyawirewirvu. Kunykuuyvu kenaap, nyaamat newattkeh. Saapaat, 'aatim, nyaamat wechuw, 'iiwaark nyanewatt nyasepir, akekwiikeh panemaawvu nyaapum shekwiirp mu'yuum chepaak waah, nya'ar weyuu, mu'yuuk 'uuyuk nya'ar hemaa, mu'yuuh maaw 'iipaym wehap hemaa.

stronger and better; then slowly he'd walk back and forth, he'd go farther and come back. So he went and then he said: "I'm all strong now," to the old woman his father's mother: "Now when you go, you bring me something." I think I heard it called *palachaa*, I don't know or . . . *'ehkat*. "Bring me that, and then also bring me some tail feathers," he said. "I will make arrows, that's what I'll do. Then close by there is some of this greasewood, bring me some." The old woman left, and the sinew she had brought he tied to the arrow, that arrow—what is it called?—*'ehkat* . . . to make rope with, she would bring that for him to make it. He used the *'ehkat* to do something with . . . to twist and make a rope, and a bow to strike with. It took him a very long time before it was finished.

While finishing he told the old woman, he told about down below, about how things had been down there, about how he had been afraid of the eagles and they had been afraid of him. How after a while they became friendly. He told about the big deer that he ate. How then when the eagle babies were growing up, well hm . . . [he pulled] their wing [feathers] off, so they didn't have any, not at all. How, as they grew bigger, they tried to fly away but couldn't. How he'd hit their wings, as he lay there. How as they were growing bigger and stronger they would have flown away if they had had wings. He told the old woman all about it, until he finished everything. [By then] he had made shoes, a bow, everything, and after a while, when he was all done and feeling much stronger, he asked his father's mother then to hide out and somehow to move away, to any place at all, even if she had to sleep outside somewhere, but under no circumstances to sleep in with the [other] people.

Puy nuyk Hattepaa Nepuuvech 'iichach wellichm tewaa. Nyawiichem kunykuuyvech akekwiih umaaw mu'yum puu 'ichvu. Nyaam: "'Ehans," wiiches. Nyawaam kunykuuy nyawaach ewiich shekwiirp 'uuyuk 'enyaak 'ekur. Aakeyuuchkeh, aakeyuuchk hemaak puy tewaakeh. Kupilly hewakm matt hemuk nyatewaachem, 'iikwiichvech myatuu-yuuwch wenyaay nyanaa nyata'urp pekwilly, siinyvech—'ehaavech wenuw tuuyaqm, tuuyaqm—puy allehwas, hellytaa chehekarrch weyuuwch te-nyewaykeh, siinyvech. . . . Kewaak tuuyiw, kewaak chepak tuuyiw, 'epal weyuuw puyyyyy. . . . 'Iiwaarm, puwk nyachikoot chehwir, achewallk pa'wii siinyvu. Siiny marwaych ewupch uusaayp. 'Ehin tewaas: "Puuch Hattepaa Nepuuvu rewiiches." "Ee, nyahemir Hattepaa Nepuuvech. 'Emat wellichm aarapm. Peyii chepakllya waacha? Umaaw, he'yaay melay 'ekurs. 'Eyipvu 'eyip. Nyip rewiih umaaw. . Ma'wii chepak, achepaachs?"

For already that Coyote was having some ideas that were evil. But when he talked to her like that, the old woman did not ask why he was saying these things. She just said: "Good." She left, the old woman went off and what she did was to hide in the wilderness far to the east. She would make herself a brush fence, fence herself in and sleep there. After she had stayed there two or three days, [one day] when the men had gone hunting and the noon hour had passed, the women—there was a river there, in fact there were two of them, there were—they were doing their wash, and parting and doing their hair, the women were. That's when he came from the south, he appeared in the south, holding his arrows [and shooting them]. . . . After a while again he'd insert the rope in the slot [to shoot the arrows], waving his hand like this at the women. Some of the women saw him and laughed. But there was one [who said]: "That sure looks like that Coyote." [But another one said]: "Gee, it couldn't be that Coyote. They threw him off in a terrible place. How could he show up here? No, he died long ago and far away. That's what I heard, I heard it. It's not like him at all. How could he have come out, or be taken out?"

Nyawiichem puy tepaak nyatenaykm waak weyiwkeh. Weyiwkm emiy tepaakeh. Nyaweyiwk 'uuchvu hiiwaattvu nyapuwk tewaach, peyii waak mu'yuuvu hemiiykm nyaweyiwk puy nyanewatt tewaakeh. Nyaam puu heyaayvu may 'iipayvech . . . ventaanvech hewak hemukm umaaw. 'Ewaa 'ehinkm nyim wehap. Nyaapum nyahunnkm weyiwkeh. Weyiw nyatuuyiw nyapaach nyaapum pehemach. 'Uyyyyy wiikeh. 'Iipayvech pehemach pu'yuu, pa'wiich nya-aawatths. Pa'wiich lapwerrti chekwaakeh. Hiiwaatt lapwerrti chekwapm newatt nyaapum puwk chap pelyak. Nyii 'iichaah 'emaaw

After she said that, he stayed there till evening and left and came back. He'd come and she [his grandmother?] was with him. When he came, he brought back some thatching brush, he did that I don't know how many times coming and going, and when he was finished he left. Now in those days people didn't have . . . two or three windows [like now]. They only had one way to go in the house. So after dark, he came. He was coming and when he arrived they [the people] were already asleep. And while the people were sleeping, he was arranging to kill them. What he did was to drop them [the bun-

'uuchm hellyapvu. Nyahellyap—haa, wekaak ewiik hellyap—nyahellyap, nyaapum 'ihinvu ewiich hiiwaatt ewiich pu'yuuch 'ily 'equllm aannak, puu nyahellyap 'ewaavu kaakap. Pa'wiich, 'ewaavu pa'waach wechuw aannakvu kaakap. Pa'wiich nyahellyapch, wenuw ewaawch, chuupar hetuuch: "'Ihpaa nyehuumaay, 'ihpaa nyehuumaayveches." Nyawiichem puully mat wemii puully nyahellyap shaawattpkeh. Wellyapk shaawattpkeh.

Shaawattp nyanesoomkm, puuch Hattepaa nyaweyiw peyii chepak kupillyvu nya'ar wemii te-kwaa. Nyaam tuuyiw, nyip my father kenaapm te'eyip 'emattvu. Nyahellyapch 'uuch hala'sii 'ii'yaaw. . . . pu'yuuches 'iiwalpch eyuus. 'Ihpaa aakatt maay wepay 'uuyaawh 'emaaw. . . . Semaan 'ehin 'uu hewak wellyap rewii may myinyuyyyy 'ehanh umaaw. . . Kwak nyay nyawaach nyawe-ruwm 'eyip. Nyip puu 'iich 'ekenaap. . . . 'Eyipch apesiiw, 'uuyaawh umaaw. Hemiiy kenaapm . . . 'eyips. Marway ewiichem kechenapm tii'eyip. Mayvu kwa'han 'uuyaawh umaaw. ◇

dles of thatching brush] at the door. He kept dropping the brush at the door until it was all used up and laid out. I don't know what he started the fire with. But when it was lit—oh yes, he used a fire drill to start the fire—when it was lit, he used one of them, he used one of the bundles of thatching brush, he tied it to a long stick, and when it burned, he ran around the house with it. That's what he did, he was there going around the house with that tied-up bundle he had made. He did that and when he had it [the house] burning, he ran and hollered and did the victory yell and carried on: "I am the eagle's son, I am the eagle's son!" When he said that, the people inside started to cry for he was burning them to death. They all died in the fire.

Now they are all dead and gone [and that's why] when Coyote comes around here, you can hear him crying at any time. He just comes around, I guess I heard my father tell about it. Where the fire was, there are now two kinds of willows growing there. . . . you can see it clearly. But where the eagle's nest is I don't know. . . . It burned for maybe one or two weeks and it was never quite the same again. . . . I heard . . . I heard a lot, but I don't remember too well. A lot of story-telling . . . I heard. There are other ways of telling about it and I heard them too. But I don't know which is the right one. ◇

The Tar Baby Story

Alejandrina Murillo Melendres, Narrator

Transcribed by Leanne Hinton

Kur'aq shin kwa'kuy shin,
gayiin nyehat nyewaaychem.
Perehaaw shin naar waar ayaw.
Ti'nya shin tramp chaw chuwaw—
hpilly—
moon chawchaw chpe'aw chwaw,
wa'aaha chpe'aw anemak tuwaa.
Perehaawhach gayiinha usaaw nyapachm moonhach pe'aaw yaw nyapaach "kpiyee wa'aa nyipi xap gayiin saawh yees."

Moonhach karkwar mawchyum.
"Kpiye nyitchtuk nyahwayhs.
Sally kwa'shin chtu—
thpilly—
nyimu'ttip nyimaawkum sally ha'kay nyichtuk ny'hwayh nyikine'mak sally ha'kayxam chtuya.
Thpillyi meellya—
"unya'maaykem nyimo'ttip nyomawkum meey ha'kay nyikyeerr nya'hwayh!"
Kiyeerr meey thpilly,
mey ha'kay kiyeerr thpilly.
"Pily nyichukaw nya'hwayh nyimo'ttip nyomaawkum!"

There was an old man and an old woman,
They had some chickens.
A fox was robbing them a lot.
One night they made a trap and put it there—
Out of tar—
They made a doll and stood it up,
They stood it at the door, left it and went away.
When the fox arrived to eat the chickens, the doll was stationed there, when he arrived. "Get away from the door there, I'm going to enter and eat the chickens."
The doll did not talk.
"Get away, or I'll hit you and kill you!"—
With one hand he hit it—
He got stuck—
"If you don't let go, I'm going to hit you with my other hand and kill you, let me alone!" He hit him with his other hand. He got stuck again.
Next, his feet—
"If you don't let go, I'm going to kick you with one foot and kill you!"—
He kicked, and his foot got stuck,
He kicked with his other foot and it got stuck.
"Now I'll bite you and kill you if you don't let go!"

Moonhach muyuk uttip imelly maaw?
Yaawham chukaw,
yaawech thpillyi—
nyipi wach 'inyaa 'inyaallyi kur'aqhach nyumaan,

kwakuyha hwak nyumaan gayineerhem naachem—

mo'kur perehaawhach tramphally neelly towa thpilly.
Waach nyapaamch,
"Aaa pi wah perehaaw pi wah gayiin keknaar kwa'yawhach!
Pily tonaq aak litmaarrjaw!"
Tonaqchaw chuwach chuwa,
chut tonaq.
'ii yupaay nyanaachem,
htpaa shin paa.
"'A'uych merare mwa miyuuch perehaaw?" 'u'im.
Perexaawhach:
Ny'to'naqchawm pi' waach chisaaw kwaxaan chak nyi'wichkm saaw u'ich—
nyimemapkum maap nyitonaq nyach ya'willy 'aarr chisaw ma'ich saaw mawh 'iyum llewaarmes.
"'Ehaaniya!"
u'ich ottip perehaawha uttip chawchem perehaawhach hatpaha tonaq chaw nyachut,

waa skan nyawaachem kwakuuyhach kur'aqham hwak nyachaq—
"kwiiiiw perehaawhach kur hetepaa wiyuch pi waa!"
nyipiwpak a'aw chutth llitmaarr chawh piach nyihat nyin'aar saaw chaws".

A'aw llitmaarr chaw hetepaha nyichut perehawech—

skan tuwaa nyaama. ◇

How could the doll let go?
He bit him with his teeth,
His teeth got stuck—
He was there until morning. In the morning, the old man, when he got up,
With the old lady, when they got up, they went to the chicken coop—
There he was, Fox, in the trap he was fallen, he was stuck.
When they arrived,
"Ahh, here he is, the fox, here he is! The one who robbed our chickens!
Now we'll take him and tie him up and burn him!"
They took him and tied him,
They finished tying him.
When they went to get some wood,
A coyote arrived.
"What are you doing here, Fox?" he said.
And Fox:
"They tied me up and here I am. They went to bring me some good food for me to eat—
If you want, I could tie you up. I am very full. I cannot eat any more."
"Okay!"
He said, and he let him loose, he let Fox loose, and when he finished, Fox tied Coyote up the same way,
Then he went off, he fled. The old lady and the old man, when they arrived—
"Looooook! The fox turned into a coyote!
Nevertheless, we'll throw him in the fire and burn him. This one robbed us and ate our chickens."
They made a fire and threw Coyote in it, and as for Fox—
He was long gone. ◇

Coyote Baptizes the Chickens

Alejandrina Murillo Melendres

Translated by Maria Aldama and Leanne Hinton

Nche'ak shin.
Gayiin shin gaay hwakem nyihat tuwach.
Gayiinhech poyiit pehkay u'wich.
Wanaach sa'mally saw aar anyiw sa'mally saw
    taniiwchyum.
Htpa shin paa malik kcham aak saw maawh
    llwarchum.
Wiiw toyaw wa'a wiish "poyiit shin nyik'inkum aak
    hash'unuph—
nyowaha maap hash'unup" wa'aw'wi hatepa'hach.
"Ehaniyaakum kaa."
Aach saaw poyiitha—
nyi'iyaaychem paach shinkum 'aayem'esh.
"Komaar,
poyiit nyi'mit aak hash'unup shin tuwach yeyllit
    mese'awhech."
Yaaw aach saw—
hashiyaaw hashunup.
Nyi'inyaaychum paach nyi'mich aa,
naach kchamell nyaach saw nyuchawch.

There was an old woman.
She had a hen and a rooster.
The hen had seven chicks.
They went about eating herbs, eating herbs.

A coyote came; he was unable to carry off all
    of them.
He saw her at the door and said, "Give me one chick
    and I'll carry it off and baptize it—
I'll carry it to my house and baptize it," said Coyote.
"Very well, take it away."
He carried the chick away and ate it—
The next day he came and took away another one.
"Comadre,
I'll carry another chick away and baptize it, your son
    is lonely."
He took it and carried it away and ate it—
He was deceiving them about baptizing.
The next day he came and carried away another,
He went and carried them all away and ate all of
    them, finished them all off.

Nyapach "iii komaar kaa kwiw minchakwaall nyakur xallunup nyoaay kwa'taay inhaas waar mu'wuwhwitchem."

Ehaniyakom kaa w'awis gaayhich.
Gayinha yaawch aa hetepahach yaawch aa sawya—

saaw nyichaw paach.
"Kompaar pill mkomaar mse'tum yiw'yus komaar maahwit' pay mayaay mowahu'ich maak minchhakwall muwiw—

ha'kwalle pay muwiwyah kur kwataay nyoaay poyiithach."
"Ehaniya" wich gaayhich waa.
Yaawj aa hatpahech aach saawye.

Nyosaaw nyochawchim nyaama',
kwnyihaatety pa "muyuuch gayiin nyehat peerdeer awatt omoyu—

Ma'ich skwich nyin'aar?"
Shmay yuwaachem aaa kwevo kwa'teeysh 'wi kuwaay lemisa chiyayuwaar.

Nyipi nam saaw nam poyiit gayiin cham gaay kcham saawye cham.
Pam nyicha'qhach tuwiw nemi yeyaaw nyaama ma'ich rarimes nyama lhoh. ◇

When he came next, he said "Ay, Comadre, go see your children; they are all baptized now; they are very big and beautiful; they want to see you."
"Very well, go," said the rooster.
He took the hen and carried her off; Coyote took her and carried her off and ate her too—
When he had finished eating her, he came back.
"Compadre, now your comadre cries for you to come; Comadre wants you to go and reunite with them, for you to go and see your children—
For you to go see your children, now the chicks are all grown up."
"Very well," said the rooster, and he went—
He took him and carried him off; the coyote carried him off and ate him too.
When he finished eating him,
The owner of the chickens came: "What happened to my chickens? They are lost, gone, what happened?
Who robbed me?"
She went to search for them. Ahh, a big cave, underneath a stone there were a lot of feathers.
They went and ate all the chicks, the hen, all of them. The rooster, all, they ate them all.
The old woman arrived and saw that, and she got furious. Now what could she do? They were all gone. ◇

Bibliography

Couro, Ted. 1975. *San Diego County Indians as farmers and wage earners.* Ramona, California: Ramona Pioneer Historical Society.

———. Forthcoming. *Mesa Grande Diegueño stories*, ed. Margaret Langdon. Banning, California: Malki Museum Press.

Couro, Ted, and Hutcheson, Christina. 1973. *Dictionary of Mesa Grande Diegueño.* Banning, California: Malki Museum Press.

Couro, Ted, and Langdon, Margaret, et al. 1975. *Let's talk 'Iipay aa, an introduction to Mesa Grande Diegueño.* Banning, California: Malki Museum Press.

Hinton, Leanne. 1976. The tar baby story. In *Yuman texts* (International Journal of American Linguistics: Native American Texts Series [*IJAL: NATS*] 1:3), ed. Margaret Langdon, pp. 101–106. Chicago: University of Chicago Press.

———. 1978. Coyote baptizes the chickens. In *Coyote stories* (*IJAL-NATS*, Monograph 1), ed. William Bright, pp. 117–20. Chicago: University of Chicago Press.

Langdon, Margaret. 1970. *A grammar of Diegueño: the Mesa Grande dialect.* Berkeley: University of California Press.

———. 1976. The story of eagle's nest. In *Yuman texts* (*IJAL-NATS* 1:3), ed. Margaret Langdon, pp. 113–33. Chicago: University of Chicago Press.

Shipek, Florence. 1975. Memorial to Theodore "Ted" Couro, 1889–1975. *Journal of California Anthropology* 2:3–4.

———. 1977. A strategy for change: the Luiseno of Southern California. Ph.D. dissertation, University of Hawaii.

———. 1978. History of Southern California Mission Indians. In *Handbook of North American Indians*, ed. William C. Sturtevant. Washington, D.C.: Smithsonian Institution. Vol. 8, *California*, ed. Robert F. Heizer, pp. 610–18.

Acknowledgments and Credits

The writing system. Adapted from Couro, Ted, and Langdon, Margaret, 1975. *Let's talk 'Iipay aa: an introduction to the Mesa Grande Diegueño language.* Banning, California: Malki Museum Press.

The tar baby story. From Hinton, Leanne, 1976. The tar baby story. In *Yuman texts* (*IJAL-NATS* 1:3), ed. Margaret Langdon, pp. 43–50. Chicago: University of Chicago Press.

Coyote baptizes the chickens. From Hinton, Leanne, 1978. In *Coyote stories*, (*IJAL-NATS*, Monograph No. 1), ed. William Bright, pp. 117–20. Chicago: University of Chicago Press.

The story of eagle's nest. From Langdon, Margaret, 1976. The story of eagle's nest—a Diegueño text. In *Yuman texts (IJAL-NATS* 1:3), ed. Margaret Langdon, pp. 113–33. Chicago: University of Chicago Press.

Photo credits: pp. 225, 226, and 246—Victor Masayesva; p. 233—Tony Celentano.

MARICOPA
Literature

SONIA MANUEL-DUPONT and HENRY O. HARWELL,
Editors

The Maricopas

Henry O. Harwell

People knew the land—its rivers and highlands—long before '49ers crossed its desert tracks, lured by California and Oregon. They fought skirmishes and battled foes (Yuma, Mojave, and Apache) long before a grateful government impressed them into service for its Indian Wars, raids against Pancho Villa, and the great European conflict. The term "Maricopa," however, is relatively new to them, a convenient fiction for talking about related Yuman groups clustered along the Gila River, from the Mohawk Mountains almost to Casa Grande, the national monument. Their own way of calling themselves is *Piipaash*, simply meaning "the People." Since whites first encountered them, they have mingled with Piman groups, with whom they shared the land's resources.

These Yumans seem to have been continually on the move. By about the first third of the nineteenth century, a number of leaders and family heads had brought their people into the Gila Valley around Sacate and Maricopa Wells. Stark ranges and majestic peaks thrust skyward here; the Sierra Estrella, dominated by *Viialxa* (Sissy Mountain) and *Viikwxas*, made greasy by Coyote's touch. Together with Pima neighbors, they cooperated in agriculture and defense.

Although this country could support them easily since they also hunted, fished and relied on mesquite, ever increasing numbers of whites (Merikyaan) soon came with their own demands for land and a rapacious greed for water, life blood of Pimas and Maricopas alike. Pestilence, too, they brought: cholera, malaria, measles, tuberculosis, and smallpox. As many children and grown-ups died, the medicine men became suspect. Water shortages and foreign disease put Maricopa culture under great stress for a time. On the move once again during the second half of the last century, groups from the Gila Valley found good places along both banks of the Salt River and on the high ground near the Salt's juncture with the Gila.

Many Maricopas believe that urban sprawl from Phoenix will soon push them out from where they now live, as white farming and ranching finally

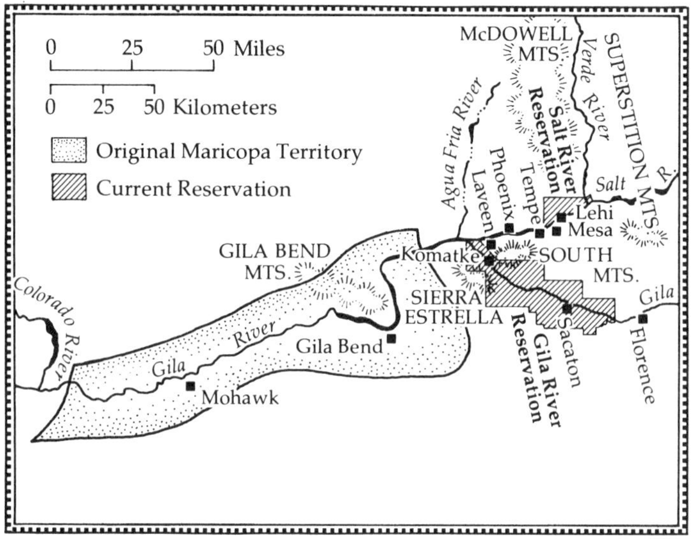

forced them into two communities to the east and southwest of the city, known as Lehi and Laveen. They number about 700 persons, not counting those living for periods of time away from the reservation. Almost all talk with reverence for the beauty of this Sonoran terrain, with its peaks and rivers, plants and wildlife (see the poem by Ralph Cameron). Many older men recall man-high grass and clear, fresh-running water filling river beds long dammed dry, pointing with dismay to the treated effluent meant to cool a nuclear reactor.

Most are very tolerant of white newcomers, but an older generation taught them important tactics in survival: "K'aavk k'ishk, k'wiim, lycheemum!" ("Be careful in what you do and say, or you'll miss out") a need underscored by the encounter with a white woman related by Philip Monohan. Although some older Maricopa are plainly distressed at the time it has taken, a younger generation is now actively entering community life with pride and hope for the future (see the text by Leroy and Ralph Cameron). Wise in new ways, they will build on the foundations set by those who have gone before, those who saw the transition from hand-cleared fields and communal labor to cement-lined ditches, tractors, farming cooperatives, and other phases of economic development. ◇

The Contributors

Ralph Cameron was born in Laveen, Arizona. At the age of six he was sent to a boarding school in California for a year but returned to Arizona to finish his schooling at Indian School in Phoenix. Feeling a lack in his education, he then enrolled in public high school to take grades 9–12 over again. Ralph Cameron spent most of his adult life in Los Angeles working in a steel factory. When he retired, he returned to Laveen, where he became an active member of his community. With many other elders, he has been worried that the Maricopa language and culture may die out with his generation. He has been actively working to record as much as possible and to begin a language program for the children.

Leroy Cameron is Ralph Cameron's youngest son. He was educated in Los Angeles, where he attended East Los Angeles Junior College and California State. He has provided the English versions for some of his father's narratives.

Henry O. Harwell, who received his Ph.D. in anthropology from Indiana University in 1979, has worked with the Maricopas since 1972. From 1972 to 1975 he studied the Maricopa language; in 1976 he added to this interest pursuits in history and culture. Since 1981 he has been an active consultant to the community in language, culture, history, and economic development.

Sonia Manuel-Dupont is currently working on a pedagogical grammar of Maricopa in fulfillment of requirements for her Ph.D. Her graduate work in linguistics has been at the University of Kansas. She also works with Henry Harwell at Laveen in an educational program on Maricopa language and cultural awareness.

Philip Monohan gained his knowledge of medicinals from his father, Mumahy (Xmamaxay, Quail's son), an old-timer who is today remembered as one of the last of the traditional doctors, or kwsithee. This calling was not undertaken or recommended lightly—even by father to son. The aspirant must already have been guided by the right kind of dream-vision.

Since federal control over their land, followed by Arizona's statehood in 1912, Indian people in the Phoenix area had to be very careful about letting on just how much they knew of the old-time medicine ways, because that knowledge was actively suppressed (principally in schools and churches). Those knowing and practicing old ways risked jail, although outsiders might not be sensitive to the dilemma involved for someone who cared about others.

Philip Monohan was always one to speak out, although not without touches of humor and a sense of outrage over what had been done to the land. As a historian, his grasp of events extended throughout the sweep of the Gila and Colorado rivers. Born in the Maricopa community near Laveen, he spent many of his younger years at Lehi with his mother's people, after her death. He knew both communities well. In the text that follows, the reservation area referred to is the Maricopa district located to the northwest of the Gila River Indian Community.

A respected elder among his people, Philip Monohan could be counted on for concern and unflagging honesty in personal and public affairs. His gentle intelligence easily probed the uninitiated, but never without humanity. He shared his knowledge of curing and community affairs willingly, trusting that a sense of history would be helpful for the younger generation. About one month after sharing the knowledge he relates here, he finally succumbed, in April 1982 at the age of 88, to the respiratory problems which had long bothered him.

The Maricopa Alphabet

Vowels

Maricopa has five short vowels and five long vowels. The short vowel sounds are represented by one letter; the long vowels are represented by two identical letters. The vowels may also occur in diphthongs, which are short or long vowels followed by the letter *w* or *y*. Below an example from the Maricopa language is given for each long and short sound and, if possible, an English word with the same or close to the same sound is also listed.

Short vowels

The vowel letters in Maricopa are pronounced as they are in Spanish.

a v*ak*

e av*e*

i xav*i*k

o iith*o*

u iix*u*

Long vowels

aa *'iipaa.* Like the *a* in f*a*ther.

ee *avee.* Like the *a* in m*a*ke.

ii *iito.* Like the *ee* in b*ee*t.

oo *iithoo.* Like the *oa* in c*oa*t.

uu *xavashuuk.* Like the *u* in fl*u*te.

Consonants

Maricopa has twenty-three basic consonant sounds. These can be represented by either one single letter (such as *k*, *m*, or *x*) or by two letters combined to form a single sound (such as *ch*, *ny*, or *th*).

ch *chiyer.* Like the *ch* in *ch*ief.

k *kapet.* Like the *k* in *k*eep.

kw *iikway.* Like the *qu* in *qu*een.

ky *thaxkyer.* Like *k* but pronounced farther forward in the mouth.

l *xaltot.* Like the *l* in *l*ot.

ly *xaly'aw.* Like the *ll* in mi*ll*ion.

m *mispo.* Like the *m* in *m*an.

n *xanmo.* Like the *n* in *n*ame.

ny *nyaa.* Like the *ny* in ca*ny*on.

p *paam.* Like the *p* in *p*ot.

q *qwaq.* Like *k* but pronounced farther back in the throat.

qw *qwaqt.* Like *kw* but pronounced farther back in the throat.

r *raak.* Like the Spanish *r* in *r*ama.

s *sarapk.* Like the *s* in *s*at.

sh *shmalyk.* Like the *s* but with the tip of tongue curled back.

t *iito.* Like the *t* in *t*op.

th *tathish.* Like the *th* in *th*ough.

v *va.* Like the *v* in *v*an.

w *iiwa.* Like the *w* in a*w*ay.

x *xat.* Like an English *h* but with more force.

xw *milxwe.* Like an English *h* but with rounded lips.

y *iiya.* Like the *y* in *y*es.

' *'ukk.* Like the sudden catch in the throat between the two English words meaning "no"—uh-uh.

Texts

Ralph Cameron, Narrator

'inyamat 'inychxa 'inychaviish

Transcription by Lynn Gordon

'inyamat thany xumarxaayly 'iyuuk vinyathiim,
xaxan thash palyk shakamp kovark.
vii vakava'osh thash waly noqampamak
chaxotilyaviik xmiik
vataym, mat nyim'oyuuvk viiva'oshk.
mat nyixamev thash kwilyshawk.
uuva'awsh as'uulyik taklasham, miyuum
chaxotilyaviik
mapis aanya walyviimak.
thany 'iyuuk vinyav'awm, nyip 'iyem'athoy thash.
xa'ash kushlyuuvevak pamm shmaanysh ashpashm
miyuuk.
aanya 'ilyviitk 'avtik
'uuva'otintiyuum
'esa 'etik.
'ayuush palyik aampsa 'etik.

My Land, My Water, My Mountains

When I was young, I saw my land as I grew up.
The rivers were many and without price.
The mountains there had not been touched.
They were beautiful, tall and big and they stood out.
The land I was born on was clean.
The rain washed it and purified it.
You saw it and it was very good.
Now it is not like that.
I see this.
This is my tradition.
A tree half fallen down with its roots showing—I
feel
I am like that,
I say we will stand again.
I see many things are left that haven't vanished yet.
The great lakes of the East are still there.

walynyuupaymxaayk.
xa kovtash thash 'inyaashpak asily
shathaakalyskiitk.
vii koxshamenysh viiva'oshxaaysa 'etik.
yaa kovevak xa kovatash vishathaakxaayk.
thany 'iyoovk vinyava'ok.
piipaa thash uuva'ok
'uuva'otintiyuum
'esa 'etik.
'ayuu kw'empa 'athawishintiyuum
'esa 'etik.
piipaa nyikur thash vathuu vathiik thany thawshik
uuva'ak
vinyathiik thany
'ilyavetntiyuum ◇

The tall mountains are still there.
The great rivers of the Northwest still exist.
We see this.
The people will walk again, I say.
We will again have the truth.
Our forefathers did this; they took this; they
progressed up until now.
I say we can do this too. ◇

sinya'ak 'inyuuxaav kanaav

Transcription by Lynn Gordon

piipaa kwchewish nyapuym, sinya'ak shentsh sinya'ak 'inyuuxaavsh kathuushpak. anyim walykormam, xumar xavakshish maxash piipak thammishk viithawtik. sinya'akinysh 'ayuunykuupay nyiaayk vunuusa, kuvartik. nyikuvarm, thany uuwintik yuuxa iim sinyavak. xaly'awsh viithawm shtuum uutr'uym iithonyik shatheyk unuuk. thash thuukathuum mashuuxank vinyathawk. thuunyik thany yoovk shinyishiq ishtik tham uumishing natamakk. tikshe anyish nyoxshmarik anyish kamiim. xaly'awinysh kawish kwinyanyekma nyimakoviik thanya nyayoovk shuupawshtik nyikoshinysh wiikathuum nyayoovk nya'avshik. tham iiwashinysh nyixuutik. ◇

West Woman

Translation by Ralph Cameron

When the creator died, one woman, West Woman, moved away along with others. Then not too long afterwards, twin boys were born. Then they kept crying. The woman was giving them everything, but nothing worked. This didn't work so she tried other things. There was a cottontail rabbit there and she took it and prepared it and she put it in front of them. They wanted to have this. Then they saw this and they fell silent and stopped their crying. The gopher had them as children. He brought it. The cottontail rabbit was mixed with other good things. When they saw this, they knew their father did this, when they saw it and heard it, and then their hearts were gladdened. ◇

tathish 'uuv kanaav (Corn and Tobacco)

Transcription by Sonia Manuel-Dupont

mkipm thuum eemk 'ayuu kanavii thowk. tathish 'etk 'uuv 'etm. piipaa xavik thash nyvum matiyaak athuum seythawm aany kanaavk nyvum matiyaak snythawk nykshuunaavk snythawk aanym makshuunaavk kawism xuut. piipaa thany aay'im viiwaynk nyikshuunaavk seythawk. tatish 'etkxapuk piipaa thash tathish thany aanya iiwaaxotkxotk thuum thuutk 'esa 'uuv mansh walymawexotm shthuum thuutk. 'uuv sekovetpatk 'iim kathot m'iim tathishsh aanysh xotk xotxotm piipaa uuwishwii. xotxotm 'iim nykthotk. tathish sekovetpatk 'iim. tathish thash kwinyavash thash nyayuuk kwinyavak chawuum kwutra'uuii xot xotm.

shamak shamunk chovaw kwinyathiik kwinyathiik kwinyathiik nyoxamiim. aanym thuum thuum 'ayuuk palysh nymank xotk. 'ayuu piipash xwinyayawm nyuuvaak 'ayuu shensh shuumathiik many aly'iithuushxaputk. aanym thuum tathishsh thuum aanya mythush. 'ayuu tathish thany nyashthuum 'ayuu a'awlyvii shvathuum thanyii chim utra'uuiik kwinyanook nyaviirk aanym tawaatm thotk tawaly kwinyanook kwinyanook aviirm mavar kekowom. thany iipash xwinyayawm thany thany nyipayk 'etm thany matly aanya 'etk. tathish thash iipaa thany wikxotkxotk 'etk 'etk. thanylyviik xwinyayuuk xwinyatapoyem xwinyatapoyem kamthuum nyaa tathish kathuum thuum nyaa 'etk xwinyatapoyem 'shlyviik.

nyaa piipaa thany 'ayuu uumayk thochish shkwiyak xwinyatapoyem thoyk. aany 'iim 'yuuk 'iim. nyaa kathawom xotxotm 'etk 'etk 'etk thuum 'uuvsh thokavik ny'etpatk. mansh aanym muwaastik.

'uuvsh sekovetk tathish ny'etpatk many mapayatik xwinyayak xwinyayak aanym xwitly mlyyamk kumkowat 'esa nyip nyanyikopaym piipaa thash nyathuum thotk tinyamnysh yam thanylyiviantik xwinyayawm nyipm shulyentik. aasily yemk nyaxwi nymnyakum nyxavik kwinyanook aanym tathish chu'ulya wiim muchawamk uumow kasathawk aasim mamtik aasily nymlypaytik 'esa nyaa nlyvamak nya'amxaaym. piipaa thash payik xokavik thuum thotk thanylyviik aanyii maam kkwilythomak. piipaa thash kitavik mimatm uuvak iipay thash shkyetuum tinyam nyikopay tinyam nyikopaym.

aanym tathishk shthuum xotm mxotm nym'iim 'ayuu piipash matashevk kinyavak many 'ayuu xuuchovuuthik nyikorwaruk chaam'uumaum walyyuumtik kathomsh shthuum nyakathok k'iim walyyuumtik. many mshthuum xa'ly shovawuushpuum kawisha kumathuum. 'esa nyaa 'uuv nyip nyathow uuchuush sepik kawom kwanook kwanook nyatinyam thany akap thuum thotk.

thany 'iim nyaa tho 'uuvsh nyaa thowuuxot xotm setathitsh mansh kwshlumakly kwmathitk thuum nymawaamkik say'iim. 'uuv say'iim shkwerk kwanook nyaviirk aanym matanyvthim. nyavuuvak thuum nyaktavik nyaaw avii komee mkanamk. vany vnyayemk thuum tathishsh vii vathuushk matly viimak nmak kathuum nya'iim iiwaany aviirk nyip kathok womkuum. nyathuu nya'avk vyemk mayvishpa kwilyyaakny matly yem xekonyi thaanym matkanaav.

tathishsh matkavaavyem nyip walyamawxotxotmak. kathum ny'iim nykthiik piipaa thash shopawuum nyip 'ayuu kọmny thany mshthomish nykthiik nyaxalyiivim aanym ny'etkwaly kawish kathuum nyathiik nyxavik 'ayuum 'esa 'etk aany muunum say'iim. thash 'ayuu chavaw xovik thash 'uuvsh tathishsh matsay'iim matwalyxotmak 'ayuu matmarixa. iivnyuuvak aanyii mank walynyiyemak. mansh shopaum shensh iiwaany manypatk aanyii mank thuum thuum. 'ayuu piipaa thokwanook matii kwnook thash tathish chavawm walyxotmak. thanylyviik lyviientik piipaa thiik kwnook shensh 'uuv chavawuum lyviik xotxotm thiik 'etk. ◇

Corn and Tobacco

Translation by Leslie Spier (1933)

Once the corn and tobacco were visiting each other. They talked about how they provided for men. The corn said, "Humans use corn more than they use tobacco." The tobacco asked, "In what way is corn more used?" The corn said, "Corn is well cared for because it is of most use. When humans prepare to go to war, the first thing they think of is taking corn, parching it on coals, and grinding it into meal. Men going to war carry it for provision. So corn helps a great deal. When they kill an enemy, I feel as though I was killing the enemy, because I feed the people well so they are able to go kill the enemy. I am more useful."

The tobacco said, "You are used only at the time they are going to war; they take not only corn, but tobacco. As for corn, when they are ready to return, they have eaten all their meal, and they come back without the corn. But tobacco comes back with people. Even when the men are home, tobacco is carried every day and night. If corn is more useful, when men are gathered in meeting, why do they not put a bowl of cornmeal right in the middle, and each take a swallow? Instead they put you aside, take tobacco and use it all night." So tobacco claimed it was more useful than corn. Then tobacco, after saying this, said he was going back to vikami' (the sacred mountain of the Mohave). Then the corn was left here alone for a while. Finally corn went away to Mexico.

The corn said, "If I am not useful, they will not call me back; humans would do without me. But tobacco will see that people will try to get me back." On account of these two plants quarreling, we do not get good results with our corn and we do not raise tobacco as well as they do to the west. ◇

Respect for the Elderly

Free translation and transcription by Sonia Manuel-Dupont

nyikor nyaeexapuk xumarsh nyishxaysh nyikwithiikxaayly 'ayuu nyashopawuum 'ayuu kanaavk.

mthooxa mkwush movanxilyaa aanya mkonaavk 'ayuu shen vathiik many 'ii xotxotm.

piipash 'ayuu 'ism ka'av mkathuushk kathuum ka'avk aanym xotm aanym miiwanyshxotm aanym miiwaanysh msperuum aanyii mank. piipaa akoy, kur'aqsh shkiyaam myuuk vunuukovarik muuwiikuum aanyii kamank mumawiim mshopauum mumawiim m'yuuwuum mumawiim mu'avm mumawiim muuwiikuum 'etk kanaavk vthiik viiwaynk viiwaynk.

vuunuxaaymmansh kwshensh xavathikxaayk piipaa shqwershqwerk 'iim. vuunuxaaym matkyavk matkyavk vuunuxaaym muthii ny'iim thany mathawk vanym thuum kawish vaka thily thanyii thawtuum thuum 'avk nymxotpatk kawish nymyaatm kawishm myemk kawishm shopauum kawishm moxayk nymnyuuvayik muxuutly thany kanaav kwathish thuum 'avtm thuum ny'entm pish ny'avk vthiik kamank shentlyviish lyshkiit kawitch wiim viny miyak.

kamathuum m'iim mvak iiyaw say'etk 'etk kanaav thamii. ◇

There is still another generation of children coming, one after the other.

When you get older there will be things you know, good things will be coming to you.

You must listen to people; think; listen; you will be happy; you will be strong. All of these things have been going on since the beginning. When you see an old lady or old man you love them, you help them. From the very beginning, you know your relations, you see your relations, you listen to them, you help them. This will go on and on and on.

We are still together, we are still all around here; we're still all here together. Things will be good again. Learn from your elders. Go in a good direction. This knowledge will go on from generation to generation. It will help you go in your life's direction. I have heard this from the beginning many times. We are like one.

It's still the same. It will always go on and on. ◇

Instructions on Hunting

Transcription by Sonia Manuel-Dupont

'ayuu matmoqwerm many mo'vaak lyvamak mo'vaak lymathoshxapuk. kawish thaxoman ka'iim mvanyk nyavamuum nymyeawuum mvaak. iipash nyshthuum kawish xotk kwalyyeshmak mera'merum

The first thing you need to do is think about going hunting. Then you make preparations to see if you have your bow and arrow and to see if they are in working order. Then when that's all done, you go

xotm. nymsha'ulym thanyk kawishm xlyqwawm thanyk aasii thiik shamak mthiim. mv'aak mkanamk ay'entik vo'vaak miyaak. nymvamum nymyaak aanym matthiksavk 'avk xuutm. miyaak miyaak miyam kawish muly'iim nyawiim aanym miyuuk aanym thuum mkisaavk. nymlypaxay 'owk mat siiyuum mat siiyuum uv'owk mvamum vumiyak vumiyak. nymavam lyxilypanik nymyuuk aanym uutiyish nymshamiim muthawk. nyimakathuum mkyiam nymsha'ork kyaam aanym aanym moxa muthowtik. ◇

out to a certain place where certain game is. When you start traveling you have to take extra real precaution to be quiet, "snishqa'iim," you have to be quiet. Then when you spot the game you're after, you have to be extra more quiet so you can get closer. As you get closer, you prepare your bow and arrow and position it, then *bang* you got your game! ◇

Some Thoughts on Modern Education

Transcription by Sonia Manuel-Dupont

Children today do learn to a certain extent, but there is something lacking, something missing because they are not really being taught about their culture and their traditions in which our people have been brought up for thousands upon thousands of years.

I have heard of and read about great empires like the Roman Empire. How great they were—and yet their traditions and culture must have been weak because they were not strong enough to survive. But we are; we're still existing and that's something that the kids and grown-ups have to know. Otherwise we won't stay here. We'll be wiped out just like a lot of other Indian tribes. There used to be two-three hundred Indian dialects in this country and now there's only a few left. That goes to show you the weakness of their culture. That is what makes you stand up to be a nation. Cooperation and learning—that's what they (the children in school) need to learn. Our tradition may seem kind of funny in ways, but it has paid off.

I am quite sure they (the children) are not well satisfied with this modern education. You need to get in there and touch on these real things, for example, some words that are real heart touching; that are real challenging. It's enough to reach down in there and make the challenge that you are going to get up and do something. That's the way it was done in the past. They (people of the past) had heard it; they'd grown up in it and when they got to the age that they were facing responsibility in the future they could go on from there.

But this modern education—it's not all there. It

will take you the modern way of making money, but it seems to me that you will have to do a little cheating here and a little lying there in that way. The Indian way wipes all that out. It (the Indian way) is all on being honest—that was another thing we were brought up in—being honest.

There's a big part of them (the children) missing now. They know there's something missing. But when you start to talk to them in these words (Maricopa) which are a part of them, then it's going to start to fill in those empty spaces. It's going to help them a lot. That's what every kid is looking for—a part of that emptiness being filled in with what he is supposed to be fully. ◇

Piipaa uuwish thany (On Being a Maricopa)

Transcription by Sonia Manuel-Dupont

piipaa uuwishk thany 'ayuuk shumay nyuuwishk vthanym nyvayiik aanym 'ayuunysh 'ayuuk 'ayuu kwaym thany 'yuuk xaxan, viis, 'ayuu uulvash thuum tamar lythiik kwathiknya chamaach aanyii mank matsh paam xuutk kwithowv.

'ayuuk shmay thany knaavk aviirk. piipaa kwinyikoor sekethinya sekiyem thany knaavk 'iim thany minymatsh thany minywish 'iim thash iiya piipaa kwchewish aviirk nyiaayxapuk kwithaw xotm aanyii mank kwnyayaak iipaa xamaly chavaatk xikoxan chavaatk nyimatsh xakily chavaatk.

piipaa kwinyikoor thash korik shamunk 'ayuu nyikopay nyiwishpatk mat thany shek 'ayuu uulyvash thuum tamar lyyaamak tamar lychuumish vokwam thany. aany shek vinya waantik pilyk, xachurk, xanpashk nymkowashish shilyshentik wiiwaam may wik thuum m'yuuk xamshiish mayk alyvo'awk vokwom thany 'yuuk shuupawm muly'aym mki kuuvash kawish kwinyathuum kathuumsh ay'uuknaavk vokwam thany muly'nyiiayiik. piipaa kwinyikoor thash mulyshishk vokwam thany 'etk kwalyemak 'ayuu piipaa kwchewo thany shamaa vinyathiik shamaa nyayuuk aany kshuvnaavuum aanysh knaavpatk uushkwik 'iim thotm aanyii mank 'ayuum nyikopaysh shimuly' thuum thutk.

piipaa uuwish thany 'ayuu nyikopay aym aviirk 'ayuush thuumtik 'ayuu muxsh nyikoor nyathuum 'ayuu nyikoor mush nyikoorsh thany watpatk matk thiik shamaank tamar lythiik shamaank 'ayuush uulyvash thuum tamar lythiik voqwam thany sook 'ayuu xavachoosh thuum chiyersh mayly uulyvak voqwam thany chiyersh kathomsh xaly thiik qwaqwamnya aany maashapatk chiish thotnthiik aanym thuuk kathowa piipaa kwinykoor vokwithiik thash xaxan thany a'urk nyishovayatik vthiik chii thash xotk thuum thany uusaavek.

piipaa nyikoor thany 'ayuu mush thash shenti-kwalythomak palyk iiyash kawish thuum aany chamaank kawompatk viiwak palyk xotm xoma'vk viwak thuum aanyii 'entk 'ayuum nyikopay 'ayuu mumaax thany ka'aavk nymkawaamkik nymaka-waam 'iim thany knaavk aviirk nymshopeik 'iima-wiim mamaam movatayuum aanyii mank mulyxuum kawis kamawaxa muuvarum kathom aanya knaav-thentik xumarik kwinyathuum thany shamaank knaavk

piipaa nyikoor thash 'ayuu nyikoor nyknaavshsh shomayiik vthiim aany aanysh 'ayuu nyikopay thany mat nyikoor vash thany nykshamaank 'ayuu knaav thash knaavk thuum kanyavaantik xamshiish vynathowum may thily tam'orum thany 'entk 'ayuu nyknaavsh kwknaav thash 'ayuum kwknaav thany msheyentik kwustomach 'etk piipaa thash piipaa kwustomach thash piipaa kwilyviinpatk mank thotm 'etk kwilyviik aanyii mank sekwathinyish aany lyvii'etpatm aanysh mank aayiishuum uu'etpatk piipaa thany 'ayuu knaavk.

anylyviik xamiik kwnyathiik thany av'k shava-ruum 'avak 'ayuu kwknaav 'avak aanyk shamaank matchievtik matcheeovk 'etm 'owvak piipaa thash wiim matwiik thany wichawk piipash knythiik 'yuuk nyarawvk thuum piipaa kwcheoovk thany chuuyav thuum thotk chuuyawvk thuum vinya thawk piipaa thash iiwaa thany nyatathuum iipaa kwcheoovk thany matawiik 'ayuu karav thany uuwik watapayiik aanyk kamank xotk iikathumwetk viiyaamk nyv'ova-rum piipaa 'ayuu koor'avm nyetlyxoxam aanym kwcheoovknysh 'ayuuny kopay uutr'uuiik 'esa viientik nyknaavk nyacheoovk vinyuuvak waly-xotmaym knaavk shavark kwathaw chashpaashm knaavk nyaxotm shavark avathawuum aany chash-paashm kshavaruum thuum thotk shuupaw thuum thotk my'etm thuum ny'etm xoxan ninyakovam aanym piipaa thash matakyaavuum 'ii 'iichaam as'ulyk kwaam nook aanym xotenyetk.

piipaa uu'iish thash choomishk vinyathawk kinyayemk uvathotuum iiyovtum vinyathuum pis anylyviik 'entk kinyayemk kawish walyxotmak 'ayuu ravsh thuukathowa xwaysh thuukathowa ka-wich nyikanaavk vithitmiyov thuum thotk.

nikors sekwathii nyish nyathuum anylyviim aany kwilyvii nyayxuutkpatk piipash vuwaam kwu-stomach 'ayuu iivovaam 'ayuu thany kwilyviik thany nyayuuk shuupaw vunuuk aviirk. 'ayuu xotsh vthiik 'ayuu xotsh kathawompem kinya'emk 'ayuu mshiithevshthawompem kinya'emk 'ayuu ravshk ka-thawompem. thany piipaa kawish viiwaynk noo-kovash thany machaawamk uukanaavk aviirk aanyii manuum piipaa thash any'owk piipaa aany'yuuk piipaa xotsh tho 'yuuk 'iim 'iim shank aylyiivanyavak thuum matly erik viinyavak viinyavak thuum saviis 'is thuum thotk kinya'emk nyatho'ntik 'ayuu mush-tothavak thawk vnya thuum thany nyikanaavk thany 'ayuu knaavsh 'etm 'ayuu knaavsh thotk thany knaav thuum thany shuupawuum matly tathomuum matshaverk shothowuum vithawtik thuum piipaa nikors sekethi thash 'ayuu shmathiik kwalythomak ny'entm 'ayuum kwustomach uuwish thash lyalyasnyak piipaa thany 'ayuu knaavk thotk vthiik thotk kwustomach.

piipaa thash ny'entm nikoor nyishovaayk nishomishpatk xakathawk kwnyathiik thuum.

'ayuu matmawiik 'etm thotk xomarsh samiik nyathiim thany nyashkwerxapuk thany knaavkxapuk piipaa nyikopay kwaam thany mumashowish vany knaavk kwanook kathom xishypanyk kathom noqemkoriim kathomsh korik nyathuuvithot'sa nyknaavk mamawiish 'etk aany miyem miyuuk womakovarik aany knaavk 'iim aanyii kiriim kathuum matmaviirk matly kovarik nyavak chomiish vokovash thash aanym matayuuwuum nyikathuum matkovaruum nyikathuum 'etk kathuumsh piipaa kathumsh shentikwalythomak palyk vinyavak thuum wuthox thotk piipaa kopays matly uuyush thutk aanyii kuwumek miyak ny'entm matmachowish vokshent thash 'ayuu nikopay matly kyevuum thuum thotk matmachowish thawpatk matakivetik viiwamk anyii muchawamk chomishsh matakivetik aanyii kowomk masperaxaaym aany kowom kawish kathom mothawk kathom samamatawak nyikoor nyathopak xutk 'iim nykopaysh xotk kwalythomak xwayk kathom vinya thiim thikawom kathom 'iim piipaa vokovarxa 'etk anylyviik xwayk nyathuum iipaa thash nyathuum shuupowuum matmawiik my'iim nyixovak xwee xwee thany thany nyayuuk winyayuuk thuum chawaamk matwiik thuum thotk thany muwaxaik thuum thany knaavk shamaak shamunk knaavkwathii matmawish thuum nywikiuu'iink nywikiiuu'iink nyuuii'uuiink nytrauuii-'uuiinyk thanyly 'iim iinyathush vinyawak thuum matwiksh sperm shapilyviik thuumowiim xwinyayaak nyithawmartik kinya'emk nyathuum kovarpatik thotk ilyshlok kwathiik thany 'iim 'ayuu thany 'entum nyknaav xwayntum matmawii thash kiinavak ny'entm xomarsh 'owk xixway thily 'ovk paam tulyxaaly kwishta kanaavk thash thawk shentik valyvak kwishta knaavk xomar thany xaviktik vinya thawk xavik thuum xomarik kwalyemik shamaank 'ayuu shkwirk iithoo theyarpayikik uushkwerik 'ayuu kxotk chuushkwerk xotuum nywiishk ooshkwerk kshovaruum iyaa thany thawk pak uukshovarik viiwaynk xomar thash nya'owvk piipaa thash ntay thash winyakovarik thany thoomay'im nyshuupawuum thuum iiwaa xotk iiwalymak thot aanysh mank xumarxan xuutk kwilywomek shamaank 'ayuu nykopay knaavk viiwaynk viiwaynk viiwaynk viiwaynk xilykushim aanym ny'entm chomish kwvash thash matly kyievk thuum thotk 'ayuu xotsh thuum aanly kwilythuumtik aanysh kovarik aanysh shmethii vuuk nypaym chewmkviyatk thuulyskiit vithawk vithawk kathomsh kathom thuum thotk vashk kwinkwathaw thany ny'entm nyawiiim xomarxaayk nykshamaank kwshkwik kwithii kwathiiny nyakwushuum thany kwinyavak aanlyvetpatk piipaa thash muchawaamk 'ayuu matxuutaly thany 'ayuu matly wiik aany nyashuupawuum vinyavak thuum vinyayak mkwinyayempk ookwish nyavamk kathuum piipaa vokovash vash thash 'ayuu 'ayuu chavowpatk 'ayuu kawish tathish'entish xomat mariik'entish kawish palyk chapeek vokwom thany chovaak thany nymnyivay'ik vivatk xotm thash vathuum aany 'iim shamaak shamank shamank thany matvokovar thany knaavk vothiik vothiik vothiik thany kamiim uuvthentik xotk xomar nyakushm nyasperm nuuwaak nyathuum lyveevsh avathiikpatm tee'uvk kwtr'oyiik kathom vimyathiik kathom 'ayuu moiish walyvetmak xomarsh matxavik shnathuum qwaqwashish qwanoga vashaw palyk kiimnam thuum tamiyuutk thash avish kovarntik nyathawm thotk thany walymiuuntum vinyathawm thuum thany thamii vawiim matkovarik vthiik thotk ny'entuum xomar uulyveevsh matly shem'otm troy'iik kinyathuum vnyathiik thuum va'xapuk vowompak matm yuuvk matlyvash skwiishk walywomak kovark 'ayuu xotk vash kovark 'ayuu xotm thash thuutm thuutm thany 'awvk vithiink nyikweshm uuvaakuum ulyveevuum matatakyem thuum xotm kwiyak nyientuum viiwaynk viiwaynk thany yavaam kush nyavaam iipaash nyathuum siny'ak 'yuuk siny'aksh shthuum aanlyviitk iipaa athawpat kwithawk kathom 'ayuu nyimank xomarsh a xomer kathom vinyavam thuum 'ayuu xumux thuum xava thiitm thuum shuupawm vinyvak thany matawiithiik ny'entum ovayiik vokovash thash matawiik xalyviik piipaash thash shensh nyawiim vovarik qwaask nyathuum koriyvm aashlyviirk nyithotm vithawm nyayuuk vithuum machotook wanook nyaviirk matawiik thuum nyashentikathotm kaem mashoverik aanyii shamaank thiik kwinyavak kathom seevemawiik wey'entik winyawamk kwinyawamk 'ayuu nykopay matm akap thuum shovaw vitiyuuk thuum chamaash thash shpatpatk vithiik vithiik nyakuush shmthuum vuwentik aalyaviik mata ev'entik 'ayuu thany shakyetm xapoonuum kawom iiwak nyash thuum wivinyawak kathom 'ayuu xotsh nyamthuum xomar thash mamawiiwa xotm nyvaak ara'oyk kwiiam thany kwkush thash nyayuuk nyavak thuum iiwaa thash nyixotpatk thany vixowash vokish shenkwish thany nyikoor piipaa nyikor sekwiyem thash thany knaavk kwathish thany nyathuum thany vawiikwash 'ayuu xotsh nyimank nyayuuk iiwa xotm amkiitiiv thuum thotk thaanya lyveshmo thamii. iipaa uuwish thany 'ayuu piipaa 'yemthoy aany shkwerk 'iim thany tshuupaawshik va iikathom aanya 'iim aany 'iim nyanikovnaavk vothit'sa makinyayemk kinyayemk xomar thash shtamathaw vnythuum matly xomarm thash shtamathawtuum mki mank thuumsh piipaa piipaash thash kia mank thuum thanysh shtamathawk nypiipaa uuwish thash mki kawishii sevuum akanamk vuwak thuum shamaak thanysh shtamathawventk xomar pisa vokovik thash 'ii matly eemak nyikoor aany knaavk vowanook kaviirm shuupawm piipash thuum mki mank ny'entm nyimatk nyishovii nyishoxash vthiik thany shuupawm asiimank kathuum aasm mnyvayiik matly nymnyuuwishk aasii mamank vmathiik mat thily mvaak 'iim thany knaavk vuthism uu'aavk shuupaw thiik vithiik pisa skovarik thany entamak kwalykshoonavuum xomar vokovik thash thany 'iim pisa thanysh shtamathaw kathuum thuum piipaa kwinyikoor thash 'ayuu kwxotm 'ayuuk 'ayuu iimsh thany thowsh thany myemk thany 'yuuk shuupawm aviirxapuk 'ayuu aanym nyishomayk piipaa xamalysh mat thily uuvaak va'a thuum thotk piipaa xamalysh mat inyavak kathuum nyip iithoiish 'iim shkwersh 'iim 'ayuu nyikopay thany shomathiik shomathiik kwinyavak thuum piipash iivthawm thuum nyoknaavk many mulythoshsh walyxotmak many 'ayuu me'esh walymiyemk kwilythiik walyxotmak thuum maxsu'kiyavxa xashukiyavaka piipaa xamaly iyemthoy thany kathuum thuum thany knaavtik vthiim iyov vinya thawm aanya shkwerish 'ayuu iiyem anxan nyikoor thany yentamak vinyathawk thuum maree iipaa xamaly yem thany iipaa xamaly kokowthii thash shamathiik thuum thuum iipaa xamaly yem thany thuu'etk vovam yoentik aanym mki thuum walyxotmak shuumiiwaa thily kawitshii thuum kawitshii thuum shomeek vovak aanyiimank 'ayuu kwithoy thany iipaa xamaly kwithoy thany vathuum lyvak thuum waly'etm thuum thotk kimam aanya walyviimak maatm piipaa shkwerii thoy thany nyishuupawm nyathuum thany wilyviimayuum ny'entm 'ayuuk xotm 'awvk 'ayuukwxotm 'awvk shamawvk vimathushk vithiink thuum nyakweshm thuum kwishuupawuum uunyik kxotm topitk nymnovayk siyem thuum thotk thany 'entik iipaa xamalysh thany 'iim piipaa thany 'iim.

manysh miyemmthoy thany walymanmakmak matm mithuum nymmiyak 'awvk piipaa 'ayuu iipaa xamaly thany walywalymuveeumayuum piipaa matach mkyem kimovatk piipaa 'ayuu shmathiish thany kimovatk 'etk thany knaavk thash walythuu-walythaw say'etk say'etk.

aanym mank shamank kwavarxanxan iipaa 'ayuu matachawk piipaa thany nyathuum thany 'ayuu ka-wish xotk 'ayuu piipaa nyikoor vash 'ayuu yem 'aym vuunuuk piipaa xamalysh ntapetk kwimiyak kwi-nyavak thuum vinyayaamk piipaa thany si'ily thuum thotk mvovarik 'ayuu mamshovark ivim nyamak ntamak walynyithuush nto aanyii kathuum aanyii kiyem thuum aanym piipaa thash 'ayuu kawis iipaa xamaly thany walyaymxapuk iipaa xamalynysh thuum matamk nyikoor paym shemk 'ayuu nyuu-wishk shemk 'ayuu shuupawuum merikyaan thuutk kathowa ntiwamtor thuutk kathowa kawish thuum kwaly thash kwinyavak thany shemk shuupaw vi-nyavak thuum thotm viothwk'sa nyip ny'entamak nyawishuum thuum kawish kwalyvinya wily'aw shthuum thotk 'esa viiwaynk nyathuum kwi-nyamiim nyathuum nyikoor thash walyviitamak nyavook kwathiik thany thash matam thash kwinya-minyk nikoorsh sekeyemaam walyuuvemak aanym merikyaan thash niktovik nyishuupawnysh piipaa thany 'yemthoy thany shuupawm 'etk thuum 'iinyaa'vak kwinyavam 'ayuuvm nyikopay mnyayk kwanook nyaviirk nyinyay viiwatm thiik muunuum piipaa kokush thash vivak matly kyevm iyook kwinyathawk 'ayuu xotsh shamalyk kwithaw thotk thany 'yuuk kiyavshik vany thooshik vi'ishk kwesko-thi'tsa kovarik kwithim thuum mataamk kashiim-xaayk kwithaw thuum 'ayuu xotsh xomar 'ayuu shuupaw xokwi aanysh shomalyk kawishsh alyviien-tik kawish muxaly nym'iim myxaaym 'ayuu nyikopay shomalyk chxotlyviitam viiwaynk thuum thiksha-maank matashuupawm matatiky'evm 'ayuu nyiko-pay 'ayuu kwaxotm kwilyviinya mishamaank mata'ayvk naak ilyuuthooshik xotamak nyikoor nyathuum alyvek xomarsh nyathiim naak 'awsh-thuum thot nyikoor nyawiim mataxapuk nyikoorsh mata'evk nyatinyam shamiim mata'evk xumarsh nyavak kwinyavak 'awtikovatk ka'awtika shkwerk 'iim k'awvkokovat kokovatm tuikyavk mata'am palyk matashuupawm mnyayemk aanym piipaa kwik shwar thash xumar thany nyikooraavk ny'entm shkwerketka'av vokowaymk kokowayn viiwayn viiwayn viiwayn okwishm pa'aam me'aanysh xamalym chulyshilym ilyvashm 'eta aanym kovauum 'ayuu muxay thany chishpashm shkwerpatk 'etk kwathiik.

piipaa 'yemthoy vokothiinya thany shaxayk uukshovaark 'ayuu kxuutk shkwerk kxuutk shamaa kamank shkwerk kxotsh vyathiik xayem nyikoor kwalythomak mapis mapisxaayk shkwer thushii iipaa kukosh thash thany shkwershxaayk thany thoxaayk thany 'eexaayk viiwaynk nymaamkam shkwer thash mat thily uuvalyskiit 'ayuu xotpersh mat thily uywalyskiitm thany thawk vasqwe'iim 'ayuu kwxotk ny'iish nyathunya'aw vashkwee 'iim 'ayuuk aasii vnychamatkilyapaxik 'ayuu koxotm thany nythushk shkwersh thanyii shkwersh ka-mavish thanyii shkwersh shkwersh avathawk matkovarik knaavk chaxotlyviik nikovk thany thawk thuum nykshamaanya nyamatsh thany 'uukshuuva-ruum thuum aanym manamtam mat kokovar thiiko-mank matakovaruum matayuuwuum mat'avuum nyikoor nyathuum alyviik piipash 'ayuuwuuvark 'ayuu mevkovark kyawom kyaak kwikat 'etm akoy kor'aqsh shav'awk xotm matkovarik nyavaam xumarsh thuum thany nyknaavk kyaak kowikat thany uuwish thash 'ovatk matmawish xosperk matathawk kwinyathawk thuum machawamk ny'entm shkwersh kwinyikoor thany shuupawsh lyshkiit kwthawkum thuuothishxash thotk piipaa inkokush nyaash thuush xotk kwilyviitk xumarsh nyivukavu kwnyayuuk nya'aavk kwiny'am mki shthuum thuum aly'etk shkim mawiyaxaxan shthot sashm vthiik kwilyvak mki shthuum thuum aly'etk vuvatk shamaka'etk thaman uulyviimak 'ayuu kopay ny'entm 'ayuu nykopay valy pax kwanook 'ayuuk savii valyapax kwanook aviirk kava 'iim walyxotmak kwashamalysh shomoshkweem 'iim thuutk miim nyaxomar thany yame'enm kawish palyk 'iim nyathaw shamulymak skwetk maki mamank mathuu thany met'sa 'owk nyishuupawm thany thushk thany 'owvk kwinyaveshk thuum uunyee komeramera thuum nymnyiimuum mat matawiik matayuuk matavamk xotkmanye komeramera thuum nymnyiim kwinyayesh kathuum shuupawsh piipash uuthuushm thash thuum 'iim ish nyathaw aly'iim miiwaa thash xotm iiwaash thash xotm aanyii mank nymatsh thash xotm matsh viivaam avii mank ayuu xotmishpa'o thuum mat thash xavasho'ii shvatlyii uuyawuum nyikoor nyathuum anyalyviik vthiim yuutk xotxotm anlyviim tivia'sa thuutuum uuthushk'shthotk matakyevk uushthot thuut timawam knaavk kiyuum. ◇

On Being a Maricopa

English by Leroy Cameron

These are some feelings and ideas on being a Maricopa. This has been put together by a Maricopa father and son, the son writing in English and the father interpreting it in his own Maricopa words.

Being a Maricopa means that each of us has an inherited right to live and enjoy our rivers, mountains, wildlife, and vegetation that is on our land. Inherited right means that our ancestors or forefathers were given the right to live on this land by the Creator before the Spanish or European ever came to this land. Our forefathers gave the land, animals, even the weather and the stars in the heavens their names. Those original Maricopa names came from the communication that existed between the Maricopa and his Creator.

Being a Maricopa means having our own types of native foods that included a variety of wild and domesticated game, vegetables, fowl, and fish that once inhabited our rivers. The Maricopa diet did not consist of a few items, but a variety of foods. Moderation in eating was emphasized, so that being overweight was greatly discouraged.

Being a Maricopa means having our own native religion which evolved around nature and the stars in the heavens. Our religious leader was called a shaman or medicine man. This person came from a long line of medicine men and, while growing up, his education in songs, stories, and medical treatments of the tribe came on a day-to-day basis. So when a person became sick, the shaman was sent for in hopes of making the person well. When a natural catastrophe or a natural phenomenon occurred greatly affecting the community, it was the shaman who would interpret the occurrence and ease or perhaps warn the community of impending danger.

Being a Maricopa means having and keeping family relationships as well as having an overall concern for the community. Belonging to someone or to a group of people is very essential to the well-being of all persons. In the past, family and community relationships were very strong because of the need to survive. Their family relationships were explained and taught to the children within their homes. Values such as family respect, benevolence, trust, cooperation, bereavement at wakes were emphasized and explained to the children as they grew up in the home. Community concern was also taught, for in the older days community cooperation was necessary for the livelihood of all. In those days farming and the raising of food was done by hand. The community working together could finish a job much faster than a few working alone.

Being a Maricopa means being culturally aware of who we are, where we came from, and where we are going. Our forefathers had a positive outlook on our culture that existed until the arrival of the European. These people did not understand the Maricopa and his culture. They told the Maricopa that he must change his ways and language. If they did not change their ways of life, they would become inferior. It was during this time that they were not given the right to express themselves, nor to contribute to the growth of America. Today things are different. We live in a time when other people want to know, understand, and listen to us. The door to opportunity and knowledge is finally open. We must also try to understand, communicate, and listen to others, most importantly, our elders.

By cherishing our traditions, values, native language, and land, that concern and love will make us more aware of who we are. It is then that we will be on the road to understanding and being Maricopa. ◇

Old-Time Medicine

Philip Monohan, Narrator

Transcribed by Hank Harwell

Philip Monohan gained his knowledge of natural remedies and curing at the source, as he relates here. His father Hmamhay (Quail's Son), whose name sounded like "Monohan" to Anglos, knew and practiced the old ways. Today he is remembered as one of the last of the medicine men, or (k)sithee. *This piece goes into detail about the use of* mily'k, *a herb mentioned in the previous selection. The general area referred to is the Maricopa district located to the northwest of the Gila River Indian community.*

Ayuu noq matknav maavsham, ayuu . . . nykor . . . nyep nymanthash'ii nyi'yuuk, nyvak 'iyuum, ayuu noq nyknavtu v'ark—ayuu kawich viyamk 'eetk 'eetknavtik. Ayuu . . . ayuu kawich chpaavk viyam anya 'eetk. Ayuu, anch hotk 'eetk anya mamaam-hotuu 'eetk.

Ayuu kawich shmash duum, anyish anya 'omaamhotm 'eetk; ayuu kawish mattoqhamiik thoom k'avanyk—anya knavk. Anya homaam wi-diik, anya piipayk thuum 'eetk.

Iivnyawak ayu kathom sav'oshnthik, anyish ayuu . . . ayuu raavk u'truy'intik: ayuu nymraavk, anya mthawha mlyulyk, kinya'em 'uvshov wiim; kamawoo mamaam piipaa shopawsh, sitheesh—anyish knavham nyathom hotm 'iim. Nymwom'k nymahotha 'ii—anya wiim withiik thuum'ii, 'iim 'eetknav.

Iivnyawak ayuu, ayuu kathom ayuu shentik knavhay'u ayuush vdik ayuu tamarsh avathik mat'i

Let me tell you a little, how quite some time ago my old Dad, whenever I would come to see him, I heard a few things he would tell me about what was growing around here. Well, he'd talk about some of the natural growths that existed. He'd say, "They're good, they're fit for you to eat."

There are some edible roots that he'd discuss; they just grew wild in these parts. He'd talk about just what we ate around here, and how we got along.

He'd go on to say that there are some (other) things growing out there, that . . . would cure whatever ailed you. When you're sick, you take and boil them, or you can use them raw; people that knew about it, or doctors—he talks about how it works real good. If you do it that way, it'll work out fine—that's how it's been done around here, so they say.

Another thing he went on to talk about was some of the weeds growing wild in this area—it's a kind

hamiik—qwnaak hamiik kathom uvathikam; anya piipaa thash nyasheek ayuu mily'iksh 'iimsheek. Anya . . . anya nyukor nyawiim, anya homarnya weytik 'ovetk ayuu raavk. Ayuu kawish 'iimha ayuu raavk nyathuum, nyathuum mitosh . . . 'ovarpak alyspermam wiim : anya weyk, anya wiim hotk 'eetmthotk, anya weetk.

Ayuu kathomish avathikam anya kakuush thash anya wetapatk; ayuu nyaraavk anyim matatruyam wiim thany. Ayuu . . . piipaach 'ovark ayuu ksitheesh hiim anyish anyi meev; anch showpawam anyish piipaa thany 'iyuuk, anyish knavk wiim . . .

Mily'ik 'uyuush thash, ayuu . . . avim t'ar athaw'a; t'ar walythoomak kwahay'u mkihamiik avantik. Ayutaavsh thash, nyathuum hwetm, noqm hwetm. Thuum hvshuk uv'awtik; ayu . . . ayu havchush alytpuypak: pilyk hachyurm hamiik. Mkipalyk alythoomak; sheyantik mki v'otsa. Anya, anya wiim nkum mat'a'amk kekyav 'etha'ametha. Anyish awaamk ipayk uv'awtik alynykovmak.

Thotsa ayuu kathom shvthawthiknthik, anyish ayuu shamaash thotk kawich athotk anyish kwinchmiyntik; anyish ayuu kathomsh vinyly'ithik kathomsh matthi'ithik. Thuunya hwelm wiim, nyathom ayuu kawish'u nyahotk nymiyemk kwinchiminy ayuuraavk kwinchiminy thany maweyk. Wiim 'etk.

Ayuu vany'ii ayuu 'uyshthany anya nywiyum nyaweyum, ayuu homara maweyum, uhwelk ovashtuum. Ayuu kathom shmash ayuu alyqolmak mat'urtm mashkyetk chmpapk; chmpapk matchyuly wiim anya nyilyulk—nyilyulyk anya hotknyahathoom: nyalyolym,nymathaw'k anya wiim hmalym maamik ayuu hmaly ma wiim; klashak nyawiim, mayma. Hotikathotk ayuu . . .

Ayuu nyimank viyam anya piipaa kuk'usha thotpatk, 'etsa thash homar, homar haweyk thotmthotk.

of desert growth around here; these people call it "mily'k." For a long time they fixed that, for a baby when he's sick. Whenever they get sick to the stomach . . . they wouldn't be strong enough to hold out: they say they'd use it to make them better.

There's something else that the adults also use; when they're sick they fix themselves right up with it. When people can't shake something, doctors knew about using it; he works with it in looking after people, and he talked about using it.

This mily'ik (plant) that I'm talking about, you find it in the open; but it doesn't grow everywhere on the bare ground, just in certain places around here. Its flower is a little red one. And it's always green; the cold doesn't kill it: hot or cold, it grows. It doesn't grow everywhere in bunches, just one by one here or there. I can say that they use it year-round. It keeps on standing and doesn't disappear.

But there are these others around here, with different roots; some are in the mountains and some are here in the flatlands. Well, those can be dug up, and some varieties would help them remedy whatever ailments they had. That's what they did, he said.

If you're going to use this plant that I'm talking about, for a child, you dig it up. Then you take and cut the roots short, not long, into four pieces; the four you take and boil—until they're boiled real good. After they're boiled, you take and strain it real clean with a cloth, and give it to him. He'll be all right.

There's others around that grownups use too, but this is strictly for babies. Now when their stom-

Athuum mitoo nyo'ik kathom ayuthawk nyasperam. Anya nyawiim hoti 'etkthany wiim—'iyuutnthotk.

Anya knavhaym hayknav hava' wiim, wiim'ii knavm piipaa shopawsh nya'iim 'a'iim 'etk.

Ayuu 'uy'ish knoaaw dany, ayuu nymasiym k'em mnyoyik waly'eemak xotk; alykawish xwiimak, walyaraavmak, walya'eemak xotk. Ayuu . . . eetsa ayuu . . . aduum piipaa dash alyawiixotntik, pisa—ayuu nyimaweydash nypalyk viny'ayam aweyv-nyvaak kawich enyadom alywotndotk. Dotsa, ayuu xoch aduum anya, anya wetpotk nkum xotk nypiipay vidiik aduum etmodotk.

Duumayu . . . itoo: piipaa kuch adotsa, ayuu kwraalyviish; dunyduny nykorim, kawich etkin-ayum anya, anya wamweetk dotk xomar'ush dany xwet. Ayuu kadom, ayuu itoosh, 'aspermak, ayu nyadany. 'Anykvarm dany aytik, nyiwetk, kwetk etndootk. ◇

ach is sour, you use it and then they get stronger. Then they're fine—I've seen it used.

This is what he tells—how they do it, how it's done and the people that know about it; that's what he says.

What I've been talking about, when you drink it, it doesn't taste bitter or anything; it's got no odor, and it doesn't burn, it's not disagreeable. But people don't use it hardly at all, nowadays—since they have a lot of other things to use, they don't use it much anymore. It's a good thing, it worked and people were raised up on it around here.

Now for the stomach: when it's an older person and he's had it sort of sour for a while and nothing else helps, they used it for that. They used it for a child's stomach too, when it wasn't strong. When they had to give them something, that's what they used. ◇

A Confidence Betrayed

Philip Monohan, Narrator

Anya . . . piipaa ayuu sinyaksh, akyan akoysh, aduum ayuu raavk. Aduum vakpaly 'ovak 'iyuum, vakpaly 'owaamk . . . asim 'iyuuk'iim nyikshkwek, piipaa ayukawish wiksxay'iim matayuraavm achpeevamakorm. "Nyukoram 'uvak'iim, 'uxo-maram. Aduuma, ksidee 'iyuuk 'ovanyk: 'kvark; 'awich 'akawoomak' iim. Nyakvaram anya, piipaa xayemtik kawish mshupo anya ka'iimnya'awk wiim 'awoom'iim?"

Iivnya'awk a'eet nyaxtaltik 'iyuuk 'eetk, ah, "'e'alyxa kawich araavm'iim ma'iim shemak," ayu 'iim. Ayu 'itonish'iim 'etk: 'itonish raavk—ayukawish maam, walyavamak etk. "Domii'etk'etk ayukawish 'akadom nyikovm, 'asper'ii nyupayk; enykopay, ninyako viyamk. Nkomo alyxotntvuvak 'iim 'eetm." "Kaduuk nyadanya nywik, nywik'iim 'awxay."

Ayu, nya 'avadiik vaak, ayu 'uy'ish any mily'ik 'uy'ish any anya xlyqwaak, 'adaw 'awiim xweyk

There was a woman, a white lady, who was sick. While I was in town I noticed her, and when I saw her (once) she asked me if there was anyone around to help her out of being so sick. "I've had this for a long time," she said, "and I'm getting desperate. I went to see a doctor, but it wasn't any use; he told me 'I can't do anything for you—nothing.' Is there anyone you know who might prescribe something I could try?"

I felt sorry for her when I heard this and I said, "I don't know what's ailing you, or what you're complaining about." Her stomach was sore: whatever she ate, wouldn't stay down. "That's why I'm telling you I can't do anything," she said, "my strength is fading; it's just all used up, gone. I'm just not feeling right." "Let me see what I can do," I said.

So when I came back here (to the reservation), I looked for this mily'ik plant I've been talking about,

wiim, 'stuum wiim, tr'uy'unuuk 'avirk 'ov'ark;kamem 'ay'm. 'Ay'm avadiik 'ovanyk 'ov'ark nyamshay shentm 'kktvek uyaamtk 'vaamak. 'Vaamam ka'etm 'iivm, "Xotk: xotk 'aly'ish'iimii. Ayuu maam xottamtish."

Alyu'eemak'iyi, xa'ee'ishm, nyadom kaminta'iivii 'vuvaak, kamevamtik; 'ayntam 'awentik. 'Awentik makkadiivam kavii'e nyvaamamtam "Xotk" hii'a, "nya xotsh" hii'e, "ayuu maam xottamam. 'Iwash xotk hiim, xotk hiim." "ah, aduuny'awk xotknydaw"—anya duunya, "nyetakinyayum" hiim: "Kvar," 'iim, "walyintkiny'eemak" 'iim.

Xo, nykshkwek hiim, any nywoomak nykshkwek hiim. "Ayuu . . . kawich aduu mawiim'iim?" 'Iim'em. "Ayuu tamash aduum." "Kadikm muyish duum—xo mkikadiish, kadomish aduum?"

"Shemadiik. 'Uyshemadiik 'iim; dotsa, anya 'ii walya'eemtik anch adootk mavawaamtik kadonya—vu'wexsh'alyadoomak,nyep'oxshalydoomak vo'aw. Ayuu matkwinyaxiirsh adotka, ayuu xanareesh maxeerk, ayuu mataamk palyk m'ay'um—adany mo'wexshalydoomak 'ishadawtsa 'wetk 'wetk, 'wetk nywixtik 'awetk.

Duum ayunywoom ayu wiim'e nydoom viwoomk: kadomish stuum viwoomak, ayuu aly'ishany anya stuuvm viwoomak—ayuu vadii mkily matskidawk sidawm Washinton hiim, asilywoomam. Konaashaviim choyoo'iim iyuuk unuuk, xot hiim; anyish kshkweshm iim'iim, "Kawich aduum mawiim mawiim'ivm"; "'ishmanyoy iimaknaavm."

Iim'em "Kvar, waly'aknaavxayum: kmawoom nyayam nshupaw wetxaya. Anyish adotk 'anamaktum anya, anya iim alyawomak many nyiwetii'etk'etk. Ayumshidee esawetkawet'ii, nkuuma anch adootum. 'Ushwely'aamak, etkinyayuum. "Nkvar—

and I got ahold of some and dug them up, gathered them together, fixed them up and took it to her. And I gave it to her and then I came back here for one week. When I returned, I asked her how she was: "Good, I think I'm ok. I'm eating better."

"Well then, I'll bring you some more," I said, and so I took her some and gave it to her. When I went back again (she said), "I feel good, tip-top—I'm eating good, and I feel fine all over." "So everything's all right then," I said and she said, "I'll pay you"—but I said, "No. Don't pay me."

But you know, she kept on after me and she asked me, "What was that stuff you used?" "Oh, it's just a weed," I said. "What's it called—where does it come from?"

"I don't know," I said that I didn't know. "Besides, I don't see it the way you're going—I'm not supposed to be doing this, it shouldn't have been my doing. It's a penitentiary offense, and the government will lock you up, they'll give you many years in jail for it—they say you shouldn't be doing it, but I just went and did it to help you out."

Well, then (she said) she had sent it off: she had gathered up what she had, I think she sent it off—over there to Washington, you know. They analyzed it and checked it out, and said "it's pretty good"; and then they asked her, "What did you use?" "That's what they said so I'm telling you."

I said, "No, I'm not going to tell you: you can find out about it for yourself. That's it and I'm just going to let it be right here, since I was just trying to do something for you. You know it's kind of dangerous to do this, but it's done and that's it." She

'alystuum anyi ninytaminim'em anyim nyaxa'erstuum, 'iim'ii. Nykvarm 'anamaktam.

Duum ayuu xatik 'voshkaduum. Ayuu marisiin das'ii xotk kw'ashk nydom iim; 'wik 'eet'a. Duum piipaa shent 'awk 'shopawm xotik aly'eetk. Anya—hii'ntam aly'mdash wiywidiik adotmkum. Anya, anya shopawm wishikwetk palyk dany lyuveela vuxishka. ◇

insisted on paying me, ignoring what I said. "No—I'm not going to take it; that's worse if I take it, I'm sure to go to jail." So I just quit (that job).

So it's a good thing, I guess. They say that medicine works pretty good. I know for sure I helped one person with it. As I said, this is what Indians have been using all along. It's the way they practiced and many followed it. ◇

Bibliography

Ezell, Paul H. 1963. *The Maricopas: an identification from documentary sources.* (Anthropological Papers of the University of Arizona, no. 6.) Tucson: University of Arizona Press.

Gordon, Lynn Martha. 1980. *Maricopa morphology and syntax.* Ph.D. dissertation, University of California at Los Angeles.

Harwell, Henry O. 1979. *Maricopa origins: an ethnohistorical approach to a riverine Yuman community.* Ph.D. dissertation, University of Indiana.

Spier, Leslie. 1933. *Yuman tribes of the Gila River.* Chicago: University of Chicago Press.

———. 1946. *Comparative vocabularies and parallel texts in two Yuman languages of Arizona.* University of New Mexico Publications in Anthropology, no. 2.

Sunn, Nick and Harwell, Henry O. 1976. An account of Maricopa origins, in *Yuman Texts,* ed. by Margaret Langdon. International Journal of American Linguistics Native American Texts Series, Vol. 1, No. 3. The University of Chicago Press. Pp. 26–30.

Credits

Photo credits: pp. 253, 254, 259, and 271—Tony Celentano.

PAMELA MUNRO and JUDITH CRAWFORD,
Editors

The Mojaves

Leanne Hinton

The home range of the Mojaves centered in the lower Colorado River valley and covered an extensive area within the present states of Arizona, California, and Nevada. This tribe has always had a strong sense of nationality, of identity as a unified tribe; therefore, settlements were small and often nonpermanent. Their location along the great Colorado River allowed extensive agriculture both in the days before contact and in the present. They were a large and powerful nation, whose access to water allowed the development of a permanency and high population density not available to the desert and mountain tribes that surrounded them. Their ability to produce an agricultural surplus made them important traders; trading and a sense of adventuresomeness led Mojaves hundreds of miles away on journeys, even as far as the California coast. They also had great military prowess in the old days, with excellent military techniques as well as superior weapons in the shape of long war bows and war clubs. Like other Yumans, the Mojaves had a strong clan system: clans were patrilineal and exogamous, with names referring to animals and natural phenomena. The Mojaves had hereditary chiefs descending in the male line. The chiefs who first confronted the American military men and settlers were remarked on by writers and historians as very strong, wise, and honorable leaders of the people. One chief, Irataba, gained national prominence in the troubled times of the late nineteenth century; he was probably the first Mojave to learn English, and in his own language was an unusually eloquent and persuasive speaker. His speeches were often attended by white men, who found themselves enormously moved by them even though they could not understand the language. Irataba traveled twice to Washington, D.C., where he had audience with President Lincoln, and was shown a review of American military troops (presumably to impress upon him that American military strength was too great to be worth fighting against). Irataba's pro-American stance made him a controversial figure, but Mojaves today view him as figuring among the great leaders of their history.

Anthropologists were greatly struck by the highly developed skills of the Mojaves in the oral arts, and much has been written by Kroeber and others on the songs, story-telling arts, and the importance of dreaming to the arts. The Mojaves believe that dreaming is the basis of all learning and experience. As Kroeber says, "Dreams . . . are the foundation of Mohave life; and dreams throughout are cast in mythological mold. There is no people whose activities are more shaped by this psychic state, . . . and none whose civilization is so completely, so deliberately, reflected in their myths" (Kroeber, 1953, p. 755). Songs and myths are believed to be given only in dreaming—a person may have heard the songs and stories many times from others, but it is only through dreams that final learning and spiritual authorization of their use takes place.

The Mojaves sing long song series at funerals and other ceremonies; in the late nineteenth and early twentieth century, these songs have spread to neighboring tribes as well, and the Mojave singers are often invited to lead the singing at wakes for members of other tribes. These song series, each of which takes anywhere from one to four full nights to sing, are depictions of sacred myths. Each song represents one point in the myth. The songs themselves are not stories, nor even usually intelligible to the lay listener; they are simply representative of some event, some character, some place, some sound, occurring in the myth.

Some of the short stories given here are from another realm of the rich Mojave cosmology, the Coyote Tales. ◇

The Contributors

Nellie Brown was born on the Colorado River Reservation and lived there most of her life except for some periods of residence in California. She attended Parker Indian School and Sherman Institute as a child. She worked extensively with both Pamela Munro and Judith Crawford; Munro's book *Mojave Syntax* and the forthcoming Mojave Dictionary by Munro, Brown, and Crawford are based on Nellie Brown's language expertise. Within the tribe, she was a highly respected authority on Mojave language and culture and was committed to the goal of seeing Mojave traditions recorded and maintained. She died in 1981, survived by her several children and grandchildren.

Judith G. Crawford, who received her bachelor's and master's degrees in anthropology at Idaho State University, Pocatello, did field work on the Mojave language in the early 1970s under the auspices of the Survey of California Indian Languages, Berkeley. She has done field work on several Yuman languages and has investigated the genetic affiliation of Yuman to other Indian languages. Pursuing one of her other interests, she obtained an M.F.A. in art at the University of Georgia in 1980 and now maintains a studio in Athens, Georgia.

Robert S. Martin was born about 1900 in Parker, Arizona, the son of Dr. Martin (the agency physician) and Bertha Gray. His wife was Rose Martin. He drove the school bus for the Indian school, and in his later years became Fish and Game Warden for the Mojave Tribe along the southern boundary of the reservation. Robert Martin was very interested in the old ways and in their preservation. He was one of the last who knew how to make cradleboards, and he also made gourd rattles and flutes. He was A. L. Kroeber's interpreter in 1953; Kroeber described him as an interested and excellent interpreter. Most of the myths collected by Kroeber (see bibliography) were translated with Martin's help. He also worked with Pamela Munro and Judith Crawford. Very much respected in his own community, he is remembered by those who knew him as very knowledgeable, full of intellectual curiosity, and blessed with a wonderful sense of humor. He died in 1973, survived by three children and several grandchildren.

Pamela Munro has been a professor at the University of California at Los Angeles since receiving her Ph.D. in 1974. She has been working with the Mojave language since 1971. Her publications include the book *Mojave Syntax* (1976) and numerous articles on Mojave; she has almost completed an extensive dictionary of Mojave, coauthored with Nellie Brown and Judith Crawford. Pamela Munro also organized a Mojave class on the Colorado River Reservation. Beyond her work on Mojave, she has worked on Tolkapaya, Yavapai, Maricopa, and Diegueño, and on numerous American Indian languages outside the Yuman family.

The Mojave Alphabet

Vowels

a *marikan*, 'English'. Like the vowel in English f*a*ther.

aa *nyahu'aak*, 'marry (of a man)'. Same quality as *a* but longer.

e *ahwer*, 'fence in'. Like the vowel in English p*e*t or Spanish p*e*so.

ee *ahwee*, 'smell'. Same quality as *e* but longer.

i *akwiny*, 'go through, go over'. Like the vowel in p*i*t.

ii *akwiich*, 'be tatooed'. Like the vowel in f*ee*d.

o *'ahot*, 'good'. Like the vowel in p*o*ke.

oo *hool*, 'five cents, a nickel'. Like the vowel in f*oa*l.

u *hayuny*, 'cricket'. Like the vowel in f*oo*t.

uu *upuuv*, 'enter (of more than one person)'. Like the vowel in f*oo*d.

Consonants

ch *chuksa*, 'head'. As in *ch*eck.

d *iido*, 'eye'. As in *th*ough.

h *'aha*, 'water'. As in *h*at.

k *kulho*, 'boat'. As in s*k*in.

kw *kwiyer*, 'airplane'. As in *qu*it.

ky *kyaanti*, 'candy'. As in than*k you*.

l *lapalap*, 'flat'. As in *l*amb.

ly *lyavii*, 'look alike'. As in mi*ll*ion.

m *machay*, 'hungry'. As in *m*an.

ny *'anya*, 'sun'. As in ca*ny*on.

p *pay*, 'all'. As in s*p*ar.

k *qampanyq*, 'bat'. Like *k* but with tongue farther back; no English equivalent.

qw *'aqwaq*, 'deer'. Like *kw* but with tongue farther back; no English equivalent.

' *'anya*, 'sun'; *nyahu'aak*, 'marry (of a man).' Like the break in the middle of the English expression *uh-uh* (no).

r *tharap*, 'five'. Flapped *r* as in Spanish pe*r*o.

s *siviily*, 'feather'. As in *s*it.

t *tiima*, 'mesquite root'. As in s*t*ir.

th *thampo*, 'bee'. As in *th*istle.

v *vatay*, 'big'. As in *v*alue.

w *iiwa*, 'heart'. As in *w*aste.

y *iiya*, 'mouth'. As in *y*es.

Texts

Nellie Brown, Narrator
Edited by Pamela Munro

Tharavayew

"Tharavayew" is the Mojave story of the man in the moon and how he got there. It is a coyote story—Tharavayew is one of Coyote's Mojave names—presented here both in Mojave and in Mrs. Brown's free English translation. "Tharavayew" contains an extended conversation with no indication of change of speaker, a rarity in a Mojave tale. (For comparison, note the occurrence of "he says" in the English version—it takes us some thinking to unscramble all the "he"'s.)

Tharavayew huktharvch, hukthar Tharavayewche thuuvak im.

Ivesk vuuvak pi'pa kwa'atay halyuuvak vuuvakt i'iima, "Hee, 'inyeche haly'a huviily 'ichips 'im, 'tahakyev'e," ikm.

Nyaa'iim i'iima pi'panych havuuv'ookt a'iim, "Kamadoomote."

"'Iduutahane 'iyemtahank 'tahakyevtane 'ichipsk imakly 'uupaame!"

"Macham mipuype nyamtakaveekmotm!"

"'Aa, 'iyemke 'ayuu tadiich 'ayuu 'chakama'awe."

Akyook iduum nyayuu apook akyook korly aadosk viidiik im, aadosk viiyamm ivesk viiyemm isaamk vuuv'oochm viidiik ichipspatk iich ichipsk

There's a man, a coyote, a man, and his name is Tharavayew.

And he goes around bragging all the time, and he says, "You know what, fellows?" he says, "you know what I'm going to do?" he says. "Well, I think I can jump over that moon! I can jump it, and get on the other side."

"I'm afraid you can't," he says; "you'd better get something, so that you'll have something to eat."

"Oh, yes," he says, "I've already had some corn and some beans and some things in my bag," he says.

And he said he was going to jump, so everybody got out there, so he ran and jumped once or twice

iyem 'asenta havikm uuyoovm uunyaqk chakavar ipooyk.

Pi'panych havuuv'oochk im, "Iyemntike korly anyoompotk," iichm.

Anyoomkum isaamkum halyvuunuuchkte, "Haly'ahly ivak," iichtm 'a'aamm'o. Tamuunaly aados-hayk haly'ahly ivatk ivak.

'Anya vidam viivatk vii'iichtke, Tharavayewch. ◇

before he really did, you know, and then he jumped.

And he never came back.

And then he still stays in that moon, they tell me.

So they call him the man in the moon, Tharavayew. ◇

Going to School for the First Time

Hayikoly 'ahav 'ahipuktaahank, nyayu 'asuupawa 'emottaahank, marikan chuukwarny 'asentm 'asuupawmotk, 'iiweek 'imuulyny aseechm pay 'asuupawmotk—havnya 'uuvaak. Huchqol nyanyaahavkum a'wemka uusma im a'wintm 'avaly nyicham hayikonych a'wiim. Nyichqathk a'wiim, 'atayemk 'upaka'eechm, nyanyatanyuuchk, nyanomakm. Thanya'idiikiki, 'iiwanych 'alaytaahank. Manyeechuvikm 'ahotm: 'atuunyuuchke. 'uupava 'iyuuk 'iduum, 'ahottaahanke. Nyamathavtm 'imanka ('anyamhanyoony 'iyuunypatka 'a'aamotntk, 'iimiivk vu'uwatka, hachorm 'idotk nyakapilym 'idotk—nyakapilym 'ithava nyany 'avutlyesk, 'amayk 'akach'iim, 'avahinmk thi'iyepmtk—'idotk 'iduum iduum), 'anyahamaruy marikan hanidal uu'wiichny nyany nyachamharuychm, 'anyamharuyk vu'uuvaatka. 'Anyamharuyk 'a'aamach iduukte duukat 'anyamharuyka'eeka vu'uuvaak. 'Uhaymottaahanka'eeth pay 'anyamharuyk 'iduum. Nyidawn nya'inak 'akalyhoqm makathk 'ichatk vu'uuvaatk—vi'idiitk 'iduum. Huchqolch vaaduunyapatk mo'wav

When I first went to school, not a thing did I know, I didn't know one word of English, when my own name was called, I didn't know it—that's how I was. When it was evening the white lady told the children to go to sleep and put them to bed. She called us, we went in to sleep, she covered us up, and she left us. I was lying there, and I was sad. It was very nice: I was covered up, I had a bed, it was very nice. In the morning I got up (I never had shoes either, I was barefoot, in winter and in summer—in summer I would break off pieces of arrowweed, I would step on it, then move on further—that's how I was), a government shoe was put on me, and I was wearing shoes. I had never had a shoe on before, but I was wearing shoes. I didn't know how to wear shoes at all. When I had a chance to sit down, I would pull them off and put them down somewhere—that's how I grew up. Most of the children were like that too when they left their families and came to school. Some still weren't weaned. When the parents had a chance to come in, they had fenced

natumakik upuuk vanyuunuuk. Kaaduuch 'ama pithahayk iduum iduume. Nyaavachkuu'eekum ahwerk a'wiitaahanm—vu'uunuuka'eek 'iduum. Imakly inakik huchqol 'ama aym; 'inyechvach idoth 'atayemchka chuuhwer imakny thu'uutpam—thinyith'iilym, nyinytatavirk, nyanyatselk a'wekum—hav'atadiipk 'iduuchich iduum. Ayim marikanvny 'amasdeetaahanm. Marikan thinya'aakny 'iyuu a'a'taymotntk mat'ar nya'uwaak, duum *school* nya'ahavtm marikan thinya'aakny 'iyuuk 'iduuke. Kaaduuch 'ahottaahanm, do'itpataahanm. Kaaduuchiche marikan 'uhaymotm suupaw pay nyatara'uym, nyamaayevk iduuntm. Kaaduuchich 'imatichev nyaytntk a'wetm—hav'idiitk 'iduum. Nyiwaamtaahan *one word* im 'asenta havikm 'asuupawka'eek. Pi'pa 'anawah imuuly pay 'asamodiik ipetm—kaa'epk vidany aseechuvaa?, 'aly'etk. Mah hav'idiitk 'idoptk 'iduum, 'iduuchm duum. Pi'pa 'ich suupawmottaahana 'alyaviik vi'ivak nya'iduuntm. ◇

the place in—that's how we were. They sat outside and gave milk to the children; even us, we'd go outside the fence—they didn't want us to, she'd follow us, she'd beat us—that's the way we were. We were scared of every white person. When I was outside I didn't see many white women, but at school I saw white women. Some were real nice, some I really liked. Even though they knew I couldn't talk English, they took care of me, most of them were like that. Some gave me medicine—that's how I was. At last I learned one or two words. Sometimes I even forgot my girlfriend's name—now how did they call her?, I thought. I was just like that, I was. I was acting like someone who didn't know anything. ◇

A Warning about Coyote

Humar 'akooch viidiiptch iduum. Viidiike 'ava ivaatm. Duum 'i'iim 'iduum, "Nyayu masuupawm hamuuvaa'a?" 'im. "'ee, 'asuupawka—vidikuvach vidach nyayu nyakunaam." *Book* e'etm. "Masuupawa vaa?" "'Asnuqm, 'ee," im. Duum 'i'iim, "Nyayu *animal book*cha. Nyayu 'ich kwanyuumeevch iduum. Huktharch viiv'awm. Hukthar vidach iduum. . . .

"'Akortaahanm satamuly vidach i'iim, 'Miv'aak thanyamiyem 'amiich nyamiyemam, hukthar huvany makavkyoota,' etm. Humar mahayny i'iim.

My grandson was coming. He just came to the house. So I asked him, "Do you know anything?" "Yes, I know things—this one here tells me things." He meant the book. "Do you know?" "A little, yes," he said. So I said, "It's an animal book. There are different things in it. There's a coyote standing there. This one is a coyote. . . .

"A long time ago the Indians said, 'When you've been walking far, you might meet Coyote.' They'd say that to a little boy. 'If you meet him, what will you say? That one says, "Child, won't you follow me

'Makavkyookm kama'iilyi? Nyahch i'iim, "Humara, 'inyep matakwerka tadiichhavaso mamaalyi vaa?" im. "'Ee, nyatakwere," e'etk iduum. "Minakik 'inakmtk; 'iyemta. 'Atakwerk," etm.'

"'A'aavchm."◇

and eat *tadiichhavaso*?"* "Yes, I'll go with you," he says. "I'll sit on your back; I'm going. I'm coming along," he says.'

"I've heard that."

(They'd say that to scare them. They didn't want them to go too far.)◇

* *Tadiichhavaso* or *tadiichkwavaso* is corn with some red and green kernels mixed into it, a delicacy.

Coyote and Crane

Robert S. Martin, Narrator
Transcribed by Judith Crawford

Nyakw'ech 'aha kwa'uurly ivak.
'Achii satok istuum.
'Achiihaan a'wetk 'achii chahnap a'wetk istuum.
Ithook vuwaam isamk.
Hukthar chudoorm, iyuuk thuwaak.
"Kaa'we ke'eeyk a'wim va?" im.
Thinyuwaak, "tha'a'wetpat'e, 'inyech!" etk.
Thinyuwaak, iyemk 'a'iis takwerakwerk, ta'akyuulyk ta'ahaank uunuuk aaviirk.
Iyemk 'ahpily iyaak kamim, iihunyk tahpilym uunuuk nyaaviirk.
Kor 'aha kwa'uurly ivak, uudoorm vivak.
'Achii chaam iyuuk vivake.
"Achii inyto'och idotm iyuuk.
"Humer valytaaytaahaanch vidiit 'iyuuk 'a'wiis, duum 'ithootahaank 'atootahaank," etk, vivak iduum.
'Achiich viyaam nomaktk, vivakete, 'achiihaan kwavalyteetahaan vidiikum, iyuukum, "nyath ta'ahaan 'a'wiith," etk.
Kor uusaaptk, nyasachooqm, 'achiihaanch ithpeertk iduum.
Kor idaawptk aawemk a'wim.

Crane sat on the river bank.
He speared fish with his beak and got them.
He got salmon and humpback fish.
He [Coyote] looked at him eating [fish], walking back and forth.
Coyote was spying on him and he saw him as he moved about there.
"How did he do it, poor thing?" he said.
As he was walking back and forth there, he said, "I can do that too!"
Then he walked around there, he went and sharpened a screwbean [branch], making it really long.
He went and fetched pitch and brought it back, and stuck it [screwbean branch] on his nose.
Now he sat on the river bank, waiting here.
He saw a lot of fish [go by] as he sat here.
He saw little fish [go by].
"Later I will see a very big one come this way and I will do [spear] it, then I'll really eat and be very full," he said, as he sat here.
A fish went by him and he let it go, and as he sat here, a very big salmon came toward him,

'Ahpily ulhuyulhuymotm.
Hamahak aawemm, 'ahaly ipuyk.
Haly'anyoomtk, 'anyook uuwaalymotm.
Kor nyamaamk. ◇

and he saw it, saying, "That's the one I'm going to get!"
By and by he speared it, and after he speared it [a second time], the salmon was too strong.
Then it took him.
He could not loosen the pitch [from his nose].
It took him down, and he drowned.
He disappeared, was gone, and never showed up any more.
Now that's all. ◇

Bibliography

Crawford, Judith G. 1976. Seven Mojave texts. In *Yuman texts* (International Journal of American Linguistics: Native American Texts Series [*IJAL: NATS*] 1:3), ed. Margaret Langdon, pp. 31–42. Chicago: University of Chicago Press.

———. 1978. Coyote and Crane (Mohave). In *Coyote stories* (*IJAL-NATS*, Monograph 1), ed. William Bright, pp. 121–23. Chicago: University of Chicago Press.

Grey, Herman. 1970. *Tales from the Mohaves*. Norman: University of Oklahoma Press.

Herzog, George. 1928. The Yuman musical style. *Journal of American Folklore*. 41:183–231. (Includes Mojave song texts.)

Hinton, Leanne. 1979. Irataba's gift: A closer look at the s>s>θ soundshift in Mojave and Northern Pai. *Journal of California and Great Basin Anthropology*, Papers in Linguistics 1: 3–38.

Kroeber, A. L. 1951a. *A Mojave historical epic*. University of California Anthropological Records, 11:2. Berkeley: University of California Press.

———. 1953. *Seven Mojave myths*. University of California Anthropological Records, 11:1. Berkeley: University of California Press.

———. 1953. *Handbook of the Indians of California*. San Francisco: California Book Co., Ltd.

Munro, Pamela. 1976a. *Mojave syntax*. New York: Garland Press.

———. 1976b. Two Stories by Nellie Brown (Mojave). In *Yuman texts* (*IJAL-NATS*, 1:3), ed. Margaret Langdon, pp. 43–50. Chicago: University of Chicago Press.

———. 1978. Molly Fasthorse's story of the great wrestling match (Tolkapaya Yavapai). In *Coyote stories* (*IJAL-NATS*, Monograph 1), ed. William Bright, pp. 121–23. Chicago: University of Chicago Press.

Acknowledgments and Credits

Coyote and Crane. From Crawford, Judith G., 1978. Coyote and crane. In *Coyote stories* (*IJAL-NATS*, Monograph No. 1), ed. William Bright, pp. 121–23. Chicago: University of Chicago Press.

Going to school for the first time. From Munro, Pamela, 1976. Two stories by Nellie Brown. Chicago: In *Yuman texts* (*IJAL: NATS* 1:3), ed. Margaret Langdon, pp. 43–50. University of Chicago Press.

A warning about Coyote. From Munro, Pamela, 1976. Two stories by Nellie Brown. In *Yuman texts* (*IJAL: NATS* 1:3), ed. Margaret Langdon, pp. 43–50. Chicago: University of Chicago Press.

Photo credits: pp. 279, 280, and 289—Victor Masayesva.

ABRAHAM M. HALPERN, *Editor*

The Quechan

Abraham M. Halpern

At the time of first contact with whites the Quechan tribe probably numbered between 4,000 and 5,000 members. Shortly before the middle of the nineteenth century, the tribe's range extended on both sides of the Colorado River from about Blythe, California, to a point just above the Colorado Delta. In 1850 a military post was established at Fort Yuma and the tribe came under U.S. Army control. Control was transferred to the Bureau of Indian Affairs when the military post was discontinued, and in 1883 a reservation was established in a tract east of the Colorado and north of the Gila rivers. In 1884, however, these lands were restored to the public domain and a new reservation area was established, primarily on the California side of the Colorado River. By a treaty signed in 1893 the area of this reservation was drastically reduced to just under 9,250 acres. The 1893 treaty was never regarded as legitimate by the tribe. After protracted negotiations, the tribe in 1979 regained control of some 20,000 acres, thus reestablishing approximately the 1884 boundaries except for certain non-Indian-owned enclaves.

The tribal members were gradually gathered within the reservation boundaries. Some of the southern division remained in residence in Mexico until about 1914, when for various reasons, among them a desire to escape from conditions created by the activities of Pancho Villa, the last of the tribe moved to the reservation. There are persistent rumors that a few Quechan still remain in Mexico in some remote area.

Traditionally, the people lived in small settlements, usually located close to water where agriculture was practicable. Despite this dispersion of the population, there was consciousness of the tribe as a whole, as well as joint action at times of war and on other occasions. Considerable seasonal mobility existed throughout the full range of occupation. Settlements were generally occupied by lineages based on male descent. Lineages in turn belonged to named clans, which were in principle exogamous.

It is not possible at this time to obtain a full and accurate understanding of the Quechan prior to white contact. The population has been drastically reduced, evidently under the impact of introduced diseases, up to and including the influenza epidemic of 1918–19. The tribal roll of 1974 contained 1,687 names. The Quechan population of the reservation in 1977 was 815; the other tribal members lived off the reservation, some as far away as Phoenix, San Diego, San Jose, or even farther. In addition to reduction of the population, concentration in a confined area, and dispersal to remote locations, the original social and religious patterns have been affected by government and missionary activities, by intermarriage both intertribal and interracial, and by proximity to Yuma, Arizona, which has undergone mushroom growth in the past several decades.

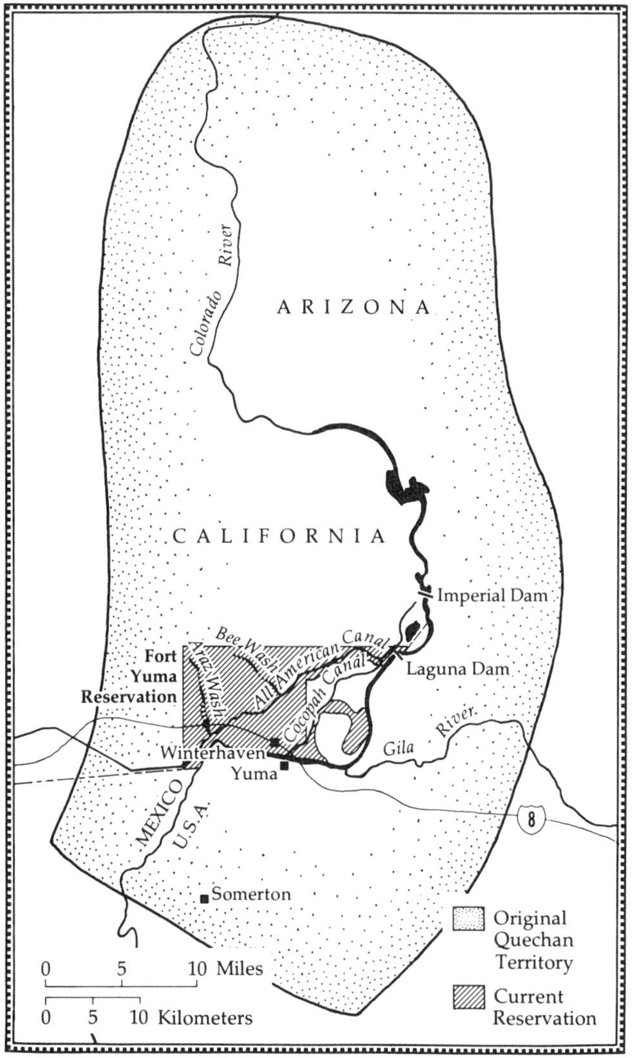

Despite the Quechan tendency to adapt comparatively easily to changing conditions, certain essential features of the Quechan ethos persist. The Quechan language remains the favored means of communication in the over-60 age group, though almost all in this bracket are bilingual. Perhaps a majority of those in the 40–60 age group remain fluent in Quechan, and a number of those in their 30s, as well as some in their 20s, are fluent to a usable degree. The clan organization, whatever its original functions may have been, is obsolescent, but there remains a strong sense of family solidarity and pride in family traditions. Most striking is the retention of a traditionally high value placed on individual freedom and individual achievement, combined with a sense of support from and responsibility to the family, and with traditional respect for the elderly. The essential core of funeral practices, always important in the culture, has persisted, though with several modifications in outward form. Native medicine has almost disappeared.

The future of the Quechan language and culture is in the hands of the 40–60 age group. Despite all the factors that promote further disintegration, and despite great differences of view in this age group, there seems to be a growing realization of the value of Quechan traditions, and a growing feeling of responsibility for maintaining them. ◇

The Contributors

Amelia Caster traces her ancestry back through several generations to a well-known warrior and tribal leader of the nineteenth century, known in the literature as Caballo en Pelo. Caballo en Pelo produced numerous descendants, so that Amelia Caster, now about 70, has a wide circle of relatives. Her late husband's family was responsible for contributing to the construction of the shield used in the karˀúk ceremonial.

Lee Emerson lived part of his adult life in the San Diego area and on the Mojave reservation, his paternal grandfather having been Mojave. At the time of his death in 1978, he was in his late 60s. Lee Emerson was very active in tribal affairs up to the time of his final illness, having performed long service as member and at one time as chairman of the tribal council. He was an industrious collector of tribal lore of all kinds and was known in the tribe as the semi-official tribal historian.

Lee Emerson's version of the folktale "Coyote and Quail" was first published in *Coyote Stories*, edited by W. Bright. It is expected that his numerous papers dealing with aspects of Quechan history from the Indian standpoint will eventually be published.

Jessie Webb Escalante is the widow of a prominent member of the tribe, known especially for his mastery of the šakwatxót song cycle. Born in the second decade of the twentieth century, she grew up in a very conservative environment and received little or no formal education. She is regarded as one of the most knowledgeable sources for folktales, songs, and other aspects of the older tradition. Translation of her narratives was made with the invaluable assistance of her daughter, Tessie Escalante.

Mary Kelly Escalanti, a woman in her middle 70s, is the youngest child of a man who is generally regarded as having been the last of the authentic ceremonial experts and shamans. The family belongs to the southern division (kavé·ly cadóm) of the tribe and formerly lived south of the border. One of her lullabies seems to be identical with a song recorded by Frances Densmore from Mrs. Charles Wilson. Millie Romero provided essential help with the translation.

Abraham Halpern was the collector and translator of all the songs and tales in this Quechan section. Born in Boston, Massachusetts, in 1914, he completed work on his Ph.D. in anthropology in 1940 at the University of Chicago. He was the first linguist to write a grammar of any Yuman language (Halpern, 1946, 1947). The beginning of his research in linguistics came through a job in the summer of 1935 with the California State Emergency Relief Administration: Halpern was hired to teach a selected number of younger Quechan a method of writing their language, with older speakers providing the data. In 1938 he made a long field trip to Yuma to pursue his studies with Quechan, this time sponsored by the University of Chicago. It was during this period that he collected the piece "Lightning." Halpern spent the war years at the Civil Affairs Training School at the University of Chicago teaching intensive courses in spoken Japanese to army and navy officers who were designated to serve in the occupation of Japan. After the war, Halpern was invited to work on General MacArthur's staff as adviser on language revision in Japan. As a result of his exposure to Japan, he decided to pursue his interest in contemporary Asian political developments, and he worked on the staff of various research institutes from 1949 until his retirement in 1978.

It was when he retired that Halpern was able to put into effect his long cherished plan to return to the study of American Indian languages, and especially to renew his ties with the Quechan tribe. He has been working intensively with speakers of the Quechan language since then, and most of the songs and tales presented here were collected during this recent period of work.

Ethel Wheeler Ortiz is the youngest of the narrators represented in this collection of Quechan material. She is descended from a prominent family, one of her uncles having at one time served as tribal judge. She has won awards for dancing to the paʔi:pá: song. Her narrative was recorded during her term of service on the staff of the Quechan Cultural Heritage program.

William Wilson, who died in 1950 at approximately 80 years of age, was a singer of considerable reputation, not only within the Quechan tribe but among neighboring tribes as well. He had mastered many songs, including Haraup (originally Diegueño), but "Lightning" was the one for which he was best known.

The Quechan Alphabet

Vowels

Quechan has six short vowels and five long vowels. The short vowel sounds are represented by one letter; the long vowels are represented by a letter followed by a colon (e.g., a:). Vowels may also occur in diphthongs, which are short or long vowels followed by the letter *w* or *y*.

Short vowels

a e i o u ə

The vowels *a*, *e*, *i*, *o*, and *u* are pronounced as in Spanish. The sixth vowel, ə, is an indistinct or murmured vowel with the sound of *a* in English "*a*lone." It only occurs after the accented syllable and is never itself accented.

Long vowels

a: e: i: o: u:

These are also pronounced as in Spanish a, e, i, o, and u, but are held longer.

Diphthongs

There are eight possible diphthongs consisting of a vowel followed by y, and another eight consisting of a vowel followed by w.

ay ey oy uy

a:y e:y o:y u:y

aw ew iw ow

a:w e:w i:w o:w

Accent

Usually there is only one accent (´) in a word, and it falls on the vowel of the stem. There are, however, a few suffixes which are accented, so that some words carry two accents: ʔanayémú 'let's go away'. There are also cases where two words are run together, each retaining its accent: vadí:mánək ('starting here') from vadí, 'here', plus amánək, 'one arises.' Native speakers who have mastered the alphabet could omit the accent mark, but for beginners it is useful to have it indicated.

Consonants

p, t, k	represent sounds similar to those of English, but rather to the sounds of s*p*eak, s*t*eam, and s*k*ate than of *p*eak, *t*eam, and *K*ate; that is, there is little or no expulsion of breath accompanying the consonant. Here again the Quechan pronunciation resembles Spanish rather than English.
c	represents the sound of *ts* in English pe*ts.*
q	represents a sound similar to *k* but pronounced much further back in the mouth, with the back of the tongue touching the soft palate.
ʔ	glottal stop, produced by closing and opening the vocal cords. This is a very important consonant in Quechan; among other things it is the sign of the first person pronoun, 'I' or 'we'.
ṭ	represents a *t* sound made with the tongue curled back and the tip of the tongue touching the top of the gums. This is the same tongue position as in making English *r*. The sound is something like *tr* in English *tr*ee.
s	as in English.
š	similar to English *sh* but with the tongue in the same position as for ṭ. The sound is something like *shr* in English *shr*ink.
x	like nothing in English except some exclamations. Similar to *ch* in German Ba*ch* or to Spanish jota.
v	similar to English *v* but made with the lips only, as in Spanish.
d	Since there is no sound in Quechan like English *d*, this letter is used for convenience to represent the sound of *th* in English *th*ey or *th*en (but not the *th* of ba*th*).
r	is a rolled sound, like the Spanish rather than the English *r*.
w, y, m, n, l	as in English
ɬ	a rare sound in Quechan, an *l* sound pronounced without vibrating the vocal cords: a breathy, voiceless or 'slurpy' *l*.
ŋ	represents the sound of *ng* in English so*ng*. In Quechan it occurs mainly in songs, also in a few words of Spanish origin: na:ráŋk, 'orange', from *naranja;* cá:ŋk, 'monkey', from *chango;* tu:míŋk, 'week', from *domingo* 'Sunday.'
f	as in English; f is found only in a few Spanish loan words, such as ka:fey, 'coffee', from *café.*

There are several consonants pronounced concurrently (coarticulated) with *y* or *w*. To retain the principle of one letter for each sound and one sound for each letter, the coarticulation is shown by using a raised ^{y} or ^{w} after another letter in many writings; for convenience the y and w are written on the line here. Thus:

t^y n^y l^y $ɬ^y$ k^y *or* ty ny ly ɬy ky

and k^w x^w q^w *or* kw xw qw

Any Quechan word that begins with a vowel is introduced by an *h* sound (aspirated attack) when it stands at the beginning of a breath group (a single word, a phrase, etc.). We do not represent this aspirated attack because the *h* sound disappears in context and no *h* sound occurs anywhere else in the word: (h)ayémək, 'he goes away', but vadám ayémək, 'he goes in this direction.' But we do have to use an *h* in some exclamations, like hḿḿ 'yes' or haʔhá· 'Oho!'

Texts

Jessie Webb Escalante, Narrator

i:wá: tu:év

paˀi:pá:c xavík su:nó:m, paˀi:pá: xa:vákəc adótk, xavík lyu:vévək, ˀu:naˀú:n, paˀi:pá: nyanyc ˀalméc alyaˀém, nyaváyk si:dáwk.

si:dáwk—ˀanyá: acpák vi:dí:m nya:yú: maṭxalykwá:yk si:dí:k.

nyi:dí:k ˀaˀí:c vi:vˀáwəm, ˀí: palyˀónəc vi:vˀáwəm nyá:nyi, axwélyk vu:nó:k, nya:yú:c maxák alyadá:wəm, nyá:nya aštú:m—ˀa:málykəc—ˀa:mályk u:ˀíc, maxák adáwk avadáwəm nyá:ny aštú:m.

ˀaˀí: a:ˀúlyk a:qwéṭk tapúyəm adáwk caváwk, adáwk caváwk vu:nó:k.

avác nyi:yá:nypatk xalykwá:kəm, kórəm alyványpatk awínypatk si:vát.

ˀamáṭəny axwélyk vu:nó:xayəm acpákəm adáwtək, acpákəm adáwtək vu:nó:k.

vu:nó:ny tavé:rək vu:nó:nyk, ˀakwéšk ˀuskaˀúsk aˀím nyi:kwé:vəm aštú:m, vi:wá:k nyavá kamémək.

Stubborn

There were two people over there, they were twins, both the same, tiny ones; those people were not tall, and they lived over there.

They were there—when the sun rose they came to hunt things for themselves.

They came; a tree stood here, a stump stood, and that's where they were digging; things were underneath it, and that's what they gathered—pack rats—what's called ˀa:malyk, whatever was underneath, that's what they gathered.

One carried a stick and beat them and killed them; then he picked them up and laid them down, he was picking them up and laying them down.

The other also went and hunted, he also stayed a little way off and also did it.

As soon as he dug the ground, they came out, and he caught them, they came out and he was catching them.

tará:k vu:nó:k a:ví:rk, kwaxaˀúyəm nyi:cadú:nək, kú:r aˀím aštú:m cacpá:ck, asó:k vu:nó:k acá:vək.

avác avawínypatk awétk.

u:šmátk, qwalayéwəm amá:nək nyá:va xalykwá:k vi:wéck adótk vu:nó:t, ˀí: palyˀónəc si:vˀawm axwé-lyk vu:nó:k, maxák adáwəm aštú:m, tavé:rək i:kwé-vəm aštú:m, ˀavá kayá:k, nyá:ny awétk vu:nó:t.

ˀaˀí:c aˀí:m xalykwá:k, u:vá:k aštú:m kamí:m tará:k vu:nó:k, a:ví:rk, maxák cadú:nt, ˀamáṭ kwaxaˀúyəny.

aštú:m asó:ck vu:nó:k acá:vək, va:wínypatk awétk, u:šmátk awétk vu:nó:k, nyá:va awíctək vu:nó:t.

vu:nó:k nya:wícəmˀašk si:dáwk, si:dáwəm xatal-wéc avá:m, ayú:tk si:vˀáwəm, "nyá:ny ˀawétapatk avˀu:vá:tk ˀamá:štapatk ˀadótk avˀu:vá:m mawétəm ˀayú:tk ˀavˀáwk ˀawítya," aˀétk si:vˀáwk.

láw aˀétk ayú:m, ˀašéntc avík avátəntik nyamlyaví:təntik u:vát, xa:vákəc aˀétkəm lyu:vév táx aˀét.

ayú:tk si:vátəm, "nyá:va ˀawétk, ˀanyá:m kwaší:nt avˀawétk—ˀasó:tk ˀadótk ˀu:vá:k. ˀanyváyk nyiˀmánək nyaˀdú:va," aˀí:m kaná:vkəm, "ˀanyá:c nyi:nya:tu:qwér ˀa:lyˀétk," aˀét, xatalwévəc.

"xóṭk." nya:ˀétk nya:dáwk vi:wá:t ˀavá u:kayá:m, kamém, nyaváy kwaˀác vi:vám ayú:k si:vát.

a:cu:yó:yk vu:nó:k, nya:yú: u:wíca, nya:yú: apú:ck acá:ck vi:wá:m, nyaša:kwí:lyk aˀéta.

tadíc apók. kwalyˀó ˀamáṭ acéwk vu:nó:k a:ví:rək, nyá:ny alypók vu:nó:k a:ví:rək, caváw caváw, ˀma:rí:k.

"avány tadíc aˀím, avány camˀi:tó:díc, avány ˀaxmáta:díc aˀím."

Then he piled them up until he had gathered tremendous heaps of brown stuff, and he took them and brought them home.

He lighted a fire and when it became hot ashes he put them into it, and soon he gathered and took them out, and he was eating them and ate them all up.

That's what the other one also did.

They slept; next morning they got up and were going off hunting these things; they were digging where the stump stood and gathering what was underneath, they gathered great piles and headed for home; that's what they were doing.

They hunted for what's called wood, and they gathered and brought it and lighted a fire, then put them under it—the hot ashes.

They gathered them and were eating and ate them all up, doing as they had done, and they slept; this is what they were doing.

Then when they were doing it in the usual way, a coyote arrived where they were and stood there watching; "That's what I also do, I also eat those, and I see that you do it," he said as he stood there.

He turned his head and looked, and there was another one there, just like the first one; they were twins, so they were exactly alike.

As he watched them, "This is what I do, what I do every day—and so I eat. I belong here and live here," one of them explained, and, "I'd like to be your follower," he said, this coyote.

"All right." When he said it and took him and brought him towards the house and arrived there, he saw that they did in fact live here.

He showed him the things he did, that he put things into containers and put them away, and he said he was preserving them.

acá:ck vi:wá:mk a:ví:rək, ˀavu:šxwí:rk acá:ck vu:nó:k a:ví:r.

nyaša:kwí:lyk aˀétəm, awím nya:yú: xatpíly ayá:k kamí:m, nyi:tałyík vu:nó:k va:wí:m u:kakwí:nək vu:nó:k a:ví:r, tapínyəm, alyavérək i:kwévək, caváw caváw vu:nó:nyk nyi:té:r awét.

(nyá:va ˀacamá:w nya:ˀí:m, ˀu:cé adáwk, nyi:takamé:k va:wím.

nyaˀpínyəm, ló:q aˀím atáq va:ˀétəm, nya:yú:c si:dáwm aštú:m alyúlyk amátk awétk.)

u:vá:t, tapéṭk, nya:nymá:m awét. a:cu:yó:yk vu:nó:k, "kawí:m" aˀím. xatalwéva a:cu:yó:yk.

"ˀí:s avík adáwəntik vi:dáwəm nyá:va ku:táq alykaˀémək," aˀím.

"nyá:va mu:táqxayəm, ˀaxwá:yk i:ná:mxa lyaví:m, nyá: ˀmašadétk," aˀétk, "nyá:va ˀu:táq alyˀaˀémətək ˀawítya."

cavúwəm vi:vát. "vadány kanaqám alykaˀémək, ˀí:s avány kawí:m," aˀét.

a:cu:yó:yk vu:nó:m, "má:, ˀayú:k ˀavák." "mawí:lymaˀémətəxa," aˀét. "xóṭk. ˀaˀávək ˀavák." aˀí:m si:vám ašmá:m si:dík.

nya:qwalayéwəm nya:mánək nya:wétəmˀášk vi:wéc. ˀa:mályk vi:wéck vi:wéck.

axwélyk aštú:m awínypatk si:dá:wk si:dá:wk, láw aˀétk ayúm, xwa:kóp aˀétəm ayú:k.

"nya:yú: ˀu:ˀícəny aˀáv alyaˀémək nya:wét kayú:k," aˀét. "ˀaxwá:y ˀu:púc adótk avány ku:táq alykaˀém, aˀét, u:táqtəm, ˀaxwá:yk maṭcapé:m ˀayú:k vaˀavák."

aˀétk si:vák nyá:sik namánək nakavék vi:nadí:t, awéck ayó:vtək nakavék vi:nadí:t.

vi:nadí:k. xatalwény nyakór u:ckyíṭk vu:nó:k a:xwešxwéšk atá:pk vu:nó:k, i:mé u:kyéṭk, i:šá:ly u:kyéṭk a:xwešxwéšk makyí nyi:yáp a:lyˀí:m a:í:m

He put in corn. He made a clay olla and that's what he put things into, putting, putting—beans.

"This is called corn, this is called melon seeds, this is called pumpkin seeds."

He kept putting them away, and he put them all in a corner of the house.

It's called "preserving", and so he went after arrowweed pitch and brought it and was sticking it on there, and in this way he put it all the way around; he warmed it and it got all hardened; he put it on and put it on until he had it all around.

(About this, when they want to eat things, they take hot coals and put the pot near them, like this. When it warms up it gets sticky and opens up, like this, and they collect the things that are there and eat them.)

Then, he just covered it. He was showing him; "Do it!" he said. He showed this coyote.

"But, there are others there, and that one, do not open!" he said.

"As soon as you open this one there might be a great battle, that's what I'm afraid of," he said; "This is the one I do not open."

He put it down, and it sat there. "Do not touch this one, but use that one!" he said.

He was showing him, and, "Aha, I see." "You are not to do it," he said. "All right. I'm listening," he said, and he lay asleep.

The next morning when they got up and when they did as usual, they went. They went and went after pack rats.

They were each digging and gathering there, and one looked around, and he saw a cloud of dust rising.

"Look! He didn't listen to what I said, and he's

maṭṭapúyk, ʔaxwá:k nyi:lóp tan i:kwévk vu:nó: nyi:yá: vu:nó:.

avá:m cá:mək a:é:vək va:wí:m, va:wé: awí: vi:wá:m, nya:yú:ny alypók vu:nó:k, kwalyʔóny alypók vu:nó:k a:ví:r, tapéṭk vu:nó:k a:ví:r. alya:kalá:ymək vu:nó:k a:ví:r.

caváwk avány avawíntik vu:nó:m, vadác apúyk vi:dík, xatalwé:vac, apúy, kyá:ṭk vi:dík.

ayá:k aštú:m tatkyá:vək vu:nó:k a:ví:rək, šamán tašáṭ.

"nyu:kaná:vəm maʔám, ʔanyá:c vadány madóxa lyaví:m, kawí:lykaʔémək ʔaʔépəm maʔámək. vadány kwaʔa:pác aʔím, vadány kwacá:nc aʔím, vadány xatpá: ʔanyá:c aʔím, ʔaší:tk ʔacá:cəm vi:dá:wk. vadány nya:mu:táqəm vadác cá:m maṭtapúyk adóxa lyaví:m, ʔaʔí:m nyaʔí:va," aʔím, vu:nó:m, "á:, ʔaʔávək ʔašu:páwk ʔawí: kwaʔáct maʔétk maʔítya," aʔétk.

"kanaqám alykaʔémək vadány. nya:manaqámək mapúytəxa," aʔím vu:nó:k namákcəm aʔávək si:vák. alyašmá:m si:dík.

nya:qwalayéwəm nya:mánək vanya:wécəntik, nya:yú: nya:wécəntik vi:wéc, ʔa:málykəva.

a:qwéṭk, tapúyk, atá:pk vu:nó:k si:dáwk. "ʔaʔí: maxalykwá:k mawí: ʔím," aʔícəm aʔávək vadány, ʔí: xalykwá: kwaʔáck su:vá:m, katánək—ʔaxóṭṭəm katánək u:šmát.

vadány va:dótk vu:nó:t. ʔanyá:c sanya:díkəntim nya:wécəntik vi:wéck, ʔa:málykəny nya:wécəntik si:dá:wk. láw aʔím ašá:mk, xwa:kóp nya:ʔétəntim ayú:m, "nya:yú: ʔu:ʔícəny aʔáv alyaʔémək, nya:wínymʔášəm kayú:k," aʔét.

láw aʔétk ayú:m, xwa:kóp aʔétəm ašá:mtək. nya:yú:k vi:nadí:t nakavék vi:nadí:t. nyamadúc xwa:kóp aʔím nyi:kwévək, maṭalytapúyk maṭa-

done it," he said. "He was told, It's what I've put war into, don't touch that!; and he's opened it, and I see a terrible battle."

He said thus, and they started from there and went on back; they went there and saw and turned back and came.

They came. Already they had broken the coyote in pieces and flung them here and there; they broke off his legs, broke off his arms, and flung them wherever they felt like; they were just making war, there was awfully thick dust all over, and shouting.

They got there and were gathering everything up, like this, went on doing like this, and put things away, put it all into ollas and covered it all. They sealed it all up.

They set it in place and did that again; this one lay dead, this coyote, dead, lying here in pieces.

They went and gathered and put him all together and set him up on his feet.

"You know I told you, I did, that you might be like this; you certainly heard me say, Don't do it! This is called Cocopa, this is called Quechan, this is called Maricopa; I named them and put them away, and they were here. If you open this, all of these might go to war, I did say," he said; and, "I heard and understood, and in fact I did it, just as you say," he said.

"Don't touch this! If you touch it you'll die," he said, and they left off, and he heard it. They went to sleep.

Next morning when they got up and when they went, they went after things again, pack rats.

They beat them and killed them and were putting them here and there. "You should go after wood," he had heard them say, and in fact he went after wood,

lya:xámək vi:wá:mk aˀávək a:í:mək nyi:yá:t, ayú:tk vi:vám, u:kavék aštú:m apók vu:nó:k a:ví:rəm, avác ˀakór apúy nyakór si:dík, xatalwény.

si:díkəm nya:yú:k, "mó:," aˀétk aštú:m, tatkyá:vək vu:nó:k a:ví:r.

"nyu:kaná:pəm maˀám vadány kawí:lykaˀémək nyaˀépəm maˀámək, ku:táq alykaˀémək nyaˀícəm maˀám. vadí mu:vá:k maˀaxóṭ tanək ˀanyma:tu:qwérək vadí mu:vá:t. ˀaˀí: mayá:k ˀaxá mayá:k mawí:m, madú: aˀétk aˀétəma. nya:yú: ˀapú:c avá:məm mu:ctáq mawí: ˀaˀí:lyˀaˀémək, nyu:kaná:pəm maˀámək vadány. ˀaxwé ˀu:púc ˀaˀí:m nyu:kaná:vəm maˀám. nyá:va nya:mu:táqm akór mapúytəxa," aˀí:m u:kaná:vək vu:nó:m aˀávək.

"ˀaˀávək vaˀu:vá:təsá:, ˀawí: kwaˀáctəm maˀétk maˀítya," aˀétk si:vˀáwt.

si:vˀáwəm, nya:štú:m u:taraˀúyk acá: vu:nó:k nya:ví:rək, nyi:namák vi:dí:t.

vi:nadí:k nya:yú: nya:wécəmˀášk vi:wéck, alydáwk awíck si:dáwk.

ˀamáṭəny axwélyk aštú:m, acá:ck va:ˀé:, a:qwéṭk matˀár atá:pk awétk vu:nó:t, ˀa:málykəva.

nyá:nya apá:vək asó:ck awétkəm, su:nó:t.

si:dáwm, ˀakór nya:wéck su:nó:ny, nya:wínymˀáštək vu:nó:k, maṭnya:tapúyəmˀášk xwa:kóp aˀét.

"á:, nya:nymá:mtək adútya, ˀu:ˀíca:, ˀu:ˀícəny nya:má:mtək adútya," aˀétəm, "ˀu:kavékənti:lyˀaˀémətəxa," aˀét.

si:dáwk nakavék katánək, ˀacu:púc aštú:m u:kavék apók vu:nó:k a:ví:rək, nya:má:m xatalwény šamán alyaˀémətəkəm.

nya:má:mtəm alykwévtək, xatalwé nyá:nyc apúyk, adú:k aˀétk.

nya:má:m. ◇

and they arrived—it was all right and they arrived and slept.

This is how they were acting. When the sun was there again, when they went again, when they went after pack rats again, they were there. One turned his head and looked 'way over there and saw the cloud of dust rising again, and, "Look! He didn't listen to what I said, and he's done it as before," he said.

He turned his head and looked, and he saw the cloud of dust over there. When they saw it they turned back and came. Thereupon there was a terrible cloud of dust, and they had been making war and beating one another and lots of shouting, as they saw, and so again they gathered everything up and put it back in, and that one was already lying there dead, the coyote.

When they saw him lying there, "Oh, well!" they said, and they collected him and put him all back together.

"You heard me tell you, you surely heard me say, Don't do this! Don't open it! you heard us say to you. Here you are getting along quite well as our follower. It was told that what you should do is go after wood and go after water. You heard me tell you that I don't want you to open these things around here that I've put things into. You heard me tell that the enemy is what's been put in. If you open this you'll soon die," they were telling him, and he heard.

"I heard, but I did in fact do it, just as you say," he said and stood there.

When they had gathered and fixed up and put it all away, they left him there and came.

They came, and they went after the things they usually went after, and they were doing it there.

They dug in the ground and gathered and placed them here and there, like this, they beat them and put them down outside, the pack rats.

That's what they were baking and eating.

They were there for quite a while until, now he was doing it as before, they were making war as before, and a cloud of dust rose.

"Yes, that's the end of my talking, it's all finished with my talking," he said, and, "We're not going to do it over again," he said.

Then they turned back and arrived, they collected and put back in all the things that had been put in, that was all, they didn't revive the coyote.

That's all, that's the end of him, that coyote died, they say that he did.

This is all. ◇

Coyote Fishes

xatalwéc si:nyváyk xalyˀáwəny nya:vé:yk si:dáwk.

"maˀa:kó:ynya, avám ˀayémək viˀyá:k ˀayú:wú," aˀétk avˀáwtəm; "é:ˀe, kadú:m." vi:yá:k.

xatalwényc vi:yá:k ˀanyá:va šadómpək vi:yá:k vi:yá:k vi:yá:k. xanyóc si:vám avá:m, láw aˀétk ayú:m, naméc alyvák, ˀací: awí:m si:vát.

si:vám ayú:k si:vˀáwm, naményc láw aˀétk ayú:t.

"ˀanyá:c vadány ˀawétk—ˀa:ˀár vadány—camˀi:tó adíc ˀkapá:lyk vˀu:nó:k ˀa:ví:rək ˀcaváwm, nyá:va ˀataˀúlyk vaˀdí:k, nyá:va ˀavák, ˀa:ˀárəm ˀalú:k vˀu:nó:k, ˀaxály ˀá:pəm kú:rəm ˀací:nyc tamaˀórək nét aˀétəm ˀadáwk, ˀa:xwéšk ˀá:pk vˀu:nó:m, ˀací:nyc tavé:rək nyi:kwévəm ˀaštú:m viˀayémək ˀasó:tk ˀawétk ˀadótkaš," aˀét.

kaná:vəm aˀávək si:vˀáwk, xatalwényányc.

"é:ˀé, nyá:ny avˀawétapatk vaˀu:vá:tk

Coyote was living there, he had Rabbit as his wife, and they were there.

"You, Old Woman, I'm going over that way to look," he said as he stood; "Ah, well, do it!" He went.

Coyote went along heading east and went and went and went. He came to a pond there, he turned his head and looked, and Wildcat was in it, he was there fishing.

He stood looking at him, and Wildcat turned his head and saw him.

"I use this—this tail of mine—I grind melon seeds up and put them down; and I come carrying them, here's where I sit; I smear them on my tail and lay it in the water, and soon it's chock full of fish; I take and flip them and lay them down; I gather great piles of fish and go home and eat them; that's my way," he said.

He stood there, that Coyote, listening to him tell about it.

"Ah, well, that's what I'm doing, too, and I eat

ʔamá:ctapatk vaʔu:vá:təm, nya:yú: ʔu:wíc tan mawétapatəm ʔaʔávək. nyá:ny ʔawétapatkəš. camʔi:tó adíc ʔa:ʔárəm ʔlú:k vʔu:nó:k ʔa:ví:rk, ʔxály ʔá:p, ʔakú:r aʔétəm ʔa:ʔárəny tamaʔórək nét aʔím ʔadáwk matʔár ʔa:lyáq. avʔawémək ʔasó:tapatk ʔadótk avʔu:vá:m, mawétapatəm ʔaʔávək, vaʔvʔáwk ʔawítya. nya:yú: ʔu:wíc tan mawí:m. á:, avʔawétk-ʔaš," aʔét.

si:vʔáwm vadác awím matʔár a:páxk vu:nó:k nya:ví:rək aštú:m.

kwaraʔákəc nyá:si a:kwí:n takavék vi:dí:t, xatal-wényanyc. ʔavá kayá:k vi:dí:k, vi:dí:k avá:t, ʔa:kó:yc ʔavák avák si:vám avá:t, xalyʔáwc, xalyʔáw ʔa:kó:yc.

avá:k aʔím, "maʔa:kó:ynya, camʔi:tó adíc kakapá:lyk."

"camʔi:tó adíc maʔétk," aʔét, ʔa:kó:yənyc aʔím.

"á:, kawí:m."

nya:ʔávək xalykwá:k su:vá:k camʔi:tó adíc si:dáwəm kapá:ly kwaʔáck vu:nó:k a:ví:rk.

"kaʔóṭk ʔanyká:yk," aʔím. aʔóṭk vu:nó:k a:ví:rk á:yk.

adáwk nya:taʔúlyk vi:dí:t, "ʔcí: ʔyá:w ʔaʔím ʔaʔétka," aʔét.

vi:dí:k xá kwa:ʔú:r anák awím á:m, a:ʔárəm alú:k vu:nó:k a:ví:rək, xály á:p.

kú:r ʔím ʔací:nyc amá:ck u:vá:k u:vá:k a:ʔárəny tamaʔórək nyi:nét aʔím aʔávək, "nya:malydópí:." a:xwéšk matʔár á:pəm, ʔací:nyc manamánək i:kwé-vəm ayú:k si:vʔáwk.

alya:nákəntik si:vák si:vák si:vák. kú:r aʔím adáwk a:xwéšk vu:nó:nyk, ʔcí:nyc maṭkwacpé: aštú:m si:vák. nya:wíntik nyamalú:k vu:nó:k nya:ví:rək alya:nák si:vák.

kú:r aʔéxayəm ʔcí: nyi:kwaná:məc si:dík.

them, too; I notice that you yourself do just what I do. That's what I do, too. I smear melon seeds all over my tail, I lay it in the water; pretty soon my tail gets chock full and I take them and drop them outside. What I do is eat them, and standing here I notice you do it, too. You do just the things I do. Yes, that's what I do," he said.

As Coyote stood there, this one did throw them outside and then gathered them.

There the old man turned and came back, that Coyote. He came towards home, he came along and got there, he got to where the old woman was staying at home, the Rabbit, the Old Lady Rabbit.

He got there and said, "You, Old Woman, grind up melon seeds!"

"You say melon seeds?" the old woman said.

"Yes, do it!"

When she heard it, she was searching and in fact she ground up the melon seeds that were there.

"Ball them up and give them to me!" he said. She made them into balls and gave them to him.

He took them and came along carrying them; "I intend to go after fish," he said.

He came and just sat by the edge of the water, and he smeared them all over his tail and laid it in the water.

Soon he felt that the fish were eating and eating and filling his tail chock full; "Now you're going at it!" he said. He flipped them and threw them outside, and stood there looking at the fish flopping all about.

He put it down again and sat, sat, sat there. Soon he caught some and flipped them until he collected lots of fish. Now he did it again and smeared it and put it down and sat there.

Right soon a great big fish was lying there.

"ka:wíc su:vá:k ˀanypaˀi:pá:va nyi:nyaštótk u:vám ˀaˀávək vaˀdíktək ˀadútya. ˀayá:k ˀayú:xa," aˀí: vi:dík, xá maxák á:mk.

vanya:dí:k kwaraˀákəny a:ˀár nyamé:vək u:vám aˀávək awím, ˀanéxí: aˀétəm aˀávək u:vá:t.

anyí:lyqətək awét. a:ˀárəny anyí:lyq té:m awétk té:m awétk vu:dí:m aˀávək si:vám, "cí: nyi:kwaná:m ˀadáwtəkˀa," a:ɬyˀétk si:vát.

a:xwéšxayəm tyútyk aˀétəm aˀávtək si:vát. si:vákəm u:spér tanək—adáwxayəm, ˀavérək tyútyk aˀétəm aˀávək si:vát. té:m awétk, té:m awétk vanya:wá:k vanya:wá:k alytá:m taˀaxánək, a:ˀársily tá:mək awét—əm aˀávək si:vát.

avˀáwk, avˀáw aˀéxayəm tyútyk aˀét. ˀmáṭ štaxpáck su:vá:t. su:vá:k su:vá:k alynú:p nú:p aˀétk si:yá:m aˀávək ˀaxányily vi:yá:m aˀávək si:vát. ˀávək si:ványk "nya:yú: kwanymée" aˀéta. aˀétk si:vát. ˀa:kó:yny aqásk, "ˀa:kó::y" aˀét.

ˀa:kó:yc aˀávək si:vák, ašmályk alywél aˀétəm aˀávək si:vát. "ˀa:kó::y" aˀétk vu:nó:m aˀávək si:vát.

ˀa:kó:yny xalyˀáwc adótk adúm, avˀáw aˀétk aˀávək si:vˀáwk, "vadám aˀétá," aˀétk avéšk. vi:dí:k avéšk kírrr aˀétk vi:dí:k vi:dí:k vi:dí:k nya:vá:k xá kwa:ˀú:r nyi:vˀáw—kwaraˀák anyí:lyq—alyˀanyéw aˀét—xányi.

ˀa:kó:yəc nyá:nyi u:vá:k amí:m u:vát. "kwaraˀáká:, kwaraˀáká:" aˀétk u:vá:t.

nyi:ríš ˀetk, vi:yémtək, apúyk nya:má:m. apáyəx. ◇

"I notice as I lie here that there's someone there gathering us people. I'll go and look," he said, and he swam under water.

When he came he was bothering the old man's tail, and he felt it, he felt that it was getting heavier.

Indeed he swallowed it. He was swallowing the tail, going a little farther and a little farther, and Coyote felt it there, and he was thinking, "I've caught a great big fish."

As soon as he flipped it he felt that it was stuck fast. Then he tried harder—as soon as it caught him he felt that it was stuck fast. The fish kept on and on going a little farther, going a little farther and really got to the end, he got to the end of the tail there, and Coyote felt it.

He stood up, as soon as he tried to stand he was stuck. He was clawing at the ground. There, there he felt himself gradually sinking deeper and deeper, and he felt that he was going into the water. He was there feeling it until, "Something strange," he said. He sat there saying it. He called the old woman, "Ooold Woooman," he said.

The old woman there heard him, she felt the faraway sound strike her ear. There she heard him saying "Ooold Woooman."

The old woman was a rabbit, and so she rose to her feet and stood there listening; "The sound's coming from this direction," she said, and she ran. She came running, hoppity hoppity she came and came and came and finally she got to the water's edge—stopped there!—swallowed the old man!—disappeared!—in the water!

The old woman stayed there and was weeping. "Ooold Maaan, Ooold Maaan," she was saying.

He was nowhere, he was gone, he was dead. Story's ended. All gone. ◇

Coyote Travels

xatalwéc si:nyváyk, "mó:, ʔamáṭ ʔanyá:va ʔa:dómp avʔayá:k ʔayú:k, paʔi:pá:c nyaváyk vi:yá:k ka:dú: ʔa:lyʔétk ʔayú:wú," aʔétk, avʔáwəm, "ʔaxá ʔa:ʔú:rk viʔyá:ta," aʔétk. "viʔayá:ta, xá ʔa:ʔú:rək."

nyamadúc vi:yá:k vi:yá:k vi:yá:k, nyamá::m ʔanyá: nyamaxávəm, kwalyʔi:nyó:ly kwašmá:c nyaváyk si:vám avá:mək. nyamá:m a:šmác aʔí: vu:nó:m ayú:k.

"mó:, vi:madí:tka."

"á:, ʔadí:tk. ʔadótk nyá:m ʔadí:tk vaʔdí:tk. paʔi:pá:c nyaváyk vi:yámək ka:dú: ʔa:lyʔí:m, nyá:ny ʔayú: ʔaʔétk vaʔdí:k ʔadótk, ʔadótkʔaš."

"té:, ʔanyá:c nyá:vi ʔadáwk vaʔadáwəm mayúm."

nyamá:m a:šmác aʔí: vu:nó:k adót.

"kamadómək mašmá:m nya:madú:m am-madótapatxa, ʔanyá:c kwalyʔi:nyó: vadány ʔakú:lyk ʔamáy alyʔvák ʔašmát, ʔadúc nyaʔdú:va."

"é:ʔé, avʔadótapatk, kwalyʔi:nyó: nyá:ny ʔakú:lytapatk alyʔavátk ʔašmátapatk, ʔadótk. ka-madómk ammu:nó:k nya:yú: ʔu:dúc tan madó-tapatəm ʔaʔávtək avʔadótapatxa."

aʔétk nyamadúc akú:lyk vi:dík. ʔanéxtək adúm wélək aʔétk ʔamáṭk apám, wélək aʔétk xálypámək adótk u:vá:t.

nyamá:m ʔanyá:yk vanya:dí:m, "kaʔávək, paʔi:pá: kwavá:ny walyu:néxəmpiny."

xacú:rəm u:sé:rpək vu:nó:nyk, é:, ka:dó:pk i:kwévək.

nyamá:m ʔanyá:y alyaʔéməxaym amánək vi:yá:k, xá a:ʔú:rək vi:yá:k. vi:yá:k vi:yá:k vi:yá:k nyamá:m

Coyote was living over there, and, "Well, I'm going toward the east and looking, I think perhaps people are living there, and I'll see them," he said and stood up; "I'm going alongside the water," he said. "Along-side the water, I'm going."

Thereupon he went, went, went, and at last when the sun had set, he arrived where the Sleepers on Short Tules lived. At last he saw that they were about to go to sleep.

"Well, you've come?"

"Yes, I've come. I just came from this direction. I thought there perhaps are people living around and about, that's what I want to see, so I just came, I did."

"Well, you can see that this is where we stay."

Now, they were about to go to sleep.

"If you have some way of sleeping, that's what you may do. We climb these short tules and stay on top and sleep, that's our way of doing."

"Ah, well, that's what I also do. I also climb these short tules and stay on them and sleep. I hear that somehow or other you yourselves do just what I do, and that's what I'll do, too."

Saying so, thereupon he climbed up and lay there. Being heavy, he flipped over and fell to the ground, flipped over and fell into the water.

Finally, when it was becoming daylight, "Listen! How very restless our visitor is!"

He shivered from the cold until, oh, it was really terrible.

Finally, while it was not yet light he got up and went, he went alongside the water. He went, went,

ʔanyá: nyamaxávəm, paʔi:pá:c nyaváyk si:vám avá:m, cakmató kwaškyínyc nyaváyk si:vám avá:m.

"mó:, vi:madí:tk."

"á:, ʔadí:tk ʔadótk ʔadótk vaʔdí:tk. paʔi:pá:c avá:yk vi:yámək ka:dú: ʔa:lyʔétk ʔadótk vaʔdí:tk, nyi:nyayú:k ʔavʔáwtək ʔaʔítya."

"vaʔtí:vtək, ʔanyá:c nyá:va ʔatí:vək ʔadútya. nyamá:m ʔa:šmác avʔatí:vəm mayúm, ʔanyá:nyc axávək vi:yám."

"kamadóm mašmánypatk madútya. ʔanyá:c nyaʔašmátk, ʔaʔí: ʔadáwk ʔackamatóny ʔu:šám, ʔaxwéṭk pómó:m aʔétk ʔu:cí:k aʔétk, ʔapínytək adópəka. ʔpínyk wé: aʔétəm ʔašmátk, ʔadúc nyaʔdú:va."

"é:ʔé, avʔadótapatk ʔašmátapatk. kamadómək ammu:nó:k nya:yú: ʔu:dúc tan madótapatəm ʔaʔáv. avʔawétapatk, nya:xacú:rəm ʔackamatóny ʔaʔí: ʔadáwk u:šáwašáw ʔawétəm, ʔaxwéṭk pó::m aʔétəm, ʔapínytəm ʔašmátapatk ʔadót. ammadótapatəm, á:, avʔadótapatk ʔašmátk ʔavák ʔadútya," aʔétəm, "á:, ʔaxóṭk," aʔétk a:šmác alytí:vək.

nyu:vá:k u:vá:t xatalwényc. nyi:dík vi:dík xatalwényc, nyamawíck ʔaʔí: adáwk cakmatóny a:šalyótk vu:nó:m, a:šalyót—a:šalyót—a:šalyót a:šalyót awétk vu:nó:təm, makyík ʔaxwéṭk pó:m aʔí:lyaʔémətəm, awétk vu:nó:t. a:ví:r alyaʔémək awétk vu:nó:k, cakmatóny a:šalyótk vu:nó:ny ʔaxwéṭk nyi:mé: awétk, va:ʔí:k aʔéta.

vadík a:dómpətək vadík a:dómpətək u:vá:tk.

"á:, paʔi:pá: kwavá:nyc xacú:r ka:ʔéməm u:vá:tk alyví:tk."

"é:ʔé, ʔadótk ʔadótk," ʔím, "ʔi:tóc ʔalá:ytəm avʔu:vá:k ʔacpámtək ʔaxávtək ʔadótk avʔu:vá:k ʔadótkʔəš," aʔím.

"é:ʔé," aʔétk vu:nó:təm, ʔanyá:yk vanya:dí:m cakmató kwarávənyc maṭcapé:k. nya:ʔávək amánək,

went and at last at sundown he arrived where people lived, he arrived where the Knee Jabbers lived.

"Well, you've come?"

"Yes, I just happened to be coming and I came. I thought perhaps people are living around and about, and I see you as I stand here."

"Here we are, this is where we are settled. Now, you can see that we sleep here."

"You also have a way of sleeping. When we sleep, we take a stick and jab our knees, and it bursts into red fire; it turns to hot coals and gets quite warm. When it gets a little warm, we go to sleep, that's our way of doing."

"Ah, well, that's how I myself sleep. I hear that somehow or other you yourselves do just what I do. That's what I also do; when it's cold, I take a stick and stab and stab my knee, and it bursts into red fire, and when it warms up, I sleep. What you yourselves do, yes, that's what I also do when sleeping," he said, and, "Yes, all right," they said, and they lay down to sleep.

Coyote stayed where he was. He lay where he lay, Coyote did, and thereupon he took a stick and was poking his knee; poke—poke—he kept poking and poking, and it never burst into red fire, but he kept doing it. He didn't finish, he kept on doing it, he poked his knee until he made it flow red, they say that it was like this.

He was turning to this side and turning to that side.

"Oh, it seems that perhaps our visitor is cold."

"Ah, well, I'm just doing something," he said; "I'm having stomach trouble, and I'm just going out and coming in, that's all I'm doing," he said.

"Ah, well," they were saying, and when it was becoming daylight the pain in his knee was terrible.

ˀanyá:y alyaˀémǝxaym a:šu:dúlyk vi:yém. vadác a:šmáck vi:tí:vǝk nyu:má:nǝk u:yó:vǝnyk, nyu:díkǝnyc ˀaxwá:ṭǝm u:yó:vǝk, paˀi:pá: kwavá:nyc ka:dómǝk u:vá:m adú:m aˀétk u:yó:vǝm, vi:yémtǝk.

vi:yá:tk a:šu:dúlyk nyamaxápk vi:yá:k, vi:yá:k vanya:yá:k vanya:yá:m, vanya:dáwk vanya:dáwk, ˀanyá:: nyamaxávǝk. paˀi:pá:c nyaváyk si:vám avá:m.

"mó:, vi:madí:tk, xatalwéc."

"hḿ:, vaˀdí:tk. ˀadótk vaˀdí:tk ˀadót. ammadú:m paˀi:pá:c manyváyk vi:má:m ˀayú:k ˀadú: ˀa:lyˀétk vaˀdí:tk ˀadót."

"ḿ:, ˀanyá:c nyá:va—ˀatí:vǝk, nyamá:m ˀa:šmác alyˀatí:vǝm mayúm. avˀawétk nya:xacú:rǝm ˀašmályk avány ˀataxpályk rú:r ˀawétǝm maṭˀatapéṭk ˀašmátk, ˀapínyk wé: aˀétk. kamadómapatk mašmác nya:madú:m madótapata."

"é:ˀe, avˀawétapat. ˀašmálykǝny ˀawétapatk ˀataxpálytǝk ló:q aˀétǝm maṭˀa:lypó:yk ˀašmát, nyaˀapínytǝm ˀašmátapatum. kamadómk ammu:nó:k nya:yú: ˀu:dúc tan madótapatǝm, ˀaxóṭ, ˀaˀávǝk vanyˀavˀáwǝm."

"á:, nyamˀadúctǝk ˀadótapatk."

"xóṭ, avˀadótapatk ˀašmátxa."

a:šmáctǝk—a:šmácǝm adú: kwaˀáck u:vá:k, ašmályk taxpálytǝkǝm ˀáy ˀavérǝk tyútyk ˀavérǝk tyútyk aˀétǝm aˀávǝk u:vá:t. u:vá:k ašmályk kwarávǝnyc, é:y, ka:ˀé:pk nyi:kwévǝm.

nyamˀanyá:yk vi:dí:m, "kaˀávka, ka:dóm ašmá:lyaˀémǝtǝk u:lyví:k u:vá:t, xatalwéc."

"á:, ˀalá:ytǝm ˀaˀávtǝk ˀu:vá:tk ˀadótkˀaš, ˀi:tóvǝc," aˀétǝm. ˀanyá:yk vanya:dí:m ašmályk u:wá:lyǝny maṭcapé:m nya:ˀávǝk nyi:skyínyk vi:yá:k aˀím, ˀanyéw aˀétk vi:yá:ta ˀu:nyém tapéṭk vi:yá:k ˀxá a:ˀú:rǝk vi:yá:t. vanya:dáw vanya:dáw

When he felt it he got up and while it was not yet light he secretly went away. These people were lying asleep, and when they got up they looked until they saw that where he was lying was bloody; they looked to see how the visitor was getting along, and he was gone.

He went, secretly he went 'way off, he went along, and as he went, as he kept going on and on, the sun went down. He arrived where people were living.

"Well, you've come, Coyote?"

"Hm, I've come. I was just coming along here. I thought I'd like to see you people living around and about, and I just came."

"Mm, this is where we are settled, and you can see that we are just now lying down to sleep. What we do, when it's cold we pull on those ears of ours and stretch them and cover ourselves and sleep; it gets a bit warmer. If you have your own way of sleeping, you may do so."

"Ah, well, that's what I myself do. I use my ear, I pull on it, it stretches out and I cover myself and sleep, when it's warm I sleep. Somehow or other you also are doing just what I do; all right, I hear it as I stand here."

"Yes, that's just what we ourselves do."

"All right, that's how I'll sleep, too."

They slept—they slept, and in fact he did it, he pulled at his ear, and, Ooh!, he felt that it was stuck fast, stuck fast. Then the pain in his ear, Oh!, it was terrible.

Then it was getting to be daylight, and "Listen! Somehow he appears not to be sleeping, Coyote."

"Yes, I'm feeling bad, that's all, my stomach," he said, and when it was becoming daylight, he felt the

vanya:dáw, ˀanyá: nyamaxávək ašxá::yv aˀét. paˀi:pá:c nyaváyk si:vám avá:m.

"mó:, xatalwéc vi:madí:tk."

"á:, vaˀdí:tk."

"é:ˀé, ˀanyá:c nyá:va ˀatí:vək nyamá:m ˀa:šmác avˀatí:vəm mayúm ˀacˀatí:vəm. ˀnyá:nyc axáv vi:kwá:m vadám ˀawétk nya:yú: ˀamadílytək vˀu:nó:k ˀavu:yá:nyəm ˀašpéṭk łyák ˀawétəm ˀapínyk wé: aˀétəm alyˀatí:vək ˀa:šmáck. ˀu:má:vk ˀawí:lyˀaˀém."

"hé:hé, avˀawétapátk. ˀnyá:nyc axávək vanya:yéməm nya:yú: ˀamadílyk vaˀu:nó:k ˀany-vány ˀašpéṭṭapatk ˀašmátəm ˀapínytapatəm ˀaˀávtək. ammawétapatəm, ˀu:wíc tan mawétapa-təm ˀaˀávək vanyˀavˀáwəm," aˀét.

"maxávək mašmátapata."

"á:, avˀadóxa."

alyaxávək šamá:w aˀí: kwaˀáck si:dík. aˀávənyk mu:díly axwí:vənyc ca:nyí:m i:wá: xá:k u:dáwəm si:dík. a:ksá:m tanək má:n aˀétk acpáktək vi:dí:k, i:yá:lypók acpámək vi:yá:k. matˀár avˀáwk cama-nyá:k vu:nó:k anyí:lyq nya:kwí:nək vi:dí:k, axávək avawétk vi:yá:k awétk u:vát.

"á:ˀá, ka:dóm xatalwé walyu:néxəm," aˀéta.

"é:ˀé, ˀi:tóc ˀalá:ytəm ˀacpámtək ˀaxávtək, ˀadótk ˀu:vá:tk ˀadótkˀaš."

"é:ˀé" ˀétk vi:tí:vəm, nyamˀanyá:yk vanya:dí:m, nyamá:m mu:dílyəny acá:vəm nyi:vák kwalaxúyəm, ˀanyá: nyamašá:mək nyi:kwévəm nya:yú:k, "paˀi:pá: kwavá:nyc amápətk u:vá:k acá:vta," aˀétka.

tatu:ví:rək, nyi:skyínyk vi:yá:təm, ˀnyá:y aˀétəm avéšk álálálál aˀétəm, ató:nyc ˀanóq alyaˀém vi:yém. vi:yém vanya:dáwk vanya:dáwk, xá va:ˀú:rək vi:yá:nyk vi:yá:nyk vi:yá:nyk, nyamá:m ˀanyá: nyamaxávək.

awful swelling of his ear and he ran away from them and went, he went along wanting to disappear. He went down the middle of the trail, he went along-side the water. As he kept on and on and on, the sun went slowly sinking down. He arrived where people were living.

"Well, Coyote, you've come?"

"Yes, I've come."

"Ah, well, we just stay here, and you can see we're about to go to sleep where we are. Now that the sun hereabouts is setting, we are making dough and with it we shut our door tight, and it gets a little warmer, and we lie down to sleep. We don't eat it."

"Aha! That's what I myself do. When the sun goes away I make some dough and I, too, close up my house and sleep, and I feel that it's warm, too. What you yourselves do, I see that you also do just what I do, as I stand here," he said.

"You, too, may go in and sleep."

"Yes, that's what I'll do."

He went inside and in fact lay there intending to sleep. He tried until the smell of the dough was too much, and it upset him, and he lay there. Slowly and carefully he arose and came out. He stood out-side and was chewing it and swallowed it and turned around and came back in, and then he went out and stayed.

"Well, how restless Coyote is, somehow," they said.

"Ah, well, I have stomach trouble, and I've been going out and coming in, that's all."

"Ah, well," they said, and when it was becoming daylight, then there was a hole where he had eaten up all the dough; when they saw that you could see the sun in the distance through it, "The visitor has

šamˀúk kwaxwí:c nyaváyk si:vám avá:m šamˀúk vu:nó:k á:pk axwí:ck, sí:::x aˀétk adáwk šú:t awétk, kwanyméc awétk, kwanyméc awétk vu:nó:m ayú:k si:vˀáwk.

"mó:, vi:madí:tk," aˀétəm, "á:, vaˀdí:tk. ˀadótk ˀadót. paˀi:pá:c si:nyváyk vi:yám ka:ˀém ˀayú:k, ˀadú: ˀa:lyˀétk ˀadótənyk, nyammadúck vi:madáwəm nyi:nyayú:k vanyˀavˀáwəm."

"té:. avˀadótkəš šamˀúk avˀawétk vaˀu:nó:k ˀaxwí:ctək, ˀu:má:vxa ˀaˀí:lyˀaˀémək, ˀaxwí:ctək ˀadótk, alyˀá:pk alyˀtaˀámtək vˀu:nó:nyk, maṭcapé:k u:vˀó:m mayúm. kamadóməc nya:madú:m mawémtapata."

"é:ˀé, avˀawétapat. šamˀúk vu:nó:k a:ví:rcəm, ˀaxwí:c ˀawétapatk ˀawím. ˀalá:ytəm ˀaˀávtəkˀaš. nyá:ny ˀawí:m ˀavˀá:xayk amˀúk amˀúk amˀúk ˀaˀétk, amˀúk amˀúk ˀaˀétk, nyá:ny ˀaškwétk ˀadúm ˀawí:lyˀaˀéməṭəkˀaš."

nya:ˀétk a:kxávək a:šmáctəm, acpámək vi:yá:k aˀépəm matˀár vu:vá:k, matˀar tu:tˀá:məny amátk u:vá:t. kú:r axávək vi:dí:tk, kú:r acpámək vi:yá:tk, avu:vá:nyk tó:k vu:nó: ˀanóq alyaˀém tanək.

"walyu:néxəmpiny," aˀét.

"é:, ˀi:tóc ˀalá:yt avˀu:vá:k walyˀanéxmət avˀu:vá:k ˀadótkˀaš."

"hm hm" aˀétk si:tí:vət.

acpámək vi:yá:k, alytu:tˀá:məny amátk amátk vanyu:nó:k acá:vək nyi:nyép, tó:k vu:nó:ny ˀanóq alyaˀém, ˀnyá:y alyaˀéməxaym alyˀanyéw aˀétk vi:yém.

"paˀi:pá: kwavá:nyc nya:yú: ˀatu:tˀá:m acá:vtək mayúm, šá:m maˀím, amáptəkəm awím acá:vək, axwí:c alyaˀémək," aˀétk. u:yó:vək su:nó:k.

avéštək ˀaxá va:ˀú:rək vi:dí:k, tó: ˀanóq alyaˀém. vi:dí:k vi:dí:m vi:dí:m vi:dí:k ˀanyá: nyamaxávət, paˀi:pá:c nyaváyk si:dáwm avá:m. nya:yú: ˀakwá:v šu:ví:k vu:nó:k.

been eating it and ate it all up," they said.

They chased him; he ran away from them and went on; it was daylight, and he ran chop-chop-chop-chop, he was not-just-somewhat full as he went away. As he kept on and on going away, he went alongside the water and went and went until at last, the sun went down.

He arrived where the Mush Sniffers lived. Standing there he saw that they made mush and put it down and sniffed it, with a sniiifffing sound, and pushed it aside, and another one did it and another one did it.

"Well, you've come?" they said, and, "Yes, I've come. I just happened to do it. I was thinking of seeing people who perhaps are living around and about, until I did it, and I see, as I stand here, that here you are."

"Ah! What we do, we make mush and sniff it, we have no intention of eating it, we just sniff it; we put it aside and dump it out until, as you see, there's lots of it around. If you are one who has his own way of acting, you may do so."

"Ah, well! That's what I myself do. When they've got the mush all made, I also have a sniff at it. I've tasted it and found it bad. I use it and as soon as I travel, I go mushywushywushy, I go mushywushy, which is what I don't like, so I don't use it."

So saying, they went in and slept, and he went out and went and stayed outside and was eating the things they had dumped outside. Soon he came along inside, soon he went along out, and he kept on until he was not-just-somewhat filled up.

"How very restless he is," they said.

"Oh, I'm having stomach trouble, that's why I'm restless."

"Hm, hm," they lay there saying.

ayú:tk si:vʔawm, "mó:, vi:madí:tk," aʔétkəm, "á:, vaʔdí:tk."

u:má:ptək adúm vadác.

"é:, ʔakwá:v mamáp alymaʔéṃək madúm, šu:ví:," aʔétk su:nó:t.

"é:ʔé, nyá:ny ʔamá:s ʔalá:ytəm ʔaʔávək ʔamá:lyʔaʔémətəkəš. kwá:avá kwá:avá kwa:avá ʔaʔépk viʔyá:nyk viʔyá:tk, mapísa xóṭ alyaʔémətəm ʔaʔávtək ʔadúm, ʔamá:lyʔaʔémətiyum."

"xóṭ, avadáwm á:m," aʔíct.

si:vʔáwk. alyu:yó:mcəxáyəm xavílyk a:cúptək awétk si:vʔáwk.

si:vʔáwk adú:k aʔétk.

nya:má:m apáyəx. ◇

He went along out, and he kept eating and eating the things they had dumped out, and he ate it up, the whole thing, he was filled up not-just-somewhat; while it was not yet daylight he wanted to disappear and went away.

"The visitor ate up all the things we dumped out, as you see; take a look over there, he was eating and ate it all, he didn't sniff it," they said. And they were looking.

He ran and came alongside the water, not-just-somewhat full. He came and came and came and came along, and the sun set; he got to where people lived. They were stewing pigweed.

He stood there looking, and, "Well, you've come?" they said, and, "Yes, I've come."

These people had already eaten.

"Ah, don't you eat pigweed stew?" they were saying.

"Ah, well, I've eaten that, but it tastes bad to me, so I don't eat it. I used to go like pigaweedle-eedle-eedle when I went along, and now I find it not good, so I never eat it."

"All right, that's all there is to it," they said.

He stood there. As soon as they weren't looking he scooped it up and sucked it in, standing there.

They say that he just stood there.

Story's ended. All gone. ◇

Coyote and Mud Hens

Mary Kelly Escalanti, Narrator

xatalwéc su:vá:kəm, xalyˀáw nya:vé:y ku:ˀéyk si:dáwk.

si:dáwəm paˀi:pá:vəc—avadúnypatk nyaváyk vi:yémək, si:dáwxayəm u:vˀáwta.

u:vˀáwtək. nya:ˀávək, "u:vˀáwk vi:dáwk nya:ˀí:va," aˀím, ˀa:kó:yənyc u:kaná:vxayəm, apátk si:dík, i:mény caqolu:qóltək si:dík.

"é:ˀé, aˀétk nya:ˀí:va. ˀamáy i:dó nalysác aˀétəm avaˀétk, é:ˀé," aˀétk adúm, nák aˀétk si:vátk.

"avnya:ˀí:m akwévəm ˀaˀávxa," a:lyˀí:m si:dík aˀétənyk, u:vˀáwk vu:nó:nyk vu:nó:nyk, vu:nó:nyk ˀaxányc í:p í:p aˀím nya:dí:m satu:kyá:nymək aˀávək u:pó:yvək aˀávək nya:dúcəm, si:vák maṭasó:tan nya:yú: u:dúcənyc avadótk adótum.

ka:wíc ˀamáy akúlyk ˀamáyəly avˀáwk vi:vˀáwxayəm, ˀaxányc avadí:təntik.

Coyote was over there, and he had Rabbit for his wife, poor fellow, and they were there.

They were there, and these other people also lived here and there, and as they were there, it rained.

It rained. When she noticed it, she said, "It's raining hard," and as soon as the old woman told him, he lay down and stretched his legs out full length.

"Ah, well, it's nothing much, just a few tear drops from the sky, as they say. Ah, well," he said, and he paid no attention.

"If that's how it is, I'll see that it will stop," he lay there thinking until it went on and on and on raining until the water came creeping up higher and higher, and they all ran for their lives, but he stayed—that's always his way of doing, sticks to his point.

He climbed up onto something and stood on top, and as soon as he stood there, here came the water again.

nya:yú:kəm vi:vˀáwxayəm avadí:k tamaˀú:r tamaˀú:r, nya:ˀí:m, ˀi:dó:c aˀím ˀaxˀá:c vu:vˀó:m, nyá:ny makyípənya, ˀaxˀá:ny akúlyk vanya:yá:k ˀamá:y alyvák.

si:díkxayəm avadí: taˀaxán tamaˀórí: tamaˀórí: vi:dí:k, nyamá:m nya:vá:kəm a:ˀárənyc ˀaqóltək adúm ˀaxály a:vályəm si:dík, a:lyu:vé:vəm si:dík, nyá:nyəm á:mək akwévəm si:dík.

si:díkxayəm—nya:yú:c xanamó:c—xanyí:lykəc adótk adú:m, alyu:nó:k xály tatu:ˀúpk vu:nó:k, ˀamáy nyu:nó:k, paˀi:pá: ˀaxály u:nó:c adótk adú:m, ˀasá:mtək ˀamáy nyu:nó:k.

malyxóny xály a:vá:lyk, i:mény awétk avu:ˀá:ny alykyí:ty alykyí:ty aˀétka, manyé:k aˀétk adú:m a:cxwá:r aˀétk vu:nó:m, aˀávək, ayú:k si:díkənyk, "kaˀdómapatlya," a:lyˀí:m si:dík.

"ka:ˀétám. u:vˀá:vəm madúck," aˀéxayəm, "á:ˀa, i:kwévək, kadí:k, kayú:k va:ˀé," aˀétkəm, malyxóny awétk, i:mény alykyí:ty alykyí:ty aˀétk vu:ˀáctək avadík.

u:vˀá:vək adú:k aˀétk vanya:dík, "á:, ˀadótapatxa."

atáqšək acénək adú:k a:lyˀétənyk, ˀaxányc ˀaraˀárək i:kwévək, maṭcapé:m adótkəm xály u:vá:k ˀaxák á:m u:xáymək—aˀétk, ašvíly ašvíly ašvíly, ṭáw aṭáw aṭáw aˀétk—anáwtək u:vák, alyapúytək adú:k aˀétəma. ◇

When he saw it, while he stood there, when it came on gradually filling up and filling up—what they call willow, and cottonwoods were standing there, and—one or the other of those—he went climbing up a cottonwood and sat 'way up on top.

While he lay there, here it really came, kept getting fuller and fuller, finally when it reached him, his tail is long, and so he lay there with it dangling in the water, halfway, then at last it stopped, and he lay there.

While he lay there—some kind of ducks—they were mud hens, and so they were swimming in it, they were on top of it, because they are water-dwelling people, they are light, and they were on top.

They splashed their wings in the water, they did something with their feet and walked on tiptoes, and because they thought that it was pleasant they were laughing; he lay there listening and looking until, "I wish I could do it, too," he lay there thinking.

As soon as he said, "How is it? Are you where one can walk?"; they said, "Yes, nothing to it. Come on! Look! Like this," and they did things with their wings and walked about tiptoeing on their feet.

As he lay there saying that it could be walked on, "Yes, I'll do it, too."

He thought he was jumping down into it. The water was awful deep, a whole lot of it, and he's in the water and doesn't know how to swim—so, he's grabbing, grabbing, grabbing at it, going plop! plop! plop!—there he was, making noises, and they say that he just died. ◇

A Snake Bit Me and an Old Lady Cured Me

ˀa:vé nyacakyíwəm ˀa:kó:yc nyu:mánək

Lee Emerson, Narrator

nyakó:r taˀaxán ˀaxu:márək vaˀu·vá·təm, ˀamaṭá·m ˀapa:xkyé:m ˀadú:k aˀícta.

nyá:nyi:míck vu:nó:m, karaˀúk u:nó:m, ayá:ly ˀu:nó:k. ˀanyá: sá:vədək u:ˀícəm, nyamá:m ayá:vəly, nya:yú: karˀúkəly ˀu:nó:k, ˀaˀí: ˀayá:k aˀét.

ˀadú:m, nyá:, ˀaxu:má:rtək ˀadúm, ˀatáy tanək vaˀa:dí:k. nya:yú: xanˀa:vá:c arúvəm ˀaštu:tú:tk ˀartu:ˀó:yk, vaˀa:dí:k vaˀa:dí:k. ˀu:nyéc ˀašéntək vi:díktəm ˀawéck ˀawéck ˀu:nó:xayəm, nyá:lyˀatanák ˀavéšk viˀayá:təm, ˀavéštək ˀadú:m ˀavˀáw alyˀaˀémət.

ˀamáṭ ˀayú:m nya:yú: šamá: lyaví:tk u:vát—ˀi:sáv šamá:c adú:k ˀa:lyˀétk ˀaˀím ˀatáqš taˀaxán, ˀa:véc adótkəm adúm, ˀa:véc si:vátkəm adúm, nyi:nyaˀatáqš taˀaxánəm atáqšapatk nyacakyíwt.

Really long ago I was a boy here, and they say I was seven years old.

They were having a funeral there, and they were conducting the karˀuk, and we were there in the river bottom. On what's called Saturday, as it was going on, we were in the karˀuk, and I went for wood, they say.

So, well, we were children, there were very many of us coming along. We were having fun collecting dried-up locusts, coming this way, coming this way. While we were going and going on the one path that was there, I went along running at the head of the others, and since I was running I didn't stop.

I looked at the ground, and there was something there like a root—I thought that it was an arrow-weed root, and so I made a big jump; it was a snake, there was a snake there, and when I made a big jump there, he also jumped up and bit me.

ˀi:má:ṭnyi sírr aˀétk, viˀayá:k. kú:r aˀétəm xu:már—nyu:nó:va nyá:nyəm—avu:nó:cxayəm maṭˀašcamá:m avˀáwəm, mašaxáytək vi:vák, ˀakúc tanək nyi:nyu:cá: vu:nó:k. ˀavá:m, nyá:nyi alycu:nák ˀaqó:l ˀawí:m, wemtaka:xá:v ˀi:wá:m u:péṭ ˀawíntik. awím nyá:nya ˀi:mény u:cˀéxk alycu:nákəny tacénək ayú:xáyəm, ˀackamató maxák tan aˀím, ˀi:mé kwasá:rək ˀaxwéṭk xanvík nyi:dáwət, nya:yú: ˀa:vé nyacakyíwənyc.

aˀím, nyá:, "ˀa:véc macakyíw kwaˀáceš maˀávək," aˀétəm, nyamá:m ˀi:wá:nyc apúyem ˀi:wá:nyc konakonakón nyi:vˀáw ˀi:wá:ny kŕŕ nyi:vˀáw ˀatkavék. nyi:míc nyu:nó:vək nyiˀu:dáwsi nyiˀu:tí:vsi ˀakayá:m ˀavéštək. nyá:sik ˀamánək ˀavéšk vaˀdí:k vaˀdí:k. nyá:ny makyí ˀu:dóm ˀašmadí:tk ˀadúm, ˀavéšk vaˀdí:k vaˀdí:k vaˀdí:k, kú:r aˀéxayəm ál ˀapám, ˀa:cnyavárək i:kwévək.

ˀapámək vaˀu:dík nya:yú·k xu:má:rəc cavu:kyá:vək vanya:yá:k, nyá:nyəm nyaˀu:mánvəc ˀaxú:ṭk avadáwəm, adú:m nyu:kaná:vcəm, vi:yá:k nyu:kavnáwk vanyu:dí:k, nyiˀatí:vək ˀacˀu:má:vily kamét.

nyamá:m kwasˀi:dé: ayá:kəm. ˀi:pá: kwasˀi:dé:, ˀa:vé šamá:c u:vá:m, N.T. aˀím amúlyk u:vá:m, nyá:nyi nya:kamícəm acé:vək vu:nó:m, paˀi:pá: kwamaxánənyc séx aˀét tanək a:kwí:nək, atóly camí:m acé:vək vu:nó:k. acé:v vu:nó:nyk nya:yú: ˀacˀaqóltəm awétkəm u:kyéṭk nya:dáwk ˀi:mény takwí:n, kwarávənyc ayá:xa lyaví:m caréq ˀím awí:k ˀéta.

There was a trembling on my body as I went along. In a little while a child—one who was standing there, at that time—one who was still alive at that time—I insult myself [by mentioning a dead relative]—was there, she was a young woman here, she was full-grown, and she was in charge of us. I got to her, and at that time I was wearing long stockings, also I was wearing bib overalls. So, about that, she rolled up my trouser leg and rolled down my stocking and looked, and right away she said that just back of my knee on my left leg there were two little red spots, where the snake had bitten me.

So, well, she said, "You can feel that a snake has actually bitten you," and then I felt scared, and I turned back, my heart was thumping and I was in shock. I ran towards the place over there where they were gathered, all camped and still conducting their mourning. Starting from that point I came this way, came this way, running. About that, I didn't know in what direction I was headed, but I came on, came on, came on running, and pretty soon I fell flat, I was all worn out.

When the children saw that I had fallen and was lying there, they went running along here—my parents were still living at that time—so, they told them, and they went and lifted me up and were bringing me and carried me to the place where we were camped and ate.

Then someone went for a doctor, a doctor man, a snake dreamer was present, one named N.T. was present, and when they brought me to him, he was treating me, and the onlookers were all standing in a real throng around me, and he set me in the middle and was treating me. He was treating me, and then he used a certain long thing [a hair], he cut it off [his head] and took it and wound it around my leg, say-

acé:vək vu:nó:nyk vu:nó:nyk avány nya:kwév, ka:wé:lyaˀém nya:yú:k, ˀa:kó:yəc u:vá:təm, ˀa:kó:y ˀa:vé šamá:c, ˀa:kó:y ˀa:vé aˀícəm, nyá:nyc ˀaˀí: ayá:k aˀétk. nyi:míck vu:nó:m ˀaˀí: ayá:c alya:xwílypatk vi:yéməm, nyá:ny aqásk aˀí:m, ka:wíc ayá:k, u:kaná:vək.

nya:ˀávək, "makamét, makamí:m, paˀi:pá: macu:xánək u:vˀócxayk a:é:vəm nya:dú:m, vadány ma:é:mək, vanya:vák ˀakú:r aˀíc matápk, paˀi:pá: kwamcu:xánəny ˀalá:yk adópəka," aˀétəm, nya:é:mcək.

ˀa:véc nyacakyíwk vanyˀadíkəm, kwasˀi:dé: ˀa:kó:y ayá:k kamí:m nya:é:məcxa ˀu:ˀícəny, paˀi:pá:nyc macu:xánək nya:kyá:vək, séx vu:vˀócəm, nyá:nyc nyu:é:m vadány, "paˀi:pá: mu:yó:vənyc ˀalá:yk adópəka," u:ˀíc nyá:va ˀakana:v ˀaˀí:m viˀavák ˀaˀépəva.

"paˀi:pá:c vu:vˀócəm mu:yú:nya, paˀi:pá:c nyá:vi, paˀi:pá: sanycˀá:kəc alyu:vˀóctək adúm, sanyacˀá:kəc alyu:vˀócəm maṭa:rˀék vanyu:vˀócəm nyá:vəc nyi:xwéṭəc adú:m awí:m u:cé:va, ˀaxóṭ alyaˀéməxa," aˀí:m nya:é:mək awétəməš. paˀi:pá:c alyu:vˀóck nyá:ny avadík šu:páwk aˀétkəm, "paˀi:pá:c ˀaxóṭ alyaˀémək, kwalašáw alyaˀémək," aˀí:m, "ˀací: nyá:vəc nyamašú·k," aˀím nyá:nya "nyá:nym ašú:m ˀacu:cé:venyc ˀaxóṭ alyaˀéməxa lyaví:k," aˀím nyá:va.

nya:é:mcək nya:wá:k xi:pán camétəm, paˀi:pá:nyc nyu:yó:v alyaˀémətəm, nyá: camí:m

ing that he was doing it to stop the pain that appeared to be going further.

He went on and on doctoring until, when they saw that he failed, he wasn't doing anything, there was an old lady, an old lady snake dreamer, called Old Lady Snake, and she was going after wood [for the karˀuk], they say; while they went on mourning, she had gone off as one among those going for wood. She's the one they called, somebody went after her and told her.

When she heard their story, she said, "You are to bring him, as long as the people are all standing looking on, they are crowded together, therefore you are to move this boy and set him down a little way off; it's quite bad for the people to be watching him," and they moved me.

What I told you about my lying there bitten by a snake, and that they went after the old lady doctor and brought her and were going to move me; and this that she said about the people looking on, standing in a throng around me; and her moving me away, saying that "It's quite bad that the people are looking at you"; I'm going to explain this here, I might say.

"That looking at you as the people stand, the people here, there are women standing among them, and they are menstruating as they stand, that's blood, and it has an effect, on the curing, it won't be good," she said, and she moved me away. She said that she knew there was that about the people standing among them, and she said, "The person is not good, is not clean"; "This one reeks of fish," she said, about that; "It reeks like that, and the curing probably won't be good," she said, about this.

They moved me, and when they took me away, they put me down nearby, and the people didn't see

nyacé:vət. nyacé:vək vanyu:nó:k vanyu:nó:k, ˀanyá: ˀapílytəm awétəm adú:m, vanyu:nó:k nya:taˀór acém awétəm adú:m, vanyˀadík vanyˀadík, ˀaxá ˀasí:lyˀaˀémək ˀacˀamá:lyˀaˀémək vaˀu:díkənyc vaˀu:díkənyc vaˀu:díkənyc, ˀanyá:c axáv acém taˀaxán, nyá:ny tan, "mó:, a:í:mək ˀaxá nya:masétxa," aˀétəm adúm, ˀaxá ˀasí: kwaˀáck. ka:ˀém alyaˀémətəm ˀadík. nyá:nyi nyacé:vək vu:nó:k.

u:yé:y tánəm nyu:yé:yk, i:šá:lyəm nyapá:sk awí:m u:taraˀúynyək acé:vək vu:nó:nyk vu:nó:nyk, nya:ví:rək nya:namák ˀacnyu:kaná:vət, ˀa:vé ˀacadó:y avány. ˀa:vé paˀi:pá:c adúnypatk aˀím nyá:va nyu:kaná:vək vu:nó:nyk vu:nó:nyk, xu:mártəm aˀétk aˀím, maṭkwi:šá:yk u:lyví:tk ˀu:ˀávanyc.

vadány nya:é:mək kú:r aˀím nya:camí:m nya:nyacé:vk vu:nó:k nya:namákəm, ˀacnyu:kaná:vtək aˀítya, ˀa:vé adó:yá. aˀím "ˀa:vévany paˀi:pá: lyavé:nypatk nya:dú:va," aˀéta. "xamí: nyu:wíc, adú:m nyi:mánək adú:m aˀí:s, ˀa:vé makwacakyíw avány, paˀi:pá: xá:k u:vá:c, paˀi:pá: nya:yú: kwaˀíc aˀáv alyaˀéməc, kwaxóṭ u:kaná:vcəm aˀáv alyaˀém ˀacku:vá:t, paˀi:pá: nyá:lyaví:c avu:vá:k, ˀašéntək avu:vá:k, nyá:nyc macakyíwk nya:wí:va," aˀéta. "paˀi:pá: ˀaxóṭ alyaˀéməc."

aˀím nyu:vá:k nyá:va ku:ná:vəny—"ˀavá nyiu:mán tan ˀa:véc avadúnypatk. ˀa:véc vi:yá:k vi:yá:k, kavá:r ka:ˀá:məc, ˀa:vé mayú:xayk matapúyk mawím, nyá:ny apúyk nya:díkəm šatamé:vək, nyavák adí:təm adúm šatamé:v vu:nó:k. kavá:r ka:ˀá:məc nyá:nyc xalykwá:k vi:dí:kəm, ˀa:vé ˀašéntəc xalykwá:k vanya:dí:k vanya:dí:k vanya:dí:k,

me, then she put me down and doctored me. When she kept on and on doctoring me, because she was doing it in the morning, because as she went on it was not quite noon, I lay there and lay there drinking no water and not eating anything, but lying where I was, lying where I was, lying where I was; just before sundown, just then, "Well, you may drink water freely," she said; therefore I did actually drink water. Without anything happening, I lay. There she was doctoring me.

She breathed her real breath on me and massaged me with her hand, and so she took care and went on and on doctoring until, when she finished, when she stopped, she told me things, about that behavior of snakes; she said that snakes are also people, this is what she went on and on telling me until, being a child, it was really marvelous for me to hear.

This thing, when they moved me a little way off and set me down, and when she went on treating me and stopped, she told me things about the behavior of snakes. So, "Those snakes are very much like people," she said. "They have offspring, to start with, but that snake that bit you was a person living apart, not listening to people who give advice, he stays about not listening to the good things they tell him. One like that, wherever he stays, he stays alone, that's the one that bit you," she said. "He's not a good person."

So, as she was there, the story about this— "Snakes also have a family they originate from. A snake goes on and on, and it never fails that, as soon as you see him you kill the snake, and when he lies there dead, they miss him; because he comes from their house they are missing him. It never fails that they search for him, and as one snake comes this

apúyk vanya:díkəm avá:k ayú:t 'ˀá:, apúyk vi:dík,' aˀét. šu:mé:vəny—taˀaxánək šamé:k aˀétkəm, xalykwá:k adáwtək. nyá:ny lyavé:k adú:k aˀím kwapaˀi:pá: lyavé:k aˀím.

"aˀétk, maṭwa:kavárapatk, matu:púyənyc ˀalá:yk aˀínypatk, aˀí: vu:dáwcənya. ˀackamá:məm, mu:kaná:vəm maˀávxa, 'vaˀavápk ˀadú:va,' aˀí:m. 'ˀanyta:sí:lyənyc sírr awím maˀávək,' nyá:nyəm mu:kaná:vək aˀím aˀí:k aˀéta. 'paˀi:pá:c vaˀaványpatk,' aˀím. ˀamáyk makacˀí:lymaˀémk matapúy alymaˀémk madú: aˀím aˀím. nyá:nyc mu:kaná:vək, 'mó:, si:ká:mək,' aˀím, manamák vi:mayém aˀím. aˀí:s madú:lymaˀéməxayəm ˀamáyk nya:makacˀí:m, mašaráytəkəm macakyíwtəxa. 'ˀawéxa lyaví:k,' aˀím mu:kaná:vək awí:k ˀéta."

vu:nó:nyk, acé:vk vu:nó:nyk nyamá:m nyi:míc vu:nó:k šamác cu:mpáp alywémək, nya:í:məm ˀankavék ˀanyvály ˀankayá:k.

ka:rétəly camí:m vu:dí:tk, nyá:ny ka:rét savíly ˀadík. ka:rétənyc ka:wíc ˀu:nyéc ˀaxóṭ alyaˀémətəm adúm, ka:ˀém akúpk nya:vám, alynályəm—kwarávənyc maṭcapé:t, xwó:ṭ kwarávəny maṭcapé: vaˀdí:nyk vaˀdí:nyk. nya:nyakamí:m avá:k nyacé:vtəntik. "nyamá:m nyu:mánək," aˀétkəm, "ˀanamák."

"ˀaxály kaˀúp alykaˀémək, mu:vá:ny xamé:ra kadú:m," aˀétəm, ˀacanyók vaˀu:dík, nyá:ny ca:mánək xeykó nyamarasí:n nyami:lú:kc ˀadú: ˀavánˀyk, ˀi:mény talpúk nyi:kwévəm, ˀaˀí: ˀaša:ˀórək, ˀaskalypóly ˀa:kxávək ˀaša:ˀórək

way, comes this way, comes this way, he gets here and sees him as he lies there dead, 'Ah, he lies here dead,' he says. They're missing him—they really do miss him, and they search for him and pick him up. It is said that they are like that, it is said that they are like human beings.

"Furthermore, they also love one another, and there are some who also say it's bad for you to kill them. You pass by at any places and you'll hear them tell you, 'Here I am,' they say. 'You hear my rattle make a whirring sound,' and it is said that that's how they inform you. 'I'm also a person here,' they say. They want you not to tread on them or kill them. That one tells you, 'Well, pass by over there!' he says, he wants you to leave him and go away. But as soon as you don't do that, and if you tread on him, he gets angry and he'll bite you; they say that he does it as a way of telling you, 'I'm likely to do something.'"

She went on and on treating me until finally they kept up the mourning through to the end of four days, and when it was all over we turned back and headed for my home.

They put me in a wagon and brought me, I lay over there in the wagon. Because it was some kind of not good road, wherever there was a hole, the wagon dropped into it—the pain was extreme, by gosh, I was in extreme pain as I came along, came along until. . . . When they brought me home, she arrived and treated me again. Finally she said, "I have cured you. I'm stopping."

"Don't go swimming yet, do it later," she said. I obeyed her, and from there I began using white man's salve-medicine. My leg was doubled up and useless, and I leaned on a stick, I put it into my armpit and leaned on it, as I stayed and stayed, I

vaˀu:vá:nyk vaˀu:vá:nyk, ˀi:ményc tík aˀí: alyˀu:vá:t, talpúk ˀu:vá:nyk ˀu:vá:nyk, kavé:ly ˀayémək.

nyá:səm ma:cawíc kavé:ly cadóməc si:dáwany ˀakayá:m, nyá:sily ˀu:vá:m nyikˀapílyəm saˀu:vá:nyk saˀu:vá:nyk, ˀi:méc aˀáv tanəm meramérək vi:dí:k. nyaˀaxóṭ, ˀamáṭ tík vaˀavˀáwk, nyá:səm ˀaxalyˀúp ˀayá:tk, ka:ˀém alyaˀémətək, ˀu:vá:nyk, avány ˀamántək.

nyaˀamántək ˀu:vá:m ˀi:mé tašpáyk ˀalú:m alyaskyí:t, ˀanóqtem ˀalú:m vaˀu:vá:nyk ˀawét, nya:má:m. nyá:si:mánək ˀaxóṭk.

vadány, maṭku:ná:v vadány maˀávci: ˀaˀétk ˀaˀét, ˀa:vé nyacakyíwəm, ˀa:kó:yc nyu:mánək, ˀaˀí:m mu:ˀáv vadány, mó: nya:má:m. ◇

remained with my leg barely touching the ground, I remained and remained doubled up until I went off to the south.

At that point I went off heading to where my relatives of the southern division of the tribe were living, and there I stayed, and I remained and remained there through the summer until my leg had feeling, it was coming to be straight. When it was all right, here I stayed barely touching the ground; at that point I went swimming and was there without ill effect until I recovered.

When I recovered I continued to limp on my leg on one side; I've been limping a little ever since, but that's all. From there on it was all right.

I wanted you to hear this story about myself, and I've told it; a snake bit me and an old lady cured me, this that you've heard me say, well, here it ends. ◇

Childhood Reminiscences

Amelia Caster, Narrator

xu:márxayk maṭá:m xamók vanyˀu:vá:m, ˀaxály nyu:taˀúpc ku:ˀé:y, nya:yú: ˀaví: ˀamáyvik ˀanyváytiyum. mapísa nya:yú:c nyi:vák vanya:vám, ˀavá u:céwxayc nyi:vák vanya:vám, nyá:ny maxáknyik ˀanyváyəm, ˀawím—

nyaˀu:mán nyá:nyc nya:wím ˀaxály nyu:taˀúpk. mi:sí:lyk nyacamí:m, awím ˀacapé:vtəm awím nyi:camí:m, ˀaxány nyi:caˀí: vi:dáwəm, kwaskyí:ly awíc, ˀi:ˀény a:sˀúlyk, ˀi:dóny a:sˀúlyk, ˀi:má:ṭ a:sˀúlyk vu:nó:k a:ví:rk—a:vxáy kwalašáwc si:vám nya:cvu:xáyk vu:nó:k a:ví:rək. ˀi:ˀény šacék vu:nó:nyk vu:nó:nyk nya:ví:rək, nya:wí:m nya:yú: ˀakwér adáwk ˀakwér nyu:pányk vu:nó:k a:ví:rək awím ˀu:vá:təm, ˀanyá: kwaší:ntəm awétk awétk vu:nó: tavˀártiyum.

u:nó: vaˀárxayəm, xu:már ˀama:wí:c makyík adí:k avá:m ˀaraˀóyck vˀu:nó:m, ˀavu:mák ˀadáwk xantapˀó:p ˀaraˀóycək vaˀdáwm, xantapˀó:p makyípəc apúyk aˀím va:ˀím ˀamcacˀí:m vaˀu:nó:nyk, vaˀdí:k, ˀxá ˀasí: ˀí:m vaˀdí:k, ˀxá ˀasí:m, ˀatkavék.

nya:tók—nyá:vəc—maṭˀašcamá:təm—ˀany-

As a child, when I was three years old, they used to bathe little me; I always lived up on the Hill. Where there's something there now, where there's a newly built house there, below that is where I lived, and—

My parent bathed me. She laid me on her lap; because I was small she laid me there; she put water there, she poured it into a pan, she washed my hair, she washed my face, she washed my body and finished—she dressed me in a clean dress that was there and finished. She combed and combed my hair until, when she finished, then, she took red pigment and painted my face with red pigment and finished; and here I was, and she always used to do it every day.

She used to do it, and a little girl relative of mine came from somewhere to us, and we were playing; we were behind the house and playing with dolls; she said one of the dolls had died and we were mourning it until I came inside, I came in to drink water, and I drank water and went back [outside].

At that point she—I insult myself—the one who

kwu:taraˀúyəny, ˀanykwataˀa:kú:cənyc cakavár apúy nyakwasá:yəm tan kamúlyk, cakavár apúy aˀím, nyayú:lyaˀémək. ˀatkavék saˀványk nyamá:m, nyaˀdí:ntixayəm nyá:vəc ˀi:ˀény láwəm ayú:xayəm, ˀiˀévac ˀonaˀón a:kyíṭk vu:nó:nyk, ˀi:ˀény u:kyenakyénək, vadí avám, ˀá:a nya:yú:k mašu:ráyənyc nyi:ná:m—

took care of me, the one who raised me was laughing fit to die and pretending to compliment me, she was about to die laughing, and she wasn't looking at me. I went back [out] and stayed there until at last, as soon as I came in again, and as soon as she turned her head and saw my hair—[my little girl relative] had been cutting my hair short [as a sign of mourning] until she had clipped it all short, up to here—and, Ooh! when she saw it her anger was great.

mašu:ráyəny maṭcapé:tk nyatapúy aˀí: vu:nó:k. nyanyúv alyaˀéməš adótas, xu:már ˀama:wí:nyc avéšk vi:yémk mašadék.

She was awfully angry and ready to kill me. She didn't hit me, but my little girl relative ran away in fright.

kwaraˀák nyá:vəc, xu:márxayəm nyapá:pəntik. ˀa:ckóycəc—maṭˀašcamá:təm pá: ˀakú:cvəc šu:kaˀúl ša:ˀá:ṭ nya:wécəm, nyapá:pk, nyá:nyanyc. ˀamí:m nyakˀu:mék ˀamí: vaˀárəm nyapá:pk. nya:yú: ˀi:dó:c avadíkəm, u:lyéškəm—ˀi:dó:nyi, manyé:k, ka:ˀém ˀa:súkər lyaví:k nyi:pácəm nyá:ny awí:m nyá:y ku:ˀéyəm ˀa:táwk, dú:ls lyaví:m ˀa:táwk ˀawím, ˀawétum.

In childhood, this old man also carried me on his back. The old women—I insult myself—when the grownups went to sell beadwork, he's the one who carried me on his back. I cried from loneliness and when I used to cry, he carried me on his back. Where there were some willows, he broke them off, and—on the willows there was something sweet, sort of like sugar, and that's what he gave me and I sucked on it; I sucked on it like candy all the time.

nya:yú: kwaraˀákənyc nya:wí:m, kapéṭəm ˀu:pú:vək ˀawécəm, nya:nyanamí:lək awím nyapá:pk amák nyatápəm ˀawécəm, vaˀawécəm nya:yú: xamályəny u:kyéṭk nyá:yəm, ˀamáynyi xamá:lyk malá:š lyaví:k adú:m, nyá:yəm ˀa:táwəm manyé: tanəm, ˀmá: vaˀártiyum.

nyamá:m ˀaxárək, nyamá:m xacú:r vanya:yá:m nya:yú:c ˀaxárək, adúm, ˀaxáy lyaví:k nyá:nyc manyé:tum. ˀacˀi:páy ˀantankór nyá:ny kamánək aˀí: ˀa:lyˀéta. ˀantankór tan ˀa:lyˀéta, nyí:lyk.

What the old man did, when we went through the brush, when he consoled me, he put me on his back and carried me, and we went, and as we went along he tore off some leaves and gave them to me; and there was something white on them, like molasses; and he gave it to me, and I sucked on it, and it was really sweet, and I always used to eat it.

Well, it was covered with honeydew; well, when fall was coming on things got covered with honeydew; and so, that's what was sort of moist and always sweet. I think it comes from those tiny insects. I think they're real tiny, and they're black.

nyakór tan ˀanyá:c ˀaxu:márxayk vanyˀu:vá:m, nyamá:m ˀašmá:w ˀaˀím nyaˀu:vá:m, paˀi:pá: kwakú:cənyc nya:ˀí:m, xatalwé nyu:kaná:vəctiyum.

ˀadú: vaˀárək ˀašmá: vaˀárək vaˀu:vá:k, xatalwénya ˀatáyəm ˀašu:páwk ˀu:vá:k nya:má:m, ašmadí:tkaˀa. nyamá:m ˀaˀkúck vanyˀavák ˀašmadí:tkaˀa, ˀi:wá: nyi:péṭta. sá: ˀnóq tanəm ˀašu:páw ˀacém alyadá:wtəm, nyá:ny ˀakaná:vtəxa.

paˀi:pá: kwakú:cənyc nya:wím, nyašalypúyəm alyˀadík ku:ˀé:yk nya:yú: i:šá:ly ˀašapúkəm nyu:kaná:vta.

nyu:kaná:vək aˀím—ˀakór tanək, máṭ nyakór taˀaxán, ˀamáṭ vadác ˀaxác tamaˀórək aˀéta. ˀaxác tamaˀórəm, vi:dáwkəm nya:yú:c—xwaškyé:vkəc, nyá:nyc—nya:yú:—ˀamáy takyé:m tanək ˀaxányc vi:vˀáwəm, xwaškyé:vkəc vanya:yá:k nya:yú:ny awí: ku:ˀé:yk. nya:yú: ku:ˀéyk caxnáp ku:ˀéyk, nya:yú:nya ˀamáyvi caxnáp ku:ˀé:yk si:vák.

a:ˀárənyc xály a:nák a:lyu:vé:vəm si:ványk, ˀaxányc nya:sáṭəm, a:ˀárənyc a:lyu:vé:vək xamá:lyk. ˀaxály kwa:nákənyc vanya:dú:m va:dú: vaˀárək adú:k aˀéta.

adú:m ˀaxányc nya:rúvəm, xarcampúkəc xi:púk taˀaxánək ˀamáṭ kwarúvənya cacpá:ckək awí:k aˀéta.

aˀétk ka:návəc aˀétk aˀítya, nya:yú:c nyá:va.

nya:ˀí:m aˀím—xi:púk kwakwamá:ṭc paˀi:pá: acéwk sanya:vák, nya:yú: masˀé: aštú:m, paˀi:pá: acéwk vu:nó:k a:ví:rək, ˀaˀáw tará:k vu:nó:k vu:nó:k vu:nó:k nya:ví:r, nyamá:m maspá:m, ˀaˀáwənyc. nya:maspá:m nya:yú:k, nya:yú: kwaxˀó:nya awí:m, kwaxˀó:ny alya:dú:nək aˀéta. paˀi:pá: u:céw avány nya:dú:nəm, vanya:wí:m ˀamáyk tará:ntik awí:m. u:kavék ˀmáyk tará:m, si:dík avadík kú:r aˀím

A long time ago when I was a child, well, when I was about to go to sleep, what the grownups did, they always told me Coyote stories.

That's what I used to do, when I used to be going to sleep, and I knew many Coyote stories, but now I don't know them. Now that I'm old I don't know them, I've forgotten them. But, there are some that I almost know a part of, and that's what I'll tell.

What the old people did, they held me in their arms, and there I lay, little me, I snuggled in their arms and they told me things.

They told me—long ago, a really long time ago, this earth was filled with water, they say. It was filled with water, and there something—the dove, that's the one—the water stood reaching all the way to the sky, and as the dove went along he did something, poor thing. He clamped his beak onto something, he was there clamping on to the sky with his beak, poor thing. His tail sat halfway into the water as he stayed and stayed there until, when the water drained away, his tail was halfway white. They say that that's how his tail used to be from sitting in the water.

So, they say that when the water dried up, the small yellow ant was the very first one that brought out the dry earth.

So, that's what the story was, about this.

Then, they said—when Kukumat was first making people, he collected mud and finished making a person; he lit a fire and went on and on and on doing it and finished; at last it died down, the fire. When he saw that it had died down, he used the hot ashes, he put it under the ashes, they say. When he had put that human figure underneath, then he lit another fire on top. He lit a fire on top again, and

adáwxayəm, avšú:m nya:yú:k, "ˀó:, ˀalá:yəš, avšú:k nyi:kwévəš," nya:ˀétk a:xwešxwéšk alyá:pk aˀéta.

nya:á:pk "ˀawíntik ˀayú:xa" aˀíntik awíntik, nyá:ny u:cá:wk awíntixayəm, tu:rá:c ca:nyí:kəm apóṃək nyí:lytəm nya:yú:k, "ˀó, nyi:kwévəš ˀa-nyóyməš" nya:ˀétk a:xwešxwéšk alyá:pəntik.

nya:wí:m amák tan vu:dí:ntik, awíntik nyá:ny u:cá:wk awíntik ˀaˀáw tará:k, vu:nó:nyk. nyamá:m nya:maspá:m kwaxˀó:nya awí:m, a:kwé:mk kwax-ˀó:nya, a:kwé:mək vu:nó:k vadí paˀi:pá:ny nya:ca-mí:m, nya:yú: masˀé: alynya:camí:m tamárək vu:nó:k nya:ví:rəm, si:vák kú:rəm adáwxayəm, adú:m, ˀakwéš tanək ˀaxóṭ taˀaxánək makyík apóm alyaˀémək, avšú:lyaˀémətəm, "má:, nyá:vəc adóˀš" nya:ˀí:m, nyá:nyc nyaˀdú:m ˀadúck aˀéta, ˀanykwacá:nvac.

aˀí:m va:ˀí:m kaná:vtəm ˀaˀávtəkˀe.

when the figure had been lying there where it lay for a little while he took it, and right away, when he saw that it was raw, "Phew! it's no good, it's awfully raw," he said, and he flung it away somewhere.

When he had thrown it away, "I'll try doing it again," he again said and did it again; he did it again in the same way, and right away the flame was too much, and when he saw that it was burned black, "Phew! it's no good, it's ugly," he said and again flung it away somewhere.

So he carried on again for the last time, he did it again as before, he lit a fire and went on until—at last when it died down, he did something with the ashes, he spread the ashes aside, and when he spread them aside and laid the person down here, when he laid the mud down there, he got it all covered over, and when it had been there a while he took it, and right away, then, it was real brown, it was just right, it wasn't at all burnt, it wasn't raw, and "Aha! this is the one," he said, and they say that that's the one we are, we Quechan.

This is how I heard them tell it.

ˀaxály maṭa:wí:r aˀím, xu:má:rxayk xály taˀúpəm, ˀanyá:c nyaˀdú:m viˀyá:k, xály ˀu:nó:k viˀyá:k ˀatavérək, xu:már ˀašént ˀanaqámək rapatk adúm, xály ˀu:nó:k ˀartu:ˀó:yk nyaˀlyvé:təm, ˀakóra.

təm, ˀakóra.

xu:már ˀi:kyíny xanatálc avám maṭˀatkyá:vək ˀartu:ˀó:yk, nyá:ny ˀu:dú:ctiyum.

ˀanyá:c ˀa:í:mək xály ˀtaˀúp ku:ˀé:yk alqáš alqáš avˀu:nó:m, xu:má:r ˀi:kyá:rny maṭˀatatkyá:vək ˀa:í:m ˀartu:ˀó:y manyé: tan ˀu:nó: tavˀártəkaš.

They call it Water Tag; in childhood they go for a swim, and I went as well; I'm in the water and I go and chase someone, and when I touch one I run away, and he goes and chases someone else somewhere; and so we played in the water, like that, long ago.

There was a poor orphan boy whom I joined and we played, that's how we always did it.

We little ones went for a swim any time, dressed just as we were, and I joined with the boys, and we used to have pleasure playing any time.

matˀár ˀu:nó:k nya:yú:nya, nya:šalyˀáyəm nya:yú: kwa:lató ˀawí:k ˀaˀím, ˀavá ˀcéwk ˀaˀím vˀu:nó:təš, šalyˀáy ˀawíck vaˀu:nó:təm.

maṭá:m si:pxú:k tanək ˀadótk kwaˀa:lyví:t xalyˀúpk vanyˀu:nó:k, xály taˀúp avˀárək vanyˀu:nó:k.

ˀaxák ˀá:m ˀu:xáyəntik, xu:márxayk, xalyˀúpk, xá ˀatapóməntik. xá tapómk, ṭáw ṭáw ṭáw, maṭnyi:ká:m aˀíntik awí:m. makyípəc anáw tanəm ˀaˀáv ˀaˀím, ˀu:ˀí:c avˀártəntik.

makyípəc anúp ˀa:kú:r ˀaˀíntim, ˀanúpəntik ˀavány ˀavány ˀavány, kór ˀayém maṭnyiˀká:m ˀaˀíntik.

ˀaxá kwa:ˀú:r nyamáṭ, ˀmáṭ masˀé: ˀa:píck vˀu:nó:nyk vˀu:nó:nyk, ˀatáytəm nyá:ny ˀa:rík ˀaqdá:yvək xály cúp ˀaˀí: vˀu:nó:ntik.

kanya:ˀí:m nya:ti:nyá:m ˀaxály nyaˀtu:ˀúpk vanyˀu:nó:m, xamˀa:ví:rc alyu:vá:təntim, ˀaxály u:vá:k nyí:lyk ˀi:laˀí:l avu:nó:m nyaˀyú:k ˀastu:kyá:nyk ˀa:cpá:ctiyum.

xu:márxayk nya:yú: ˀacayér sataˀóc ˀxalykwá:k viˀyáməny viˀyáməny viˀyám, ˀa:ná:lyc u:vˀáwəm ˀa:í:mək, ˀatáṭc adótk, ˀa:í:mək ˀakú:lyk, ˀacayér sataˀócəny ˀaštú:m—ˀantakórəs awétk, ˀaštú:m ˀcawémk, ˀacnyi:ˀu:má:yk vˀu:nó:nyk nyaˀkú:ctiyum. nyaˀkú:cəm ˀacacayéməc tavˀártəkˀaš.

I'm telling that we were out [of the water] and when it was sandy we used some fine sand, we were building houses, using sand.

It seems that I was a full eight years old when we went swimming, when we used to go swimming.

Also, I knew how to swim; in childhood I went swimming and I also "burned water" [splashing water against one's sides by rapidly crossing the arms in front of the body]. "Burning water," pop! pop! pop!, they try to beat each other. We tried to hear which one made a real loud noise, we also used to try that.

We also tried which one could stay under water longest, and I also sank down and stayed and stayed and stayed, so that we could beat each other in lasting a long time.

The ground at the water's edge, we plastered down muddy ground until, when there was a lot, we slipped and slid on it and dropped down into the water.

Sometimes we went for a swim in the evening, and there was a water snake in it, too, and when we saw him there in the water, black and peeping his head out, we always ran away and got out.

In childhood I went around here and there, here and there, hunting birds' eggs; where a mesquite tree grew, without hesitation—it's thorny—without hesitation I climbed it and gathered birds' eggs—even though they were tiny I gathered and took them home, and I fed them things until, now, they always grew up. When they were grown I used to let them go.

nyakór tan, ˀaxu:márxayk, vaˀawéc—xavík vaˀawéck, nya:yú: xá cu:míc avadíkəm, nyá:nyəm

A long time ago, while I was a child, two of us were going, where there was some kind of ditch,

ˀanxakyí:xayəm nya:yú:c—xamác—nyikacpák ayérək vi:yám, nyaˀayú:k viˀayá:k nya:yú: kapéṭəny ˀatamánxayəm, nya:yú:c—šataraˀú:rəc alyadáwk, ˀatáy tanək alydáwk avadáwəm ˀayú:k ˀaštú:m ˀanyvály ˀacawémxayəm, aˀím "ka:ná:rək, šalyˀáy kawím ka:kwé:mk avku:nó:k, ka:ná:rək," aˀícəm nyaˀaˀávək ˀawím, nya:yú: ˀaˀí:—ˀanˀí: ˀantanakórəc vi:dáwəm ˀacatárək vˀu:nó:k, nyaˀa:ví:rək, ˀamáy ka:wíc ˀatapéṭəntik, mašu:kwá:ly ˀawí: ka:wíc ˀawí:m ˀtapéṭk, ˀawí:m ˀatamárək, šalyˀáy ˀawí:m ˀatamárək vˀu:nó:k ˀa:ví:rək.

vi:dáwk šamác xavík xamók nyi:yá:xayk šatarém, mancacˀí: vu:nó:m nyaˀˀávkəm, ˀaxwélyk ˀaštú:m, ˀanyxáṭk ˀu:vá:tum. nya:yú: xalyˀasmó u:má:vk vu:nó:taš.

and as we crossed it, something—a quail—came out of there and flew past, and when I saw it I went and as soon as I lifted up some brush, there were some eggs in there, very many were in there, and I saw them there, gathered them, and as soon as I took them home, "Bury it! Take sand and spread it out and bury them!" they said; and when I heard them, then I got the ground all spread out, laid the eggs in there, and on top some sticks—little tiny sticks that were there, I laid them crosswise, and when I finished I covered them over with something else, I covered them with cloth or something, and I buried them, buried them all over with sand.

They were there for two or three days and right away they hatched, and when I heard them chirping I dug and gathered them and kept them as pets. They ate flies.

nyakór nya:ˀí:m, "xu:má:rəc nya:yú: xamá štaˀuraˀú:r kamá:lykaˀémək," aˀím, paˀi:pá: kwakú:cənyc nyá:ny alyúlyk amá: vaˀárək awím, camóšk aˀéta. awí: vaˀárək awím, nyá:ny xu:márəny aˀím, "kamá:lykaˀémək," aˀím. "mi:dónyc sacasácúm, nyí:lyk sacasácúm," aˀím. aˀí: avˀárəm, xu:má:rənyc u:má:v alyaˀém avˀárək adótum.

kanya:ˀí:m xu:má:r ˀi:kyíny aˀím, "kamá:lykaˀém maṭkamavsú:cúm," aˀíntik. aˀí: avˀárəm maštadá:vk u:má:v alyaˀém avˀárək. va:wí:m awétəmaš.

xantapˀó:p—mašu:kwá:ly awí:m, awím, acéwk nyawé:ycəm nyamˀaraˀóyk. sanycˀá:k awím, xu:nmá:r awím acéwəm ˀaraˀóyəm—ˀí:s ˀi:pá: nyu:céwxəny u:xáymək aˀím awíc alyaˀéməm, nya:má:m sanycˀá:k ˀa:ckóycəm, nyamˀaraˀóyk ˀaványk ˀaványk ˀaványk, maṭˀakaná:vək ˀacaqwérək ˀaványk ˀaványk ˀaványk, nyamá:m

In the old days they said, "Children, do not eat quail's eggs!" The grownups used to boil and eat that, chomping, as they say. They used to do it, and they told the children, "Don't eat it!" they said. "Your face might be freckled, it might be black and freckled," they said.

Sometimes they told a boy, too, "Don't eat it! You might wet yourself." They used to say so, and they were afraid and didn't used to eat it; that's the way they used to do.

Dolls—they made them for me of cloth, and I played with them. They made women and little babies, and I played with them—but, they didn't know how to make men, so they didn't make them, only women and old ladies; and I played and played and played with them; I talked and told them about myself on and on and on, and at last when I was

nyaˀpúyk ˀaštú:m, ˀu:taraˀúyk ˀa:sˀótk ˀaca-váwnyək. ˀaraˀóy nya:xalyvím ˀaštú:m ˀaraˀóyk ˀawétəm, nyakó:ra.

ˀawím xu:márxayk ˀaví:ly ˀu:vá:k u:ˀé:yəly ˀu:vá:k, nya:yú: pa:pél ˀa:ckyíṭ ku:ˀé:yk, ˀawím nyamˀaraˀó:yənyc nyaˀa:ví:rək, ˀa:ná:rək ˀu:vá:nyk ˀaraˀóy nya:xalyvím ˀaxwélyk ˀaštú:m ˀaraˀóyk ˀawétəm, ˀacvé:m ˀaxavík.

nya:wí:m—xantapˀó:p ˀatáy tan nyawé:ycən-tim, va:wí:m adík awí:m, šapú:r awí:m—ˀakwílyk nyamˀaraˀó:yəntik ˀu:vá:təntikaš.

kwaraˀákənyc vanyu:vá:k nya:yú: xanˀaé: aˀím avadík, xa:víly kwa:ˀú:r avadík, manavís tank ava-díkəm nyá:ny adáwk awím, ˀaša:k adáwk axásk u:xoraxórək a:kyéṭk vu:nó:k awím, xantapˀó:p acéwk nyawé:yəntim nyamˀaraˀóyəntik ˀawétkˀaš.

ˀaví:ly nyaˀu:vá:k, nya:yú: mu:díly ˀacéwk ˀaˀím, masˀé: ˀu:xárək ˀawím, ˀu:tapatá:pk ˀacá:ck, mu:díly manyé:c adú:k ˀaˀím. nya:yú: na:ráŋk xamály ˀakackyéṭk ˀamáynyi ˀacá:ck vˀu:nó:k ˀa:ví:r—ˀawétum.

xu:márxayk ˀnyá:c ˀavéšk ˀaráwk aˀíck, aˀícəm, ˀavéšk ˀaráwtiyum. xu:már ˀi:kyínyc avu:vá:ny-patəm, ˀacavakyévək ˀanyá:c ˀu:ṭáwəš.

tired I gathered them, fixed them up, wrapped them up and put them away for a time. Then, when I felt like playing, I gathered them and played, long ago.

So, as a child I was on the Hill, I was in school, and I cut out paper [dolls]; when I was finished playing, I buried them until, when I felt like playing, I dug them up and played, I together with someone else.

So—they also made very many dolls for me, making cradles and cradle hoops—and I also played at cradling [the dolls].

When the old man was there, the stuff they call driftwood that was there, there by the river's edge, that was very soft, that's what he took, and he took a knife and carved and whittled and so made another doll for me, and I played with it.

When I was on the Hill, I made bread; I stirred mud and made it into patties and set it here and there, and I said that it was cookies. I chopped up orange peels and put it on here and there and finished —I always did so.

As a child, I was a fast runner, they said, I always ran fast. There was a boy there, too, and we ran and I beat him.

ˀaxu:márxayəm ˀi:má:ṭc mavís tantiyum. mavís tanəm, vaˀu:vá:k, nya:yú: ˀi:šá:lyəm ˀav-ˀá:tk—wélək ˀaˀím, nya:yú: ˀí: kwalxóc u:vám ˀa:xkyé:vtək.

ˀa:ná:lyc u:vˀáwəm nyá:ny ˀastu:wí:n ˀi:mény ˀasawénk, ˀi:ša:lyənyc, ˀamáṭk ˀawí:m,—ˀó:y, ˀu:púyxəc adú:s, ˀašu:páw alyaˀémək, nyá:va ˀadú:m vaˀu:vá:təm xu:márxayk. ˀu:vá:m, ˀi:má:ṭənyc mavís tanək.

When I was still young, my body was very limber. It was limber, and there I walked on my hands—I somersaulted over a bench that was there.

Wherever there was a mesquite tree growing, that's what we hung from, I hung by my legs and with my hands I touched the ground,—Ooh! I might have gotten hurt, but I didn't know it; this is what I did when still young, and my body was limber.

paˀi:pá:c manyvá nya:vá:m, "ka:féy kasí:m," aˀétum xi:púk, "ka:féy kasí:m." makyík aˀétk, "ˀackamá:m" aˀí:ly aˀém—nyá:ny aˀí:lyaˀémək. ˀacamá:w aˀí:m vi:vátəs aˀétk, "ka:féy kasí:m," aˀím.

kwacá:nəc nyakór nya:dú:m, xu:már a:lyˀák vanyu:nó:k, "kanák avkavák," nya:ˀí:m, xu:márənyc anák nák aˀétk aˀím u:vám—acémk xu:márənyc ka:wíc ayú:k—i:šá:lyənyc ka:dóm—"kayú:k, i:šá:lyənyc va:dóš," nya:ˀí:m, ˀa:kó:yənyc láw aˀím ayú:k aspá:k aˀím—su:páwk ašnyícq aˀí: vaˀárək adótum.

xu:márxayk, maṭˀašcamá:m nya:lyˀák vaˀdáwəm, paˀi:pá:c avu:vá:k i:šá:lyənyc avˀalá:y—ˀanašéntək i:šá:lyc canpé:vək nyá:nya, i:šá:ly kwavatáynyi avám, nyá:ny ˀayú:k ˀi:wá:nyc apúy tanəm, "kayú:k kayú:k kayú:k," ˀaˀím. ˀa:kó:yənyc láw ayú:k aspá:k aˀím nyaˀyú:k nák ˀaˀím ˀaváš.

"paˀi:pá: ku:nyáq alykaˀémək, paˀi:pá kaštamadé:lykaˀémək. paˀi:pá: kackavár alykaˀémək. nya:yú: ˀalá:y kaˀí:lykaˀémək. mama:wí: wakakavárək. mu:taraˀúyk mu:kaná:vək. nya:yú: ˀaxóṭ manyu:wíck nya:dú:m má:yk mawétxa. nya:yú: mu:wíc wakakavár alykaˀémək. mama:wí: kayú:k ku:tá:rək. mama:wí: nya:yú:ny ˀaxóṭ nya:kawí:m nyi:kaxavík. kaxalyˀéš alykaˀémək. nya:yú: nya:kawí:m ká:yapatk, nyi:kaxavík."

When a person comes to your house, they always say "Drink coffee!", first [they say] "Drink coffee!" They never say "Eat things!"—they don't say that. They mean that they want him to eat something, but they say "Drink coffee!"

The Quechan in the old days, when they had a child with them, said "Sit somewhere!," and the child sat down and kept quiet there, and—by chance the child sees something—something's the matter with someone's hand—when he says, "Look! His hand is like this!," the old woman turns her head and looks and blinks at him—he understands and always leaves off.

In childhood, [one by whom] I insult myself took me with her and we were somewhere, and a person who was there had something wrong with his hand—he had another small finger growing on his thumb, and on seeing that I was startled and said "Look! Look! Look!" When I saw the old lady turn her head and look and blink, I sat there in silence.

[They said:] "Don't make fun of people, don't ridicule their looks! Don't laugh at people! Don't say bad things! Love your relatives! You are to explain things to them correctly. If you have something good, you are to give it to them. Don't cherish things that you own! Consider your relatives and share with them! If you have something good, divide it with your relatives. Don't be greedy! Whatever you have, give them too, divide with them!"

ˀaví:ly nyaˀu:vá:k u:ˀé:y ˀayá: avˀárək vanyˀu:vá:m, vanyˀu:vá:k, xu:mártək vaˀu:vá:k, ˀaˀnóq tanək alyˀu:vá: vaˀárək ˀaˀítya.

nyu:nó:nypatk, ˀantankórək vu:nó:nypatk,

When I stayed on the Hill, I used to go to school, and then, when I was a child, I used to be the very littlest of them.

There were also others, little bitty ones there,

ˀasa:ráp ka:ˀém vaˀárək vˀu:nó:tum, xu:má:rəc ˀartu:ˀó:y ku:ˀéyk.

šu:páw alyaˀémək adótəs, xu:má:rək ˀu:vá:tk kanya:ˀí:m makyí ˀadík ˀašmá: ku:ˀé:ytək, nya:yú:šk vanya:dí:m ˀašmáxa lyaví:m, makyí ˀadíkəm nya:wí:m, mašatxá: kwavašáwəny *Miss Ehrman* aˀím u:vá:m, nyá:nyc nya:nyayú:k nyadáwk nyu:kavnáwk vi:wá:k, nyacamí:m ˀašmá: ku:ˀé:yk, avˀadíkənyk, ˀnyá: nya:xávəm nyadáwk nyatacénəm ˀacˀamá: ˀayá:k ˀadótum.

ˀayá:k kanya:ˀí:m u:varˀély nyaˀayá:m *Mr. Crouch* aˀím kwaranˀákəc u:vá:k nyá:nyənyc nyi:nycawá:m xeykóly ˀa:yém, tu:míŋkəm adótəm xeykóly ˀa:yém, ka:wíc šu:páw alyaˀémətəkəm alyˀvák ˀašmánti ku:ˀé:yk savám, avawétəntik, adáwk nya:paqá:nyk vu:dí:nyk vu:dí:nyk vu:dí:nyk, ˀaví:ly nyakamí:m nyatašmác—ˀaˀáv ˀašu:páw alyˀaˀém ˀašmátk ˀaˀím, šu:páw alyaˀémətəka.

ˀaˀétk ˀaˀím ˀaˀnóq tantəm awí:m nyapá:pk sa:wí:m awícxa ˀa:lyˀéta, ˀu:ˀáva. ˀmaṭá:m xu:mxú:k ka:ˀém u:ˀé:y ˀayá:k ˀaˀítya.

pa:cxí:rəc u:vá:k awí:m nya:kxávəck awícəš. aˀí:s nyu:nó:ntik, kwu:nó: avác ˀakú:c tanək a:kxávəm ˀayú:tkˀaš. maṭá:m ša:xú:k aˀétk, ˀamáṭá:m si:pxú:k aˀím, nyá:nyc a:kxávək vu:nó:m ˀayú:tk ˀu:vá:tkˀaš.

ˀu:vá:tkum ˀanyá:c u:ˀé:y ˀayá:k ˀu:vá:tk ˀadótk ˀadúm, u:ˀé:yənyc ˀamé:m alyˀvátk nyá:nya. ˀamé:təm alyˀvák ˀacˀu:xáyk nyi:ˀná:m vaˀu:vá:tk ˀaxu:márxáyk. ˀackwšányc ˀaxóṭ ka:ˀém aˀítya.

vanyˀu:vám *Somertónək* vu:cadí:nypatk kamétaš. kavé:ly cadóm kamí:m, vu:nó:m ka:ˀíc i:ˀényc ˀaqóləm, i:ˀény acúk awícəm, améta. i:ˀény wa:kavár ku:ˀé:yk aˀétk aˀím, amét, amét, améta.

nyá:ny mapís avadú:lyaˀémək. xó, nyakór va:wí:m avawí:m, paˀi:pá:c i:ˀény ˀaqóləm, šaréq a:kyíṭk vu:nó:nyk, mapísa mari:ká:nəc i:ˀényc

too; there used to be maybe five of us there, and we little kids played.

I didn't even know anything, but I was young, and sometimes, little me, I lay down somewhere and slept; when it came on to be afternoon I might fall asleep wherever I was lying, and so the girls' matron, Miss Ehrman by name, was there; and she's the one who, when she saw me, she took me, picked me up, took me [upstairs] and laid me down; and, little me, I lay there asleep until, when the sun went down, she took me and brought me downstairs, and I went for my meal.

Sometimes when I went to church, an old man, Mr. Crouch by name, he's the one who took us all, and we went to town; I was one of them but didn't understand anything, and again at that time I went to sleep; he did the same thing, took and lifted my limp body and brought me along and along and along until, when he brought me to the Hill, he laid me down to sleep—I didn't hear it or know it, I was asleep or something, didn't know it.

And so, since I was very small, I think that's why they were going to carry me on their backs, so I've heard. I went to school at perhaps six years of age.

There was a policeman, and they were the ones who put me in. But, there were others, those who were quite old, whom I saw enter. Some were ten years old, some were eight years old, they were the ones I saw entering.

Then, I went to school, and I was in a high grade at school, there. I was in a high grade and I knew how to do a great many things while still young. I guess my head was good.

Then, they also brought in some [children] from Somerton. They brought [children of the] southern division of the tribe, and a certain one, his hair was

nyaˀqóləm nyamá:m, kwacá:nəc a:kavékəntik; i:ˀényc nyaˀqólənti avadíkəm, ka:dómk maṭu:cú:k aˀí: vu:nó:k awítya, nyamá:m.

xu:márək u:ˀé:yəly ˀu:nó:k makyík ˀackaˀa:yém alyˀaˀémək. nyá:lyˀu:nó:k vaˀu:nó:nyk vaˀu:nó:nyk vaˀu:nó:nyk vaˀu:nó: u:ˀé:yəly nya:cakxávəm alyˀu:nó:k vaˀu:nó:nyk, nyamá:m nyikˀapílyc vanya:dí:m, nyamá:m ˀpú:ṭkˀaš. ˀapú:ṭk saˀu:nó:nyk ˀa:kavéktəntik.

nyamá:m u:ˀé:yəly ˀa:wayá:xənyc nyamnya:lyví:m ˀa:kavék alyˀu:nó:k vaˀu:nó:k, kanya:ˀí:m —ˀanyá:c nyakór ˀasakyínyəš. ˀsakyínyk ka:ˀéx ka:dúntəm ˀadútya ˀašmadí:tk, ˀadótk, ˀadótkˀaš.

ˀacˀayú: ˀaˀétk. xu:márxayk, ˀmáṭá:m si:pxú:k ka:ˀém, vu:vá:nypatəm, nyamxavik ˀawéck *Winterhaven* nyá:ny ˀkatánək nyá:nyi ˀu:nó:k vˀu:nó:m nyi:nyu:ckavéktəkˀaš. tu:rtí: ˀamáck ˀaˀávkəm, *Deweyc* nyá:nyváyk u:vám nyá:ny ˀkatánək ˀacˀamáck, nya:yú: ˀma:rí:k ˀacašáyəm a:waé:c ˀamáck. tu:rtí: ˀamácəm, nyaˀtúcəm nyi:nyu:ckavékcəpəka.

Matron nyamá:m nyi:nyxí:rək. nya:yú: ˀavály nyi:nyšapéṭk. ˀackamác alykaˀémək nyi:nyˀíc ku:ˀéyəm vaˀdáwəm, ˀanyá: nyaˀašéntəm nyaˀwéc ku:ˀé:yəš.

nya:yú: xu:má:r ˀi:kyá:rənyc avu:nó:k nyá:nyc satu:kyá:nypatk.—nyá:nyc sakyínyk adúm—adáwk awím, kamí:m, nya:yú: ˀavá ˀacu:má:v atónyi šavˀáwəm, nya:yú: ˀašá:k vatáy tanəm i:mény axérc ku:ˀé:yəm nyá:nyi:vˀáwk, u:vˀáw vaˀártəməš. avˀáwk u:vá:nyk, "ˀá: avadú:m ˀasatkyá:nyk ˀu:vá:m nyayú:k nyamá:m." nyamá:m nya:kwaraˀákəm namákcəm vu:vá:k adútya.

nyá:nyəm amí:m, nya:ˀí:m amí:m a:ckyíṭc ku:ˀé:yəm amí:m aˀétum.

long, and they clipped his hair, and he cried. The poor child loved his hair, and so he cried, and cried, and cried.

They don't do that nowadays. Well, in the old days that's what they did, a person had long hair, and they grabbed him and cut it off until, now, when the white men's hair is long, at last the Quechan are going back again; if their hair is long again, is there any way they are going to clip it again, at last?

When we were in school as children we didn't go anywhere. We were there and stayed and stayed and stayed and stayed; when they entered us in school, we were there and stayed there until finally when summer came on, at last we scattered. We stayed away until we went back again.

Finally, when it was time for us to go to school, we went back and were there and stayed, and sometimes—long ago, I ran away. What reason there might have been to run away, I don't know, I just happened to do it.

I wanted to see things. There was another child, still young, perhaps eight years old, and together we arrived over there to Winterhaven and stayed there, and they sent us back. We tried eating tortillas, and we arrived there at where the Deweys live and ate things, we ate beans fried with lard. We ate tortillas, and when we were full, they sent us back.

Well, then the matron locked us up. She shut us up in a room. They told poor little us, "Don't have anything to eat!"; there we were, and we went through the whole day [without food], poor things.

Boys that were there were the ones who also ran away. X—he was the runaway—they caught him and brought him and stood him in the center of the dining room, they locked really big irons onto the

nyaˀu:vá:k u:ˀé:y ˀa:ví:rək nyaˀu:vá:nyk ˀaví: ˀu:vá:k nya:nymá:m nyaˀkúck vanyˀu:vá:m, ˀmaṭá:m ša:xúk ˀmáy ˀašéntək ˀaˀím, nyaˀu:vá:m, *Riverside* nyawémcək, *Sherman* nyawémcəm saˀu:vá:k xalyˀá cu:mpápəm ˀtakavék ˀavá:k.

ˀaví:ly ˀu:vá:ntik ˀu:vá:nyk ˀu:vá:nyk ˀu:vá:nyk nyamá:m nyikˀapíly nya:vá:m nyamá:m ˀaˀkúck aˀétk awí:m, nyamá:m ša:xúk ˀamáy xavíkəm nya:yú:k nyamá:m, "vi:kayémək u:ˀé:y kayá:k makyí kayémk," ˀmaṭá:m xu:mxú:k nyá:yc ku:ˀé:yəm, *Phoenix* ˀu:vá:k saˀu:vá:nyk saˀu:vá:nyk saˀu:vá:nyk, ˀavá: ˀanyka:ˀá:məc, saˀu:vá:nyk saˀu:vá:nyk saˀu:vá:nyk, nyamá:m ˀmaṭá:m xu:mxú:k ˀa:ví:rk, u:ˀé:y ˀa:ví:rəntik. ◇

poor boy's leg, and there he stood, where he used to stand. He stood until [he said,] "All right, then, they'll see that I do nothing but keep running away." At last when he got old they gave up on him, and he stayed around here.

At that time he cried; when he cried, they whipped the poor boy, and he always cried.

There I finished school and stayed until—I stayed at the Hill and at last when I was grown, I'd say eleven years old, when I was there, they sent me away to Riverside, they sent me away to Sherman [Institute], and I stayed there four months and then came back home.

Again I stayed on the Hill, stayed and stayed and stayed until at last when it came to summer, they said that at last I was grown up, and so, when they saw that I was twelve years old, at last [they said,] "Go away and go somewhere to school," and they allowed poor me six years; and I was in Phoenix and there I stayed and stayed and stayed, I never came home, there I stayed and stayed and stayed until at last I finished six years, I finished school again. ◇

Quechan Songs

ˀamó / Mountain Sheep Songs

Mary Kelly Escalanti, Singer

1. ikáya wanú:mpanú:mp
   ma:kár imán

ˀaví: nya:nyc nómsanóms, arkáy arkáy aˀétəma.
arkáykəm, nómsanómtək, arkáy arkáy, adú:m nyi:vˀáwk si:vˀáwk aˀí:k aˀétəma.
ˀamáṭəny tayá:mk ayú:k vi:vˀáwk, vanya:vˀáwk avány, ˀašéntənti nya:švá:rək, ˀamáṭ amák alyu:yémxəny a:švá:rək aˀím, aˀím avˀáwk.
xi:púk ˀamáy alyavˀáwk nyá:vik, alyavˀáwk ˀaví: kamadá:v nyi:kúlyk madá:vək aˀétəma.
nómsanóms, arkáy arkáyk makyík, nyá:ny aˀím.

1. (Song is untranslatable.)

That mountain is rough and slippery, so they say.
It's slippery, and it's rough, slippery, so he's standing there on it, they say that [the song] says.
He stands there looking far off across the place, and as he stands there, when he sings another one, he sings about how he's going to go away beyond the place, and he stands there.
At first he stands on top, here, he stands on it and has trouble climbing the difficult mountain.
It's rough and slippery somewhere, that's what he says.

2. matˀárəm kwayá:vi
   inyá: nyayá:ka

ˀamáy nyi:vˀáwkəm, ˀamónyc ayú:k vanyu:vá:k, ta:dú:mək matˀár kwaxóṭ avayú:k sanyu:vá:k, "ˀatá-

2. (Song is untranslatable.)

Standing on top there, the mountain sheep is looking, turning this way and that, and looking at the fine place out beyond, and there he says "I'm

qšətəxa" aˀí:m sanyu:vá:k, atáqšək avík a:xkyé:vək, matˀár kwanymék avˀáwk, ayú:k, — aˀím sanyu:vá:k.

nyamadúck avˀáwk kaná:vək, "ˀamáṭənyc maṭkwi:šá:yk nyama:yá:vək vi:díkəš. "ˀadóxa," aˀím si:vˀáwk, nyi:táqšək.

aˀétk u:vá:k, adú:k aˀéta. ◇

going to jump," and he jumps across from there and stands in a different place beyond and looks.

Thereupon he stands and describes it. The land is excellent as it extends alongside. "I'll do it," he stands there saying, and he jumps onto it.

He's telling it, it [the song?] says that he does so. ◇

Locust Songs

Ethel Ortiz, Singer

nyakór xu:márək vanyˀu:vá:k, xanˀa:vá: ˀaxaly-kwá:k vanyˀu:vá:k, nya:yú: ˀanyxáṭ ˀá:y ˀaˀím, šakwi:lá:, nyá:va, ˀaxalykwá:k—ˀi:dó: ˀakavá:yk—vu:vá:m nyaˀayú:k, anyórək xá:m adú:m nyí:lyk kanya:ˀí:m ˀaxwéṭk, nya:ˀí:m ˀadáw ˀaˀím vanyˀu:vá:k ˀa:švá:rək.

kwá:c—nya:nyi:lyí: nya:nyi:lyí:,
kwá:c—nya:nyi:lyí: nya:nyi:lyí:

nyaˀadáwk ˀanyxáṭ ˀá:yk. nyiˀayá:k kwanymé ˀayú:ntik, ˀxwéṭc u:vá:m nyaˀayú:k, ˀaˀíntik.

kwá:c—nya:xwaṭí: nya:xwaṭí:,
kwá:c—nya:xwaṭí: nya:xwaṭí:

nyamá:mək. ◇

Long ago, when I was here as a child, I hunted for locusts to give to a pet I had, a mockingbird; this is what I hunted—I went around from one willow to another—when I saw one there, they are differently colored, black and sometimes red, and so, when I am about to catch one, I sing.

Black locust, black locust

When I catch it, I give it to my pet. Going along there I again see another one; when I see a red one there I again say

Red locust, red locust

That's all. ◇

Lullabye

Mary Kelly Escalanti, Singer

mantáy mantáy	Your mother, your mother
tadíca yavéra	the Hard Corn
šakwá:l kanáciyá:a, kanáciyá:a	told her to, told her to husk it

When I sang that, I go just like that [hand movement], and they go to sleep.

I think it means, in American, they wanted her to go do something about the corn, your mama's gone to do this and do that. tadíc ˀavér—that's that corn. šakwá:ly—that means peel it. I think that's what it meant.

Another one?
When they cry, they sing—

ˀá:táṭ axá:wəlya	thorn went in
ˀá:mály vi:kwadíkəc	mesquite that lies there
ví:kwá:məc mu:šá:m mamí:k mí	that are around stuck you, and you're going to cry
ká:dúcəc kamawá:m mamí:k mí	something did something to you, and you're going to cry

aˀéta, nyá:va. [This is what they say.] ka:wícənyc kamawéməm mamí:v aˀím, ka:wícəc mu:šám, tamár ˀasi:má:c mu:šám, va:ˀí:m aˀí:k. [? You must be crying because something did something to you, something stuck you, some wild brush stuck you, this is what it says.]

I only have these two.

Salt Song

Amelia Caster, Singer

Did any of these old people ever tell you a song, like telling about how they got the salt?

I used to sing that when I was a little girl. They used to ask me to sing that.

ˀasˀí: vadá:c vadá:c makyí:ly adí:kəm mayá:k mamá:k mawí:va, mawí:va

ˀa:ná:ly kwa:péṭ atóly adí:kəm ˀayá:k ˀamá:k nyawí:va, nyawí:va

nya:dú:m ˀanyá:c ˀayá:k ˀamapéṭ tóš

ša:kwalí:t, ˀa:vé mu:kwépš

nyamá:m, nyiksi:kwayá:ny ˀu:xáymək. [That's all, I don't know what goes on from there.]

Something about:

cakwšány xavašú:, qól qól, qól qól

or something like that. I think it meant a duck, these wild ducks, that have bluish heads. [Mallard?]

ša:kwalí:t, I don't understand what it means. They said, ša:kwalí:t, ʔa:vé mu:kwépš. ʔa:vé—you know ʔa:vé [snake]. mu:kwépš—it seems like "untie it" [You pull it loose.]

My grandfather just sings it to me. He teaches me that. It's just a story. A lot of words in there are understandable. There are words there I don't understand. I think it meant:

ʔasʔí: vadác makyíly adíkəm mayá:k mamá:m mawí:m [Where was this salt lying that you went and got it and ate it?]

ʔa:ná:ly kapéṭ atóly adíkəm ʔayá:k ʔamá:m ʔawéš [It was lying in the middle of a mesquite thicket, and I went and got it and ate it.]

nya:dú:m ʔanyá:c ʔayá:nypatk [In that case I'm going, too.]—ʔama:péṭ tóš.

tóš—I don't know what that means [Perhaps, in the middle of the place?]

The other part I forgot. I know there's ʔa:vé mu:kwépš. cakwšányc xavašú:, qól qól, qól qól—that's the duck. You know, the head is bluish. cakwšányc qól qól means, like, it's round. ◇

Excerpts from the **Lightning Song**

William Wilson, Singer

The Lightning Song was composed by William Wilson's father, Charles Wilson, as described in Frances Densmore's Yuman and Yaqui Music. *Although William Wilson had taught the song to several other members of the tribe, by 1980 none of them remained alive. The version of the song from which the present excerpts are taken was recorded manually in 1938 by A. M. Halpern from William Wilson's dictation. The translation depended critically on the assistance of the late Bernard Jackson.*

In this narration, the singer as a rule first described the actions of the protagonist and then sang a series of songs relating to the same actions. The majority of songs consist of one line of verse sung to a fairly long melodic pattern and accompanied by a gourd rattle to mark the rhythm. Some songs have two lines, and a few have three lines of verse. Usually, but not always, the melodic pattern is the same for all songs in a series, whether the song consists of one, two, or three lines of verse. The gourd accompaniment is, for some songs, an iambic double beat; for others, a dactylic triple beat.

The excerpts presented here are just that: only excerpts. Like all song cycles, when sung in full, Lightning takes all night, from sundown to sunup. The excerpts are (1) the introduction; (2) the vision of lightning, which would be sung just before midnight; (3) the morning songs, which come just before and at sunrise.

(1)

u:rávəc mu:ˀíc avác ka:wíc adú:m ˀaˀí:m walyaˀémək, ˀakwéc xamá:lyk.

avkwavác nyá:nyi nyá:nyi:mánək acéntaˀa; xu:már ˀacadú:m kwa:lyavé:, ˀu:tí:š vadámá:m a:vkyéwk, ˀi:pá xašˀéṭ ˀašéntəm alya:é:vək. vanya:vˀáwk aˀí:m, ˀanyép ˀanyu:rávəc ˀadóˀaš.

acénək vanya:vˀáwk, ˀacˀakaná:vək ˀamáṭ kwaˀaqólva ˀa:kxápəxa. ša:várəc adú:m aˀétkaˀa. ˀašéxa, u:rávəc aˀétxa.

That thing that you call "lightning" is nothing else but a cloud that is white.

The one who is there started there and descended. Wonder Boy—he carries nothing but a bow, and he has one unfeathered arrow to go with it. Standing there he said, "It is I whose lightning it is."

Having descended, he says, "I will go throughout the length of this earth describing things." He said that it was a song. "I will name it, and people will call it 'lightning.'"

(2)

nyi:šadómpətək vi:yá:w aˀétk vi:yá:tk.

He is going along with the intention of heading only in one direction.

nya:ša:m akwi:vawk
nya:ša:mk inya:miyu:k
nya:ša:m ika:na:vk

He stands and looks from afar
He looks from afar and sees
He looks from afar and describes

nyá:ny nyamáṭk aˀét, ˀasá kwapáynya, kaná:vtək vi:wá:k aˀéta. avá:mək ayú:m xamá:lyk ˀéq ˀamé:k vi:vˀáwəm, makórəly u:vá:k i:mák, aˀétk kaná:vtək aˀét.

That land belongs to him, he says, "Fog Bearer [San Jacinto Peak]," and he went off describing it. He arrived there and saw it; it stood there as a high white mass; he is on its summit dancing and so he describes it.

minya:ma:ṭ iša:kupay
    nya:i:ša:mk avi:nyavawk
minya:ma:ṭ iša:kupay
    nya:i:ša:mk avi:nyaya:k
minya:ma:ṭ iša:kupay
    nya:i:va:mk avi:nyavawk
minya:ma:ṭ iša:kupay
    xamu:wa:lyk inya:miyu:k
minya:ma:ṭ iša:kupay
    maŋau:kork anye:muva:k
    nya:i:ma:k avi:uva:k

He stands and looks from afar at San Jacinto Peak
He goes along looking from afar at San Jacinto Peak
He arrives at San Jacinto Peak and stands
He sees that San Jacinto Peak is white
He stays on the summit of San Jacinto Peak and is dancing

kwe:xuyaw nyakwexu:yaw

Ball of cloud

ˀakwé avác ˀanya:xá:pk amánək axyá:w aˀétk vi:dí:m ayú:k aˀét kaná:vək vi:vˀáwk.

That cloud comes from the west in the form of a ball of vapor, and he sees it and stands describing it.

kwe:xuyaw kanyama:yu:

He sees the ball of cloud

ˀakaná:vxa aˀét kaná:vəm aˀí: vi:vˀáwk.

"I will describe it," he says, and describing it he stands there speaking.

kwe:xu:yawk inya:ka:na:vk

He describes the ball of cloud

ˀakwé kwašént kaná:vtənti vi:vˀáwk. ˀakwényc vi:dí:k ˀamáy lyu:vév alyu:vá:k maṭmaxávək u:vá:k. mó:, ˀakaná:vxa, aˀétk a:švá:rək vi:vˀáwk.

He stands describing the same cloud. The clouds came along and stayed in the middle of the sky passing in and out amongst one another. "Well, I will describe it," he said and stood there singing.

kwexiye:r nyakwexiye:r
kwe kwiya:ny akwe kwiya:ny
kwe ma:yany akwe ma:ya:y
kwe ma:yany inyaka:na:v

Spotty clouds moving about
Clouds going
Clouds in the distance
He describes the distant clouds

ˀakwé ˀasác u:ˀícənyc análÿk i:má:ṭk apá:m, aˀávək vi:yá:k, nyakaná:vxa, ˀasác maˀétk maˀítya. aˀí:m kaná:vək vi:vˀáwk.

The so-called "foggy cloud" drops and falls on his body, and he feels it as he goes along. "I will describe you, you are fog," he says and stands describing it.

kwe:saen inya:miyu:kaum
kwe:saen inya:kana:vkaum
akwi:yaa:m inya:miyu:kaum
akwi:yaa:m inya:kana:vkaum
kwe:yumpi:yump kwe:yumpi:yump
  inya:mi:yu:k
  anye:mawvam
kwe:yumpi:yump kwe:yumpi:yump
  inya:ka:na:vk
  anye:mawvam

He sees the quivering foggy cloud
He describes the quivering foggy cloud
He sees the cloud passing
He describes the cloud passing
He is looking at the clouds as they turn this way
  and that
He describes the clouds turning this way and
  that

nya:lyaví:m ˀakwé kwašént ˀakaná:vxa, aˀétk vi:vˀáwk. ˀamáyəm tayá:k ayú:m, ˀakwényc komakómək a:kyévək vi:díkəm ayú:k. savíly u:vá:t aˀí:m adútya, aˀétk kaná:vək vi:vˀáwk.

"In a similar way I will describe the same cloud," he says. Glancing toward the heavens, he saw the cloud in the form of narrow strips that were almost joined together. It was there that he wanted to be, so he stood describing it.

kwe: kau:m aku:vany
kwe: kau:m aka:na:vk

Cloud strips are there
He describes the cloud strips

kwe: nyu:r aku:vany
kwe: nyu:r ika:na:vk

Colored clouds are there
He describes the colored clouds

ʔakwé kwaʔašéntəc ʔanya:xá:pk á:pəm, ti:nyá:m tík aʔétk vi:díkəm, u:ráv á:pəm nyikcacénəm u:rávú, u:nó:m ayú:k kaná:v vi:vʔáwk.

The same cloud being placed in the west, it became pitch dark there, and lightning was placed there and brought straight down from there, so that lightning should flash. He saw it happening and stood describing it.

u:ra:v nyi:yu:k
kwiti:nya:m au:ra:vk
u:ra:v ika:na:vk

He sees lightning
Lightning flashes in the darkness
He describes lightning

(3)

aʔí:m va:ʔí:m, ku:ná:v ʔa:ví:rək, aʔétk vi:yá:k. vi:yá:k makyény cu:vá:m makyény u:yú:xəc alykwadóməny ʔadú: ʔaʔétk viʔayá:xas ʔakaná:pí:m ʔadútya. aʔétk kaná:vənti vi:vʔáwk.

Thus, "I have finished the story," he says and goes on. "I am going to do that which is impossible to attain and not to be seen, as I will go on, but I will fully describe it," he said and stood there describing it again.

vu:varm anyi:yu:k
vu:varm ika:na:vk

He sees its impossibility
He describes its impossibility

aʔí:m va:ʔí:m vi:yá:m kwampányqəc maṭawéмək vi:yémək ʔanya:xá:pk a:dómpək, xu:márəny nyi:tí:šk, kwati:nyá:m adáwk i:dóm a:péṭəm, nya:ʔávək vi:yá:k, nyašu:páwtʔaš. paʔi:pá: ka:wíc nyawíyú:m, kwampányqəc mawétk mawítya. aʔétk kaná:v vi:vʔáwk.

Thus he goes on; a bat goes off roving, heading west, and deceives the boy; he takes the darkness and spreads it as a screen in front of him; when he senses it he goes along, "I know you. What person are you that would do it to me, you are Bat that are doing it," he said and stood describing it. [It is nearly dawn, but the bats were trying to make him believe it was still night. This is probably a reference to the darkness before the dawn.]

nyumcu:kye:k a:nyumcu:kye:k
kwiti:nya:m anyu:mi:dawk

He clumps it together
He takes darkness and clumps it together

nyumcu:kye:k a:nyumcu:kye:k
kwiti:nya:m anyu:mi:dawk
nyumcu:kye:k inya:ka:na:vk

He describes taking darkness and clumping it together

aˀí:m va:ˀí:m, ku:ná:v ˀa:ví:rək, aˀétk vi:yá:m, ayú:m ti:nyá: ka:lycéšqəc mašaxáyc ˀavá u:cavákw vi:vám, nyamacpámək vi:yá:m, nya:nya:dáw aˀí:m kwadúc, aˀétk. avkadí:k, ˀanyá:c nyá:vi ˀavák viˀavák. ˀanyá: kwaxávəm paˀi:pá:c avá:k vi:kwu:nó: kayú:k. ˀanyˀavác waˀi:páyk. aˀétəm aˀávək kavárək. sanyaˀák ˀaˀí: kaˀaˀémək avˀá:mək ˀadú:m? ˀa:í:mək viˀanykwá:mənyc viˀayá:k makyík ˀadóxa. ˀaˀétk viˀayémək ˀadútya. aˀí:m vi:vˀáwk kaná:v vi:vˀáwk.

Thus, "I have finished the story," he said and went on; he looked, and Flying Fox Maiden has located her house there [the flying fox is the symbol of flirtatious or promiscuous women; people who dream of it become promiscuous]; he comes out there and goes along; "That's the kind of man who's going to court me," she said. "Come over here! This is where I stay. See how people come here at sundown and are around and about here. My house becomes lively." He hears her saying so, and he refuses. "How can I have intentions toward women where I pass by? I am going along as the one who passes here unheeding, and I go away though I don't know where I will be," he said and stood describing it.

minya:va:c a:wi:ŋi:payk
minyu:nya:c a:wi:ŋi:payk
minya:va:c a:kwi:ŋi:ni:x
minya:va:c atu:ŋu:lya:x
nyanu:ma:k avi:nya:ya:k
minya:va:c atu:ŋu:lya:x
nyaka:na:vk avi:nya:ya:k

The house is lively
The road is lively
The house is quiet
He strokes the house, leaves it and goes on
He strokes the house, describes it and goes on

[He speaks of the house as quiet in an ironic way. He says that he strokes, or affectionately pats the house though he doesn't actually do so. He means to show that he approves of it, that he recognizes the pleasure of sex, but he has business to attend to. As a serious-minded man he does not permit himself to be diverted.]

aˀí:m va:ˀí:m nyi:namák vi:yá:k, vi:yá:k aˀávək vi:yá:m, davˀórtəm aˀávək vi:yá:k, kaná:vək vi:wá:k.

Thus saying, he left it and went on and noticed something as he went; he feels drowsiness and goes off describing it.

do:vo:ŋo:rk ido:voŋo:rk
do:vo:ŋo:rk inya:miyu:k
do:vo:r alyu:va:mk
do:vo:r ika:na:vk

He is drowsy
He sees the drowsiness
He stays here drowsy
He describes drowsiness

aʔí:m va:ʔí:m, ku:ná:v ʔa:ví:rək, aʔí:m vi:yá:m acpák vi:vʔáwəm ayú:k kaná:vək vi:wá:k. ka:wíc madúwú:m ? xamšéc madótk madútya. ammadú:m macpákəm paʔi:pá: kwapaʔi:pá:yc mayú:k qwalayéwk adú:m adú:va maʔáctəxa. nyakaná:pí:m ʔadútya. aʔétk kaná:v vi:vʔáwk.

Thus, "I have finished the story," he says as he goes on; he sees something emerge and stand there, and he goes off describing it. "What might you be? You are Star. Human beings who see you as you come out will say of you, 'It must be close to dawn.' I am describing you," he said and stood describing it.

šakwa:ŋkye:c a:mayma:vawk
šakwa:ŋkye:c inya:mi:yu:k
šakwa:ŋkye:c inya:ka:na:vk

They stand clustered in the sky
He sees them clustered
He describes the cluster

aʔí:m va:ʔí:m, ku:ná:v ʔa:ví:rək, aʔí:m vi:yá:k aʔávəm ti:nyá: xamá:lyc acpák ʔamáy a:xakyé:vək vi:díkəm ayú:k kaná:vənti vi:vʔáwk.

Thus, "I have finished the story," he said and he went on and noticed something; White Darkness emerges and crosses the sky; he sees it there and stands describing it again.

nya:msa:vm axu:wayk
ka:may amayixwany
nya:msa:vm ika:na:vk

Whiteness flecked
Heavens are hazy above
He describes whiteness

aʔí:m va:ʔí:m aʔávəm vi:yá:m xatalwéc aʔávək qwalayéw alypá:m, aʔétk kaná:vək u:vá:m aʔávək, ka:wéc maʔíyú:m? maxáy ma:kwanaméɬ maʔétk maʔítya. nyakaná:vəm ʔadútya. nya:ʔétk vi:vʔáwk.

Thus, he heard something; Coyote noticed [Milky Way] going along and mistook it for dawn and described it; [Wonder Boy] heard him there; "What might you be? Indeed you are Showoff Boy. I am describing you." So saying he stands there.

yalymu:pa:k iyalymupa:k
yalymu:pa:k inya:miyu:k
xata:lwa:c inya:ŋamsa:vk
    nya:ka:na:vk anyemuvany
yalymu:pa:k inya:kana:vk

You have mistaken it
He sees you mistake it
Coyote is there describing dawn
He describes you mistaking it

aʔí:m va:ʔí:m vi:yá:k aʔávəm ʔamáyəm naxakyí:k ʔanya:xá:pk nadómək, vi:ná:məm aʔávək, nyiʔašu:páwʔaš nyiʔakaná:vəm ʔadútya. nyašék šalypotc ʔaʔí:m nyašéxas, paʔi:pá: kwapaʔi:pá:yc nya:mašék ma:šaxwéṭc aʔét mašéctəxa. aʔí:m kaná:v vi:vʔáwk.

Thus, going along he heard something; they cross through the sky heading west; he hears them, "I know them and am describing them. I name you saying 'šalypot,' but though I name you so, when human beings name you, they will name you saying 'ma:šaxwét,'" he said and stood describing it. [The bird referred to was not a resident of the area but occasionally appeared when migrating. It was regarded as a sacred bird, though the powers it conferred were not known to the narrator.]

šaŋalypo:c a:may nu:wa:mk
šaŋalypo:c i:nya:mi:yu:k
šaŋalypo:c i:nya:ka:na:vk

šalypót pass in the sky
He sees šalypót
He describes šalypót

aʔí:m va:ʔí:m vi:yá:k aʔávəm ayú:m ti:nyá:m cakyá:ṭk anákmətək. mó:, ʔanyá:yk vi:dí:m adótʔaš, aʔétk vi:yá:k. ʔakaná:pí:m ʔadútya, aʔétk kaná:v vi:vʔáwk.

Thus he went on and noticed something; he looked, and the darkness is broken by jagged rays and patches of light. "Well, it's getting to be light," he said and went on. "I am describing it all," he said and stood describing it.

kwi:ti:nya:mk inyaxaukyi:v nyaxaukyi:vk
kwi:ti:nya:mk inyaxaukyi:v nyami:yu:k
nya:miyu:k inyamaiyu:k
kwi:ti:nya:mk inyaxaukyi:v nyaka:na:vk
nya:kana:vk inyaka:na:vk

Darkness goes across
He sees the darkness going across
He describes the darkness going across

aʔí:m va:ʔí:m vi:yá:k ayú:m, ʔamáyvəc ʔaxwá:k tán aʔétk vi:vám, ʔakaná:pəntim ʔadútya. kaná:vənti vi:vʔáwk.

Thus, he went on and saw something; the sky was hazy and motionless there; "I am again describing it all." He stood describing it again.

mayakupa:rc amiŋi:xwa: miŋi:xwa:k
mayakupa:rc amiŋi:xwa: miŋi:xwa:k
nya:miyu:k inyamaiyu:k
mayakupa:rc amiŋi:xwa: miŋi:xwa:k
nya:kana:vk inyaka:na:vk

It is hazy at the end of the sky
He sees it hazy at the end of the sky
He describes haziness at the end of the sky

aˀí:m va:ˀí:m vi:yá:k aˀávəm, qwalayéw alyá:mpətəm amánək amétk, u:vá:m aˀávək, nyakaná:vəm ˀadútya. šakwˀi:lá:c u:ˀíc maˀétk maˀítya. aˀí:m kaná:v vi:vˀáwk.

Thus he went on and heard something; it still was short of dawning, and something arose and cried; he hears it there and, "I am describing you. You are what they call 'mockingbird,'" he said and stood describing it.

šakwi:la:c a:nyemi:mank
šakwi:la:c inya:mi:mi:k
šakwi:la:c inya:xu:kyi:vk
šakwi:la:c inya:ka:na:vk

Mockingbird arises
Mockingbird cries
Mockingbird flies straight up and down
He describes mockingbird

aˀí:m va:ˀí:m vi:yá:m, aˀávəm nya:lyaví:m, maxwá:c amánək u:vá:m aˀávək, nyakaná:vəm ˀadútya. aˀétk kaná:v vi:vˀáwk.

Thus saying he went on, and he noticed something similar, he noticed a badger arising, and "I am describing you fully," he said and stood describing it.

šamaxwa:c avi:u:vany
šamaxwa:c a:nyemi:mank

Badger is there
Badger arises

aˀí:m va:ˀí:m, ku:ná:v ˀašéntətəm mamúly ˀakaná:pí:m ˀadútya. kaná:vtənti vi:vˀáwk.

Thus, "I am describing its name fully in a single telling." He stands describing it again.

nya:muly ika:na:vk

He describes its name

aˀí:m va:ˀí:m, ku:ná:v ˀa:ví:rək. aˀí:m vi:yá:m, vi:yá:k ka:dóm walynyi:yéməly, paˀi:pá: qwalayéw aˀávəc amánək maṭcaváwk amétk vi:vám aˀávək, ma:madí:c u:ˀíc maˀétk maˀítya. nyašéyí:m ˀadútya. cu:šá:m kwaˀanyá:y ˀaˀét nyašétxa. ˀaˀétas paˀi:pá: kwapaˀi:pá:yc nya:mašék ma:madí:c maˀíctəxa. aˀétk kaná:vənti vi:vˀáwk.

Thus, "I have finished the story," he said and went on, but before he had gone very far he heard there a person who senses dawn and arises, takes his position and cries; "You are what they call 'Owl.' I am naming you. I will name you by saying Sunlit Farscanner. I say so, but when human beings name you they will call you 'Owl,'" he said and stood describing it again.

nyu:ša:m ikwa:nyayk
nyu:ša:m ika:na:vk

Sunlit Farscanner
He describes its looking afar

aˀí:m va:ˀí:m aˀávək vi:yá:m, ˀamáy vu:vá:k xakyí:vək u:vá:m aˀávək, ka:wéc maˀíyú:m ?

Thus, he heard something as he went on, he heard it as it stayed up above and flew up and

qwalayéw kwaʔanyá:yəm ʔu:rú:c maʔétk maʔítya. kaná:vənti vi:vʔáwk.

ka:may axu:kyi:v
šayu:ru:c a:nyemi:mank
šayu:ru:c inya:mi:mi:k
u:ru:c inyaxukyi:vk
  xa:tpa:c inyaxukyi:vk
u:ru:c ika:na:vk
  xa:tpa:c ika:na:vk

aʔí:m va:ʔí:m nyamʔanyá:yəm xamšé kwacu:pá:c vi:kwadí:vəc maṭa:ví:rək ʔanya:xá:p tadómpətək vi:yá:m ayú:k, nyakaná:vxa. kaná:vənti vi:vʔáwk.

xamu:ši:c a:may nu:wa:mk
xamu:ši:c a:may vu:xwi:rk
xamu:ši:c a:may nu:yi:vk
xamu:ši:c a:maym u:nyayk
xamu:ši:c a:maym nya:va:k
  nyaka:na:vk a:nyemu:vany

aʔí:m va:ʔí:m̀ nyamá:m nyamʔanyá:yk kóx aʔí:m. ʔa:vé:c nyavá šamé:k avéšk axávək u:vá:m ayú:k kaná:v vi:vʔáwk.

minya:va:c i:kwaŋa:nyayk
minya:va:c i:kwaŋa:nyayk
  inyaka:me:k a:vi:u:vaŋ

kaná:vək nya:ví:rək aʔí:m, mó:, ʔamáy ʔaxávi viʔavʔáwk. axávək vi:yá:k ʔamáy vadí u:vá:k u:vá:m, ʔaʔanyéw alyʔaʔémək ʔu:vá:m nyaʔávəctəxa. ʔanáwk vaʔu:vá:txa. nyaʔakwí:m ʔanáwtəxa.

down; "What might you be? You are Nighthawk of the Sunlit Dawn." He stood describing it again.

It flies up and down in the sky
Nighthawk arises
Nighthawk cries
Nighthawk flies up and down,
  Coyote jumps up and down
He describes Nighthawk, he describes Coyote

Thus, it became light, and the stars which have emerged and come this way dwindle and go along heading west; he sees it and saying, "I will describe you," he stood describing it again. [He is telling of the morning star.]

Stars pass overhead
Stars wandering overhead
Stars pass overhead
Stars trail across the sky
Stars trail across the sky
He describes stars sitting in the sky

Thus, at last it becomes light blue daylight. A mouse that is anxious to get home is running around and entering; he sees it and stands describing it.

Its house is sunlit
Its house is sunlit, it is anxious

When he finished the story he said, "Well, I will enter the sky and stay." He went and entered and is staying here above, "I shall not disappear, but you will hear me as I stay about. I will be making sounds. When it clouds up, I will make sounds.

nyu:rávəm nyá:nyəm ˀakaná:vtəxa. ˀi:má:ṭ vadác vadú:m aˀétəm ˀanáwtəxa. ˀanyˀi:pá vi:kwadík vadány nyaˀakyéməhk u:rávtəxa. nyampaˀi:pá: kwapaˀi:pá:yc nyaˀávək šu:páwtaˀa.

u:dóxəny nya:vá:m ˀamáyva nya:xávək avˀáwk aˀítya.

cu:pa:k anyiyuwa
cu:pa:k ika:na:vk◇

When lightning flashes, that's when I will describe things. When this body of mine changes position, I will make sounds. When I shoot off this arrow of mine that lies here, lightning will flash. Thereupon human beings will understand when they hear it."

When he reached his destined state, when he entered the heavens, he stopped.

He sees sunrise
He describes sunrise◇

Bibliography

Densmore, Frances. 1932. Yuman and Yaqui music. *Bulletin of the Bureau of American Ethnology*, no. 110.

Emerson, Lee, and Halpern, A. M. 1978. Coyote and quail (Yuma-Quechan). In *Coyote stories*, ed. William Bright (International Journal of American Linguistics: Native American Texts Series [*IJAL: NATS*], Monograph 1), pp. 124–36. Chicago: University of Chicago Press.

Forde, C. Daryll. 1931. Ethnography of the Yuma Indians. University of California Publications in Archaeology and Ethnography, vol. 28, no. 4.

Halpern, Abraham M. 1946, 1947. Yuma. *International Journal of American Linguistics* 12: 25–33, 147–51, 204–12; 13: 18–30, 92–107, 147–66.

———. 1976. Kukumat became sick—a Yuman text. In *Yuman texts* (*IJAL-NATS* 1:3), ed. Margaret Langdon pp. 5–25. Chicago: University of Chicago Press.

———. 1980. Sex differences in Quechan narration. *Journal of California and Great Basin Anthropology* 2: 51–59.

Harrington, J. P. 1908. A Yuma account of origins. *Journal of American Folklore* 21: 324–48.

Credits

Photo credits: pp. 291 and 292—Helga Teiwes (courtesy of Arizona State Museum, University of Arizona, Tucson); p. 335—Abraham Halpern.

[illegible]